RADIO CULTURES

For Bruce,
With special thanks!

Michael

PETER LANG
New York • Washington, D.C./Baltimore • Bern
Frankfurt am Main • Berlin • Brussels • Vienna • Oxford

RADIO CULTURES

The Sound Medium in American Life

EDITED BY
Michael C. Keith

PETER LANG
New York • Washington, D.C./Baltimore • Bern
Frankfurt am Main • Berlin • Brussels • Vienna • Oxford

Library of Congress Cataloging-in-Publication Data

Radio cultures: the sound medium in American life / edited by Michael C. Keith.
p. cm.
Includes bibliographical references and index.
1. Radio broadcasting—United States.
2. Radio broadcasting—Social aspects—United States.
I. Keith, Michael C.
PN1991.3.U6R328   791.440973—dc22   2007043470
ISBN 978-0-8204-8865-3 (hardcover)
ISBN 978-0-8204-8648-2 (paperback)

Bibliographic information published by **Die Deutsche Bibliothek**.
Die Deutsche Bibliothek lists this publication in the "Deutsche
Nationalbibliografie"; detailed bibliographic data is available
on the Internet at http://dnb.ddb.de/.

Cover design by Joshua Hanson

Radio is eminently worthy of the social researcher's time.

—*Paul Lazarsfeld*

Table of Contents

Part II. Pulpits, Politics, and Public Interests

Part III. Archives, Curricula, and Afterthoughts

Foreword

FRANK CHORBA

Radio Cultures celebrates the role radio has played in shaping the United States' social consciousness. Americans began listening to radio in great numbers by the mid-1920s. During the subsequent decades, thousands of personalities have emerged on the airwaves, contributing to our sense of national culture and folklore. Indeed, if one were asked to list some of radio's most significant benefactions or services to the public it might be best done through a survey of its extraordinary personalities.

As the 1920s began, millions of country folk moving into the nation's cities found themselves disconnected from their old ways of life and security. Seeking a sense of belonging and community, they were among the first listeners to radio. For them, radio offered a unique personality that reinforced their traditional values. In 1922, Will Rogers appeared on pioneer station KDKA. Departing from his wealthy upbringing, Rogers spoke to his audiences in the persona of a simple country cowboy from the plains of Oklahoma.

His listeners, especially in the cities, included people whose simple country backgrounds gave them a commonality with immigrants of various European nationalities. Rogers's humor encompassed the current social issues of the day while roasting key personalities and offering advice. His style was freewheeling and was perfected over years of ad-libbing as a vaudeville entertainer. He said whatever came into his head while rambling from one anecdote to another without any concern for time. His programs were live, unedited, and tremendously popular with millions of country folk who identified with his homespun humor.

Will Rogers was America's first radio commentator. He demonstrated the power of radio. For the first time in history, one person speaking into a microphone could talk to millions of listeners. His 1924 series titled *Fifteen Minutes with a Diplomat* on *The Eveready Hour* was the first commercially sponsored pre-network hookup.

By 1930, Rogers's annual income was $600,000. His final radio series was the *Good Gulf Show*, which aired at 9:00 p.m. on Sunday evenings between 1933 and 1935. Because of Rogers's immense popularity, President Franklin D. Roosevelt's *Fireside Chats* followed Rogers's show. When Rogers died in a plane crash in Alaska in August 1935, Columbia Broadcasting System (CBS) went off the air for 30 minutes as a tribute to his life.

The entire nation was affected by the Depression as industry, mining, and the banks collapsed. The angst was further deepened in 1933 as farmers from Texas to the Dakotas were severely affected by a devastating drought. Hundreds of thousands of families were displaced by the Dust Bowl.

My father quit school in ninth grade to find what little work he could to support my grandparents. He walked the railroad tracks into the country-side and hunted groundhogs to keep from starving. I remember him talking about the *Amos 'n' Andy* program. He claimed that the show kept people together. It gave them something to look forward to each day.

Freeman Gosden and Charles Correll were the creators of *Amos 'n' Andy*. They were white actors familiar with minstrel traditions. Historian Elizabeth McLeod (2005) called them the pioneers of modern entertainment. Theirs was the first serial program devised for radio broadcast. Beginning in 1926, the situation comedy became so popular that some 40 million listeners tuned in between 1930 and 1931 to episodes involving Andy's romance with the Harlem beautician Madame Queen. Elizabeth McLeod noted that the program profoundly influenced the development of dramatic radio.

Correll and Gosden created an intimate, understated acting style requiring careful modulation of the voice that differed sharply from the broad techniques of live stage actors. The performers pioneered the skill of varying the distance and the angles of their delivery into the microphone to create the illusion of a group of characters. Listeners could easily imagine that they were in on a conversation among close friends. Critics considered the Negro stereotypes of Amos and Andy a link in a heavy chain shackling the Negro to the past. However, Erik Barnouw (1968, 111) noted that the stereotype proved durable. It was said that the program was so loved that department stores piped in the broadcasts so shoppers would not miss an episode. Movie theaters scheduled their features to end before the broadcast (Buxton & Bill, 1972, 14).

In the late 1930s, radio participated in another cultural convergence, involving Orson Welles and the infusion of classical drama over radio. Between 1935 and 1937, Welles appeared in the *March of Time* series and portrayed Lamont Cranston, the invisible character, on the *Shadow* mystery program. His splendid voice and stellar reputation with the cultural elite won him opportunities for classical roles. During 1937, he appeared on the CBS Summer Shakespeare series and Mutual's *Les Miserables*.

In 1938, CBS approached Welles with a proposal for a weekly one-hour series of classic dramas. Actors from Welles's existing stage group, the Mercury Theater, were hired. The series began as *First Person Singular* and was later renamed *The Mercury Theatre on the Air.* The original title referred to an innovative narrative approach used by Welles in which he acted as the narrator while building himself directly into the drama.

The Mercury Theatre on the Air was a pioneer program of quality drama and experimental radio presentations. Welles's narrative first-singular approach made it possible for him to adapt lengthy novels into one-hour radio dramas. As the narrator, he would quickly move from one point in time to another and then reassume the role of the story's main character.

In close association with Howard Koch and John Houseman, Welles wrote, directed, and performed in the productions. The presentations included *Huckleberry Finn*, *A Tale of Two Cities*, *The Magnificent Ambersons*, and *Dracula*. The Mercury Theater was praised by critics, but ratings were low. However, a broadcast of the H.G. Wells tale *The War of the Worlds*, on October 30, 1938, propelled Orson Welles into American folklore.

The War of the Worlds program was presented in the format of a news broadcast; the program's early minutes were deliberately dull. Events slowly accelerated into an excited pace as the aliens killed their first victims. Listeners tuning in late panicked after hearing the announcer reporting news of a hostile attack. The next morning, *The New York Times* headline claimed "Radio Listeners in Panic, Taking War Drama As Fact."

All across the nation people were telephoning newspapers to ask what they should do. The Associated Press sent out an explanatory bulletin to its member papers. Police stations were swamped with calls. Priests received calls from people seeking confession. Some people dug old World War I gas masks out of closets. Sailors on shore leave in New York City were summoned back to their ships. In Indianapolis, a woman rushed into a church service screaming that the world was coming to an end; she had heard it on the radio (Barnouw, 1968, 87–88).

After World War II, radio listeners experienced a cultural transformation as the big band era ended and the first teenage-oriented culture emerged. A new type of music—rhythm and blues—was crossing racial boundaries. In 1951, Alan Freed became a disc jockey at WJW AM in Cleveland. Leo Mintz, a local record store owner, talked Freed into playing R&B records, which previously had been known in the trade as "race records" and were sold mostly to juke box operators in black neighborhoods (Sullivan, 1965) Freed agreed and named his late-night program *Moondog Rock and Roll Party.* The name quickly became associated with the music.

Alan Freed's show began with the howling of a dog and the theme song "Blue for a Red Boy" by Todd Rhodes, followed by music requests. He began promoting dances featuring the music he was playing on radio. He was an organizer of a show called the *Moondog Coronation Ball* at Cleveland Arena on March 21, 1952. The event is recognized as the first rock 'n' roll concert. It ended early because 21,000 teenagers overcrowded the arena.

Freed was among the first people to promote racial integration among youth at a time of deeply rooted racial strife. In September 1954, he moved to WINS radio in New York City. He was also eventually syndicated in 40 markets across the nation.

His stage shows continued to be sensations. In 1958, Freed was arrested and blamed for a riot at his *Big Beat* show in Boston. His concerts were banned in Newark and New Haven. Rock 'n' roll music was condemned by public officials as immoral and was cited for promoting juvenile delinquency. Freed was outspoken in defending his fans and the music. *Ebony* magazine claimed that he was ridiculed and subjected to threats and harassment by the government for airing black artists (Chappell, 2001).

In 1959, while at WABC radio, payola rumors surfaced. The station asked him to sign a statement denying that he had ever accepted payola; he refused and was fired. In 1962, he pleaded guilty to commercial bribery. Although he received only a $300 fine and a suspended sentence, his career was over.

Alan Freed's death in January 1965 marked the passing of an era. He called himself "King of the Moondogs" and was the man responsible for bringing rock 'n' roll to worldwide popularity as tapes of his programs were broadcast in Europe. In 1986, Alan Freed was inducted into the Rock 'n' Roll Hall of Fame along with some of the black artists he helped to popularize, including James Brown, Chuck Berry, Sam Cooke, Fats Domino, and Little Richard. In 2002, his ashes were moved to the museum. The plaque that marks his grave reads simply, "Alan Freed 1921–1965."

As mainstream radio began playing rock 'n' roll in the 1950s, a converging counterculture movement fueled by hard-core pacifists began to form a new kind of radio broadcasting (Lasar, 1998). Lewis Hill organized Pacifica Radio (KPFA-FM) in Berkeley, California, in 1949. KPFA was the first listener-supported FM community radio station.

Hill was a Quaker and a conscientious objector. His goal was to promote social activism and antiwar protests. In 1950, he criticized the Korean War and pledged on the air not to cooperate in the war effort and to resist the draft.

Named after the philosophy of pacifism, the Pacifica station gradually grew into a national five-station network by 1977. Historian Matthew Lasar (2004) claimed that Lewis Hill fostered what he called a "pacific world in our time" through the encouragement of public dialogue.

Hill determined that a noncommercial station could survive if 2% of its audience were willing to pay a subscription. In its early years, the "2% theory" was a cornerstone of Pacifica Radio. Hill published his views on listener-supported radio in *Voluntary Listener Sponsorship*, written in 1958.

From the beginning, the station mixed highbrow classical music with folk and jazz. However, the station's first staff members were never remotely proletariat except in sympathy. KPFA's early programming was aimed mostly at university audiences (Whiting, 1992).

As FM receivers became popular in the 1960s, the Pacifica stations became sources of information for the Vietnam antiwar movement, the Berkeley Free Speech movement (1964), and the student uprising at Columbia (1968).

KPFA's broadcast archives feature controversial figures from several decades, including minority activists and alternative ideologues. Philosopher Alan Watts was on KPFA from 1954 until his death in 1973. Poet Allen Ginsberg and Lawrence Ferlinghetti appeared beginning in 1955. In 1958, the nuclear arms race was debated on the air by Nobel Prize–winner Linus Pauling and Hungarian-born Edward Teller, the father of the H-bomb. In 1963, I.F. Stone and Bertrand Russell opposed the Vietnam War on the air. Pacifica aired interviews with Che Guevara just before his death in 1965.

Lewis Hill's influence extended beyond Pacifica Radio. He created the Broadcast Foundation of America, the direct antecedent of the Public Broadcasting System (PBS), which brings listener-supported radio and TV to every American.

By the 1980s, social transformations were occurring as America moved away from the Vietnam era. The word "yippie" entered the lexicon to refer to the rise of a new middle class of college graduates with greater purchasing power. The era was characterized by the emergence of conservative political power as Ronald Reagan took office.

In radio, regulatory changes contributed to the rise of talk-show host Rush Limbaugh. He is credited for reviving AM talk radio after audiences declined in the 1970s. The wave of right-wing talk hosts who dominate today's radio was spawned by Rush Limbaugh.

In 1988, after four successful years at KFBK-AM in Sacramento, Limbaugh moved to WABC-AM in New York City. His quick rise in popularity followed the 1987 Federal Communications Commission (FCC) repeal of the Fairness Doctrine, which required stations to provide contrasting views on controversial issues. The FCC ruling triggered an avalanche of one-sided political AM talk shows. The shows are targeted at a niche audience of adult listeners and are inexpensive to syndicate via satellite.

As a master showman, Limbaugh is the staple and most influential voice for ultraconservative Republicans. His program was first nationally syndicated in August 1988. He is credited with being the catalyst for the 1994 Republican congressional victory, igniting conservative political power that only recently has been declining (Fund, 1995). As of 2005, Arbitron ratings showed that Limbaugh had a minimum weekly audience of 13.5 million. This was the largest radio audience in the United States ("Latest Top Host," 2005).

The Rush Limbaugh Show is syndicated by Premiere Radio networks, a property of Clear Channel Communications. American Forces Radio also carries the first hour of Limbaugh's show overseas. In November 2005, Limbaugh began an "Adopt a Soldier" program. Military personnel anywhere in the world can register and receive a donated subscription to Limbaugh's premium Web site ("Rush 24/7") and the *Limbaugh Newsletter.*

Limbaugh is a creative humorist who uses various phrases to amuse his audience. Listeners are called "dittoheads," referring to his request that callers just say "ditto" rather than waste time with introductions. He refers to himself as "The Doctor of Democracy."

His presentations are highly controversial, raising questions about accuracy and honesty. He is viewed as relying heavily on propaganda (Larson, 1997) and as drawing from the skills of gossip columnists such as Walter Winchell (Pratte, 2004). According to William S. Swain (1999), to use labels such as propagandists for Rush Limbaugh is simplistic. We need to study the real effects of Limbaugh's show on his listeners.

Regardless of your view of Rush Limbaugh, he is one of the most popular radio talk-show hosts in modern times. The National Association of Broadcasters gave him the Marconi Radio Award for Syndicated Radio Personality four times. In 1993, he was inducted into the Radio Hall of Fame.

The seven personalities discussed in this foreword represent various transitional eras in the history of American Radio. We began and closed with two radio commentators, Will Rogers and Rush Limbaugh. The common bridge between them is radio. Rogers and Limbaugh have demonstrated the enduring power and presence of radio as a political and social voice in our lives.

In American culture, there may have been other fictional broadcasts and films that equal the sensation aroused by *Amos 'n' Andy* and *The War of the Worlds*, but none have surpassed them in brilliance or impact. Freeman Gosden, Charles Correll, and Orson Welles amplified a special characteristic experienced only through radio—the "theater of the mind."

Alan Freed and rock 'n' roll marked the transition between the first and second half of the 20th century. Radio not television brought teenage music into our lives and into America's popular culture.

Lewis Hill, a Quaker and pacifist, created the first counterculture radio station. Since 1949, Pacifica Radio has been a voice for free speech, human dignity, and equality. Can you remember Vietnam, civil rights marches, student protests, feminists, and hippies? Look up the Pacifica Radio timeline on the Web. It documents the history of America's counterculture.

As this book makes obvious, radio is very special. It speaks to us. It challenges our imagination and conscience. It invites us to surf through its many voices and sounds, and it provides us with information and enjoyment. To be turned on, it simply requires we turn on ... the radio.

References

Barnouw, Erik. (1968). *The Golden Web: A History of Broadcasting in the United States, Volume II—1933–1953.* New York: Oxford University Press.

Buxton, Frank & Bill Owen. (1972). *The Big Broadcast 1920–1950.* New York: Viking Press.

Chappell, Kevin. (2001). How Blacks Invented Rock and Roll. *Ebony*, June, 146.

Larson, Mary. (1997). Rush Limbaugh Broadcast Demagogue. *Journal of Radio Studies*, 4, 189–202.

Lasar, Matthew. (1998). Hybrid Highbrow: The Pacifica Foundation and KPFA's Reconstruction of Elite Culture, 1946–1963. *Journal of Radio Studies*, 5 (1), 51–67.

———. (2004). Pacifica Foundation U.S. Non-commercial Radio Network. In *Encyclopedia of Radio* (p. 1057). Museum of Broadcast Communications. Christopher Sterling, Chicago: Fitzroy Dearborn Publishers.

Latest Top Host Figures. (2005). *Talkers Magazine.* Retrieved from http://www.talkers.com/talkhost.htm. April 16, 2007.

McLeod, Elizabeth. (2005). The Original Amos 'n' Andy: Freeman Gosden, Charles Correll and the 1928–43 Radio Serial [Book summary]. Retrieved from http://www.midcoast.com/~lizmcl/aa.html. April 22, 2007.

Pratte, Alf. (2004). Limbaugh, Rush 1951: U.S. Talk Show Host. In *Encyclopedia of Radio* (p. 866). Museum of Broadcast Communication. Christopher H. Sterling, Chicago: Fitzroy Dearborn Publishers.

Sullivan, James W. (1965). Alan Freed, Rose & Fell to Music of Rock 'n' Roll. *New York Herald Tribune* (Obituaries), January 21.

Swain, William S. (1999). Propaganda and Rush Limbaugh: Is the Label the Last Word? *Journal of Radio Studies*, 6 (1), 27–40.

Whiting, John. (1992). The Lengthening Shadow: Lewis Hill and the Origins of Listener-Sponsored Broadcasting in America. *Dolphin*, 23, 190.

Introduction

MICHAEL C. KEITH

The launch of radio changed the country in both subtle and profound ways. From its experimental origins before World War I to regular broadcasting after the war, it began to transform how Americans spent their leisure time and acquired information. As radio took over the parlor, it became the principal means for passing the time between work and bed. Indeed, daily life was altered by the transformation of wireless technology into a new household utility.

In the first decade of radio broadcast operations—the 1920s—women and minorities were marginalized by Anglo male dominance, and radio reflected this unfortunate reality. Not surprisingly, women and minorities, namely African Americans, were portrayed according to the prevailing social biases of the time—as radio reflected the cultural status quo. Women were depicted on the air as domestic caregivers—housewives and mothers—and blacks and other minorities were represented as second-class citizens to be ignored or stereotyped (just consider the hugely popular *Amos 'n' Andy* for one obvious example). Yet, paradoxically, the presence of women and minorities on radio (even in stereotypical roles) would ultimately help these maligned groups overcome the limitations imposed on them—albeit not for a very long time. Eventually women and minorities would utilize radio to address their equitable participation in the life of the nation.

The importance of radio as social instrument and catalyst became amply evident in the 1930s and 1940s on two fronts in particular. When the Depression placed the nation in the quicksand of financial despair, President Roosevelt turned to radio to galvanize people behind his administration's plans to reverse the harrowing descent. On some 30 occasions, FDR spoke directly to America's citizens over the airwaves. The overwhelming response demonstrated the power of broadcasting at crucial moments in history. So did the unintended panic created by Orson Welle's infamous *The War of the Worlds* broadcast in late 1938. Just two years later, Edward R. Murrow broadcast courageous reports from a bombed-out London, tuning America to its own fast-approaching war. Never before had Americans been instantaneously transported to battlefronts from the comfort of their own parlors. Radio became the first and primary source of news during World War II, an indispensable means for staying abreast of world, national, and local events. In a few short years, radio became a vital part of the American experience.

As television steadily usurped radio's status as home entertainer after 1948, the audio medium struggled until it developed an enthusiastic audience among young people who cherished the portable receivers that brought them the latest pop music and hip deejays. Top 40 radio's impact on the youth culture was immense on several levels. Radio empowered teens in ways hitherto unimaginable—and perhaps, for adults, undesirable—by instilling in them a sense of connection, exclusivity, and entitlement. Radio spoke to young people in their own language and influenced their attitudes and behavior in lasting ways.

As the public's consciousness about civil rights was raised in the late 1950s and through the 1960s, radio was seen as one means of vocalizing needs by marginalized segments of the population. One of the most extraordinary examples of radio's new value in addressing social inequities is the story of Native American radio. By the late 1960s, the nation's indigenous community had been watching the Black Power movement with keen interest and decided to emulate its strategy for addressing social wrongs. One positive way to reverse the negative influence of mainstream culture (and media) on its languages and traditions was to build its own radio stations on reservations. Today nearly three dozen radio stations are licensed to Native Americans and they help maintain the legacy and heritage of their listeners as well as promote their social and economic well-being. There is arguably no greater example of how a public medium can be used as a force for necessary change. Native American radio is a growing force and offers a strong case for why the radio medium deserves scholarly examination as an instrument of change.

Radio made its presence known in another way in the 1960s through the signals of stations standing in opposition to the status quo in the radio industry itself as well as in society. Essentially, the radio programming phenomenon known variously as underground, progressive, alternative, and freeform was spawned by two key factors: a disdain for formula radio (specifically Top 40) among a handful of young and rebellious broadcasters and the cultural upheaval over Vietnam and civil rights that characterized the period. In the first instance, the highly formulaic hit music radio sound—featuring two-and-a-half-minute doo-wop tunes and frenetic deejays—that dominated the AM airwaves had finally driven some radio aficionados and practitioners to chart a different course. This powerful though short-lived revolution in radio found sustenance in and gained inspiration from the counterculture movement that was sweeping the country's colleges. Rock music began to reflect the antiestablishment sentiments of the nation's young people, thus further fanning the flame of discontent that gave rise to commercial underground radio. This was radio designed and oriented "for the people" that gave the new programming genre its uniqueness and cachet. Stations promoting an anticorporate and antigovernment mindset were rare in commercial radio. Audiences were not accustomed to hearing deejays speak out against the military-industrial complex, big business, and social inequality while advocating love and sometimes even the use of mind-altering drugs. Nor were listeners acquainted with commercial radio that aired a broad spectrum of music (albeit rock and roll) in thoughtful and evocative sets emphasizing quality and substance over quantity and banality.

Noncommercial stations (mainly affiliated with colleges) offered programming that contrasted with mainstream commercial outlets and the gestalt that informed them, but their audiences were tiny compared with those of their commercial counterparts. Indeed, as underground radio sought to reflect deeper social issues, educational stations on the lower end of the FM band attempted to address civil inequities through programs for marginalized groups, such as gays and lesbians. As noted in *Queer Airwaves*, "The story of gay and lesbian broadcasting is only beginning to be told ... The 60s and 70s gave way to several radio shows, mainly on non-commercial radio stations that engaged in a dialogue with the gay community." (Johnson/ Keith, p. 8) This was not happening on television or in the commercial part of the broadcast radio dial. Indeed, "[q]ueer radio would push forward and feverishly combat the stereotypical attitudes and hate propaganda targeted toward gays and lesbians into the present." (p. 9).

Sadly, hate broadcasts found a place on radio in the 1980s and 1990s with shock jocks (who found it great sport to denigrate women, gays, and minorities) and right-wing extremists (who spewed virulent racist and homophobic rhetoric). In this sense, radio again reflected society in providing both good and evil. From the 1930s national broadcasts of the anti-Semitic Catholic priest Charles Coughlin to the racist ranting of neo-Nazis and white supremacists, such as David Duke and Ernst Zundel (recently incarcerated in Germany for his denial of the Holocaust), in the last decade of the 20th century, radio has been exploited for malevolent purposes. Fortunately, the positive service of radio has far outweighed the iniquity. However, the potential of the medium to shape views of a vast audience appeals to those with agendas that strike the mainstream as harmful and even dangerous.

Two movements in the past couple of decades again demonstrate how integral radio is to the social and cultural machinations of the country. Political talk radio has influenced some voting decisions, and in the early

1990s it actually influenced the outcome of several state elections and the composition of the U.S. Congress. This is yet another poignant example of radio's role in reflecting society. To the chagrin of liberals, talk radio has been largely dominated by social and political conservatives. Political pundits argue that without talk radio, the leadership of the country might have been significantly different. So should we credit or condemn radio for giving us the politicians we have? Radio has clearly had an influence on the nation's history.

A more recent radio development with potential sociopolitical bearing is low-power FM (LPFM for short), which has its roots in clandestine broadcasts that have appeared from time to time. These unauthorized and thus unlicensed stations provided alternative music and public affairs programs. Staring in the mid-1970s, a long period of deregulation has relieved broadcasters of many former obligations, most notably the Fairness Doctrine (dropped in 1978). The subsequent rise of one-sided right-wing broadcasting was one factor behind the rise of illegal low-power outlets. Micro or pirate stations, as they were initially labeled, were inspired to enter the airwaves to address what they perceived as radio's shortcomings, including a decline in public service content. Their goal was to provide highly local and community-oriented programming, something they felt traditional radio was not providing owing to its bottom-line obsession. Micro stations sought to provide an alternative to profit-obsessed, big business radio and even mainline public stations. These illicit broadcasters felt justified in airing without authorization because they believed they were exercising their constitutional rights of free speech and providing an important public service, which, after all, was the principle behind the issuance of broadcast licenses in the first place. The government saw things differently and in the name of actual or potential interference forced most of these stations off the air. At the start of the new century, the FCC created tiny LPFM licenses to meet the obvious demand for more voices. However, faced with resistance from the odd bedfellows of commercial and public broadcasters, these are issued only in limited numbers and largely in rural regions, mostly to church and civic groups. This action has frustrated the community of micro broadcasters, who, left out of the mix, have in some cases continued their illegal broadcasts.

Beyond the shores and borders of the United States, radio's social and cultural role has been no less notable. In developing countries, the medium has typically served (and continues to serve) as the primary information source, and in some third world countries its use is of singular importance as print media are often unavailable or unreliable. It is hard to calculate the value of radio to NGOs in Tanzania attempting to address gender discrimination (spousal abuse and genital mutilation) or the influence of community radio in Mongolia seeking to increase "opportunities for citizen participation and encourage social accountability" (Developing Radio Partners, 2007). Radio brings people and cultures together in sparsely populated and remote locales around the globe.

Drawing from the legacy of radio studies pioneers Paul Lazarsfeld, Hadley Cantril, and others, and in keeping with Michele Hilmes's and Jason Loviglio's *Radio Reader* (2002) and Susan Squier's *Communities of the Air* (2003) seeks to examine the many facets of radio's participation in American culture from the perspective of several leading scholars. Distinguishing this particular volume from the formidable works cited above is its focus on the relationship of certain minority or so-called fringe groups with radio at different points in its development and history. To this end, Susan Brinson launches the volume with an assessment of how communication regulators have failed African American station ownership efforts as a consequence of mainstream partisanship. Donald Browne follows with an examination of the ways in which linguistic minorities have utilized radio, Roberto Avant-Mier discusses the medium in terms of its multifaceted influence in the Hispanic community through popular music traditions, Bruce Smith explores the unique mission of radio in remote and often impoverished Native American communities, Donna Halper addresses how radio gave public voice to women, Phylis Johnson tells the affecting story of gay and lesbian radio, and underground radio pioneer Larry Miller reflects on the contribution of 1960s counterculture programmers.

Increasing the volume's scope are Tona Hangen's assessment of religious radio's effectiveness in fulfilling its mandate to broadcast in the "public interest, convenience, and necessity," Elizabeth Fones-Wolf's analysis of the efforts of labor unions to overcome the corporate world's domination of the airwaves, National Public Radio news anchor Corey Flintoff's perspective on the challenges confronting public radio, Louise Benjamin's study of the government's actions and reactions to indecent broadcasts, Robert Hilliard's investigation of hate speech in mainstream and far-right-wing programs, Peter Laufer's evaluation of talk radio's influence on contemporary society, Douglas Craig's overview of the way in which radio provided Americans with a new form of political debate, and Lawrence Soley's disquisition into the passion and plight of unlicensed low-power radio stations.

Rounding out the volume are Cindy Welch's account of the use of radio to inspire young readers, Barbara Calabrese's examination of the existence and value of radio studies in the communication classroom and curriculum, Michael Keith's survey of cultural studies in radio, and Christopher Sterling's perspective on the future of terrestrial radio as new and evolving audio technologies draw listeners from the medium.

Despite the recent spate of laudable scholarly studies of radio, the subject has been slow to gain traction and acceptance in academic circles and curricula. Yet it does seem the tide has turned, and this fact is encouraging to anyone who recognizes and appreciates the significant role the medium has played in the daily ebb and flow of society and culture since its arrival nearly a century ago. As the great radio dramatist Norman Corwin once wrote, "Sometimes the obvious is the most difficult thing to recognize."

Note

Portions of this introduction appeared as an invited editorial in the September 2007 issue of the *Journal of Broadcasting and Electronic Media* and are reprinted here with permission from Lawrence Erlbaum.

References

Developing Radio Partners. Retrieved from http://www.developingradiopartners.org/newsroom/html, March 28, 2007.
Johnson, Phylis & Keith, Michael C. (2001), *Queer Airwaves: The Story of Gay and Lesbian Broadcasting*. Armonk, NY: M.E. Sharpe.

Part 1 Listening to Other Voices

As Americans used radio to help make their mass world personal, its intrusions no longer felt so disempowering, and the possibility of counting in that world no longer seemed so impossible.

—Bruce Lenthall

1. Radio's Covenant: The Regulatory Failure of Minority Ownership of Broadcast Radio Facilities

Susan Brinson

"In a society dominated by centralized sources of information and imagery, in which economic imperatives and pervasive values promote the search for large, common-denominator audiences, what is the fate of those groups who ... find themselves outside the mainstream?" (Gross, 1995, 61). This intriguing question is central to the chapters in this anthology, all of which focus on the ways in which "mainstream" values were either perpetuated or challenged through radio. As other contributors to this volume recognize, the "economic imperatives" to which Gross refers are a powerful way through which the mainstream communicates values and attitudes to the public. Virtually since its inception, broadcast radio was constructed as a commercial enterprise. Nearly every aspect of its structure was, and continues to be, built on the foundation of making money. Network systems, advertising, and programming all developed with profit in mind. One of the most fundamental business aspects of radio broadcasting in the United States, however, is the licensee, the person or group to whom broadcast frequencies are granted. The process of radio station licensing affects the economic imperatives of nonmainstream groups.

Throughout its history of broadcast regulation in the United States, the Federal Communications Commission (FCC) fundamentally protected mainstream interests. One of the least obvious, yet most successful, ways in which it accomplished this goal was through controlling radio station ownership. With the sole power to determine who received the valuable licenses and frequency assignments, the FCC was more than just a "traffic cop" of the airwaves. The power to determine who received a license was also the indirect ability to influence the content of broadcast programming. Although the FCC did not specifically choose content, it chose the people who programmed those messages. Thus, the commission sat in the preeminent position for determining whose viewpoints had access to the airwaves. Though liberal and conservative licensees and politicians historically fought over a wide variety of regulations, they never questioned the more fundamental issue of access to the frequencies. That was a given. Rather, their debates focused on the degree to which regulations protected their perspectives *within* the dominant paradigm. In other words, if you were a media corporation or a wealthy white male who supported free enterprise and democracy, your chances of winning a broadcast license were infinitely better than if you belonged to a minority, were female or openly gay, or were a member of a labor union or the Communist Party (Brinson, 2004; Classen, 1994; Godfried, 2002; Horwitz, 1997; Williams, 2002). Thus the messages communicated through radio almost exclusively represented values and attitudes within an ideology that privileged the wealthy/white/heterosexual male perspective. Effectively ignored among the battles over licensing procedures or content were the groups of people who did not own broadcast facilities and whose perspectives were not communicated through one of the most powerful and pervasive media in the United States.

Very few of the thousands of broadcasting licenses granted by the FCC were awarded to minorities. Jesse B. Blayton became the first African American radio station licensee in 1949, nearly 30 years after the start of the broadcasting industry and certainly long after radio was fully established as a medium that was both owned by and communicated the interests of white America (Minority Ownership, 1979). By 1978, less than 1% of broadcast properties in the United States were owned by minorities (Minority Ownership, 1979). An industry that was central to U.S. economic and political systems and considered one of the great tools of democracy effectively excluded minority groups from access to its airwaves. The representations and voices of minorities that were communicated on radio were filtered through the lenses, and served the interests, of wealthy, white, heterosexual, male America to the virtual exclusion of other perspectives.

With few exceptions, the issue of minority access to broadcasting remained uncontested until the late 1960s. In 1968, the Kerner Commission released the results of its investigation into the 1967 "race riots" in Newark and Detroit. The commission's analyses focused partly on the widespread belief among minorities that broadcasting represented the values and attitudes of white America to the exclusion of minority citizens (*Report of the National Advisory Commission*, 1968). The FCC ultimately responded to the report by creating a policy in 1978 intended to increase minority ownership of broadcast facilities. Three decades later, however, minority ownership accounts for only 3.5% of total ownership (http://www.fcc.gov/ownership).[1] With nearly 30 years for its accomplishment, why has the FCC's clearly stated goal to increase minority ownership of broadcast stations failed? The answers lie in a complex combination of economics, judicial review, and politics. Potential minority owners face the widespread and persistent inability to secure the necessary capital to purchase a radio or television station, and FCC policies intended to ameliorate these obstacles faced fluctuating judicial reviews until they were ultimately rejected as unconstitutional. Finally, the past 30 years reveal fluctuating political commitment to increasing minority ownership of broadcast facilities. Ultimately, the FCC became the point of intersection at which competing economic, legal, and political forces manifested themselves. This chapter provides a historical background for contextualizing minority ownership and explains the current lack of ownership as the result of economic barriers, judicial decisions, and politics.

Conspicuous Problems and Potential Solutions

Motivated by the Kerner recommendations, the FCC took a hard, critical look at its licensing practices. In 1978, under the leadership of Democratic president Jimmy Carter, the FCC issued its "Statement of Policy on Minority Ownership of Broadcasting Facilities" (1978). The commission declared that its policy measures were not effectively addressing minorities' concerns about the media and focused its attention on the "dearth" of minority owners. "It is the licensee who is ultimately responsible for identifying and serving the needs and interests of his [*sic*] audience," the commission determined (1978, 981). Committed to increasing minority ownership, the commission recognized the economic barriers facing potential minority owners and established guidelines intended to help alleviate those obstacles.

Access to capital is the foundation on which media ownership rests. One of the most significant and long-term impediments preventing minorities from broadcast ownership is the difficulty of amassing large amounts of capital. Radio stations are extremely expensive to purchase and maintain; thus it is critical for potential buyers to find lenders willing to loan significant sums. From 1978 to the present, minorities consistently faced widespread discrimination in acquiring capital despite the fact that many had (and have) extensive successful business experience and some operating capital of their own, and were prominent and well-respected businesspeople in their communities. Applicants often faced protracted negotiations during which lending institutions undervalued collateral and potential earnings, required personal guarantees and assets as additional collateral, and assumed a paternalistic attitude toward the applicant. Adding insult to injury, lending institutions often rejected minority applications while approving applications from white people with similar collateral and qualifications.

The problem has not abated. Successful and potential licensees continue to report that systemic barriers minimize or prevent their entry to the broadcasting market (Whose Spectrum, 2000).

Beginning in 1978, the FCC developed policies to help overcome these discriminatory practices, including maintaining lists of minorities interested in purchasing stations, creating preferential "credits," adopting a distress sale policy, issuing tax certificates, and working with the Small Business Administration. The three FCC policies that held the most promise for encouraging minority ownership were preferential credits, distress sales, and tax certificates.

Preferential Credits

In 1965 the FCC revised its comparative hearing guidelines and determined that it would consider the following issues to determine licensing: diversification of control, full-time participation by station owners, proposed program service, past broadcasting record, efficient use of the frequency, and character (Whose Spectrum, 2000). Between 1971 and 1974, however, federal court decisions forced the commission to consider the race of the competing applicants as well (Policy Statement, 1965). As a result, in 1975 the agency created a system by which minority applicants were granted "credits" that weighed the licensing decision in their favor, (*Citizens Communications Center et al. v. FCC*, 1971; *Garrett v. FCC*, 1975; *TV9, Inc. v. FCC*, 1974). The preferential credits policy immediately increased the number of minority-owned stations, and the commission continued it until the mid-1990s.

Distress Sales

The distress sale policy was developed and implemented in 1978. Station owners who were in conflict with FCC rules and found their licenses in jeopardy were given the option of avoiding costly comparative hearings by selling their stations at reduced "distress sale" prices to minority purchasers. The lower purchase price accomplished two significant objectives: potential minority applicants did not have to acquire as much purchasing capital, and lending institutions were more willing to make a loan on a station priced below market value. A key stipulation required that the minority purchaser had to have an aggregate of at least 50% of the controlling interest of the station. The idea seemed to work; at least 25 stations were acquired by minorities between 1978 and 1982 as a result of the policy (Stavitsky, 1992).

Tax Certificates

To encourage station owners to sell their properties to minority purchasers, the FCC utilized a certificate program in which sellers were allowed to defer capital gains taxes temporarily if they sold to a minority. It was a policy favored by the broadcasting industry as it sellers reaped significant tax benefits (Honig, 1984). More important, it was successful in accomplishing the goal of increasing minority ownership of broadcast facilities. Minority broadcasters reported to the FCC that the "tax certificate program was the single most effective program in lowering market entry barriers and providing opportunities for minorities to acquire broadcast licenses in the secondary market" (Whose Spectrum, 2000, 106; see also Krasnow & Fowlkes, 1991). By late 1994, at least 281 radio and television stations had been purchased by minority owners as a result of the tax certificate incentive (Notice of Proposed Rulemaking, 1995).

Thus, the FCC embarked on the path of increasing minority ownership of broadcast facilities by providing solutions that were intended to address the economic barriers faced by minority applicants. Despite its intended goal, however, and the successes of the preferential credits, distress sales, and tax certificates, by 2003 minority ownership had not exceeded 3.8%. If the programs showed early promise, what happened? The answers lie in judicial reviews of FCC policies and the influence of partisan politics on commission policymaking, both of which combined essentially to eliminate programs for increasing ownership.

The Judicial Seesaw

The growth and decline of minority ownership of broadcast facilities from 1978 to 2007 is closely linked to several legal challenges. In the early 1970s, judicial decrees forced the FCC to develop policies to promote minority ownership and federal court decisions upheld the constitutionality of those policies. Between 1971 and 1975, the DC Court of Appeals encouraged the commission to grant "enhancements" to minority applicants on the basis of their race (*Citizens Communications Center et al. v. FCC*, 1971; *Garrett v. FCC*, 1975; *TV9, Inc. v. FCC*, 1974; see also Honig, 1984; Kleiman, 1991; McGunagle, 1991; Meeske, 1976; Stavitsky, 1992; Triebold, 1991; Wilde, 1990). These judicial exhortations prompted the commission to hold a conference in April 1977 to ascertain the various barriers impeding minority acquisition of broadcasting stations, which later culminated in the "Statement of Policy on Minority Ownership of Broadcasting Facilities" (1978) and the resulting distress sale and tax certificate policies. As already established, these policies showed early promise in achieving the FCC's goal of increasing minority ownership.

Under the Reagan administration, however, the federal courts began to waver in their commitment to preferential policies. The first indications came in the DC Court of Appeals' decision in *Steele v. FCC* (1985 in which the Appeals Court struck down an FCC decision granting preferential treatment to a female applicant and asserted that the commission exceeded its statutory authority in doing so. In a strongly worded majority opinion, the court gave a preview of a growing sentiment against preferences in general. Although the case focused on female ownership, the court's castigation of the commission was interpreted to include other minorities as well. As a result, the legal foundation on which minority preferences rested seemed less solid. Although the Supreme Court continued to uphold preferential treatment for minorities (particularly in *Metro Broadcasting, Inc. v. FCC*, 1990), the constitutionality of those policies was finally decided by the Supreme Court in *Adarand Constructors, Inc. v. Pena* (1995), in which governments' use of preferential credits on the basis of race was severely limited. The Supreme Court asserted that a "strict scrutiny" must be undertaken of racial classifications in decision making and, furthermore, that "such classifications are constitutional only if they are narrowly tailored measures that further compelling governmental interests" (*Adarand*, 1995, 227). The Court specifically stipulated that FCC minority preferences were unconstitutional (p. 227).

Thus, when one asks why FCC policies to increase minority ownership have not succeeded significantly, a partial answer is provided by fluctuating judicial decisions that initially supported the policies but ultimately rejected them as unconstitutional. The policies were halted before accomplishing any substantial change, despite the fact that they showed promise for increasing minority ownership of broadcasting facilities. Another aspect of the answer lies in the intersection of politics and policymaking.

Politics, Public Interest, and FCC Policymaking

A complete account of the lack of minority ownership must incorporate an analysis of the FCC as a political agency. Past analyses of minority ownership focus on the FCC's failure to license more minorities (Honig, 1984; Meeske, 1976; Owens, 2004; Wilde, 1990). It is true that increasing minority ownership is the FCC's responsibility, but only to the extent that it is the regulatory agency overseeing the broadcast industry *within a political context*. The degree to which the commission is committed to any policy is directly related to the political party in control of the executive branch of the federal government. Thus, although the FCC is statutorily directed to regulate "in the public interest," how that concept is defined differs according to political philosophies. As Rowland (1997) explains, political conservatives assert that the public interest is best served by protecting business interests first. If the profit-oriented engines are allowed to run according to their own best interests, the public will inevitably benefit. A pro-business atmosphere will result in a well-served and well-protected public. Political liberals define public interest from a polar opposite perspective, arguing that a government's responsibility is protecting its citizenry from the damaging consequences of business interests who care more about profits than the effect of their practices on the public. Thus, political liberals assert that a government agency charged with serving the public interest should serve the public, not business.

Although all FCC decisions assert that the commission's policies serve "the public interest," a close reading reveals that decisions during politically conservative periods tend to protect business interests whereas decisions during politically liberal periods tend to promote public interests (Brinson, 2004; McChesney, 1993; Powe, 1987). Such is the case with the FCC's vacillating dedication to increasing minority ownership. The period during which the commission created and implemented the distress sale and tax certificate policies (1978–1981) coincided with Democrat Jimmy Carter's presidency (1976–1980). The decline of the distress sale policy, including judicial challenges to it, coincided with the Republican presidencies of Ronald Reagan (1980–1988) and George H.W. Bush (1988–1992) but was mitigated by Democratically controlled Congresses.[2] Recommitment to increasing minority ownership returned to the FCC when Democrat Bill Clinton assumed the presidency (1992–2000), the effectiveness of which was limited by a Republican-controlled Congress between 1994 and 2000. The FCC under the Republican administration of George W. Bush (2000–present) appears fully committed to protecting business interests.

1978–1980: Early Commitment

When the commission issued its "Statement of Policy on Minority Ownership of Broadcasting Facilities" in 1978, its basic argument was the importance of increasing minority ownership for the greater good of society. The commission took a strong stand in asserting that minority ownership of broadcast facilities benefited all U.S. citizens, not just minority groups, and was a goal that served the public interest. A year later the FCC reiterated its position that "achieving greater diversity" ensured "that the needs and interests of all Americans are served," a goal to which the agency was fully committed (Minority Ownership, 1979, 5). The fact that this commission implemented the preferential credits, distress sale, and tax certificate policies, which resulted in an immediate increase in the number of stations owned by minorities, testifies to the FCC's commitment under a Democratic executive to serving the public interest by increasing minority ownership.

1980–1992: Retrenchment

When Republican Ronald Reagan assumed the presidency in 1980, he brought to the executive branch a deep commitment to protecting business interests, most obviously manifested in a dedication to government deregulation. Reagan appointed Mark Fowler, a man who was equally devoted to deregulating the broadcasting industry, to chair the FCC. Fowler believed that the FCC's regulatory perception of broadcasters as public trustees should be discarded for a perception of broadcasters as "marketplace participants" (Fowler & Brenner, 1982). Fowler believed that the public trustee model resulted in a regulatory maze, violations of the First Amendment, and the undermining of the free market. Clearly, then, the newly formed Reagan administration and its commission chair intended to develop broadcast regulations with business interests paramount. Thus began deregulation of the broadcast industry.

Deregulation manifested itself, in part, in a declining commitment to increasing minority ownership of broadcast facilities. The first policy to go was the distress sale, which was accomplished by clearing the "regulatory underbrush" created by 50 years of policymaking (McGregor, 1990). With fewer rules to govern their conduct, station owners were less likely to commit rules violations; thus fewer stations found themselves in trouble with the FCC. Less trouble resulted in fewer distress sale possibilities. Only 10 distress sales were approved by the commission between 1982 and 1986, whereas at least 25 distress sale transactions occurred between 1978 and 1982 (Stavitsky, 1992). Lack of interest on the part of potential minority buyers did not account for the sudden drop. Instead, it was lack of commitment on the part of the FCC. Clearly Fowler himself did not favor minority preferences, as indicated by his belief that "the victims of this are the innocent white people who are denied an equal opportunity to compete for a commission license" (Lotteries for LPTV, 1983, 11). Although the Supreme Court continued to support policies such as distress sales and preferential credits, the FCC informally eliminated their use. This move was consistent with a pro-business, antiregulatory perspective as it replaced agency support for diversity initiatives with the assumption that the marketplace would resolve the problem, *if* the market perceived it as a problem.

Failed Recommitment: 1992–2000

The tax certificate policy remained in effect and was widely used by the commission. Between 1978 and 1994, at least 281 radio and television stations changed hands as a result of tax certificates. Why didn't the "marketplace" regulators attack this policy as well? In truth, the policy was supported by the industry because it directly benefited station owners, who received sizable capital gains tax deferrals for selling their stations to minority purchasers.

Shortly after Democrat Bill Clinton's inauguration in 1993, the FCC recommitted itself to increasing minority ownership. In a notice of proposed rulemaking, the commission sought new ways to widen the inroads created by tax certificates with the intent of "maximizing the diversity of points of view available to the public" (Notice of Proposed Rulemaking, 1995, 2788). The notice requested comments regarding measures to increase diversity of viewpoints and economic opportunities for minorities, particularly by enhancing the tax certificate program, which the agency recognized as the most used program, and a particularly effective one, for increasing minority ownership. Thus, the FCC of the mid-1990s changed its direction from what it had been under Fowler and repositioned itself to promote the public's interest via minority ownership.

The plan was immediately thwarted when the Republican-controlled Congress voted to repeal the tax certificate policy (Dewar, 1995; Stern, 1995). In an effort to offset the loss of tax revenue resulting from another legislative measure, both the House and the Senate quickly amended the Self-Employed Persons Health Care Deduction Extension Act to eliminate the FCC tax certificate program (Self-Employed Persons, 1995). When the Act was passed in mid-1995, it halted a very successful program that was the most effective tool in increasing minority ownership (Krasnow & Fowlkes, 1991). Thus, by 1995, the three FCC programs that contributed the most toward increasing minority ownership of broadcast facilities were gutted by either direct or indirect political or judicial action.

On the heels of the loss of the three programs, the goal of increasing minority ownership was further complicated by passage of the 1996 Telecommunications Act. The most sweeping revision of communications legislation since the Communications Act of 1934, the Telecommunications Act of 1996 contained policies that further eroded efforts to increase minority ownership. In particular, the virtual end of ownership caps opened the door for further media conglomeration. The result was a substantial rise in the purchase of stations by conglomerates looking to increase their market domination. The price of stations rapidly escalated, with the two-pronged effect of limiting potential purchasers to conglomerates and forcing most potential minority purchasers out of the bidding process: they simply did not have access to the kind of capital needed to buy the stations. The twin effect of the repeal of tax certificates and the passage of the Telecommunications Act has been virtually to terminate the growth of minority ownership of broadcast facilities.

Given these assaults, the FCC commissioned a historical study to analyze the state of minority ownership of broadcast facilities in the United States. Published in December 2000, on the eve of a transfer of power from

Democrats to Republicans, the study offered a grim picture (Whose Spectrum, 2000). The study concluded that since elimination of the tax certificates and passage of the Telecommunications Act, "the barriers to entry have been raised so high that, left standing, they appear virtually insurmountable. Minority ... ownership in these industries is diminishing at such an alarming rate that many we spoke with felt we had passed the point of no return" (pp. 132–133).

The numbers bear this out. Minority ownership accounted for 2.9% of total ownership in 1998, a percentage that had remained nearly constant throughout the 1990s, despite the fact that more than 500 new television stations launched between 1993 and 1998. A peak minority ownership of 3.8% was reached in 2000 (449 of 11,865 stations), but the number is currently declining. In 2005, minority ownership of broadcast facilities was 3.6% (460 of 12,844 stations).

Continued Retrenchment: 2000–present

At the time of writing, it seems likely that minority ownership will continue to decrease under the current Bush administration. In its 2002 biennial review, the commission asserted its continuing commitment to minority ownership, then decided to increase national ownership caps to 45% of the national audience (In the Matter of, 2003). Although the decision met with widespread, bipartisan criticism, it nonetheless signaled the FCC's current commitment to regulating in the interests of business.

Implications and Conclusion

This chapter began by questioning the impact of the economic imperatives of radio on nonmainstream groups and focused attention on radio station ownership. The interesting research of other contributors to this anthology demonstrates the tenacity with which marginalized groups found ways to express their cultures through radio, but their causes certainly were not helped in any significant way by the FCC. Despite brief periods during which the FCC attempted to increase the diversity of voices on radio through ownership policies, the agency failed in reaching its goal.

Why did the FCC fail in its mission to increase minority ownership of broadcast stations? The three-part answer lies in economic barriers, judicial renderings, and political opposition. In the mid-1970s the FCC followed its liberal definition of public interest and created policies intended to increase minority ownership of broadcast facilities. After the early 1980s, however, its policies were increasingly interpreted and dismantled by conservative politicians and judges. Strong conservative influences in the executive, legislative, and judicial branches successfully undermined attempts to increase minority ownership. The marketplace barriers that always existed (but were somewhat weakened by liberal FCC policies) were reinforced by judicial interpretation and public policy to reaffirm the grip of those who communicated the dominant worldview. Today broadcast facilities remain firmly controlled by major corporations whose ability to contain mass-communicated messages that threaten the bottom line is enhanced by an FCC that protects the economic imperatives of the industry.

The past three decades have witnessed fluctuating attitudes about minority citizens and the ways in which discriminations could and should be resolved. One thing is clear, however. The Kerner Commission's exhortation that "it is time to make good the promises of American democracy to all citizens—urban and rural, white and black, Spanish-surname, American Indian, and every minority group" (*Report of the National Advisory Commission*, 1968, 2) has not been achieved.

Notes

1. The FCC does not distinguish between radio and television stations in reporting its minority ownership data. In 2004 and 2005, minorities comprised at least 50% of the ownership group of 460 of the 12,844 broadcast facilities in the United States.
2. Democrats fully controlled Congress from 1986 to 1992 and controlled the House from 1981 to 1992. The Senate was controlled by Republicans between 1981 and 1986.

References

Adarand Constructors v. Pena. (1995). 515 U.S. 200.

Brinson, S.L. (2004). *The Red Scare, Politics, and the Federal Communications Commission*. Westport, CT: Praeger.

Citizens Communications Center et al. v. FCC. (1971). 447 F.2d 1201.

Classen, S.D. (1994). Standing on Unstable Grounds: A Reexamination of the WLBT-TV Case. *Critical Studies in Mass Communication*, 11 (1), 73–91.

Dewar, H. (1995). Senate Rejects Minority Radio, TV Tax Break. *Washington Post*, April 4, A7.

Fowler, M.S. & D.L. Brenner. (1982). A Marketplace Approach to Broadcast Regulation. *Texas Law Review*, 60 (2), 207–257.

Garrett v. FCC. (1975). 513 F.2d 1056.

Godfried, N. (2002). Identity, Power, and the Local Television: African Americans, Organized Labor and UHF-TV in Chicago, 1962–1968. *Historical Journal of Film, Radio and Television*, 22, 117–134.

Gross, L. (1995). Out of the Mainstream: Sexual Minorities and the Mass Media. In G. Dines & J.M. Humez (eds.), *Gender, Race and Class in Media* (pp. 61–69). Thousand Oaks, CA: Sage.

Honig, D. (1984). The FCC and Its Fluctuating Commitment to Minority Ownership of Broadcast Facilities. *Howard Law Journal*, 27 (3), 859–877.

Horwitz, R.B. (1997). Broadcast Reform Revisited: Reverend Everett C. Parker and the "Standing" Case (*Office of Communication of the United Church of Christ v. Federal Communications Commission*). *Communication Review*, 2 (3), 311–348.

In the Matter of the *2002 Biennial Regulatory Review*. (2003). 18 FCC Rcd 1.

Kleiman, H. (1991). Content Diversity and the FCC's Minority and Gender Licensing Policies. *Journal of Broadcasting and Electronic Media*, 35, 411–429.

Krasnow, E.G. & L.M. Fowlkes. (1991). The FCC's Minority Tax Certificate Program: A Proposal for Life after Death. *Federal Communications Commission Law Journal*, 51 (3), 665–678.

Lotteries for LPTV. (1983). *Broadcasting*, April 4, 31–32.

McChesney, R.W. (1993). *Telecommunications, Mass Media, and Democracy: The Battle for the Control of U.S. Broadcasting, 1928–1935*. New York: Oxford University Press.

McGregor, M.A. (1990). Connections among Deleted Underbrush Policies, FCC Character Standards, and State Criminal Law. *Journal of Broadcasting and Electronic Media*, 34 (2), 153–170.

McGunagle, D.L. (1991). *Metro Broadcasting, Inc. v. FCC*: The Constitutionality of Minority Ownership Preferences in Broadcast Licensing. *Detroit College of Law Review*, 4, 1375–1399.

Meeske, M.D. (1976). Black Ownership of Broadcast Stations: An FCC Licensing Problem. *Journal of Broadcasting*, 20 (2), 261–277.

Metro Broadcasting, Inc. v. FCC. (1990). 110 S.Ct. 2997.

Minority Ownership of Broadcast Facilities: A Report. (1979). Federal Communications Commission, Office of Public Affairs, EEO-Minority Enterprise Division (December).

Notice of Proposed Rulemaking, In the Matter of Policies and Rules regarding Minority and Female Ownership of Mass Media Facilities. (1995). 10 FCC Rcd 2788.

Owens, W.L. (2004). Inequities on the Air: The FCC Media Ownership Rules— Encouraging Economic Efficiency and Disregarding the Needs of Minorities. *Howard Law Journal*, 47 (3), 1037–1071.

Policy Statement on Comparative Broadcast Hearings. (1965). 1 FCC 2nd 395.

Powe, L. (1987). *American Broadcasting and the First Amendment*. Berkeley: University of California Press.

Report of the National Advisory Commission on Civil Disorders. (1968). New York: New York Times.

Rowland, W.D. (1997). The Meaning of "the Public Interest" in Communications Policy, Part One: Its Origins in State and Federal Regulations. *Communication Law and Policy*, 2, 309–328.

Self-Employed Persons Health Care Deduction Extension Act. (1995). Public Law 104–107, 109 Stat. 93.

Statement of Policy on Minority Ownership of Broadcasting Facilities. (1978). 68 FCC 2nd 979.

Stavitsky, A.G. (1992). The Rise and Fall of the Distress Sale. *Journal of Broadcasting & Electronic Media*, 36 (3), 249–266.

Stern, C. (1995). Tax Certificates Gone. *Broadcasting*, April 3, 10.

Triebold, E.L. (1991). The Court Meets Half-Way on Affirmative Action: *Metro Broadcasting, Inc. v. Federal Communications Commission*. *Journal of Corporation Law*, 16, 653–691.

TV9, Inc. v. FCC. (1974). F.2d 929.

Whose Spectrum Is It Anyway? Historical Study of Market Entry Barriers, Discrimination and Changes in Broadcast and Wireless Licensing, 1950–Present. (2000). Office of General Counsel, Federal Communications Commission (December).

Wilde, B.R. (1990). FCC Tax Certificates for Minority Ownership of Broadcast Facilities: A Critical Re-examination. *University of Pennsylvania Law Review*, 138, 979–1026.

Williams, J. (2002). Broadcast Segregation: WJTV's Early Years. *American Journalism*, 19, 87–103.

www.fcc.gov/ownership/data.html. Retrieved March 1, 2007.

2. Speaking in Our Own Tongues: Linguistic Minority Radio in the United States

Donald Browne

Notwithstanding a general absence of scholarly attention to the subject,[1] the ways in which linguistic minorities have utilized radio to express themselves are well worth consideration as part of what comprises radio in the United States, where such minorities now account for approximately 20% of the total population. These minorities' negotiation of space in the electronic public sphere has not been simple, in part because the U.S. government at times has been uneasy about their presence in that sphere. That presence also raises questions about whether such media usage does or does not contribute to the "public good" and to "quality of language." I open with a historical account of three eras in the development of linguistic minority radio in the United States, then consider audience impact, potentially problematic content issues, and offer some conclusions.

Brief History: In the Beginning and on to World War II

As the 20th century opened, a relative trickle of émigrés, most of them from Europe, became something more akin to a river, with millions of "new Americans" streaming into the United States. Newspapers in the languages of their ancestral homelands appeared in many of the nation's larger cities, where a majority of the émigrés had settled. There was one problem: many émigrés could not read or write the languages of their mother tongues. Illiterates could rely on family or friends who *could* read, but such assistance was not always available.

By the time radio broadcasting became established as a medium for household use, some illiterate émigrés had learned to read and write, most often in English. Their children were doing so already. Still, many of them continued to speak their ancestral native languages. The advent of an explicitly oral medium might have provided hope that there soon would be broadcasts in Italian, Spanish, and other languages. What they expected to receive from those broadcasts probably was less clear, since the medium was in its infancy and still in the process of discovering itself.

By the mid-1920s,[2] there was a linguistic minority presence in the electronic media. Certain local radio stations, usually in the larger cities, broadcast a weekly "Polish [Italian, German] Hour." Such programming usually featured music from the ancestral homeland, perhaps a live performance by a local German/Polish/Italian group or soloist, and a community calendar, all held together by a host or hostess who spoke the language (Migala, 1987). Many stations were short on original program material and revenue sources even after the networks first emerged, and émigré groups might pay for the airtime.

The earliest documented record of an extended (i.e., not "one-shot") ethnic minority program that I have discovered is for a Polish language program produced by John Lewandowski and broadcast by WJAY (Cleveland) for a few weeks in 1926,[3] with continuous broadcasts starting in 1927. In Chicago, the *White Eagles Hour*, broadcast for several weeks in 1927, became a continuing program in 1928 (Migala, 1987, 206, 124). Both Chicago and Cleveland had large Polish populations, as did Detroit, Milwaukee, New York City, and other metropolitan areas, which led to the rapid growth of Polish language radio during the pre–World War II years. Programs usually ran for an hour or less on any given day, and typically featured Polish popular music. Some services provided religious programming, others ran material for and even by children, and a few producers tried their hands at radio drama and comedy[4] (Migala, 1987, passim). Some had sponsors and carried commercials.

Such also was the typical pattern for other "large" minority language services (Italian, Spanish, Yiddish, German), but not all linguistic minority groups fared as well. Opportunities for airtime were rare if the group was small, and particularly if it was non-European. Appearances of such groups usually were limited to special events, such as times of celebration or "national days." Money was a common problem, particularly as the Great Depression settled in. Nevertheless, individuals and groups continued to find support for introducing new programs, occasionally to the dismay of others who already were on air in the same language and feared that competition might drive down *their* audience base (Steffanides, 1974, 112–116).

There were various motivations for establishing such services,–some of them financial, some egotistical, a few educational (teaching foreign languages) or religious, and at least one tactical.: The Chicago Federation of Labor (CFL) radio station, WCFL, began to add foreign languages to its program schedule in 1928—just two years after its debut. Godfried (1997, 113) claims that those programs "demonstrated a continuing CFL commitment to make the federation a center of ethnic activity … [r]ecognizing the importance of the ethnic dimension in working-class Chicago. …"[5] Ethnic newspapers also sometimes sponsored radio programs featuring "their" languages, in part to publicize the newspapers themselves.

Educators had realized by the early 1920s that radio could be a vehicle for helping students to learn foreign languages (Lumley, 1934, v). Professors Hendrix (1932), Lumley (1934), and Engel (1936) each conducted a survey of stations broadcasting *instructional* programs in foreign languages. However, only two to three dozen stations reported their activities on any of the surveys. Spanish, German, and French predominated, with occasional appearances for Italian, Portuguese, and Chinese, and with one station offering Esperanto.

After World War II began in September 1939, the Federal Communications Commission (FCC) and the Federal Bureau of Investigation (FBI) discussed ways of "neutralizing" harmful effects from U.S. foreign language broadcasting (Ban on Broadcasts, 1940), although the FCC chair, James Fly, seemed reluctant to actually ban such activity (FCC Head Cold, 1940). As Italy joined the war on Germany's side in June 1940, the National Association of Broadcasters met to consider how stations carrying foreign language broadcasts might monitor their output. Those stations claimed that they already were prepared to do so, by reading scripts in advance, monitoring transmissions, and keeping scripts on file (Horten, 2002, 69–70). The FCC conducted a survey of such stations late in 1940 (Federal Communications Commission, 1940). It found that approximately 200 of the 850 licensed stations in the United States carried foreign language broadcasts, but that another 57 stations had stopped doing so. Most stations operated at 250 watts or less and provided such services for just a few hours per week, but nearly 50 stations with higher power carried 10 or more hours per week, predominantly in European languages (Horten, 2002, 70).

Support for closer supervision came from other quarters, as well. The *New York Times* (Radio Safeguard Asked, 1940) reported that

"The National Council on Freedom From Censorship, an affiliate of the American Civil Liberties Union, urged the Federal Communications Commission today [August 25, 1940] to promulgate a regulation requiring radio stations to have recordings made of all foreign language broadcasts in this country."

Even before the United States entered the war, the American Legion passed a resolution condemning foreign language broadcasting at its fall 1941 convention (Legion Stand Protested, 1941).

The first substantial research on program content was conducted in February 1941 (Arnheim & Bayne, 19421), when individuals at 59 "listening posts" throughout the United States monitored more than 800 hours of foreign language broadcasts over seven days. The survey's "best estimate" of total airtime devoted to foreign language programs during the week came to nearly 1,460 hours, with approximately 300 hours in "other languages," but data presentation and analysis were confined to Italian, Polish, Spanish, Yiddish, German, and Lithuanian, for reasons not explained by the authors. As expected, music (most of it from the home country) was the primary form of content—nearly 75% of the total. Drama came in second, with 12% (but nearly 25% of Italian programming), and news occupied 8.6%. Some monitors stated that music often emphasized nostalgia, and probably would not be attractive to younger listeners. Others noted "amateurish" presenters and criticized the haphazard organization of many of the programs.

One interesting aspect of the survey's findings came in the (unsystematic) monitor analysis of the largely national and international newscasts, which took up just 2% of the total program time on German broadcasts but more than 11% on Italian and Polish broadcasts. Some of the monitors went beyond their mandate to cover the nature and source of each news item by indicating what they themselves thought of the "slant" of the news, particularly for Italian and German newscasts. Several commented on the presence of "pro-fascist" or "pro-Nazi" items, and some reported on conversations they had had with local listeners regarding trends in that regard (more of it now than earlier? less?). The consensus was that there was less.

It is not clear whether the survey results were shared with U.S. government officials, but certainly FCC interest in Italian and German broadcasts increased during 1942. As Horten (2002, 71–82) indicates, the FCC and the Office of War Information (OWI) Foreign Language Division pressured station managers to remove certain individuals from a number of German and Italian programs, and in some cases to drop the programs altogether. The pressure came in various forms, one of which was issuing temporary licenses to some stations carrying foreign language broadcasts and then prolonging the process of station license renewal. Often there were hints that removing a certain individual or program might be helpful.

Sometimes the pressure was more direct. For example, in 1942 the Foreign Language Radio War Control [sic], the "internal watchdog committee" of foreign language broadcasters belonging to the National Association of Broadcasters (NAB), directed WGES Chicago's station manager to remove two Italian language broadcasters if he expected to have his station's license renewed (Horten, 2002, 82). The committee had no authority to remove a license, but as Horten (2002, 74) indicates, it did have a close working relationship with OWI, which in turn had some influence over the FCC. The manager complied.[6]

Others also raised questions regarding content. *Variety* (Government Still Skeptical, 1941) stated that

> With the U.S. [government] riding herd, but not forbidding, as a general thing, the foreign programs, license holders should double, redouble and then intensify their supervision. Fifth columnist scripters and announcers are on the loose. The station owners run the risk of losing their investments if unable to vouch for every interpreter.

Accompanying this opinion piece was a brief report on two radio station in Duluth, Minnesota that carried Finnish broadcasts noting that "they are experiencing difficulty over continued use of Finn programs since declaration of war between U.S. and Nazi forces. Many protests have come to the stations and into open via 'Letters to the Editor' in dailies."

Once the United States had declared war on Japan, Germany, and Italy, the Foreign Language Radio War Control drafted (May 1942) a code calling upon all foreign language radio services in the United States to ensure advance approval of all scripts, monitor all programs, investigate and fingerprint all personnel actively engaged in the broadcast, and take full responsibility for program content and for the loyalty of service personnel. The U.S. government Office of Censorship incorporated the code in its own Code of Wartime Practices for American Broadcasters and included provisions that there were to be "no deviations" from the scripts, adding that "these scripts or transcriptions with their translations should be kept on file at the station" (U.S. government, Office of Censorship, 1942, 8). The office also acquired the power to censor scripts and to demand the removal of those scripts violating the code.

Several contemporary publications offered examples of "pro-fascist" broadcasting by both Italian and German language stations, including *Variety* (Foreign Stations "Confess," 1942; Anti-Nazi Germans, 1942), Arnheim and Bayne (1942, 23–26, 34), Carlson (1943, 117–118), and Friedrich (1942). Smith (1942, 601) observed that "most of the employees interviewed at the stations now carrying foreign programs in Boston had no idea at all of the content of the programs." Horten (2002, 71–74) notes several claims of "pro-fascist" broadcasts but casts doubt on the reliability of a few of them.[7] A congressional hearing turned up evidence of a fascist and a Gestapo (Nazi) agent employed by stations in New York City but also of erroneous accusations in other instances (U.S. Congress, 1943, pt. 1).[8]

The FCC never required that all foreign language programs be recorded, although it did expect stations to be prepared to supply evidence of specific knowledge of program content, particularly when confronted with allegations that certain individuals (usually Italian or German) exhibited pro-fascist bias. Even as the tide of war turned in the Allies' favor, OWI and the FCC continued to exert pressure on the foreign language broadcasters.

However, congressional investigation of the FCC (U.S. Congress, 1943) concluded that much of the pressure was either unwarranted or excessive and that the commission and the OWI had gone far beyond their mandate in employing it not only to punish stations for carrying possibly seditious material but also to ensure that they carry "pro-American" foreign language programs produced by OWI.[9] As a result, OWI was prohibited from producing such programs (Horten, 2002, 82–85), although foreign language stations generally continued to exhibit a pro-American stance.

Postwar America: McCarthy, the Demise of Network Radio, and "New Americans"

There is no record of a linguistic minority–owned and –operated radio station during the first 25 years of American radio.[10] An early breakthrough came in 1946 with the purchase of New York City AM radio station WHOM by two Italians who already owned a prominent Italian newspaper in New York City. They soon converted it into a largely Italian language service (NYC AM Radio History, 2007, 6). A Hispanic American businessman purchased a station in San Antonio that same year and turned it into a Spanish language service (Meyer, 2001).

However, linguistic minority–owned and –operated stations remained relatively few in number, for three main reasons. First, few banks or other potential sources of financial support were willing to risk loans to would-be ethnic minority broadcasters; they were an unknown quantity and so were the services that they intended to provide. Second, specific groups, particularly the many "new American" refugees from Eastern and central Europe, were not all that numerous in most U.S. cities, and size of audience did matter to potential investors. Third, the commercial model remained dominant, so that it was difficult to sell investors on a venture that did not include commercially experienced administrators and staff. Since very few surveys (and none by "reputable" organizations) revealed anything about the size and purchasing habits of such minorities, there was little solid evidence that would encourage investors to back such stations.

The immediate post–World War II years did see two developments that provided some encouragement for linguistic minorities seeking electronic media outlets. FM radio commenced just before the war, but even after the war and with investors regarding radio as a sound investment, FM was shunned by many of them. Noncommercial services thus faced less competition for licenses, especially in the smaller cities. In addition, the FCC set aside a portion of the FM spectrum for noncommercial services and began to license low-power (10–100 watts) radio stations, which lowered the costs of equipment and power.

Given the suspicions directed at foreign language radio services before and during World War II, one might have expected more of the same as Senator Joseph McCarthy and others began to search for Communists in the late 1940s. Commercial radio and TV networks were prominent targets, as was the U.S. government's multilingual radio service, Voice of America. Certainly there were signs of nervousness among ethnic broadcasters. In 1947, two stations in Detroit and in Brooklyn cancelled a total of (apparently) more than 20 foreign language programs, and when their backers sought airtime on other stations in the New York City area that carried such programs, they were told that no airtime was available (Konecky, 1948, 41). Konecky (1948) also notes that WHOM (NYC) cancelled two Polish language programs, and states that there was

> [a] deliberate policy of banning foreign language programs from American broadcasting. [This] marks one of the most dangerous developments of bigotry in radio history. This danger is increased by the fact that behind the suppression of national group radio lurks the House ... Un-American Activities Committee.(p. 40)

While he offered no direct evidence to support that contention, he did point out that in 1946

> [t]here were rumors that legislation was being framed ... for the purpose of abolishing foreign language broadcasts and ... newspapers. ... No subsequent action took place at that time but when the 79th Congress assembled in January [1947], the Wood-Rankin Committee ... [proposed] "that all newspapers in the United States printing matter in a foreign language must print translations of that matter in parallel columns. Failure to comply would result in loss of second class mailing privileges." (p. 40)

That proposal never became law, and Senator McCarthy and the FCC appear to have had little concern over ethnic radio as a possible source of Communist propaganda.[11]

The creation of FM and the expansion of radio station licensing, combined with the gradual though never total withdrawal of the major broadcast networks from the provision of programming to local radio stations, actually assisted the growth of linguistic minority radio. More and more stations were eager to fill out their schedules by selling airtime to various users, including minority groups, especially during the less popular hours and days. As one example, Migala (1987, 111) indicates that stations carrying programs in Polish more than doubled in number (from 85 to 190) between 1958 and 1980 and that hours of broadcasting in Polish nearly doubled (from 281 to 547).[12] Once FM had become notably more popular than AM, it was easier for foreign language broadcasters to purchase AM stations, eventually giving rise to full-time Chinese, Korean, Japanese, Vietnamese, Polish, Italian, and Russian stations.

However, as "format" radio became dominant by the late 1950s, some linguistic minority programming risked being sidelined. Most format stations sought to maintain uniformity of program type throughout their schedules, making it awkward to insert 15-, 30-, or 60-minute programs in "foreign" languages that often had very different content. Surveys conducted by the American Council for Nationalities Service (ACNS) (1956, 1960) and by the Language Resources Program (LRP) (1960) on the extent of foreign language radio indicate growth in total hours of such programming but a decrease in average per station hours per week devoted to it, owing to an industry-wide increase in number of stations (Warshauer, 1966/1978, 76–79). Anecdotal evidence presented in many of the accounts appearing in this chapter and my own admittedly unsystematic listening to foreign language broadcasts at the time suggest a slight increase in total airtime coupled with more frequent relegation of those broadcasts to the less desirable time periods and days. The ACNS and LRP surveys also indicated the presence of broadcasts in a number of "exotic" languages, such as Turkish, Albanian, Maltese, and Hindi. They provided no details on when those services commenced, but it is likely that at least some of them were the result of a post–World War II influx of "new Americans."

That influx received a considerable boost in 1965, when U.S. immigration law was liberalized through removal of the "national quotas" system and addition of preferences for family integration and skilled labor. As Zhou and Cai (2002) indicate, the effects of those changes on Chinese wishing to emigrate were profound, in terms both of increased numbers and of diversity of occupations, educational levels, economic status, and so on. They also note the rapid growth of Chinese language media services starting in the 1970s, with a full-time Chinese language radio station (Chinese Radio Network) in New York City by 1976 and several more in Los Angeles, San Francisco, Dallas, and Boston since then—one of them bilingual (LA English and Chinese Radio). Few of the "newer" foreign language groups were large enough to warrant full-time services, but the growth in program services for them is mirrored by their increasing presence in the annual reports appearing in *Baron's Radio Directory*.

In 1978, Theodore Grame conducted a major (but not comprehensive) survey of ethnic radio in the United States. He visited 16 geographically "representative" states, recorded 152 programs from nearly 60 stations, and interviewed 18 broadcasters "at length." He noted (1978, 169–170) the presence of programs by more than 50 "national" groups (including "Polka" programs) most with material in their own languages, including even "exotics" such as Haitian [Creole?], Maltese, Ruthenian, and Ute. He concluded that ethnic radio was both vigorous and varied, praising it for its "adamantly local" character and even for its occasional touches of "amateurism." He also was optimistic about the future

> The ethnic broadcaster is surrounded with new programs: bilingual education, bicultural training, multicultural festivals, participation by government and foundations. One cannot say, of course, what the future of these new arrivals may be, but we can predict stability—and possibly growth—for those ethnic broadcasters who, Sunday after Sunday, year in and year out, tenaciously pursue their often thankless cultural task. (p. 143)

The 1970s and 1980s also brought a substantial expansion in the activities of Native American broadcasters, who often saw radio as key to the preservation and extension of their own languages. There had been small-scale efforts along those lines as early as 1941, when University of Oklahoma radio station WNAD began a weekly program hosted by a Sauk/Fox announcer (*Indians for Indians*, 1943). A Native American pirate station operated sporadically from Alcatraz Island between 1969 and 1971 (John Trudell, 1994, 439). The first licensed Native American stations came on air in 1971 in Red Springs, North Carolina (WYRU), and in Bethel, Alaska (KYUK). As Daley and James indicate regarding KYUK, it took persistence plus political and financial support at local, state, and federal levels to initiate such a service in a poverty-stricken corner of Alaska. Language was an important motivation: a commercial religious station (KICY) in Nome offered broadcasts in Eskimo, perhaps as early as 1960, but the dialect was almost impossible for Bethel's residents to comprehend (Daley & James, 2004, 147–149).

Native American radio stations were assisted by grants from the Corporation for Public Broadcasting's (CPB's) Minority Station Improvement Project[13] and the National Telecommunications and Information Administration's (NTIA's) Minority Station Start-Up Fund, but such support was not available to stations that were not minority owned and operated, and certainly not to linguistic minority groups using small amounts of airtime. Nor were Native American stations required to carry specified amounts of Native American language programs.

Corporate Consolidation of Radio and Arrival of New Technologies

The 1990s ushered in a number of new technologies that multiplied the available media outlets for linguistic minority programming while reducing costs. They also brought major changes to the radio industry itself, as the FCC began to relax its rules on the number of stations any single corporation could own. Minority groups feared that the low-rated commercial stations that many of them had relied on as outlets for their particular language services would be swept up by major corporations such as Clear Channel, which in all likelihood would regard those services as incompatible with their corporate models. We have no statistics that would indicate whether their fears were justified.

At roughly the same time, the advent of satellite transmission made it much easier for individual stations to bring in signals from the ancestral homelands. However, even if those sources provided the latest news, music, and other material from the homelands, they could not reflect the daily experiences of listeners in the United States. Apna, an Indian popular music service based in India (www.apnaradio.com), offers Hindi, Punjabi, and Pakistani music and encourages listeners around the world to contact it via e-mail with requests and comments, but it does not feature Indian American music groups. The advent of the World Wide Web[14] has made it even easier to listen to such stations and has enabled a few U.S. linguistic minorities to develop low cost Web services, such as the Pacific Broadcasting Service (www.voiceofhawaii.org), a Hawaiian language music and culture service, or to establish discussion groups on Usenet (Paolillo, 1997). There are no precise numbers for such services and no comprehensive indications as to which languages are represented through that medium.

Satellite radio has been vital to the development of a Native American radio network: American Indian Radio on Satellite (AIROS, www.airos.org) provides a daily newscast featuring information about Native American activities across the United States. It also has a daily discussion show, *Native America Calling* (www.nativeamericacalling.org), in which studio guests and program hosts discuss important issues relating to Native American health, economy, governance, religion, and so on. However, it is an English language service and leaves the utilization of tribal languages to the roughly 25 Native American radio stations, many of which carry little programming in those languages (Browne, 1996; Keith, 1995). Satellites are sometimes used for sharing material among foreign language services—for example, to link the 40-plus stations owned by the Asian American radio service of Multicultural Broadcasting.

As of the time of writing, there are thousands of linguistic minority radio services available to U.S. listeners,[15] if Spanish language and non-U.S. Web services are included. They range from low-power stations to Web services, from languages such as Cajun (French)[16] that are available in a limited number of locations to languages available in nearly every major metropolitan area in the country, and from languages available once a month for 30 minutes to languages available for 20 or more hours per week. It is usually difficult to find out which languages are on air where, when, and for how long, much less what sorts of presentations they offer, although popular music seems to be far and away the dominant format. Web searches such as "radio programs in Hindi, Japanese, Greek, and so on" or "Polish-American radio" may or may not assist in finding them, and once they are located, they often turn out to be relays of material originating in other countries and intended for a worldwide audience.

The combined (incomplete) lists of specific foreign languages available through radio in *Broadcasting & Cable Yearbook* (2007) and in *Baron's Radio Directory* (2006) total 34, more than half of them "Western" languages. *Baron's* reports list many languages in double digits (and Polish on 140 stations). A few foreign language services, such as Haitian Creole, have secured airtime by "leasing" sideband frequencies of FM stations, and there is at least one Haitian Creole pirate radio service (Smerd, 2003). There are full-time Korean, Chinese, Japanese, Vietnamese, Russian, and Polish stations, usually commercial AM stations. The quantitative picture for linguistic minority radio seems positive.

In certain respects, linguistic minority radio has been consistent over time: "popular" music predominated in the initial years and has continued to do so. Local news was either a minor or a nonexistent component for most of the early services and seems even less important to most of them now.[17] The monetary support of linguistic community businesses, institutions, and other services, whether through advertising or sponsorship, has remained important over time. On the other hand, talk shows, virtually absent until the 1980s, seem to have become significant forums for many linguistic communities. Utilization of the Web, modest at present, appears to be growing and should present stations with further opportunities for community involvement.

Impact

We have little empirical evidence regarding audiences for linguistic minority stations, whether members of the minority groups, students of specific languages, or the broader public. Those who have been active participants (Migala, 1987; Steffanides, 1974) make numerous but generally undocumented claims regarding impact, as do academics. Cohen (1992, 135) states, "Radio, moreover, helped ethnic groups to overcome internal divisions based on European political geography and to become more unified communities of Chicago 'Italians' or 'Poles' by the late 1920s," but offers no empirical evidence to support the claim. Lopata (1976, 84) notes that Polish language media in the United States assisted the assimilation of immigrants and their descendants by presenting news of American events and political activities, especially when they used English in the stories, but, again, without empirical evidence. Godfried (1997, 169) observes that "a decade of restrictive immigration policies, the emergence of second- and third-generation ethnic Americans, and a reorientation of ethnic institutions gradually made ethnic programming [in Chicago] less and less important," but he offers no supporting evidence.

Churchill's February 1940 questionnaire-based study of Italian, Polish, Russian Jewish, and German communities in New Jersey (Churchill, 1942) contains some information on the relative utilization and trustworthiness of various media sources, and "ethnic radio" appears to have been quite heavily used by first-generation members (N = 1,202), among whom 37% said that they listened "often" (once a week or more), whereas just 10% of the second generation (N = 842) made that claim. Where preferences were concerned, 39% of the first-generation sample favored local radio with foreign language programs over the commercial networks or "other local" stations, but only 5% of the second generation expressed that preference (appendix 1, tables 4 and 5). Trust proved more difficult to discern, since a fair number of respondents chose not to address that dimension, but Churchill's conclusion was that "there is decidedly more listening to foreign programs and reading of foreign language newspapers than there is trust in them. This is true even among first-generation immigrants who evidence more trust than the second generation" (appendix 1, p. 20).

Roche (1982) surveyed (1974–1975) Italian Americans living in two suburbs, one ethnically homogeneous, the other ethnically heterogeneous (N = approximately 130 for each), of Providence, Rhode Island. Where media utilization was concerned, he discovered, much as Churchill had, that listening to foreign language programming declines rapidly over the generations. Such listening among blue-collar first-generation respondents was "frequent" (once a month or more) for both samples: 75% for homogeneous, 60% for heterogeneous. By the second generation, the figures had dropped to 13.9% and 13.7%, respectively, and by the third generation to 6.9% and 11.1%, leading Roche to observe that his overall findings offered little support for Hansen's (1952) contention that the third generation would be more ethnically engaged than was the second (Roche, 1982, 300). Kutay (1933, 121–122) noted similar behavior regarding the preferences of a Bohemian (Czech) community in Nebraska; each succeeding generation indicated less and less interest in hearing Bohemian music on the radio.

In his study of Greek Americans in Illinois, Seaman (1972) found that 43% of his sample (N = 950) stated that they listened to Greek-American programs "often," while another 20% or so claimed to listen "occasionally." He observed that a number of his survey respondents sometimes spoke negatively about the quality of the Greek and of the programming in general and that recently arrived Greek Americans generally seemed to look on those programs with "disdain" (p. 69). The chief reason for the latter opinion appeared to be quality of spoken Greek but could have stemmed from perceived lack of relevance, and even "outdatedness."

We do have a broad indication of the relative popularity of ethnic minority media through a survey ($N = 1,895$, of whom 780 were "Hispanic") conducted in 2005 for New California Media and other partners. Thirty-seven percent of Hispanics and of African Americans surveyed considered themselves to be "primary consumers" (they preferred ethnic radio), with 13% of Asian Americans, 5% of Native Americans, and just 1% of Arab Americans making the same claim. When secondary consumption of ethnic radio was included, figures increased to 54%, 58%, 18%, 14%, and 2%, respectively (Bendixen & Associates, 2006, 10, 13). Among Asian Americans, Vietnamese (31%), Koreans (21%), and Chinese (20%) identified themselves as primary consumers of ethnic radio, with Asian Indians far behind at 3%, and Japanese and Filipinos at 0%. Secondary consumption figures increased to 44%, 26%, 26%, 13%, and 6% for Vietnamese, Koreans, Chinese, Asian Indians, and Filipinos, respectively, but remained 0% for Japanese. For Native Americans it was 14% and for Arab Americans 2%.

In terms of the Internet, 76% of the Arab Americans indicated that they had access to it, followed by 67% for Asian Americans, 49% for African Americans, 46% for Native Americans, and 24% for Hispanics. When asked whether they visited ethnic Web sites and mainstream Web sites for any purpose, the figures were 45% and 31% for Arab Americans, 35% and 32% for Asian Americans, 17% and 32% for African Americans, 16% and 30% for Native Americans, and 10% and 14% for Hispanic Americans.

With regard to reliance on ethnic media or on mainstream media for most of their information about their "native country" or about issues important to their ethnic community, ethnic media generally came out ahead. For Hispanics, the pairings were 82% and 14%, for Arab Americans 60% and 38%, for Asian Americans 54% and 41%, for Native Americans 49% and 41%, and for African Americans 35% and 53%. When asked which of the two they relied on for information about politics and government, however, the figures generally favored mainstream media: 60% and 33% for Arab Americans, 66% and 28% for Asian Americans, 60% and 27% for Native Americans, and 66% and 21% for African Americans. However, Hispanics favored ethnic media by a wide margin of 64% to 31%. Although those preferences might seem predictable for the most part, the African American response to the first question seems puzzling given the considerable amount and variety of African American media available, and the Hispanic American response on the second question raises the issue of whether those respondents were thinking primarily in terms of U.S. politics and government, which has implications for sense of membership in U.S. society.

Major Issues: What Are They Saying About Us and Themselves?

One of the more common criticisms raised by those who question the value of linguistic minority electronic media services is the "secrecy" issue: How can members of the mainstream society be certain that the individuals and groups expressing themselves through those services are not advocating Communism, anarchy, separatism, or the political and religious causes of their ancestral homelands?

Certainly, there may be messages that are distasteful or disturbing to nonspeakers, but in my own studies of community, ethnic, and linguistic minority radio services, I have yet to discover an instance of anything that represented a clear and present danger to the public.[18] The nearest example would be the 1965 Spanish language broadcasts of two Florida radio stations that allegedly incited Cuban refugees to riot. The FCC fined both stations and gave one of them a short-term renewal (FCC Fines WMIE, 1965).[19] Viswanath and Arora (2000, 46) contend that the South Asian linguistic minority press in the United States in fact tends to minimize conflict that could have destabilizing effects within and beyond its communities.[20] Still, there are numerous instances, both in the United States and elsewhere,[21] of preemptive steps considered and sometimes taken by governments to minimize, if not eliminate, the risk that linguistic minority radio might be used to express hatred or incite demonstrations.

Are They Divisive?

The issue of whether foreign language and indigenous media hinder or assist mutual understanding, shared goals, and so on between linguistic minority groups and mainstream society is difficult to assess where radio is concerned. I am unaware of any scholarly studies that deal specifically with radio's influence in that regard. The Bendixen & Associates (2006) study reported earlier indicates that ethnic groups rely on both ethnic and mainstream media for information. That should provide those groups with some understanding of, if not agreement with, mainstream society. Whether there is reliance on mainstream *and* ethnic media on the part of mainstream audiences we do not know, but it seems doubtful.

Linguistic minority radio can serve as an outlet for unrepresented (by mainstream media) opinion, particularly in times of stress brought on through conflict between a given minority community and mainstream authority. For example, in May 1999, following the allegedly accidental bombing by North Atlantic Treaty Organization (NATO) forces of the Peoples' Republic of China embassy in Belgrade, Public Service Broadcasting's

(PBS's) *The News Hour with Jim Lehrer* reporter Spenser Michaels interviewed (May 14) several Chinese American media staff and community figures and provided excerpts from Chinese language talk shows in San Francisco. One caller to San Francisco Chinese Radio said, "The American people are like monsters. Their lives are more precious. Others are not. We Chinese should help Chinese." When a caller offered support for U.S. policy in Yugoslavia, other callers ridiculed him. Arnold Chen, a U.S.-born Chinese American community leader, noted that "there is a segment of our community that have [*sic*] not been able to voice their opinions. And this radio station allows them an opportunity to espouse their views, and their viewpoints are shared by many in the community" (Michaels, 1999).

One could imagine that some mainstream Americans who supported U.S. policy in Yugoslavia might side with the ridiculed dissenter and might resent the other callers' lack of due respect and appreciation for their new homeland. That sentiment might or might not be shared by "native-born" Americans, including Chinese Americans, who also expressed their anger over the bombing, but that illustrates another possible dimension of the place of linguistic minority radio in mainstream society: a two-valued attitude that may accord a perhaps grudging acceptance of contrary opinion when expressed by those who "sound American" (and speak English) but reject such opinion when expressed in other languages or even English accents.

Ethnic/linguistic minority radio stations have begun to cooperate on issues of mutual concern, such as the immigration legislation considered by Congress in 2006–2007. As Miller (2006) indicates, those stations played an important role in turning out Hispanic and Asian American marchers in New York City and in Los Angeles to demonstrate against the legislation. Whether the mainstream public would regard such broadcasts as positive or negative is a matter of opinion, but this does illustrate minority use of radio to assist the process of integrated participation in a democratic society.

Whom Do They Represent?

Because most linguistic minority radio activity is not full time, there are few statistical data filed with the FCC that indicate staff gender or position. Earlier anecdotal accounts show a heavily male cohort but also include occasional mention of women as program presenters. Later accounts indicate a greater presence of women, and I have noted numerous female disc jockeys on Asian language radio services. Arnheim and Bayne (1942) and Grame (1980) both noted that much of the music offered through "European" linguistic minority services was of a "nostalgic" variety, suggesting that older individuals might have been in charge of selecting it. In a number of the

European language services that I have listened to in the United States and elsewhere, the frequent dominance of such individuals has led to a decline in audience numbers, sometimes to the point where their programs appeal to few if any listeners.[22]

How Well Do They Express Themselves?

The "expression" issue generally concerns the quality (or "purity," to some critics) of the spoken language. Complaints emerged quite early, as in this article from the Polish newspaper *Dziennik Chicagoski*, March 20, 1937:

> In this multitude of Polish programs, there is certainly too high a percentage of ... cultural hideousness. There are programs that violate, by far, the limits of aesthetics. There are programs so badly hosted, so idiotically planned, that they evoke only pity and a feeling of shame. (Migala, 1987, 125)

Lopata (1976, 84) speaks of the Polish media as having "slipped into such a combination of regional, lower-class and Americanized language by World War II as to shock the new immigration [*sic*]," but indicates "a marked improvement in the 'purity'" of media use of the language in the 1940s as Polish war refugees "with intelligentsia backgrounds" joined Polish media staffs, "becoming editors or programme announcers and even starting their own publications or radio stations." Seaman (1972, 69) states, "Unfortunately, the Greek-American programs do not serve as a model of standard Greek, on any stylistic level whatever, and this fact is generally realized by the Greek community [in Illinois]." Although there may be differences of opinion among members of linguistic communities where the need for "purity" is concerned, it is an important issue to many of them.

Another expression issue concerns "indecent" speech. A few Spanish language services have been notified, and on occasion fined, by the FCC for their "indecent" broadcasts. WAZX in Smyrna, Georgia, was fined $7,000 for the comments made by its *el Manero* talk show hosts regarding teen sex and masturbation (FCC Fines Spanish-language Stations, 2002). Gurza (2004) notes that the FCC has only two[23] Spanish speaking investigators for 705 Spanish radio and TV stations and may be missing a great deal: "LURID talk with guests and callers about sex acts. Scatological references complete with sound effects. Derisive jokes about homosexuals. ... [D]aytime indecency has developed mostly under the radar of mainstream moral monitors." However, one problem (not limited to Spanish, as Arabic certainly has it) in translating "indecent" language is that some of the terminology may be indecent to Spanish speakers from some countries and innocuous to those from others (Spanish-language radio shock jocks, 2004).

Conclusion

Given the many obstacles that foreign language radio has had to overcome—scarcity of funding (especially from government), suspicions regarding loyalty, criticism of language usage, apparent difficulty in attracting second, third, or later generations of audience members—perhaps it is a wonder that such activity continues and, furthermore, shows signs of embracing new technologies. But if there still is a real problem in terms of reaching younger listeners, that has serious implications for the future, and not only in the United States: that has been a recurring refrain in my discussion with foreign language broadcasters in other countries as well.

No one claims to have discovered the magic formula for attracting such listeners, but some of the productions emanating from indigenous linguistic minority groups—Irish, Welsh, Inuit, Maori, in particular—show some promise. Most of those efforts have been supported in part through government funding and strengthened by the presence of institutions, especially educational, that support the daily use of the language (Browne, 2005, 156–166). Those groups have been quite effective in arguing that because they are indigenous people, the government *should* support them.[24] Nonindigenous linguistic minorities cannot make the same argument.

What arguments can they make? One might begin with the simple fact that the United States clearly is becoming a more multicultural society, then remind the mainstream population of the virtues of such a society, ranging from its positive effects on international economic and political cooperation to its enrichment of cultural experiences, including culinary variety, for the entire population. In addition, while this is a more sensitive issue, the services can facilitate minority participation in society by enabling their communities to express such things as experiences with discrimination or dissatisfaction with the way in which the "new homeland" is treating the "old homeland" (the Chinese talk shows) or treating *them* (the 2006 immigration demonstrations).

How might foreign language radio services reach the mainstream population with a message stressing the benefits of cultural enrichment when most of its members cannot understand Polish or Chinese, let alone Hmong, Punjabi, or Tagalog? One way could be to seek out U.S. educational institutions where such languages are taught and offer to make programs available to them, perhaps with reciprocity in the form of programs produced by the language students and broadcast by the station. Another way would be to cultivate ties with mainstream media, seeking their help in publicizing what a given ethnic community is doing, which would include some attention to ethnic media. Yet another approach would be to develop Web pages with content in both the foreign broadcast language and in English—something that also might be helpful to those members of the linguistic community who lack command of the language.

The governments of Australia, New Zealand, Canada, the Netherlands, and Great Britain have all been more supportive of linguistic minority radio (and TV) services than has the United States, with Australia providing a specific category of licensing for ethnic radio. The experiences appear to have been positive in each case. They offer a number of "model" approaches that the U.S. government might consider. In most of them, the minority groups have lobbied for such support, assisted by NGOs and well-placed supporters within government, as well as members of the mainstream population (Alia & Bull, 2006; Browne, 1996, 1999, 2005; Molnar & Meadows, 2001; Roth, 2005). Mainstream public support does seem to matter.

Joshua Fishman contends (Hornberger & Puetz, 2006, 229) that minority language communities need to foster a greater sense of economic support for those languages from *within* the community, whether through funds, goods, or services, to lessen (but not eliminate) dependence on governmental support.[25] The larger (mainstream) community might join in that support, for reasons already noted, but is unlikely to do so unless it becomes more aware of the presence and value of services such as linguistic minority radio. Fishman and colleagues (1985, 220) also state that such support should begin "in early childhood and be continued throughout one's adult life." They may be correct, but linguistic minority radio services will need to find ways to make themselves more attractive to younger listeners if they are to ensure their long-term futures.

Notes

1. Spanish language radio and TV have received some attention from academics. Since Chapter 3 of this book covers that subject, I have limited myself to using a few specific examples here.
2. Casillas (2006) reports Spanish language broadcasts as early as 1922.
3. Cohen (1992, 135) states that several stations (WGES, WSBC, WEDC, WCRW) in Chicago were "explicitly devoted" to ethnic programming by 1926 and that others carried "nationality hours" but provides no details on the precise nature of their programming. NYC AM Radio History (2007) provides sketches of New York City radio stations starting in 1920. It indicates, if not by precise dates, that there was considerable linguistic minority broadcast activity (unspecified) by the mid-1920s, all of it apparently in European languages.
4. Sies (2000) notes that there was a high level of activity in Yiddish radio dramas and comedic sketches by the 1930s in New York City.
5. Godfried (1997, 114) notes a decline in the number of WCFL's weekly foreign language broadcast minutes from 1934 (400) to 1936 (300). Whether that was a common experience among stations carrying foreign languages during the Great Depression we do not know. Anecdotal evidence indicates instances of both decline and growth.

6. When the congressional subcommittee investigating the FCC raised the question of FCC censorship with the FCC senior field attorney in New York City, James L. Guest, it did so in light of the provision of the Communications Act of 1934 forbidding such a practice. Guest's evasive responses appear to have left subcommittee members convinced that the FCC *was* exercising a form of censorship (U.S. Congress, 1943, 286–288).

7. The manager of a New York City multicultural radio station, WBNX, testified to a congressional subcommittee that a local newspaper (PM) called him to protest that a speaker on a German language program had just said that "Hitler is God" and threatened to take the complaint to the FCC. The manager verified that the complaint was false. He told committee members, "It shows, to my mind, the vulnerability of the present scheme in radio, where a 3-cent stamp will carry [baseless] complaints down to the Federal Communications Commission or some other war control board" (U.S. Congress, 1943, 835).

8. Cross-examination of Guest by the subcommittee's General Counsel (see n. 6) regarding one alleged "pro-fascist" announcer at WHOM runs from pages 291 to 360 and is replete with Guest's obfuscation and claims of ignorance. Similar instances arise in Part 1 of the hearings, leaving doubts as to the credibility of several such accusations.

9. According to Horten (2002, 76–79), OWI produced two series for the foreign language stations: *You Can't Do Business with Hitler* and *Uncle Sam Speaks*. Horten notes that groups such as the Mazzini Society (Italian Americans) and the German-American Congress for Democracy also produced at least two "pro-American" series.

10. There is considerable debate over the question of how much difference ethnic minority ownership makes in employment and programming practices. Craft (2003: 147–153) concludes on the basis of a survey ($N = 91$ for ethnic minority respondents) that such ownership does make a difference in employment of minority staff, but influence on program content is more difficult to discern (p. 155).

11. A few sources do suggest that the FCC may have discriminated against applicants who intended to feature foreign language broadcasting, but they do not indicate specific political motivations. Warshauer (1966/1978, 88, n. 8) notes that an FCC hearing examiner argued in a 1958 case involving a TV license for Buffalo, New York, that an applicant's "proposal to present 5.8% of its programs in foreign languages was less calculated to serve the public interest" than the two competing proposals but adds that the commission did not accept that opinion. She mentions another instance of possible FCC discrimination in 1963, but provides no details on it. Grame (1980, 127) notes the FCC's contention that multilanguage (35!) radio station WHBI (New York City) did not merit renewal of its license because it was unable to show that management was aware of the content of each and every one of those services—a decision remanded to the FCC by the U.S. Circuit Court of Appeals in 1978. Fishman (1966/1978, 382, n. 12) states that "language loyalists had concluded that the decision of the Commission that a number of factors must be considered 'in determining the suitability of foreign language programming' was evidence of 'intercover' federal policy to discontinue such programming wherever possible."

12. Migala does not identify his source for these figures, but they appear to be from *Broadcasting & Cable Yearbook*. When I have checked figures from that source, they are incomplete, in that many stations carrying foreign language broadcasts either do not supply information on them to the *Yearbook* or supply them in aggregate form—for example, "multicultural," with no indication of which languages are included or how many hours each is on air. Grame (1980, 62) is sharply critical of the *Yearbook's* omission of many multicultural stations.

13. Some of the CPB funding to public radio stations in general, including qualified ethnic minority stations, is recurring. Native American stations in particular are heavily dependent on it, and rumors of sharp cutbacks in CPB annual appropriations are the cause for great alarm at those stations, as I have noted when visiting several of them. Replacement funding is very difficult to come by.

14. Cunliffe (2007) says little about Web radio per se but offers an interesting appraisal of the opportunities and challenges posed by the Internet so far as minority language groups are concerned.

15. One of the great frustrations in conducting the present study was the difficulty of locating accurate and complete information on the overall state of linguistic minority radio in the United States. Three studies were conducted in the 1930s (Engel, 1936; Hendrix, 1932; Lumley, 1934), two in the 1940s (Arnheim & Baynes, 1941; FCC, 1940), three in the late 1950s and early 1960s (ACNS, 1956, 1960; LRP, 1960), two in the late 1970s to early 1980s (Fishman, 1985; Grame, 1980), one in 1988 (Downing, 1989–1990, 1–19), and one in 2005 (Bixenden & Associates, 2006), but none is comprehensive. There also are studies of specific cities (Jeffres & Hur, 1979), states (Wynar, 1981) and languages (Migala, 1987; Seaman, 1972).

16. See Browne (1994) for a brief description of Cajun radio activity, most of it in Louisiana, where more than 20 stations carry some Cajun language programming.

17. Little Saigon Radio (www.littlesaigonradio.com) does have a daily newscast that includes reports on activities involving Vietnamese in its three U.S. locations (Los Angeles, San Jose, and Houston).

18. There are occasional allegations that foreign language broadcasts are used to circumvent the law. Such a claim arose in a September 4, 2005, form letter prepared by United Patriots of America and addressed to FCC Commissioner Kevin Martin, to be used by whoever cared to download it and sign it. It stated, "I have it on good authority that Radio Station KROM (FM) in San Antonio TX [a Spanish language service] has repeatedly told their listening audience the whereabouts of immigration agents and the likely areas of immigration raids for the day in the San Antonio area." It "protest[s]" the FCC license renewal for KROM" and closes by stating that disciplinary action in this case "will put *all* foreign language broadcast entities on notice that the content of their broadcasts is subject to scrutiny and can affect their ability to have their licenses renewed by the FCC" (italics mine). Retrieved from www.unitedpatriotsofamerica.com/Home/Popup_Article_Details/Params/articles/118, April 2, 2007.

19. Socuro (1996, 38–39) notes opposition faced by those Cuban American Spanish language radio stations in Miami that took a more moderate position on dealing with Cuba. The problems included denigrating comments about those stations by more "hard-line" Cuban American stations, the car bombing of one "moderate" station's reporter, and a takeover of that station for a brief period by a group of armed men wishing to broadcast their own views.

20. A possible exception noted by Hua (2005) is a Chinese language U.S.-based radio network, Sound of Hope, with reports critical of the Chinese government as well as talks by staff members who are Falun Gong practitioners.

21. In 1940, an executive at the British Broadcasting Corporation (BBC) considered imposing a requirement that all Welsh language scripts be translated into English and sent to London for scrutiny in advance of broadcast. He and other head office executives feared that some of the material might induce national disunity ("Welsh separatism") or be subversive. The requirement never was imposed (Davies, 1994, 133).

22. The station manager for Radio Pacific 2000 in Sydney, Australia, was faced with the problem of too many older people dominating the airwaves of his Pacific Islander–oriented community station, so he required that each presenter over 40 wishing to continue on air include a much younger individual as production assistant and sometime presenter for her or his program (Huakaa, 2001).

23. Some sources claim that the commission has only *one* Spanish language investigator in its "obscenity enforcement bureau." See Spanish-language radio shock jocks (2004, 2).

24. That has helped in the case of Native American radio but does not appear to have done so for Hawaiian language radio, which remains confined to bits of airtime on a few stations and to Web services featuring Hawaiian music.

25. Government support at any level may come with strings attached. University of Louisiana-Lafayette radio station KRVS received substantial financial support from the state legislature for increasing its Cajun language programming, but the legislator who had spearheaded the appropriation also expected the station to heed his "suggestions" regarding program content (Spizale, 2005).

References

Alia, Valerie & Simone Bull. (2006). *Media and Ethnic Minorities*. Edinburgh, UK: Edinburgh University Press.

Anti-Nazi Germans Take Over Show. (1942). *Variety*, September 9, 24.

Arnheim, Rudolf & Martha Collins Bayne. (1941). Foreign Language Broadcasts over Local American Stations: A Study of a Special Interest Program. In Paul Lazersfeld & Frank Stanton (Eds.), *Radio Research 1941* (pp. 8–64). New York: Duell, Sloan and Pearce.

Ban on Broadcasts by Aliens Discussed. (1940). *New York Times*, February 18, 9, 12: 5

Bendixen & Associates. (2006). *Ethnic Media in America: The Giant Hidden in Plain Sight*. Miami: author.

Browne, Donald R. (1994). French Language Radio in the United States. In Claude-Jean Bertrand & Francis Bordat (Eds.), *Les Medias Francaises Aux Etats-Unis*. Nancy: Presses Universitaire de Nancy.

———. (1996). *Electronic Media and Indigenous Peoples: A Voice of Our Own?* Ames: Iowa State University Press.

———. (1999). *Electronic Media and Industrialized Nations: A Comparative Study*. Ames: Iowa State University Press.

———. (2005). *Ethnic Minorities, Electronic Media and the Public Sphere: A Comparative Study*. Cresskill, NJ: Hampton Press.

Carlson, John. (1943). [Avedis Derounian]. *Under Cover*. New York: Dutton.

Casillas, Delores Ines. (2006). Sounds of Belonging: A Cultural History of Spanish Language Radio in the United States, 1922–2004. Unpublished doctoral dissertation, University of Michigan.

Churchill, Charles. (1942). The Italians of Newark, A Community Study. Doctoral dissertation, New York University. Reprinted, New York: Arno Press, 1975.

Craft, Stephanie. (2003). Translating Ownership into Action. *Howard Journal of Communication*, 14 (2).

Cunliffe, Daniel. (2007). Minority Languages and the Internet. In Cormack & Hourigan (Eds.), Multilingual Matters,2007. London: Avon, Minority Language Media

Daley, Patrick & Beverly James. (2004). *Cultural Politics and the Mass Media: Alaska Native Voices*. Urbana: University of Illinois Press.
Davies, John. (1994). *Broadcasting and the BBC in Wales*. Cardiff: University of Wales Press.
Downing, John. (1989–1990). Ethnic Minority Radio in the United States. *Howard Journal of Communication*, 2 (1), 1–19.
Engel, E.F. (1936). The Broadcasting of Modern Foreign Languages in the United States: A Survey. *Modern Language Journal*, 20 (6, March), 356–358.
FCC Fines WMIE For "Incitement." (1965). *Radio-Television Daily*, March 21, 5.
FCC Head Cold on Lingo Ban. (1940). *Variety*, September 18, 26.
Federal Communications Commission. (1940). *Analysis and Tabulation of the Returns of the Commission's Questionnaire Concerning Broadcasts by Licensees in Languages Other Than English*. Washington, DC: author.
Fishman, Joshua. (1966/1978). *Language Loyalty in the United States*. Janua Linguarum No. 21. The Hague, the Netherlands: Mouton. Reprinted, New York: Arno Press.
Fishman, Joshua et al. (1985). *Ethnicity in Action: The Community Resources of Ethnic Languages in the United States*. Binghamton, NY: Bilingual Press/Editorial Bilingue.
Foreign Stations "Confess." (1942). *Variety*, May 20, Sec. 1, 31–32.
Friedrich, Carl. (1942). Foreign Language Radio and the War. *Common Ground*, 3 (Autumn), 65–72.
Godfried, Nathan. (1997). *WCFL: Chicago's Voice of Labor, 1926–1978*. Urbana and Chicago: University of Illinois Press.
Grame, Theodore. (1980). *Ethnic Broadcasting in the United States*. Washington, DC: American Folklife Center, Library of Congress, Publication No. 4.
Gurza, Agustin. (2004). Ay, caramba! Spanish-Language Radio Stations Filled with Raunch. *Alemeda Times-Star*, August 30. Retrieved from www.freerepublic.com/focus/fr/1203373/posts, April 2, 2007.
Hansen, Marcus. (1952). The Third Generation in America. *Commentary*, 14 (November), 492–500.
Hendrix, W.S. (1932). Foreign Language Broadcasting in the United States. *Modern Language Journal*, 17 (2), 91–96.
Hornberger, Nancy & Martin Puetz. (Eds.). (2006). *Language Loyalty, Language Planning and Language Revitalization*. Clevedon, UK: Multilingual Matters Ltd.
Horten, Gerd. (2002). *Radio Goes to War*. Berkeley: University of California Press.
Hua, Vanessa. (2005). Dissident Media Linked to Falun Gong. *San Francisco Chronicle*, December 18. Retrieved from www.sfgate.com/cgi-bin/article.cgi?f=/c/a/2005/12/18, April 7, 2007.
Huakaa, Inoke Fotu. (2001). Station manager, Radio 2000, personal interview, Sydney, March.
Indians for Indians. (1943). *Time*, 41 (May 31), 40.
Jeffres, Leo & K.K. Hur. (1979). *Ethnic Communication in Cleveland: An Exploratory Study of Ethnics and Mass Communication in Cleveland, Ohio*. Cleveland: Communication Research Center and Ethnic Heritage Studies Center of Cleveland State University.
Keith, Michael. (1995). *Signals in the Air: Native Broadcasting in America*. Westport, CT: Praeger.
Konecky, Eugene. (1948). *The American Communications Conspiracy in Standard Broadcasting, Frequency Modulation, Television, Facsimile, Short Wave, Newspapers*. New York: Peoples Radio Foundation.

Kutay, Robert. (1933). *The Story of a Bohemian-American Village.* Louisville, KY: Standard Printing Company.

Legion Stand Protested. (1941). *New York Times*, September 28, 31.

Lopata, Helena. (1976). *Polish Americans: Status Competition in an Ethnic Community.* Englewood Cliffs, NJ: Prentice-Hall.

Lumley, Frederick. (1934). *Broadcasting Foreign Language Lessons.* Monograph No. 19, Bureau of Educational Research. Columbus: Ohio State University Press.

Meyer, Vicki. (2001). From Segmented to Fragmented: Latino Media in San Antonio, Texas. *Journalism and Mass Communications Quarterly*, 78 (2), 291–306.

Michaels, Spenser. (1999). An Angry Voice. *The News Hour with Jim Lehrer*, May 14. Retrieved from www.pbs.org/newshour/bb/europe/jan-june99/chinese_embassy_5.14, April 8, 2007.

Migala, Jozef. (1987). *Polish Radio Broadcasting in the United States.* Boulder, CO: East European Monographs.

Miller, Lia. (2006). To Marshal Ethnic Forces, Start at Ethnic Radio Stations. *New York Times*, April 10.

Molnar, Helen & Michael Meadows. (2001). *Songlines to Satellites.* Annandale, NSW: Pluto Press.

NYC AM Radio History. (2007). Retrieved from www.angelfire.com/nj2/piratejim/nyca-mhistory, April 26, 2007.

Paolillo, John. (1997). Toward a Sociolinguistic Survey of South Asian Cyberspace. Paper presented at the Annual Conference of the American Association for Applied Linguistics, Orlando, FL.

Radio Safeguard Asked. (1940). *New York Times*, August 26, 17.

Roche, John. (1982). Suburban Ethnicity: Ethnic Attitudes and Behavior among Italian Americans in Two Suburban Communities. *Social Science Quarterly*, 63 (1, March), 295–303.

Roth, Lorna. (2005). *Something New in the Air: The Story of First Peoples Television.* Montreal: McGill/Queen's University Press.

Roucek, Joseph. (1945). Foreign Language Broadcasts. In Francis Brown & Joseph Roucek (Eds.), *One America* (pp. 384–391). New York: Prentice-Hall.

Seaman, P. David. (1972). *Modern Greek and American English in Contact.* The Hague, the Netherlands: Mouton.

Sies, Luther. (2000). Entry 9227: Foreign Language Broadcasts. In *Encyclopedia of American Radio, 1920–1960* (pp. 205–206). Jefferson, NC, and London: McFarland & Company.

Smerd, Jeremy. (2003). Radio Free Flatbush. *New York Press*, November 3. Retrieved from www.nypress.com/print.cfm?content_id=9125, May 21, 2007.

Smith, Jeanette. (1942). Broadcasting for Marginal Americans. *Public Opinion Quarterly*, 6 (Winter), 588–603.

Socuro, Gonzalo. (1996). *Cubans and the Mass Media in South Florida.* Gainesville: University Press of Florida.

Spanish-Language Radio Shock Jocks Present Obstacle for Regulators. (2004). *Jewish World Review*, February. Retrieved from www.jewishworldreview.com/0204/spanish_shock.asp, May 21, 2007.

Spizale, David. (2005). General manager, KRVS, personal interview, Lafayette, LA. May.

Steffanides, George. (1974). *America the Land of My Dreams: The Odyssey of a Greek Immigrant.* Fitchburg, MA: Self-published.

Trudell, John. (1994). In Cynthia Kasee (Ed.), *Notable Native Americans*. Detroit, MI: Gale Research.

U.S. Congress, House of Representatives, Select Committee to Investigate the Federal Communications Committee. (1943). *Study and Investigation of the FCC, 78th Congress, vol. 1*. Washington, DC: U.S. Government Printing Office.

U.S. government, Office of Censorship. (1942). *Code of Wartime Practices for American Broadcasters*. Washington, DC: U.S. Government Printing Office, June 15.

Viswanath, K. & Pamela Arora. (2000). Ethnic Media in the United States. *Mass Communication and Society*, 3 (1), 39–56.

Warshauer, Mary. (1966/1978). Foreign Language Broadcasting. In Joshua Fishman (Ed.), *Language Loyalty in the United States* (pp. 75–91). The Hague, the Netherlands: Mouton. Reprinted, New York: Arno Press.

Zhou, Min & Guoxuan Cai. (2002). Chinese Language Media in the United States: Immigration and Assimilation in American Life. *Qualitative Sociology*, 25 (3), 419–441.

3. Heard It on the X: Border Radio As Public Discourse and the Latino Legacy in Popular Music

Roberto Avant-Mier

"... The efficacy and social significance of mass media do not lie primarily in the industrial organization and the ideological content, but rather in the way the popular masses have appropriated the mass media and the way the masses have recognized their identity in the mass media."

—*Martín-Barbero (1999, 346)*

In 2000, the U.S. Census determined that Latino/as (and/or Hispanics)[1] in the United States now constitute its largest minority, accounting for at least 12.5% of the total U.S. population (Guzmán, 2001). This news was significant in different ways, one of those being that Latino/as had surpassed blacks/African Americans as the largest minority group in the United States. Other important findings were that the Latino/Hispanic population had increased by 57.9% between 1990 and 2000 and that the Latino/Hispanic population now represents much of the total youth population (under 18) in the United States (Guzmán, 2001).

Worth noting for the controversial "Latino" category, the 2000 Census was the first to include the category "Latino" as opposed to "Spanish/Hispanic," as in the previous Census. The salience of this fact is that it reflects a discursive change in our national constructions of race and ethnicity. Of course, such discursive slippages have been a consistent part of the U.S. Census for decades. Census categories before 1970 did not even include "Hispanic." Moreover, the censuses of 1950 and 1960 considered only "persons of a Spanish surname," although the 1930 Census treated "Mexican" as a racial category instead of the more specific cultural/ethnic category that it is today.

Other issues surrounding the Census included the construction of categories such as "Spanish," "Hispanic," and "Latino." These three markers are collapsed as a single category (i.e., "Spanish/Hispanic/Latino") in the most recent Census. This is problematic in that within our national discursive constructions, "Spanish" is supposed to mean the same as "Hispanic" and/or "Latino," and yet people of these groups often differentiate them. A person who calls herself or himself "Spanish" often does so specifically because she or he dislikes other terms such as "Hispanic" and/or "Latino/a." Likewise, while some people dislike the term "Hispanic" because it either essentializes or it is a word that exists only in U.S. English, others dislike the term "Latino" for its essentializing nature or because it is a word more commonly used in Spanish. Further complicating this situation, some people eschew either "Hispanic" or "Latino" in favor of more specific identity signifiers and markers, opting for "Puerto Rican," "Cuban," "Nicaraguan American," or perhaps "Mexican American" (to name just a few). In any case, I propose that this evidence reveals how U.S. culture is ambivalent about where Latino/as fit in and about how to deal with a burgeoning U.S. Latino/a population.

Although the issue of Latino/a identity is beyond the scope and spatial constraints of this chapter, I submit that the issue of Latino/a identity in the United States is an issue that warrants further investigation with regard to the question of how Latino/as fit into mainstream U.S. culture and to the role that mass media such as radio have played in cultural processes. In this chapter, I use *Heard It on the X*, a 2005 compact disc release by Los Super Seven, as an entry point into the conversation about Latino/as and American culture, as well as the role of border radio as public discourse that informs the discussion.

Revisiting the "X" stations and Border Radio

The "X" radio stations, as they were known, were the high-powered AM radio stations whose call letters began with X because they were broadcasting from the Mexican side of the United States/México border, from high-powered transmitters that would have made them illegal in U.S. territory. Sometimes reaching as much as a million watts of radio power, the X stations such as XER (which later became XERA), XEG, XERB, XERF, XEAW, XEMO, XEMU, XEAK, XTRA, and XELO were among various "outlaw" X stations, considered as such also because of how they defied the logic of borders and other practical limitations for broadcasting in a time when radio practices were still being defined.

Country music legend June Carter Cash, in an anecdote about when she and her family lived in Del Rio, Texas, tells that by blasting so much wattage the X stations were so powerful that you did not even need a radio to listen in: you could hear border radio "on any barbed wire fence in Texas" (Fowler & Crawford, 2005). The stations were known to be so powerful that they could blast radio power far beyond the Texas/México border and far up into the U.S. plains states, into the Midwest, and "anywhere in the nation." Others attest that the X stations reached as far away as Canada, Europe, Japan, and New Zealand, while still others jokingly suggest that the stations were putting out so much wattage that they affected birds as far away as Australia, Finland, and Java. A more interesting fact, I contend, is that the X stations played music that could not be heard on mainstream radio stations in the United States. In addition to the religious orientation and commercial pitches for many outlandish products that dominated airtime on the X stations, the X stations exerted a different kind of power when they began to play music to attract listeners and became the first radio stations on Earth to play "western" and "hillbilly swing," along with blues, R&B, and other "race" music. Regional Mexican and other Latin American music was sometimes heard as well, and the fact that listeners were exposed to all of these contributed fundamentally to the new popular music genres that resulted (e.g., country and rock 'n' roll).

In the spring of 2005, the Grammy Award–winning supergroup Los Super Seven (or, Los Super 7) released a compact disc as a tribute to "border radio." *Heard It on the X* was the third album by Los Super Seven, and the title was culled from a somewhat famous but now forgotten song from 1975 called "Heard It on the X" by the Tex-Mex rock/blues band ZZ Top:

> Do you remember, back in 1966,
> Country Jesus, hillbilly blues, that's where I learned my licks.
> Oh, from coast to coast and line to line, in every county there,
> I'm talking 'bout that outlaw X, that's cutting through the air.
> Anywhere y'all, Everywhere y'all,
> I heard it, I heard it, I heard it on the X.
> ("Heard It on the X," from 1975's *Fandango!* by ZZ Top)

Although the collaborative effort of Los Super Seven acknowledged ZZ Top through liner notes, the version by the popular music supergroup is more noteworthy as the lasting acknowledgment of and testament to the role of border radio for the community of listeners formed by it between the 1930s and 1960s as well as border radio's impact on American culture.

Although the details and implications of border radio have been discussed previously in radio studies (Fowler & Crawford, 2002), (Kahn, 1996), the current analysis focuses on *Heard It on the X* as a contemporary cultural text and a form of intercultural public discourse that further illuminates the Latino/a legacy in American popular music as well as the effect that border radio had on the radio listening community and even race relations in the United States. Widely acclaimed and much loved, *Heard It on the X*'s most remarkable aspect was the disc's focus on paying tribute to the influence of border radio on country and rock 'n' roll music (and popular music in general) and on U.S. culture in general. As Bentley (2005) notes about the disc,

> The dozen songs on the album cover the entire breadth of the lone star state in such a way that listeners get a direct blast of history from artists that helped create it, as well as those who learned from its roots. The way those lessons are taught is musical heritage at its most heartening.

As *Heard It on the X* suggests, and as the following analysis reveals, the X border radio stations were integral to the changes taking place in an ever-growing and rapidly evolving U.S. culture between the 1930s and 1960s and a great deal of popular music that followed. By featuring the music of poor and working-class whites along with blacks/African Americans and Latino/as, the X stations allowed radio to become the first mass medium that was truly multicultural, and therefore allowed border radio to have a lasting effect on American culture.

Radio and communication scholar Michael Keith (septemper, 2007) asserts, in connection with the role of radio in the United States, that "the world's first electronic mass medium had performed a unique, if not profound, role in the life of Americans for three quarters of a century." Rothenbuhler and McCourt (2002) tell us, "By providing new venues for expression of regional, class, and ethnic identities, radio played an instrumental role in a series of major transformations, if not revolutions, in American culture" (p. 368). Likewise, Benedict Anderson makes the following argument about radio and nationalism:

> Invented only in 1895, radio made it possible to bypass print and summon into being an aural representation of the imagined community where the printed page scarcely penetrated. Its role ... generally in mid-twentieth-century nationalisms, has been much underestimated and understudied. (2006, 54)

It could be said, therefore, that border radio deserves further attention as a public discourse that was produced by a multicultural setting in Texas and that it anticipated and likely contributed to multiculturalism and inter-cultural communication in the United States in the decades that followed. The implications, of course, are that *Heard It on the X* represents a radio listening community that anticipated the end of the Jim Crow South and preceded the integration of U.S. culture and society, and thus signifies the lasting impact of the sound medium of radio on American life.

Moreover, a deeper analysis of *Heard It on the X* (and the border radio that it commemorates) reveals significant connections to Latino/a music and culture. I propose a corollary that it also should be recognized how Los Super Seven's *Heard It on the X* simultaneously recalls the "Latin" legacy in U.S. popular music and its effect on American culture as it was mediated through radio. Thus, *Heard It on the X* also provides an opportunity to reconsider the history and role of Latino/as in U.S. culture. In a time of burgeoning significance of Latino/a peoples in the United States—from the emergence of Latino/as as the nation's largest minority to irrational fears about a growing number of Spanish speakers (and "losing English"), from political efforts to capture Latino/a voters to the building of border walls, from heated debates about immigration reform to questions about the value of ethnic assimilation in a time of intense globalization—*Heard It on the X* illuminates an important radio community (an integrated culture predating modern country music, rock 'n' roll, and other popular music), serves as a vital corrective to radio and popular music history with regard to the contributions of Latino/as and Hispanics, and provides a rich background for the conversation about the place of Latino/as in the United States.

Los Super Seven

All-star supergroups in popular music have been around for decades, and bands such as Blind Faith in the 1960s, the Traveling Wilburys in the 1980s, the Texas Tornados and Damn Yankees in the late 1980s/early 1990s, Los Super Seven and Audioslave in the late 1990s, and contemporary rock bands Velvet Revolver and Scrap Metal in the 2000s continue to be well received by fans. Most of these bands received much critical acclaim and made mountains of cash in the process, yet music critic Ed Ward describes Los Super Seven as "the only supergroup that doesn't suck" (2005). Although such a candid characterization might be based upon esoteric aesthetic judgments, I would suggest that if such a statement has any truth, it might be related to Los Super Seven's far-reaching musical range as well as the diversity of artists and musicians who are part of the collective. Los Super Seven could actually be called Los Super 75-or-more, and their musical styles include country, blues, folk, Tex-Mex rock, *corrido*, *cumbia*, *mariachi* and *ranchera*, *norteño*, *jarocho*, *bolero*, *son*, and many others.

Los Super Seven began in 1998 with the release of their self-titled first disc, which featured the first lineup of seven main artists.[2] In the 13 songs on the first album, which were mostly in the vein of regional Latin music— *cumbia*, *ranchera*, *conjunto norteño*, *tejano*, and combinations thereof—the artists blended the sound of different Latin music genres into a contemporary musical effort that recognized the importance of traditional music and important artists of the past.[3] For the second album by Los Super Seven,

Canto (released in 2001), producers reshuffled and came up with another all-star lineup.[4] As a result of the addition of three international music stars, the 12 songs on the second disc featured a more expanded version of Latin music, including Brazilian, Peruvian, Cuban, and other Latin American songs in addition to the regional Mexican styles that were already part of the supergroup's repertoire. Likewise, the influence of U.S. country music remained strong, as did the tendency toward genre blending.

When *Heard It on the X* was released in 2005, Los Super Seven all but gave up the façade of being an all-star band of just seven members. Not only was the deck reshuffled once again, but previous members returned and the new lineup included more Super Seven newcomers (but established stars).[5] The result was a list of at least ten "Super Seven" members, although that number also underreports the numerous other musicians, producers, and contributors who were part of the *Heard It on the X* effort. And this fact, I contend, is significant given that the tribute disc invokes a radio community that was influenced by border radio and Tex-Mex culture, which included Latin music alongside hillbilly and western swing music and even blues. In the following pages, I describe some important songs from *Heard It on the X* that reveal intriguing connections to Latino/as in U.S. culture and simultaneously signify the place of Latino/as in contemporary U.S. culture.

Blues Music and Tex-Mex Culture

One of the important social-cultural connections illuminated on 2005's *Heard It on the X* is a song by the aging blues musician Clarence "Gatemouth" Brown, who covers the song "See That My Grave Is Kept Clean." While the musicians and producers of *Heard It on the X* were wise to include Brown, an important link to blues music and African Americans on border radio of years past, they might not have been aware that the significance could be extended to include the Mexicans and Latin Americans who influenced early blues artists. While the predominant influence of African/African American culture is obvious in histories of blues music, a lesser-known fact remains that early blues musicians were also influenced, albeit ever so slightly, by Mexican culture.

For example, the song "See That My Grave Is Kept Clean" was actually written by one of Texas's original blues musicians, Blind Lemon Jefferson, who is considered one of the main figures in "country blues," one of two central figures of "Texas blues," and one of the earliest and most important bluesmen of the 1920s. Existing evidence suggests that various unknown guitarists among Mexican workers in the rural Texas area where he was raised likely influenced Jefferson and that those Mexican musicians probably played intricate *flamenco* guitar patterns that contributed to what was known as Jefferson's unique playing style. Although Clarence "Gatemouth" Brown's song on the *Heard It on the X* album was just a cover of an old blues classic, the significance is such that Brown's song connected him and the other artists on *Heard It on the X*, as well as a larger community of listeners to the border X stations, to the earliest of African American blues musicians but also to unknown Mexican and Latin American musical influences.

As I recalled this historical footnote about Blind Lemon Jefferson, I was reminded that when it comes to the legacy of African American and Latin influences and the multicultural dialogue that defines U.S. popular music, some historical clues shift the conversation to include the legacy of Robert Johnson. The blues music legend has been noted by scholars to have had tremendous influence on popular music in the United States and especially rock 'n' roll (Garofalo, 1997; Marcus, 1997), although he is probably best known for the Faustian legend of having sold his soul to the devil at a cross-roads in exchange for being the world's greatest blues guitarist. Yet historical evidence surrounding some of his recordings tells us that Johnson might also be considered important for how he forged his own dialogue with Latin music culture in South Texas through the late 1920s and early 1930s.

Years ago, I took notice of a small part of Robert Johnson's musical legacy, a 1930s song titled "They're Red Hot," in which Johnson can actually be heard singing about a traditional Mexican food—hot *tamales*. "They're Red Hot" is a song that has been performed and recorded countless times by blues artists, so, on the surface, Johnson's interpretation sounds like another version of a timeless blues classic that has been reworked and recorded by several different musicians over several decades. However, it is intriguing that despite this question about Johnson, the words "hot *tamales*" do not appear in similar songs by other artists. In other artists' interpretations of "Red Hot," the line "Hot *tamales* and they're red hot" is replaced by "My gal is red hot." So for others, "red hot" is a reference to the physical beauty of the singer's "gal," whereas for Johnson, "red hot" is a reference to hot *tamales*. Today, the song can be heard with "hot *tamales*" in more recent renditions that follow Robert Johnson, such as Eric Clapton's tribute to Robert Johnson, *Me and Mr. Johnson* (2004). Yet, I continued to wonder why Johnson was singing about hot *tamales*, and questions emerged. What could account for Johnson's lyric—using a Spanish word denoting Mexican food in a blues song? Is there any explanation for the change in the lyrics? Why would Johnson, a black man from Mississippi who played blues, be singing about traditional Mexican food?

To put these questions in better light through an interesting connection to border radio, Fowler and Crawford (2002) recall how former Texas governor W. Lee "Pappy" O'Daniel actually used border radio to further his campaigns for the governorship in the 1930s. As Fowler and Crawford note, it was quite natural that public figures with access to high-powered radio stations drifted into politics (p. 159). "Pappy" O'Daniel made his fortune through radio but also used border radio to get elected. He was known all over as "Pass the Biscuits, Pappy" O'Daniel because of his association with Hillbilly Flour products, which were heavily advertised on radio at the time. Since he used his own border radio station (broadcasting from México to circumvent U.S. politics) for political advantage, it was suggested that his famous phrase should be changed from "Pass the Biscuits, Pappy" to "Pass the *Tamales*, Pappy" (p. 183). In other words, for Texans of the 1930s, *tamales* served as a kind of discourse that implied "México." Still, the question remains: Why did the Mississippian Robert Johnson write a song about hot *tamales*?

As far as Johnson's connection to *tamales*, a clue exists in the liner notes to Johnson's *Complete Recordings* (1990), which indicate that he traveled to San Antonio and Dallas, Texas, for recording sessions in 1936 and 1937. The liner notes in the *Complete Recordings* indicate that Johnson recorded his Texas sessions in between recording sessions of Tex-Mex/Tejano artists such as Las Hermanas Barraza, Andres Berlanga, and Francisco Montalvo. Could it be that Johnson may have interacted with these artists and later changed a line or two in his songs—as blues musicians were prone to do? Eric Rothenbuhler (2007) reminds us about early blues artists that picking up on regional variations in musical style, assimilating multiple styles, and adapting to one's locale and audience were all standard practices for early blues musicians. Likewise, the art of entertaining a crowd, lyrical improvisation, and being clever with the audience were all critical parts of being a blues entertainer (pp. 68–71). Moreover, Rothenbuhler's recent research suggests that Johnson even learned from records and radio, revealing not only that the radio medium may have influenced Robert Johnson through the various musical styles that he was exposed to but also that Johnson composed his music and lyrics "for" the radio and records (p. 65). The significance of these details, however, is in the fact that the supposed grandfather of blues and great-grandfather of rock 'n' roll had contact with Mexicans and/or Mexican Americans in south Texas and, through "They're Red Hot," might have changed some lines as a result of that interaction with Tex-Mex culture.

It is worth noting that these two blues legends are but two brief examples of the many blues artists who could have had some form of interaction or engagement with Mexicans or other Latino/as in the United States. What this evidence suggests is that Latino/as can lay claim to having played some part in the formation of U.S. popular music, whether through musical notes and instrumentation, as in Jefferson's case, or through lyrics, as in Johnson's case. This assertion allows me to construct a history of popular music in terms of a cultural dialogue with Latino/as and other multicultural influences and avoids typical dichotomous histories of popular music that feature only black and white streams of influence. Beyond this, I contend that when these dormant features of early 20th-century life were mediated through radio, the interracial and intercultural nature of border radio and the various X stations awakened a multicultural spirit in popular culture and fomented the integrated, multicultural character of a rapidly changing U.S. culture—a culture that always included Latino/as.

Western Swing, Hillbilly Music, and Country

In addition to blues music, other genres that are commemorated on Los Super Seven's *Heard It on the X* are western swing and hillbilly music, and a direct correlation can be made between the emergence of border radio and the roots of country and western music in the 1930s and 1940s. As Kahn (1996) avers, "The earliest stations to showcase hillbilly music were in the United States, but by the early 1930s, stations began broadcasting hillbilly music from just across the Mexican border" (p. 206). Although music was not being regularly broadcast over U.S. networks during this period, by the late 1930s hillbilly and gospel constituted a great part of what was coming across from border radio broadcasting, and they were becoming more popular (p. 207).

Related to this fact, one of the greatest contributions by Mexican radio stations and border radio to popular music in the United States was the way they affected the careers of the famous Carter Family. As Kahn recognizes, "The Carter Family is one of the most famous recording groups to emerge from the American country music scene" of the 1920s, 1930s, and 1940s (1996, 205). What is not commonly known is that the Carter Family's fame resulted from their recording career in conjunction with their radio performance career, which aided in spreading their music and fame.

Their recording career began in the late 1920s and continued through the 1930s, and their broadcast days on Mexican radio lasted until 1942. The Carter Family actually lived in San Antonio, Texas, and traveled to places such as Del Rio, Texas, and Monterrey, México (in the state of Nueva León) and several other border stations that dotted the Mexican-American border. It was around this time that the family began to grow, and the several Carter children would carry on the Carter legacy in country music. Critical to the success of the Carter Family was the innovation of recording their shows instead of relying on live performances. According to Kahn, because radio shows were usually performed live, the earliest recordings and rebroadcasting of radio shows began on border radio to save the artists and announcers from early morning performances and, of course, early morning commutes to the stations on the Mexican side of the border. Although this practice was precipitated by the very nature of border radio stations, it eventually spread throughout the entire broadcasting industry after World War II (1996, 208).

In addition to such innovations in the radio broadcasting industry, the Carter Family's fame also contributed to the working out of a power struggle that was occurring between the United States and México over broadcast frequency allocation. In this sense, not only did border radio contribute to the fame and success of early country music pioneers; it also contributed to popular music in different ways, such as recorded programming, and forced the United States and México to work out solutions to frequency allocation problems at the time most critical to radio as a mass medium.

In yet another articulation of early country music to border radio and Latino/a music and culture, another significant cut from the 2005 *Heard It on the X* album is the song "My Window Faces the South," featuring Lyle Lovett's vocals on a cover version of an old 1940s tune by the pioneering country music act Bob Wills and His Texas Playboys. According to Starr and Waterman (2003), an important part of the "western" element in country music was the western swing music style that amalgamated Texas cowboy songs, German and Czech polkas, and Texas-Mexican *corridos*, *conjunto acordeon*, and Mexican *mariachi* music (p. 149). As Starr and Waterman note, the most famous figure in western swing music was Bob Wills, who achieved success as the bandleader for Bob Wills and His Texas Playboys. Starr and Waterman also remind us that the Texas Playboys' biggest hit was a 1941 song called "New San Antonio Rose," which was a hit song on the country charts and the pop charts (p. 150). "New San Antonio Rose" was later covered by Bing Crosby and went even higher on the pop charts, but the Texas Playboys' version included a trumpet duet "in the style of a Mexican *mariachi* band" (p. 151). As Starr and Waterman attest, the incorporation of such Latin American musical influences is part of what allowed western swing to exert a permanent influence on country music and Bob Wills to be considered one of the pioneers in country and western music (p. 151).

The early *mariachi* influence of Bob Wills and His Texas Playboys on the emerging country sound can be extended to what eventually came to be known as "rockabilly"—something between country music and rock 'n' roll—and the music of country and rockabilly legend Johnny Cash. The *mariachi* influence is probably best remembered in the exploding trumpets that drive Cash's 1963 song "Ring of Fire." However, the sound of *mariachi* trumpets would surface elsewhere in the 1960s and 1970s.

The use of *mariachi* trumpets, Mexican/Spanish guitar, marimbas, *bolero* beats, and other "Latinized country rhythms" that began with western swing music in the 1930s and 1940s and survived through country and western music can be found in many examples that followed in the late 1960s and into the 1970s. Concerning this "Latin tinge" in North American popular music, Roberts (1999) cites several tracks on the 1968 album *I Believe In You* by Mel Tillis and various 1970s songs such as the Amazing Rhythm Aces' "Third Rate Romance, Low Rent Rendezvous," Linda Hargrove's "Mexican Love Songs," Maria Muldaur's "Say You Will," Captain Hook's "Making Love and Music," and Michelle Phillip's "There She Goes." Roberts adds that there were more subtle examples of the Mexican tinge in Hoyt Axton's "The No No Song," "When the Morning Comes," and "Flash of Fire," as well as Crystal Gayle's "Someday Soon," "Talking in Your Sleep," "Too Good to Throw Away," and "Wayward Wind" (pp. 196–198). Of course, the Mexican influences on country and country rock music were even more obvious in the music of Latino/as Linda Ronstadt, Johnny Rodriguez, and Freddy Fender (p. 198). Freddy Fender's music is often labeled "country-rock," "South Texas Rock," and "Tex-Mex rock 'n' roll" (Lipsitz, 1994b; Mendheim, 1987; Roberts, 1999).

Not unimportant in popular music history is Herb Alpert, whose signature sound was defined by *mariachi* trumpets and who scored several pop music chart hits by tapping into the *mariachi* legacy in the United States. Alpert, of Ukrainian heritage, was classically trained in the trumpet and could have easily focused on other music styles such as classical or jazz; he had even dabbled in rock 'n' roll circles. Thus, it is noteworthy that he chose the *mariachi* aesthetic to give his own music some Latin flavor. Steve Otfinoski (1997) notes how Alpert actually traveled to Tijuana, México, to record bullfighting sounds that were later dubbed onto his signature song "The Lonely Bull." He then started billing himself as "The Tijuana Brass," and "The Lonely Bull" ended up at number 6 on the charts in November 1962. As Otfinoski tells it, by 1966 Herb Alpert and the Tijuana Brass were "more pervasive than any British rock group," scoring top-selling albums and winning Grammy Awards, and they eventually went on to score a string of hits throughout the 1960s and 1970s and even produced other *mariachi* pop acts (pp. 182–183).

In rock 'n' roll lore, Johnny Cash's "Ring of Fire" can be connected to other notable examples of *mariachi* influence through songs such as "Rocks Off" by The Rolling Stones, which was released on their 1972 album *Exile on Main Street*. Although this album remains a rock classic and is often cited as a favorite of rock 'n' roll aficionados, "Rocks Off" is not often remembered for *mariachi* trumpets and comes off as an otherwise unremarkable rock music piece. Yet, *mariachi* trumpets in "Rocks Off" can be included in a genealogy that connects Bob Wills, Johnny Cash, The Rolling Stones, Herb Alpert, Bing Crosby, Patti Page, Elvis Presley, and many others to more recent and contemporary rock, alternative rock, alt country, and indie rock acts such as Lyle Lovett, the Neutral Milk Hotel, Calexico,[6] DeVotchKa, Sufjan Stevens, Spoon, and the White Stripes[7] (among countless others). Importantly, songs such as "Ring of Fire," "Rocks Off," and others are linked in an important genealogical chain that extends far back into the days of border radio, attesting further to the influence of border radio on American culture. Moreover, such songs provide a fresh perspective on U.S. popular music, recognizing early examples of a *mariachi* legacy, and, thus, the interplay of Mexican and Latino/a culture with U.S. culture.

Rock 'n' Roll and Buddy Holly's Latino/a Connections

For further connections between the radio community invoked by the *Heard It on the X* release and Latino/a culture, one does not need to look very far. The 2005 tribute to border radio also featured a rendition of "Learning the Game," sung by country artist Rodney Crowell and performed by several other Super Seven artists. "Learning the Game," however, is actually an old tune by Buddy Holly. Holly, a West Texas rock 'n' roller, is acknowledged as a pioneer in the development of rock 'n' roll because of his use of electric guitars (revolutionizing the popular music industry in the 1950s), although I submit that the music of Buddy Holly might have been more influential in other ways. Holly also provides yet another link between *Heard It on the X*, border radio, and the unknown popular music history that further elucidates the influence of Latino/as on American culture.

First, the life (and death) of Buddy Holly can be connected to none other than Ritchie Valens (born Richard Valenzuela), the Mexican American artist most famous for the 1959 hit "La Bamba." Valens and Holly were making hits at the same time and touring together in "The Winter Dance Party" of January 1959. On February 3 of that same year, they also boarded a plane together that crashed in an Iowa cornfield, killing both. Interestingly, like Valens, Buddy Holly was said to have injected rock 'n' roll with Latin influence. Although many note how Holly's music had a unique sound that nobody could account for or explain and others state that "not even the performers could explain just what it was or where it came from" (Goldrosen & Beecher, 1987, p. 160), several scholars recall that Holly was considered to have a "Tex-Mex" sound that some speculate was a result of his West Texas roots (Geijerstam, 1976).

The "Tex-Mex" sound is evident in Holly's hit song "Brown Eyed Handsome Man." Although Holly's was a cover of a Chuck Berry song in which Berry was probably insinuating brown-skinned handsome man[8] (see also Lipsitz, 1990, p. 115), the guitar riff that Buddy Holly applied in his version of "Brown Eyed Handsome Man" sounded much more like the "Tex-Mex" sound for which Holly was known. Perhaps not coincidentally, the riff in "Brown Eyed Handsome Man" sounds much like the riff for the 1958 song "Tequila" by The Champs—another early rock 'n' roll song with an obvious connection to Mexican culture (Garofalo, 1997; Mendheim,

1987; Otfinoski, 1997). In other hit songs by Buddy Holly such as "Not Fade Away," a rock 'n' roll classic that has been covered countless times by rock and country artists, one can hear a 1-2-3 1-2 rhythm commonly known as the "Bo Diddley beat." Yet research reveals that although Bo Diddley is usually given credit as the originator of this famous beat, it is actually a product of Latino/a influence on American music. Musicologists have noted its basis in the five-beat clave rhythm associated with Afro-Cuban music, and others extend the origination of the "Bo Diddley beat" to African rhythms or Moorish influences in Spanish music (Avant-Mier, forthcoming).

Exact origins are obviously difficult to ascertain, but I suggest that what matters more is that Buddy Holly's connections to Latin American music can be seen through more than just one song. In the same vein, noteworthy is the fact that Holly married Maria Elena Santiago shortly before his death. In Holly's biography, Santiago reveals that when the couple were living in New York, Buddy had been playing Latin American and Spanish records and trying to copy the music and guitar riffs. Santiago also adds that Buddy was learning Latin American songs with the intention of recording them and that Buddy even wanted to learn Spanish (Goldrosen & Beecher, 1987, 123).

As rock historians know very well, the tragic death of Buddy Holly deprived the world of the foremost practitioner of the "Tex-Mex" sound in rock 'n' roll. In the same plane crash, rock enthusiasts also lost Ritchie Valens, who was not only a contemporary of Holly but also perhaps an influence. Together, they might have been the champions of Latin-influenced rock 'n' roll music, perhaps even the fathers of what much earlier could have been called a "Latin" rock music. These historical facts are investigated here to say not just that Buddy Holly should be remembered as a Latino rocker but also that Holly's connection to Ritchie Valens, along with his "Tex-Mex" sound and his interest in Latin music, is an indication that the Latino/a connection to rock 'n' roll music began quite early in the genre's history—in fact, much earlier than mainstream accounts are willing to acknowledge.

Unfortunately, the Valens and Holly stories ended in tragedy, but their music and influences have not been forgotten. Not only did their music retain lasting significance, but their stories reveal investments in Latino/a identity. By connecting rock 'n' roll with Latin music, they solidified the connection between Latino/as and rock 'n' roll music that would reach beyond the 1950s—and beyond national borders. The example of Buddy Holly presents us with a case of Latino/a music influences upon Buddy Holly, who in turn put his own influences on the vast community of border radio listeners who were listening to radio waves that originated on Mexican soil. It was a case of a dialogic cross-cultural and intercultural communication that happened at the level of public discourse and was mediated through radio.

Interestingly, when Los Super Seven included their homage ("Learning the Game") to Buddy Holly's West Texas music and his "Tex-Mex" sound, they simultaneously connected all of the Super Seven artists, musicians, and collaborators to a larger community of African Americans/blacks, various working-class whites, and various other Tex-Mex/Tejano/Mexican Americans throughout Texas and elsewhere who were so profoundly affected by border radio and the various cultures that came together through its frequencies.

Conclusion

My analysis of *Heard It on the X* and of the connections between border radio and Latino/as (and the lasting impact of both on American culture) ends here. However, it is worth noting that the Latino/a resonance in Los Super Seven's tribute to border radio could go further. Other examples included on *Heard It on the X* are a cover of "Let Her Dance," an original song by Bobby Fuller, a native of El Paso, Texas, who also championed the "Tex-Mex" sound and paralleled the life of Buddy Holly with his own early and tragic death; a cover of "Talk To Me," a song that was made famous on border radio through Sunny and the Sunliners, another rare example of Mexican Americans in rock 'n' roll, although further success in the rock genre so eluded them that the band returned to performing *tejano* and *norteño* music thereafter; "I'm Not That Kat (Anymore)" and "The Song of Everything," two songs written by the Texan Doug Sahm, who achieved success with "The Sir Douglas Quintet" by posing as a British rock band, hiding the fact that several band members were Mexican Americans, and denying their obvious Mexican and Latino/a musical influences (Avant-Mier, forthcoming); and, of course, "Heard It on the X," a song written by Texas blues rockers ZZ Top, who themselves were so affected by border radio that they wrote a song about it and who provide many important links to Mexican or Latino/a culture through their own musical and lyrical references. Likewise, other "Super Seven" stories that deserve further attention include that of Raul Malo, the singer/front man for The Mavericks (one of the most popular and top-selling country acts of the 1990s), who can be seen as negotiating his connections to country music and his Cuban and Latin American heritage at the same time. Another interesting "Super Seven" story would be that of Mexican American country star Rick Treviño, who has been an integral part of every Super Seven album and can be seen as negotiating his own country music identity with regard to his own Mexican American identity and Latino/a heritage.

In sum, the evidence provided by the example of *Heard It on the X* stands as a testament to Latin-influenced blues artists, to *mariachi*-influenced western swing music, and to "Tex-Mex"-influenced rockabilly and rock 'n' roll. Given such examples, it is remarkable that significant Latino/a contributions to mainstream U.S. culture and popular music continue to go unrecognized and unacknowledged. Nevertheless, *Heard It on the X* further underscores my assertion of American culture's debt to the Latino/a influence in popular music through border radio and, therefore, to the lasting effect of the sound medium of radio on American culture. Furthermore, whereas my contention has been that Latino/a influences on North American music have been minimized, this latter point underscores my argument that Latino/a connections to American popular music can be linked to issues of identity and the preliminary remarks in this chapter with regard to the place of Latino/as in contemporary U.S. culture and issues and tensions related to assimilation.

The incorporation of Mexican *mariachi* sounds into country and western and rock 'n' roll reflect a significant trend in U.S. culture throughout the first half of the 20th century (i.e., assimilation). Rather than decry sounds as particularly "ethnic," artists and musicians were able to parallel the acculturation processes that were happening in wider cultural contexts. Adopting and using Mexican sounds was not only a recognition of the presence of another community of people in Texas but also perhaps an appreciation for them and their culture. It could be said that the example of *mariachi*-influenced country music reflects a tendency in mainstream U.S. culture to minimize "ethnic" characteristics to make them more palatable to mainstream U.S. audiences. Although Elvis Presley's co-optation of African American music is remembered as an early example of this, and rapper Eminem can be seen as the most recent example, the case of *mariachi* trumpets in country and western and hillbilly music recalls how this has been happening since much earlier in U.S. history.

In conclusion, I introduced at the outset of this chapter the question of Latino/a identity and how it serves as a reminder that mainstream U.S. discourses seem unsure about what Latino/as are, who they are, and how they should be understood. Yet even after further analysis, new questions are raised about the role of radio and the possible impact(s) of radio and other mass media on the future relationship with Latino/a culture. First, how will formatting changes in recent decades affect ethno-racial relations in America's future? In addition, since Latino/as now constitute emerging radio markets, how will new radio formats impact American culture in decades to come? Will Latino/as be further assimilated through mass media such as radio? Or will emphasis on local, regional, and ethnic markets hinder assimilation? Similarly, in the age of niche marketing, "narrowcasting," and market segmentation for many different media, could current industry trends possibly result in less interaction between Latino/as and other Americans and foster an environment of mediated tribalism instead of intercultural communication? Finally, will Latino/as ever be recognized for their lasting impact on American culture, and will they ever be included in conversations about mainstream U.S. culture, rather than always being positioned as threatening outsiders, aliens, immigrants, and invaders?

I submit that if xenophobia and intercultural fear had won during the days of border radio, North Americans would have feared that their children would lose blues music or hillbilly swing to Mexican and Latin American music. Moreover, like current fears about losing English, border radio listeners in the United States might have feared that future generations of youth would be forced to play in *mariachi* bands. However, analyzing contemporary cultural texts such as *Heard It on the X* and revisiting the story of border radio, as well as radio's lasting impact on American culture, tells us that what actually happened was something much more interesting. As border radio historians Fowler and Crawford (2005) recently reminded us in their *Heard It on the X* liner notes, "Today, hispanic broadcasters dominate la frontera. Gringo broadcasting outlaws have migrated to cable television, the internet, and satellite radio. But the spirit of the X lives on, echoing through the universe." Likewise, the effects of border radio continue, echoing through America's radio waves.

Notes

1. The 2000 Census uses the category "Spanish/Hispanic/Latino." However, throughout this chapter I will employ the term "Latino" to denote a more neutral identifier that approximates "Spanish/Hispanic/Latino" or, perhaps, "Latin American." As such, my use of "Latino" reflects a pan-American, pan-Latin view of culture, without regard for nationality. Further, following Johnson (2000), "Latina/o" will be used here consistently, emphasizing the masculine and feminine forms together to "avoid androcentric interpretation of the term" (p. 167). Thus, throughout the rest of this research the term "Latina/o" indicates people from various Latin American (Central American or South American) nations, although it is important to reiterate that I also use the term "Latino/a" to indicate a person from the United States. In other words, I employ the term "Latino/a" irrespective of national citizenship. For more on the term "Hispanic" and "Hispanic peoples," see Johnson (2000). Rinderle (2005) also provides an excellent literature review of the uses and origins of various labels such as "Hispanic," "Latino," "Chicano," and "Mexican American."
2. The original Los Super Seven lineup included Joe Ely, Freddy Fender, David Hidalgo, "Flaco" Jimenez, Ruben Ramos, Cesar Rosas, and Rick Treviño.
3. Likewise, one important standout track on the first album was a thoughtful and sorrowful cover of an old folk song by folk legend Woody Guthrie about immigrants and deportation, "Plane Wreck at Los Gatos (Deportee)," which seemed to commemorate Woody Guthrie and U.S. folk music at the same time as it commemorated the plight of immigrants and migrant workers.
4. While David Hidalgo, Cesar Rosas, Ruben Ramos, and Rick Treviño remained from the original Los Super Seven lineup, the new Super Seven included international pop

music superstar Caetano Veloso from Brazil, whose extensive legacy included decades' worth of MPB (Música Popular Brasileira), *Tropicália, bossa nova,* folk, and rock, as well as international fame, political activism, and a reputation as one of the most important Brazilian musicians of all time. Another piece of the Super Seven puzzle was the Peruvian Susana Baca, whose contributions stemmed from her background as a contemporary interpreter and proponent of Afro-Peruvian music and culture. The final piece of the puzzle was the U.S. country star Raul Malo, whose time as a front man of the Mavericks placed him in one of the most successful and popular country acts of the 1990s. Interestingly, since the late 1990s, Malo had increasingly focused his musical efforts on Cuban and Latin music and, therefore, on his Cuban-American culture and identity.

5. Among the returning Super Seven members for *Heard It on the X* were Joe Ely and Freddy Fender, and the new additions included Delbert McClinton, John Hiatt, Lyle Lovett, Rodney Crowell, and Clarence "Gatemouth" Brown.

6. Interestingly, Calexico actually features *mariachis* during their live performances, and, perhaps fittingly, Calexico were actually included in the *Heard It on the X* project, playing on at least 7 of the disc's 12 cuts.

7. On their latest (2007) release, the White Stripes cover Patti Page's 1950s song "Conquest," presumably because of the trumpets that appear on Page's original recording, which suggests that Patti Page's music can also be included in a list of *mariachi*-influenced U.S. pop music.

8. This point is a mere suggestion about how Buddy Holly may have identified with the song. Holly was likely able to identify with the song because of the reference to brown eyes but also with brown-skinned minority populations. Moreover, it is worth noting that such changes in lyrics have happened with other songs in rock 'n' roll history, such as Van Morrison's "Brown Eyed Girl," in which Van Morrison's original lyrics were about a brown-skinned girl. Interestingly, "Brown Eyed Girl" has also been linked to Latin music through its rhythm and instrumentation

References

Anderson, B. (2006). *Imagined Communities: Reflections on the Origin and Spread of Nationalism.* New York: Verso.

Avant-Mier, R. (2008). Latinos in the Garage: A Genealogical Examination of Garage Rock, Rock and Pop Music. *Popular Music and Society,* 32 (1).

Bentley, B. (2005). Liner notes. *Heard it on the X* [compact disc]. Cleveland, OH: TELARC International Corporation.

Fowler, G. & B. Crawford. (2002). *Border Radio: Quacks, Yodelers, Pitchmen, Psychics, and Other Amazing Broadcasters of the American Airwaves.* Austin: Texas Monthly Press.

———. (2005). Liner notes. *Heard it on the X* [compact disc]. Cleveland, OH: TELARC International Corporation.

Garofalo, R. (1997). *Rockin Out: Popular Music in the U.S.A.* Boston, MA: Allyn & Bacon.

Geijerstam, C.A. (1976). *Popular Music in Mexico.* Albuquerque: University of New Mexico Press.

Goldrosen, J. & J. Beecher. (1987). *Remembering Buddy: The Definitive Biography.* New York: Viking/Penguin.

Guzman, B. (2001). Census 2000 brief: The Hispanic population. The United States Census 2000. Washington, D.C.; U.S. Census Bureau. Retrieved February 3, 2006 from the World Wide WEeb at: http://www.census.gov.

Hilmes, M. & J. Loviglio. (Eds.). (2002). *Radio Reader: Essays in the Cultural History of Radio*. New York: Routledge.

Johnson, F.L. (2000). *Speaking Culturally: Language Diversity in the United States*. Thousand Oaks, CA: Sage.

Johnson, R. (1990). Liner notes. *The Complete Recordings* [compact disc box set]. Columbia Records/CBS.

Kahn, E. (1996). The Carter Family on Border Radio. *American Music*, 14 (2), 205–217.

Keith, M.C. (1997). *Voices in the Purple Haze*. 51(3)Westport, CT: Praeger

———. (2002). Turn On … Tune In: The Rise and Demise of Commercial Underground Radio. In M. Hilmes & J. Loviglio (Eds.), *Radio Reader: Essays in the Cultural History of Radio* (pp. 389–404). New York: Routledge

———. (2007). The Long Road to Radio Studies. *Journal of Broadcasting and Electronic Media*. 51 (3) 1–7

Lipsitz, G. (1990). *Time Passages: Collective Memory and American Popular Culture*. Minneapolis: University of Minnesota Press.

———. (1994a). *Dangerous Crossroads*. New York: Verso.

———. (1994b). *Rainbow at Midnight: Labor and Culture in the 1940s*. Urbana and Chicago: University of Illinois Press.

Marcus, G. (1997). *Mystery Train: Images of America in Rock 'n' Roll Music*. New York: Plume/Penguin.

Martín-Barbero, J. (1999). The Processes: From Nationalisms to Transnationals. In J. Hanson & D.J. Maxcy (Eds.), *Sources: Notable Selections in Mass Media* (pp. 345–353). Guilford, CT: Dushkin/McGraw-Hill.

Mendheim, B. (1987). *Ritchie Valens: The First Latino Rocker*. Tempe, AZ: Bilingual Press.

Otfinoski, S. (1997). *The Golden Age of Rock Instrumentals*. New York: Billboard Books.

Rinderle, S. (2005). The Mexican Diaspora: A Critical Examination of Signifiers. *Journal of Communication Inquiry*, 29 (4), 294–316.

Roberts, J.S. (1999). *The Latin Tinge: The Impact of Latin American Music on the United States*. New York: Oxford University Press.

Rothenbuhler, E.W. (2007). For-the-Record Aesthetics and Robert Johnson's Blues Style As a Product of Recorded Culture. *Popular Music*, 26 (1), 65–81.

Rothenbuhler, E. & T. McCourt. (2002). Radio Redefines Itself, 1947–1962. In M. Hilmes & J. Loviglio (Eds.), *Radio Reader: Essays in the Cultural History of Radio* (pp. 367–387). New York: Routledge.

Squier, S.M. (2003). *Communities of the Air: Radio Century, Radio Culture*. Durham, NC: Duke University Press.

Starr, L. & C. Waterman. (2003). *American Popular Music: From Minstrelsy to MTV*. New York: Oxford University Press.

Ward, E. (2005). SWSX Records: Los Super 7—*Heard It on the X* [music review]. *Austin Chronicle*, March 18. Austin, TX: Austin Chronicle Corporation.

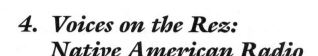

4. Voices on the Rez:
Native American Radio

BRUCE SMITH

Mainstream radio in the United States has been highly formatted since television became popular in the 1950s. Stations typically target audiences with a
particular type of music or talk. Formats give stations an identity and enable
listeners to rely on the consistency of the programming on a given station,
day or night. There are some exceptions to this approach to radio programming. Many college, community, and public radio stations broadcast more
eclectic programming. Another exception is Native American radio.

Native American radio stations try to serve entire populations—those
living on an Indian reservation or in the Alaska Bush.[1] Audiences are
young and old, English speaking and not, young people trying to echo
popular culture and those living in more traditional ways. Native stations
reflect the diversity of people, tastes, and lifestyles within the boundaries
of the indigenous community they serve. There are rock and rap music,
country and western, traditional music, and powwow broadcasts, music by
contemporary Native American recording artists, local and national news,
information about Native communities, and call-in and talk shows about
issues of local interest. It all blends into a mix that is quite unlike the sound
most radio listeners today are accustomed to hearing. Native stations program not to a single musical taste but to the diverse needs of an often
marginalized people of ancient origins who are using radio to maintain a
sense of community and foster the preservation of indigenous languages
and cultures. Radio stations owned and operated by Native Americans[2] are
a relatively recent development. The first Native stations went on the air
in the 1970s, more than half a century after KDKA began broadcasting in
Pittsburgh. Radio historian Michael Keith has observed that despite radio's
"astronomic rise to prominence in the 1920s and 1930s (and virtual ubiq-
uity by World War II), Native Americans were essentially left unserved and
ignored by broadcasters" (Keith, 1995, 3).

In some cases, radio signals were available from distant communities, but the programming was not targeted to Native listeners. In Alaska, powerful AM stations from the state's urban centers were the only radio voices that were accessible to Natives living in the Alaska bush.

Radio stations that could be heard in Native communities presented music and information that had little to do with Native culture or Native problems. Media portrayals of Natives were often unflattering. Stories concentrated on old stereotypes and current social problems without offering balancing insights about problem solving and healing or success stories (Greer, 1991). The media stories that Natives heard about themselves were tales of pain and conflict. None of the programming attempted positively to reinforce Native cultures or languages (Keith, 1995; Smith & Cornette, 1998b).

Stories in mainstream media have portrayed Natives as socialist, spiritual, or troublesome. The alternative press has used the plight of Natives to assail capitalism and racism. Environmentalists have sometimes criticized Natives for exploitation of the land when tribes pursued economic development of tribal resources (Hill, 1992). The media gatekeepers who selected the stories and framed their point of view have seldom been Natives. Natives were the subject of mainstream media news but seldom had a voice of their own.

Canadian researcher Marianne Stenbaek (1982) addressed the important issue of giving voice to indigenous people. Her particular concern at the time was Canada's Inuit Eskimo population. She drew the connection between access to and control of media and the political empowerment of indigenous people. "To be master of one's own media," she said, "is to be master of one's own fate."

In the 1960s, the civil rights movement and a general climate of social activism fostered a dialogue about access to media by minority groups, including Native Americans. The American Indian Movement (AIM), in particular, gave impetus to the development of radio stations owned and operated by Natives (Keith, 1995). Following AIM's 1972 seizure of Wounded Knee, South Dakota, a dialogue began in Native communities about the power of radio and television and the need for Native Americans to have a media voice. It was not until the early 1970s, however, that stations owned and operated by Natives began to emerge.

Charles Trimble, an Oglala Sioux and principal founder of the American Indian Press Association in 1970, noted a widespread concern among Natives about

> the lack of proper interpretation of events and priorities in Indian affairs on the part of the mass media. All too often, the mass media will give extensive coverage to sensational and relatively unimportant events in Indian affairs while completely ignoring ... more significant needs and events. (Report on a Planning Meeting, 1970)

Interest in Native radio was motivated by more than concern about the fairness of news coverage in the mainstream media. Many Natives were also concerned about the impact of mainstream media on indigenous languages and cultures (Browne, 1996; Keith, 1995; Smith & Cornette, 1998b). Alaska linguist Michael Krauss, for example, likened Western media to a "cultural nerve gas" that overwhelms indigenous languages and cultures and serves as a force for the assimilation of indigenous people into the majority culture (Lewan, 1999).

Browne (1996) argued that indigenous media around the world are vitally important in the effort to "rescue" endangered languages. Indigenous media, he said, can increase self-esteem, combat negative images in the mainstream media, foster cohesion among indigenous people, and serve as a visible and audible symbol that indigenous cultures count for something through their possession and operation of modern technology.

In a traditional Lakota Sioux community, the *eyapaha* was the person who circulated through the camp sharing information about plans for the day. He was the camp newscaster and bulletin board wrapped into one. Today, that oral tradition serves as a model for Native radio, according to Leonard Bruguier, director of the Institute of American Indian Studies at the University of South Dakota (Smith & Cornette, 1998b). Bruguier says that the telling of the day's happenings and the validation of Native culture and language lie at the heart of Native radio. "This is what radio is today," Bruguier says. "Indians have a strong oral tradition and radio has become the new 'voice of the people'"(p. 21).

The Stations

There are multiple claims to being the first Native station on the air (Keith, 1995). WYRU-AM in Red Springs, North Carolina, is generally acknowledged to have led the way, beginning operation in 1970 as a service of the Lumbee Tribe.

The first noncommercial Native station, KYUK-AM, went on the air in 1971 (Brigham & Smith, 1993). KYUK serves Yup'ik Eskimos in southwest Alaska. Other stations in rural Alaska followed in 1973 and 1975, and more were added during the 1980s. Today ten Native stations serve Indian, Eskimo, and Aleut populations in a vast region of Alaska from the Arctic to the Aleutian Islands.

KYUK was the first of many radio and television stations in rural Alaska created under the direction of the Alaska Educational Broadcasting Commission, later renamed the Alaska Public Broadcasting Commission (APBC). The goal was to create and operate stations in rural areas where few or no other broadcast services were available. State policy in Alaska in the

1970s and 1980s encouraged the development of Native radio with generous funding for both the construction and operation of stations. The comparative prosperity of Alaska stations for many years was in stark contrast
to the small budgets and staffs of most Native stations in other states. The
fact that Alaska's is an oil-based economy took its toll on station funding in
the 1990s, however, when funding cuts necessitated some restructuring of
station operations.

Outside Alaska, stations are all located on Indian reservations. Many
are controlled or funded in part by tribal councils. Most Native people in
North and South Dakota, for example, are within listening range of one
or more Native-owned stations. South Dakota has four stations serving the
Lakota, Dakota, and Nakota (Sioux) nations. North Dakota has three stations that reach the diverse populations of the Mandan, Arikara, Hidatsa,
and Chippewa tribes.

In addition to the many stations in Alaska and the Dakotas, there are six
Native stations in Arizona, four in New Mexico, two in Oregon, and one each
in California, Colorado, Montana, Washington, Wisconsin, Wyoming, and
New York. Thirty-one of the 33 stations are located west of the Mississippi
River.

Many of the stations straddle state borders, serving Natives in more than
one state. CKON in New York is unique. It straddles the border of the United
States and Canada, serving the Mohawk Nation (Allen, 2006). The station
operates with only 250 watts, and some call it a pirate station because it has
refused to seek licensing from either the Canadian Radio Television Commission (CRTC) or the U.S. Federal Communications Commission (FCC).
It is governed by a proclamation by the Akwesasne Mohawk Nation. Although
this unusual status is acknowledged by the CRTC, the FCC has refused to
recognize the station (Fairchild, 1998). The refusal of U.S. federal authorities to recognize CKON has made the station ineligible to receive operating
funds from the Corporation for Public Broadcasting (CPB) (Keith, 1995).

Since 1971, approximately ten stations, most noncommercial, have
been launched in each decade, bringing the total number of stations operating in 2007 to 33 (Native Public Media, 2007). Along the way, two Native
stations dropped from the ranks. WYRU, the first Native broadcast station,
was sold to non-Native interests and reformatted as a gospel station targeting a mainstream audience. WASG-AM, a commercial station owned by the
Poarch Band Creek tribe in Atmore, Alabama, went off the air in 1993. Its
commercial failure was blamed on insufficient support from the non-Native
community (Browne, 1996).

The good news is that few Native stations have failed. Most operate
with small budgets and staffs and make extensive use of volunteers. Lack
of funding is consistently cited by station managers as the biggest problem
they face (Keith, 1995). Federal grants from the CPB provide a nucleus of

revenue for most stations, but not all. Alaska stations also receive operating grants from the APBC, an agency of the state government. Some stations receive direct funding from tribal governments or indirect funding via program underwriting. Tribes with successful casino operations seem to be most likely to have sufficient resources to provide funding to radio stations.

Grants from different sources provide the financial foundation for station operations. Local fundraising augments revenues. Fundraising is more difficult and less lucrative in rural communities with subsistence economies where incomes are low. On-air fund drives, for example, which are a major source of revenue for mainstream public and community radio stations, are less productive for Native stations. Reservation and village populations are small, and there is little discretionary income for charitable donations. As alternatives, stations organize benefit events such as concerts, solicit underwriting from local businesses, and in some cases participate in gambling activities such as bingo to supplement their income.

Programming on Native stations includes traditional stories and music, public service announcements, and other information in both English and local dialects. Stations have become forums for discussing local problems on news, public affairs, call-in programs, and local government reports. Entertainment programs include both traditional and mainstream popular music. Often the variety of music that is broadcast spans the spectrum from rap and rock to ancient drum music, said to carry the heartbeat of Mother Earth.

Two Profiles

Two Native radio stations are representative of others. Their profiles provide insights into the history and workings of stations. KILI-FM, on the Pine Ridge Reservation in South Dakota, is a good example of reservation-based radio. KYUK-AM, serving the Yup'ik Eskimo people on the Kuskokwim delta of southwest Alaska, is representative of Native radio in Alaska's bush.

KILI-FM

KILI refers to itself as the "Voice of the Lakota Nation." Its Web site says, "KILI means 'cool' or 'awesome' in the Lakota language. KILI Radio is cool, but it's much more than that. It's a vital force of preservation for Lakota people and our culture" (KILI, 2007).

For travelers along the wide-open prairie between Sioux Falls and Rapid City, KILI is the clearest radio signal available. The station is popular on three reservations: the Cheyenne River, Rosebud, and Pine Ridge.

The Pine Ridge Reservation is the eighth largest in land area (10,000 square miles) and covers roughly the land area of the state of Connecticut. It is home to 40,000 residents. The terrain is a mixture of barren badlands, rolling grassland hills, and prairie scattered with occasional clusters of pine trees. The largest community on the reservation is the village of Pine Ridge, with nearly 6,000 residents. Most reservation residents live in isolated rural locations where there are few improved (paved) roads. The isolation is compounded during heavy rain and snowstorms, when roads can become impassable.

KILI broadcasts from Porcupine Butte, located just north of Wounded Knee, site of the 1890 massacre of 150 men, women, and children by the U.S. Cavalry. A protest siege was staged there in 1973 by members of AIM.

Members of AIM were involved in the creation of KILI. Press coverage of the siege in 1973 persuaded AIM leaders of the need for a locally owned media voice on the reservation. The station was created, however, as an independently licensed entity with a self-appointed board of directors. The goal was to insulate it from politics both on and off the reservation (Keith, 1995; Tom Casey, personal communication, November 1, 1996). The actual licensee is Lakota Communications, Inc., a 501(C) (3) nonprofit corporation.

The station's relationship with AIM created a stigma early on. Radio historian Michael Keith reported on a conversation with KILI's first manager, Dale Means. Means said that when the station went on the air, the *Rocky Mountain News* published a headline that read, "Terrorists Erect Radio Station" (Keith, 1995). Although politics motivated early efforts to create a station and have erupted occasionally ever since, the station prides itself on its independence and ability to air controversies on the Pine Ridge fully (Conciatore, 1995).

On the air since 1983, KILI conceives of itself as a *community* station. Community radio in the United States typically presents information and music of local interest that is ignored by the corporate radio stations. Community radio has a commitment to local service and relies heavily on volunteers as participants. At KILI, there is substantial involvement by community volunteers, and the station tries to provide C-Span like coverage of major events on the reservation, including tribal council meetings, powwows, government hearings, and sporting events.

Much of the programming on KILI is in the Lakota language. The station sees itself as an important partner in the preservation of the language. The station's morning program, for example, is called the *Morning Wakalyapi Show*. The all-Lakota-language program presents traditional and contemporary Native American music with news and information of interest to the Lakota. Other programming includes *News of the Lakota Nation*, *News from around the Reservations*, *Health News from the Porcupine Clinic*, and drum music in the evening. There is also country, rock, blues, and even some rap music. The station broadcasts more than 60 public service announcements daily and reads birthday and funeral announcements. Discussion programs about the schools, health and welfare, and jobs on the reservations are also standard fare.

The station's Web site describes the diversity of its programming:

Our program schedule is designed to *serve all age groups and interests* on the reservations:

- A grandmother in Medicine Root, South Dakota, awakens to the sounds of the Porcupine Singers
- A Lakota rancher from Kane Creek listens for the weather
- A young father in Wanblee waits to hear job announcements
- A young teenager in Kyle waits to hear rock and roll (KILI, 2007).

Funding for the station's operations comes from an annual grant from the CPB, program underwriting, and local fundraising. The station also organizes special events. Benefit concerts in Rapid City, for example, have netted as much as $33,000. Donors to the station live all over the United States. Many gifts are from people off the Pine Ridge who support the station's mission. The station refers to donors as "allies." One especially interesting source of funding for the station in the past was an annual fund drive on WILB, a black station in New York City, which in a single year raised almost $30,000 for KILI.

The station suffered a setback in April 2006 when its broadcast antenna was destroyed by lightning, silencing the "main source of communications to an entire reservation" (Melmer, 2006). For two months, the station could originate only Internet broadcasts. Then, for a year, it transmitted with a low-power 300-watt system that could reach some listeners 15 to 20 miles from the station (Steen, 2006). What started as a $70,000 emergency evolved into a $200,000 project, requiring extensive fundraising and a grant of almost $139,000 from the federal Public Telecommunications Facilities Program and a $46,000 grant from the state of South Dakota. The station replaced not only the damaged antenna but also its tower, transmitter, and transmission line before it returned to the air in early 2007 (PTFP, 2006).

Losing its high-powered signal for a year was a major challenge for KILI, but the event also dramatized the value of the station and its importance to its audience. Tom Casey, business manager and development director for the station, observed, "People won't take us for granted after this" (Steen, 2006). One listener said of the station, "Since KILI has been off we don't know anything anymore. We don't know what's going on anywhere" (Melmer, 2006).

KYUK-AM

Alaska Natives do not reside on reservations. Instead, they live in villages and are shareholders in both village and regional corporations. The Native corporations operate businesses that generate income for the benefit of Native shareholders. The Alaska Native Claims Settlement Act of 1971 created this different structure for Alaska Natives. The settlement extinguished Native claims to almost all of Alaska in exchange for approximately one-ninth of the state's land plus $962.5 million in compensation.

Soon after the Settlement Act of 1971, KYUK-AM went on the air in Bethel, Alaska. KYUK provided what Alaska broadcasters call "sole service," the only radio service available to an audience. Bethel is located on the tree-less tundra about halfway between Anchorage, Alaska, and Siberia. There are no roads or trains to Bethel. Even marine access is seasonal. Air transport is the only way in and out for much of the year, and even it is not always reliable.

> In the winter of 1989, for example, the temperature and barometer plunged so low that instruments on jets ceased to function, causing all planes to be grounded. Less than a month later, the eruption of a volcano between Bethel and Anchorage put so much ash into the atmosphere that all aircraft were again grounded. Such events, though uncommon, cut Bethel off from the outside world. (Brigham & Smith, 1993, 102)

Travel by road is limited to only a few miles of mostly unpaved roads. In winter, the nearby Kuskokwim River freezes solid and is maintained as a state highway, making village-to-village driving possible. Travel by boat in summer and dog team or snow machine in winter are the other common forms of local transportation.

KYUK serves 52 Yup'ik Eskimo villages with a combined population of 20,000. The station's 56,000-square-mile service area in southwestern Alaska is the size of the state of Ohio. Although radio signals from Anchorage, Nome, and the Soviet Union could occasionally be heard in the evening in Bethel, interference and fading problems were severe. A 10-watt Air Force Radio network repeater station at a nearby radar facility reached only a small portion of Bethel and none of the nearby villages. Commercial media development in such a remote and poorly populated region was judged not viable. State government decided that if it did not nurture the development of radio in such places, it was not likely to happen (Brigham & Smith, 1993).

The mission of KYUK is "To educate, stimulate and inform as well as provide cultural enrichment, entertainment, opportunity for public access, and language for cultural survival." Its call letters were chosen because "YUK" means "person" in the Yup'ik Eskimo language.

Providing sole broadcast service for much of its audience, KYUK must literally be all things to all people. The sort of specialization that is common among radio stations elsewhere is not possible in Bethel. As 85% of KYUK's audience is Yup'ik Eskimo, the station relies heavily on its own bilingual staff to produce programming, about 70% of which originates locally.

One unique type of programming on KYUK and other bush stations is point-to-point transmissions that serve as a kind of substitute for telephones and two-way radios, which are uncommon in much of the bush. KYUK transmits personal messages from one person to another on a program called *Tundra Drums*, which "helps villagers locate lost children, stolen boats and snow machines, make funeral arrangements, learn flight schedules, announce Bethel jury selection and exchange friendly greetings to those who live beyond the reach of telephone or newspaper" (Brigham & Smith, 1993). It is easy today to take the ability to communicate for granted in an era of cell phones and other telecommunications technologies. Some people complain that they feel too accessible because they can be reached any time, any place. *Tundra Drums* is a reminder that not all Americans have access to communication media. The program and others like it around Alaska are still valued highly by isolated people trying to stay in touch with one another in the bush.

Weather forecasts, live coverage of the Bethel City Council meetings, fur and fish prices, local news in English and Yup'ik, play-by-play sports commentaries, and political debates are other regular services. Music programs range from mainstream popular to home-recorded Yup'ik gospel. The most popular programs, however, are call-in talk shows. Broadcast in English and Yup'ik, *Yuk to Yuk*, features guests discussing local issues of importance. *Talk Line* invites discussion on everything from gossip to heated local controversy and was once billed as "the show you hate ... and hate to miss!" There are also statewide news and public affairs programs such as *Talk of Alaska*, *Alaska Voices Live*, and *Alaska*, and the long-running statewide 30-minute evening newscast *Alaska News Nightly* from the Alaska Public Radio Network. An automation system helps KYUK to deliver more hours of service, especially overnight, at minimal cost.

With much of its operating budget coming from state and federal grants, KYUK finds itself each year at the mercy of governors, legislators, and the price of North Slope crude oil on the world market. As the fortunes of Alaska's economy rise and fall, so too does support for Native stations such as KYUK.

The traditional fundraising techniques used by public broadcasters outside Alaska have not proved to be successful in Bethel. With only 20,000 people in its service area, most of whom have little cash income, traditional on-air pledge drives yield little revenue. The largest source of local revenue is gaming. KYUK obtained a Gaming and Raffle Permit from the state in

1983. In an area devoid of most forms of organized entertainment, bingo and pull-tab gambling are popular pastimes and have netted KYUK profits of more than $80,000 a year. The station runs the local bingo operation one or two nights a week.

National Programming

For many years, there were no national radio programs by and about Natives. Each station was on its own to create programming. Although locally originated programming still dominates schedules, today stations also have access to national programs delivered by satellite. Since 1987, *National Native News* has been broadcasting newscasts to more than 160 noncommercial radio stations across the United States. The five-minute daily newscasts were produced originally by the Alaska Public Radio Network. Today they are a service of the Koahnic Broadcast Corporation in Anchorage, Alaska, and are distributed by Public Radio International (Koahnic, 2007). In addition to Native-owned stations that carry the newscasts, *National Native News* is also heard on many non-Native stations.

Koahnic Broadcast Corporation ("Koahnic" is an Athabascan word in the Ahtna dialect that means "live air") is a major player in Native American radio. It operates KNBA-FM, in Anchorage, the only urban Native station in the United States. In addition to *National Native News*, Koahnic also produces *Native America Calling*, a daily live call-in program about issues of interest to Native communities, and *Earthsongs*, a program of contemporary music by Native American musicians. Koahnic also provides training to Native American journalists and producers with the goal of increasing the number of Native Americans who are engaged in media careers.

Another source of national radio programming by and about Natives is American Indian Radio on Satellite (AIROS, 2007). AIROS operates a full-time Internet radio service, AIROS.org, that bills itself as "All Indian Internet Radio, Everyday, Everywhere." The Webcast is a service of Native American Public Telecommunications (NAPT) in Lincoln, Nebraska, which also produces and distributes video programming (Native American Public Telecommunications, 2007).

Since 1977, NAPT, which was formerly named the Native American Public Broadcasting Consortium, has been helping to develop and distribute Native-produced programs to Native and mainstream media. In 1993, it received federal funding to create a new satellite interconnection system (AIROS) to distribute national Native radio programs more extensively.

Other sources of national Native radio programming include NativeRadio.com, Native Public Media (nativepublicmedia.org), and Native Voice One (nv1.org), which is also available on Sirius Satellite Radio.

Conclusion

Ownership and operation of media enterprises are empowering Native Americans. In Canada, First Nations[3] broadcasting has been seen as part of a decolonization process (Native Broadcasting, 1986; Smith & Brigham, 1992). Broadcasting raised the status of indigenous languages and cultures and bolstered self-esteem among Natives. In the United States, Native radio has given indigenous communities a forum for dialogue about important issues, a venue for presenting traditional and modern music by and about Natives, and a sympathetic platform for nurturing language and culture. It also connects people who inhabit rural regions in western states where communication is a challenge.

For many years, Native stations operated largely in isolation from one another. Today, Native radio operations are interconnected by satellite networks. They benefit from collaborative productions and ambitious training programs. Audio services are available not only from over-the-air broadcasters but also on the Web. Listeners who seek access to information and entertainment by and about Native Americans can access radio programming from New York to Alaska.

Although Native stations continue to suffer from a frustrating lack of resources, they give voice to Native people and communities. The motto of KLND-FM, on the Standing Rock (Lakota) Reservation in northwest South Dakota, sums up the value of Native radio in America: "Wolakota Wiconi Waste," which means, "Through unity a good life." Radio unifies local communities and the larger community of Native Americans across the country. Radio validates and helps to preserve indigenous languages and cultures. The oral culture of Native Americans has embraced radio as a modern *eyapaha* or voice of the people.

Notes

1. Bush refers to any community not on the road system. More specifically, it generally refers to communities in the north and west of Alaska that are inhabited by Eskimos and Athabascan Indians.
2. Various terms are used to identify indigenous people in the United States. In the lower-48 states, the terms "Indian," "American Indian," and "Native American" are all used. In Alaska, the preferred term is "Native American," which refers to the three distinct indigenous groups who live there: Indian, Eskimo, and Aleut. When referring to themselves, individual Native Americans usually name their tribal connection first: Lakota, Tlingit, Cherokee, Inupiat, and so on. Variability in the choice of terms requires some flexibility and sensitivity. In this chapter, the terms "Native American" and "Native" are used because they are the most inclusive.
3. "First Nations" is a Canadian term of ethnicity that refers to the aboriginal peoples located in what is now Canada.

References

AIROS Native Radio Network. Retrieved from http://www.airos.org, May 10, 2007.

Allen, K.N. (2006). Homeland Insecurity. *Cultural Survival Quarterly*, 30 (3). Retrieved from http://www.culturalsurvival.org/publications/csq, May 10, 2007.

Brigham, J.C. & B.L. Smith. (1993). KYUK in Bethel: Pioneering Native Broadcasting in Alaska. *Northern Review*, 11 (1), 101–117.

Browne, D.R. (1996). *Electronic Media and Indigenous Peoples: A Voice of Our Own?* Ames: Iowa State University Press.

Coleman, A., L. Morgan, & B. Smith. (1997). Radio's Influence in the Alaskan Bush: Cultural Transmission or Diffusion? *Journal of Radio Studies*, 4, 7–14.

Conciatore, Jacqueline. (1995). On the Plains, a Station That "Knows Where It Lives." *Current*, December 18, 71–74.

Fairchild, C. (1998). The Canadian Alternative: A Brief History of Unlicensed and Low Power Radio. In S. Dunifer & R. Sakolsky (Eds.), *Seizing the Airwaves: A Free Radio Handbook*. Oakland, CA: AK Press. Retrieved from http://www.akpress.org/1997/items/seizingtheairwaves, May 10, 2007.

Greer, S. (1991). Media Education and Native People. *Winds of Change*, 6 (4), 36–44.

Hill, R. (1992). The Non-Vanishing American Indian: Are the Modern Images Any Closer to the Truth? *Quill*, May, 35–37.

Keith, M.C. (1995). *Signals in the Air: Native Broadcasting in America*. Westport, CT: Praeger.

KILI. Retrieved from http://www.lakotamall.com/kili, May 10, 2007.

Koahnic Broadcast Corporation. Retrieved from http://www.knba.org, May 10, 2007.

KYUK. Retrieved from http://www.kyuk.org, May 10, 2007.

Lewan, T. (1999). TV's Vast Wasteland Reaches Vast Tundra. *Associated Press*, May 24.

Melmer, D. (2006). KILI-FM Radio Off the Air. *Indian Country Today*, May 22. Retrieved from http://www.indiancountry.com, May 30, 2007.

Native American Public Telecommunications. Retrieved from http://www.nativetelecom.org, May 10, 2007.

Native Public Media. Retrieved from http://www.nativepublicmedia.org, May 10, 2007.

PTFP. (2006). Radio Awards. Retrieved from http://www.ntia.doc.gov/ptfp/projects/2006/grants, May 30, 2007.

Smith, B.L. & J.C. Brigham. (1992). Native Radio Broadcasting in North America: An Overview of Systems in the United States and Canada. *Journal of Broadcasting and Electronic Media*, 36 (2), 183–194.

Smith, B.L. & M.L. Cornette. (1998a). Electronic Smoke Signals: Native American Radio in the United States. *Cultural Survival Quarterly*, 22 (2), 28–31.

———. (1998b). Eyapaha for Today: American Indian Radio in the Dakotas. *Journal of Radio Studies*, 5 (2), 19–30

Steen, J. (2006). Voice of Lakota Nation on Air, Awaits Equipment. *Rapid City Journal*, July 19. Retrieved from http://www.rapidcityjournal.com, May 30, 2007.

Stenbaek, M.A. (1982). Kalaallit-Nunaata Radioa: To Be master of One's Own Media Is to Be Master of One's Own Fate. *Etudes/Inuit/Studies*, 6 (1), 39–47.

5. *Speaking for Themselves: How Radio Brought Women into the Public Sphere*

Donna Halper

When Eunice Randall was born in October 1898, the role of women was undergoing a dramatic change. Eunice was too young to have heard of Belva Lockwood, a successful lawyer who not only won the right for women to argue cases before the Supreme Court but who ran for president in 1884. Lockwood wrote for a number of magazines and journals of that time, offering an eyewitness account of women's expanding opportunities. She spoke of her disappointment that women's suffrage had not yet been achieved, but, on the positive side, she observed that increasing numbers of women were now attending college. Moreover, despite opposition from certain conservative men, many of these educated women were able to find work in professions as diverse as law, medicine, business, and journalism (Lockwood, 1888, 1893).

Another important change in society involved new technology. The 1890s was a decade of amazing inventions. Thanks to moving pictures, people who had seldom traveled long distances could watch scenes from Moscow or Paris or New York City appearing on the screen at their local theater. And as early as 1896, they could also see what celebrities looked like. The president of the United States, William McKinley, made a brief film appearance that year, and after he was assassinated in 1901 the film of his state burial was watched nationwide (Auerbach, 1999, 797). Then there was the wireless telegraph, which began making news during 1899, as Guglielmo Marconi conducted a series of successful experiments. Though not as entertaining as a movie, the wireless offered something that businesses desperately wanted: the ability to transmit Morse code messages across long distances in a timely manner, without having to worry about telegraph wires falling down during bad weather. As the wireless was perfected, the military, ships at sea, weather forecasters, and news reporters were among the many who found it invaluable. In addition, it did not take long before other inventors, notably Reginald Fessenden, began attempting to send voice, not just Morse code. Sending and receiving messages across long distances was not reserved for professionals; it was also an exciting hobby for amateurs. By 1909, newspapers and magazines had frequent articles about boys who were amateur radio operators (it was assumed that only boys were interested in wireless technology). These young men built their own radio sets and communicated with others in faraway places. Moreover, reporters were impressed that at such a young age, these boys had mastered what seemed to be such a complex new technology (Morton, 1909).

It is unlikely that Eunice Randall was following the growth of wireless telegraphy or telephony when she was a little girl, and she probably did not know that there were girls in other cities learning to use the wireless. It was not that Eunice had no interest in new technology; she did not have much exposure to it. Her family's farm in Mattapoisett, Massachusetts, several hours from Boston, did not even have electricity. As for Belva Lockwood's observation that more young women were attending college, that mainly applied to upper-middle-class families in the bigger cities. Eunice did not come from a home where a college degree was a priority. Her father expected her to learn the skills a future farmer's wife would need to know—cooking, sewing, helping to take care of the animals— all of which could be learned by the time she graduated from high school. Mr. Randall never expected that his daughter would leave Mattapoisett to seek a career, nor did he encourage her to do so.

In the spring of 1917, Belva Lockwood died. She was 85 years old and had only recently stopped traveling across the country campaigning for women's suffrage. Because she lived just before the birth of commercial radio, the only way for her to get her message across was through newspaper and magazine articles and frequent speaking engagements. By now, there were many supporters of women's suffrage, yet the vote still had not been won. Lockwood remained upbeat, however, telling reporters on her 85th birthday that she knew women would achieve the right to vote very soon. Meanwhile, Eunice Randall graduated from high school and made a courageous decision for a young woman of her social class. She left the farm to attend art school in Boston. It was not long before she ran out of money, but rather than going back to Mattapoisett, she chose to stay in the city and tried to find a job. Her timing was excellent: the United States had just entered the world war, and many factories that never would have hired a woman suddenly needed employees. Eunice found work as a draftsman (or, as she insisted on being called, "a drafts lady"), making technical drawings for a company that manufactured radio receivers. AMRAD was located in Medford Hillside, several miles outside Boston. The company had its own experimental radio station, called 1XE, and, when the war ended, the station resumed broadcasting. Since getting hired by AMRAD in 1918, Eunice had become fascinated with amateur radio, and she studied Morse code so that she could communicate with other ham radio operators. Although the men in the factory at first were not happy about her being there, the quality of her work soon won them over (Randall, 1964, 111). She became part of a team of AMRAD employees who spent their days making and repairing radio receivers, and then, several nights a week, they would send out broadcasts to the amateurs who were "listening in." By late 1919, the young woman from a farm in Mattapoisett had become the first woman radio announcer in Massachusetts.

However, as mentioned earlier, Eunice was not alone in developing a love for the new medium of broadcasting. As she studied hard to improve her Morse code and learned the basics of radio construction, other young women were following a similar path. It was not easy for them to get involved, given that the common wisdom said technology was much too complex for women to master. Few high schools, even those with ham radio stations, encouraged female students to take courses in electronics or physics, and even fewer let the girls study carpentry. Despite those obstacles, some girls found ham radio interesting and decided to learn the necessary skills to build their own station. One of the youngest lived in Seattle, Washington. Winifred Dow was 14 years old when she visited a local amateur and became intrigued by the way he could send messages to people in faraway places. Getting a ham radio license required passing a difficult examination, which included showing proficiency in wireless telegraphy. Few women had tried to take the test, but that did not stop Miss Dow. She passed it on her first try and received the call letters 7FG. Winifred Dow was the first female in the Pacific Northwest to be a licensed wireless operator, and her story was considered so unusual that the amateur radio magazine *QST* devoted a full page to it (One of the Young Lady Operators, 1917, 70).

In Hartford, Connecticut, there was another successful woman amateur, Miss Cecil Powell. She had begun working as the secretary to respected inventor and ham radio devoté Hiram Percy Maxim when she was in her early 20s. By her own admission, she knew nothing about radio technology and had not expected to be interested in it, but within months she was hooked. She began studying to get her amateur license, and, after obtaining it, along with the call letters 1WX, she decided that other women might find it easier to learn ham radio if they had a woman as their teacher. By the summer of 1917, Cecil was giving classes to a number of local women, so that they too could take the required exam. Mr. Maxim thought this was such a good idea that he and his wife let her use their home to hold classes. Not all of the students who signed up planned to be hobbyists; some wanted to help in the war effort, as the military was in dire need of trained radio operators. Since this was a noncombat position, women were encouraged to apply. Miss Powell did a commendable job as an instructor—every one of her students passed (Miss Powell's Radio Class, 1917, 7).

Even though every major city seemed to have at least one female wireless operator, ham radio had quickly become a male fraternity. The belief that technology was too difficult for women would persist, and in some advertisements of the early 1920s it became a selling point. As radio receivers began to be mass-produced and available at department stores, receiver manufacturers created advertisements that showed a woman turning the radio dials; the implicit message was that this receiver was so simple to use that even a woman could do it. Although young women such as Cecil Powell and Eunice Randall found acceptance as hams, they were the exceptions; by and large, the men and boys who dominated the field wanted to keep it their own. As Susan Douglas points out, amateur radio was a place where it was okay for men to engage in activities generally associated with women—chatting and befriending each other. Moreover, if wireless telegraphy and telephony were activities best suited to males, then

> safe from superiors, sequestered from women, and free to abandon the codes of politeness and civility, young men could act out their deep-seated need for interpersonal communication, for contact and a sense of community, for eavesdropping and for gossiping, while regarding all these needs as distinctly masculine. (Douglas, 1992, 50)

Despite the many gains women had made by 1920, society's expectations were still very traditional. Even the women who studied for the professions were supposed to give that up once they married, returning to the confines of the domestic sphere and devoting all their energies to their family and their home. Since women had first entered the world of college and career, there had been ongoing resistance from conservatives, especially members of the clergy who believed that the Bible required women to focus their life only on marriage and motherhood. But it was not just the clergy who opposed careers for women. A surprisingly large number of journalists and educators expressed similar views, although their versions used a more secular argument. Rather than quoting scripture, they quoted some of the era's psychologists, who claimed there was proof that women were intellectually inferior to men or too emotional to be successful in business. Moreover, they concluded that since women lacked the ability to manage the stresses of most occupations, they should happily accept their "natural" role as homemakers. A good example of this type of article is "Preparing Girls for the Business of Marriage," by Mrs. Stanley Lewis (1923). Mrs. Lewis contrasts the "militant" woman with the "normal" woman, and, in addition to asserting that true fulfillment is found only in marriage and children, she suggests that women should take only those courses that will make them better at their domestic duties.

Among the authors of the "women should stay at home" articles, there were some well-known literary figures, including H.G. Wells. In one essay, he accused modern women of acting like "aggressive pseudo-men" and he asserted that feminism had caused a growing antagonism between men and women (quoted in *Current Opinion*, November 1, 1924, 625). In addition, while men wrote the majority of the essays, it is interesting to note that Mrs. Lewis was one of a number of female authors dispensing advice about how a "normal" woman should act. (Given the vehemence with which they advised women not to seek careers, it is ironic that these female essayists, most of whom wrote regular articles for magazines, seemed unwilling to follow their own advice.) In addition to telling young women that they were going against the Bible if they chose to have a professional life, the popular press continued to warn women that if they graduated from college, they would never be able to find husbands, and, if they did marry, they would end up divorced. (It suffices to cite two of many examples: "Some Failures of American Women" by Mrs. Newell Dwight Hillis, 1910, and Willis J. Ballinger's "Spinster Factories: Why I Would Not Send a Daughter to College," 1932.) Although there were frequent antifeminist articles in the press, the new medium of radio broadcasting was about to give women a way to answer their detractors. Because of radio, women would be able to speak for themselves, and their voices would be heard nationwide.

Should Women Be Announcers?

During 1920, 1XE was moving away from experimental broadcasts for amateurs and hobbyists. There were several pioneering commercial stations on the air, notably Pittsburgh's KDKA and Detroit's 8MK (later known as WWJ), and 1XE joined them, broadcasting regular programs of live music, sports scores, and talks. Eunice Randall performed a variety of important jobs at the AMRAD station. She did some engineering and repaired the equipment when it broke (which it often did). She also helped to design and test new features for the radio sets that AMRAD manufactured. Her technical expertise was recognized by the Boston newspapers, which referred to her as the "girl wizard of Medford" and noted that there were few other women doing what she did. When she took her turn on the air, she played phonograph records and read the news, which included the stolen car reports from the local police. She also read the bedtime stories for children several nights a week, and occasionally, when a scheduled guest failed to show up, she and another engineer would sing. Eunice's name and photograph appeared frequently in the Boston newspapers, as well as in the newspapers of New Bedford, the city nearest to her Mattapoisett home. Where magazines often portrayed women as objects, passively displaying their beauty, Eunice was usually shown at work, either holding a piece of radio equipment or speaking into a microphone (*QST*, July 1922, 56). In addition, what is especially interesting about the coverage was how favorable it was: for example, the *Boston American* praised her "rich and modulated voice" (June 3, 1922, 4) and the *New Bedford Sunday Times* called her a "pioneer girl in the radio field" and noted that she was becoming famous in other cities as well as Boston (April 30, 1922, 35). Women announcers were something new, and the average person did not associate the female voice with leadership or authority. Traditionally, men had been the famous orators, from Plato and Aristotle in ancient Greece to Jefferson and Lincoln in American history. Perhaps because radio announcers in those early years were mainly involved with entertainment, listeners found it somewhat less threatening when they heard a woman speaking to them. That may explain why Eunice Randall received such a positive response: she read well, she had good diction, and she sounded like a friendly big sister.

In radio's early years, versatility was essential, and most female announcers performed as many jobs as Eunice Randall did. However, the most important of their duties was being able to sing or play an instrument. In New York radio, vocalist Vaughn DeLeath was known as the "Original Radio Girl" for her 1920 performance over inventor Lee DeForest's experimental station. She was one of the first performers on the Westinghouse station WJZ in 1921, and she entertained on several other New York stations, in addition to writing songs and making a number of recordings. She became known for a singing style called "crooning." In 1923, she was named the program director at New York's WDT, which meant she booked all the performers, and she also announced her own songs. This was a common practice in early broadcasting; stations had limited budgets, and many performers provided their own announcing. Station owners did not seem to be concerned about whether the people they hired to run the station were male or female, as long as they could perform at a moment's notice and could find other performers who would work for little or no pay.

In Chicago, Judith Waller was one of the few early program directors who was not a singer or recording artist; she had been working in the advertising business when was contacted by the owners of a new station, WGU, at the Fair Department Store. It was 1922, the radio craze was sweeping the country, and when she was asked to run the station, even though she had no experience, she agreed to give it a try. Recalling that first radio job, she said, "[I]t was a one-man station, and that one man was *me*." She created the station's policies and procedures, found performers who would volunteer their time even though there was no money to pay them, did all of the announcing, and, in her spare time, answered listener fan mail. At her next job, for station WMAQ, she was able to hire another announcer so that she could concentrate on finding talent and doing station publicity (Eskew, 1930, 57). Although Judith Waller decided she preferred to work in management (she would ultimately be promoted to director of public service programming for NBC), there was one other woman in Chicago who made a name for herself exclusively as an announcer on one of radio's first morning shows. Halloween Martin was a former newspaper reporter who got a job at station KYW in 1929. Radio had not yet developed the kind of morning show we are accustomed to today, and Halloween's program was remarkably modern. She gave the time, temperature, traffic reports, and weather; she took requests, and she kept the music up-tempo. Her show was called the *Musical Clock*, and radio critics as well as fans loved it. The critics referred to her as "the girl with the musical voice" and praised her for sounding both friendly and pleasant, as well as for brightening up their morning. When KYW left Chicago in 1934, fans wrote and called to demand that another station hire her, which WBBM did in 1935. Halloween Martin had a long career and remained popular until the day she retired from broadcasting.

However, the kind of acceptance Eunice Randall and Halloween Martin received did not occur in every city. Women who were singers and also announced did not have much problem with the audience or the critics—at a live performance in a club, a woman might chat with the audience before each selection, so hearing a woman talking about a particular song was not regarded as unusual. Society had long since become accustomed to female performers, and a glance at any program schedule in the early 1920s showed that many radio entertainers were women. (The only complaint the critics had was not about women who did their own announcing but about the fact that some stations had too many sopranos and not enough variety; e.g., Rider, 1928.)

Another type of announcing women seemed to do without much negative comment was giving educational talks. This was an era when having a certain amount of educational programming was mandatory, and local schoolteachers were sometimes invited to come in and deliver short lectures. Some universities began giving extension courses by radio, and the majority of the professors who spoke were men, but sometimes a woman would discuss music, art, or literature. And speaking of literature, women writers were active participants in early radio. In Boston, Amy Lowell read some of her poetry on the air at 1XE /WGI, novelist Fannie Hurst gave readings on several stations in New York, and in most major cities members of the League of American Pen Women were regular guests. At a time when the majority of Americans still did not go to college and the idea of studying online was the stuff of science fiction, it must have been exciting for listeners to turn on their radio and hear a famous author or a well-known poet speaking directly to them as they sat in the comfort of their living room. The role of "story lady" was also considered appropriate for women—Eunice Randall was one of many who helped parents to get their kids to go to sleep. But even in those early days when radio stations could not pay salaries and almost anyone who wanted to volunteer was able to get at least one chance to broadcast, women who wanted only to announce encountered considerable resistance. Bertha Brainard was an experienced and knowledgeable theater critic who did a program called *Broadcasting Broadway* on Newark's (and later New York's) WJZ radio in 1922. But when her boss, program manager Charles Popenoe, was interviewed for a 1924 article about women announcers, he said that women did not sound as good as men, and were it not for Miss Brainard's expertise, he would not have kept her on the air either (Mix, 1924b, 393). And in the same article, another program manager, Corley Kirby of WWJ in Detroit, went even further; he said that women were totally unsuitable as announcers, that their voices were unpleasant, with an "offensive nasal quality," and that when they read, they sounded "terrible" (Mix, 1924b, 392–393).

Several months earlier, a record store owner had written a letter to the editors of *Radio Broadcast* saying announcing was not a good job for women, since women needed to be seen to be appreciated, and just hearing them would not be enough to hold the audience's interest (Mix, 1924a, 333). *Radio Broadcast* had hired Jennie Irene Mix in 1924 to be a columnist and editor, one of the few women in such a position at any of the radio-oriented magazines. Miss Mix had many years of journalism experience, first as the music critic for the *Toledo Times* (Ohio) and then as a book review editor and a music critic at the *Pittsburgh Post*. She was an accomplished musician herself, and she loved opera and classical music. One of her favorite topics of discussion was whether radio was broadcasting enough "good music," as opposed to popular dance music. But she also began to use her position at *Radio Broadcast* to defend women announcers. In her columns, she mentioned that the current state of the art in microphone technology distorted higher-pitched voices, giving men a natural advantage. She also noted that until fairly recently, women had little experience as public speakers, and it was that inexperience that was showing rather than some inherent fault that doomed women to eternal failure on the air. She told her readers about some women announcers she had heard who sounded quite pleasant and natural, and she praised a few who had shown great improvement. In addition, she pointed out some faults of various men announcers (Mix, 1924a, b). What was unique about this interaction was that Miss Mix was referring to male and female announcers whom her readers could listen to and judge for themselves. They could also offer their own assessments, both to the magazine and to those announcers. This was an example of print and broadcast working together, with the listeners able to get involved too. In addition, although I do not know whether Miss Mix went on the radio herself, I do know that there were other radio editors who did go on the air in the 1920s; they responded to written questions from listeners and they discussed what was happening with the most popular shows.

Where Women Were Accepted

In early radio, one common form of listener feedback was the "applause card," which was mailed to the announcer or performer directly. Some announcers and musicians had personalized cards made up, with pictures that showed them posed in front of a microphone, and local record stores distributed the cards to eager fans. Meanwhile, radio was making it possible for listeners to express their opinion about what (and who) they wanted to hear. Moreover, since many of the listeners were women, appealing to the "female audience" became part of the equation in determining what sorts of programs to put on the air. Perhaps that is one reason male program managers quickly substituted male announcers for the women who wanted to announce—the belief was that women would not listen to another woman and would much prefer to hear the deep voice of a male announcer. Whether or not this was true—and the research for it was mostly anecdotal—by the time the networks came along in 1926–1927, most of the women who were radio stars were singers, and they had no problem gaining popular acclaim from both men and women. Among the most beloved of the female vocalists was Jessica Dragonette, who sang operetta and semiclassical music on network shows such as the *Philco Hour* and the weekly *Cities Service Concert*. She became one of radio's highest-paid performers, and by the mid-1930s, her listening audience was said to be more than 66 million fans (Fraser, 1980, B15).

Many aspiring female performers in small towns all over the country dreamed of being discovered and achieving the kind of fame that Vaughn DeLeath and Jessica Dragonette had attained. Being a woman was not seen as a detriment to stardom, nor was beauty a requirement the way it was for movies or the stage. On radio, looks were second to talent. Even a woman who was considered overweight could find success as a radio singer, as the popular recording artist Kate Smith proved. She weighed more than 200 pounds but told reporters she was perfectly happy and saw no need to diet (Gurman & Slager, 1932, 90). And music was one of the few areas that did not exclude African Americans: even in segregated America, black entertainers performed and became successful on radio. As early as 1923, the great blues singer Bessie Smith was heard on WSB in Atlanta, and by 1933 Ethel Waters was offered her own network program. According to the *Chicago Defender* newspaper, she was paid $1,250 a week (Ethel Waters Gets Contract, 1933, 5).

If a woman could not sing she might appear as an actress in a soap opera or radio drama. The characters were frequently stereotypic—saintly heroines and evil villainesses—but the sponsored shows enabled the performers to develop a loyal following (soap opera fans identified strongly with their favorite characters) and make a respectable salary. One of the women with longevity in the soap opera genre was Virginia Payne, who starred as "Ma Perkins." Her character was a kindly widow, always ready to help others, and the Cincinnati-born Payne played the role for 27 years, having first gotten it in 1933, when she was only 23 years old. Her acting skills would ultimately earn her more than $50,000 a year (Dunning, 1998, 422). And speaking of earning power, many of radio's most successful soap operas were produced by the husband-and-wife team of Anne and Frank Hummert, each of whom earned more than $100,000 a year at the height of their radio careers (Thomas, 1996, 27). One other acceptable, and often lucrative, role for women was as radio comediennes. The cultural myth of the "Dumb Dora," the stupid or scatterbrained woman, had been a staple in vaudeville, and when it was brought over to radio, it became equally popular. Among the best known in this genre was Gracie Allen, who performed her comedy with her husband George Burns as her straight man. During radio's golden age in the 1930s, there were also other women comics, including Fanny Brice (with her character "Baby Snooks," the bratty kid who asked annoying questions) and everyone's favorite Jewish mother, Gertrude Berg, the star of the comedy-drama *The Goldbergs*. Through radio, a number of talented women were given a vehicle for displaying their skills to a national audience, giving them the kind of status and celebrity that had previously been reserved for men.

There was one other option for women who wanted to be on the air. Since radio's earliest days, most stations had set aside several hours in the mid-morning for what came to be called a "women's show." By modern standards, the topics that were assumed to be of interest to women, such as advice related to cooking, sewing, and child raising, might seem stereotypic, but many women of the 1920s and 1930s were housewives who stayed at home while their husband worked, and they had little opportunity to get free advice from experts. One of early radio's chief selling points, used by advertisers when persuading people to buy a radio receiver, was that it made the world a little smaller and could serve as a friend to those who felt lonely or isolated. In addition to the print ads that showed how women found their sets easy to use, advertisers depicted women as grateful for how radio had improved their life (Patnode, 2003, 295–296). The women's shows came to be regarded by listeners as a source of good information, and the women who hosted these shows, as well as their guests, were thought of as friends. The radio critics, most of whom were male, did not have much to say about women's shows, and we may assume they did not find these shows very interesting. But there was certainly no debate about whether women were suitable to serve as hosts and announcers. Actually, the idea of focusing on the female audience was not new. Newspapers and magazines had been doing this for years. There were syndicated female advice-givers on the women's pages of newspapers, and they addressed some of the same issues that would be heard on the radio. The big difference was how radio raised the profile of the women hosts. Mrs. Julian Heath (her first name was Jennie, but she always preferred the more traditional version) had founded the National Housewives League in 1912. The league was an organization that educated homemakers about how to make purchases that were more economical; it advocated for affordable prices, calling the newspapers' attention to stores and companies that overcharged, and even boycotting these stores when the group felt dramatic action was needed (Dudderidge, 1912, 1230). Mrs. Heath was a passionate believer in fair treatment for housewives, but, interestingly, she opposed using political means and even belonged to an anti-suffrage club. Mrs. Heath never had a problem getting publicity for the National Housewives League, and the newspapers often gave its activities coverage. Yet when she began broadcasting regularly on New York radio in 1924, her opinions on home economics were suddenly heard by thousands of women who had never attended a meeting of the league. She began getting invitations to speak at radio expositions, and at the height of her popularity in the mid-1920s, she was getting several hundred letters a day (Mrs. Julian Heath Dies of Heart Disease, 1932, 15).

Many other radio homemakers who went on the air later in the 1920s benefited from the creation of national networks such as NBC and CBS. Doing a popular women's show made celebrities out of the women hosts as well as many of their guests. However, radio did not just bring stardom. Hosting a women's show could also be lucrative, as sponsors began using the radio homemakers to deliver testimonials about their products. As Michele Hilmes has pointed out, the advertising agencies had become very much aware of the purchasing power women had, and they wanted to direct their sales pitches in a way that would appeal to housewives (Hilmes, 1997, 32–33). Choosing a radio homemaker seemed ideal. She would be perceived as a credible source of information, and the audience would trust her. Ida Bailey Allen, whose National Radio Homemakers Club was heard on CBS, was one of those trusted sources. Her show was certainly an example of what Benedict Anderson famously referred to as an "imagined community," since her audience could receive a membership card, get a newsletter, and even win prizes for the best recipe of the month. As Mrs. Allen wrote, she first went on the air in 1923, not fully aware of the great potential radio had. After just one talk, she received so many letters—many of which were from hundreds of miles away—she quickly realized the possibilities:

> [I]n radio education [lies] the mass solution of many of the home problems of the country ... Today, women no longer need to feel lonesome in their homes because they have no means of contact with the world outside. By the turn of a dial, they can invite cheerful music and interesting, helpful speakers. (Allen, 1930, 1)

By her many fans, Mrs. Allen was certainly considered a helpful speaker. On her daily show, listeners heard live music from an orchestra, consumer news, guests such as Senator Arthur Capper (who discussed current events), and, above all, plenty of recipes that conveniently mentioned her sponsors' products, notably Pillsbury's Best Flour and Royal Gelatin Dessert. In addition, those fortunate listeners who lived in New York might be able to watch the show or get a tour and meet Mrs. Allen herself (Allen, 1930, 74). It was a far cry from the days when Mrs. Allen wrote cookbooks and operated a small cooking school in her home.

Speaking for Themselves

Although the 1920s were a decade of great social change for women, some things remained the same: educated women still were paid substantially less than men, married women were not expected to remain in the workforce, and in a segregated America black women were often completely excluded from the chance at a better life. The arrival of radio did not eradicate all of society's problems, of course, but some of radio's earliest proponents had seemed to expect miracles from the new medium. Sarah Wilson writes about what she calls "a powerful discourse of technological utopianism," which placed great hope in radio's ability to "bring together the geographically and culturally scattered nation. Respected thinkers such as John Dewey, Herbert Cooley, and Robert Park believed that radio offered the means to create a new public united by channels of communication" (Wilson, 2004, 262). In America, radio had been envisioned by some as a medium of education, but it quickly turned into a medium for entertainment and commercialism. Still, it would be wrong to say that radio had no influence on its listeners other than providing them with a harmless escape from their worries. Radio education did not die out entirely: there were some widely respected national programs that dealt with important issues, such as *America's Town Meeting of the Air*, and a number of stations continued to provide lectures by famous professors. As radio gradually developed the ability to cover world news, many stations began to offer political commentary as well. And here too, women found a way to let their voices be heard. As might be expected, the majority of the news reporters and commentators were male, since the common wisdom was that men would listen only to another man talking about sports or politics (Hilmes, 1997, 143). Despite that belief, during the mid-1930s, two women were able to break through and become successful: Kathryn Cravens on CBS and Dorothy Thompson on NBC and Mutual. Cravens became known for human-interest stories and profiles of newsmakers, and Thompson covered hard news, commenting on such hot-button issues as the rise of fascism and the dangers of anti-Semitism. At a time when the voice of authority was nearly always male, it is interesting to note that the critics praised both women for being knowledgeable about their subject matter and for having voices that people could easily listen to. The importance of these women commentators should not be overlooked. Neither seemed to think of herself as a spokesperson for all women; in fact, Thompson had a very conflicted relationship with feminism, at times seeming to support the ideal of equal opportunity and at other times writing that she would not want her daughter to have a career. However, because of these two women, the myth that only men knew anything about (or cared about) current events was successfully challenged.

Another way that radio impacted the culture was in letting women advocate for the causes they cared about. Not all of the women who spoke on the air were relegated to the women's shows, although a number of those shows had some high-profile female guests, such as aviator Amelia Earhart, who was also a guest on several network news shows, talking about her latest adventures. Some of the women who spoke on the air were not famous or high profile, yet they developed a loyal group of listeners by providing shows with useful information for a general audience. A good example of this occurred in New York when the head of the Municipal Reference Library, Rebecca Browning Rankin, began a series of educational talks over station WNYC, stressing how the reference library was a wonderful resource and demonstrating this fact through the interesting content of her talks (Seaver, 2001, 294). Both locally and nationally, radio stations provided women the chance to talk about their work and their ideas. In Boston, the world-renowned astronomer Annie Jump Cannon gave a series of radio talks over WEEI about some of the stars she had discovered and classified. If the myth about women was that they were not interested in science, listening to Cannon or Earhart surely made an impression on the audience. If they thought libraries were stuffy, even the critics said that Rankin's talks were interesting and well delivered (Seaver, 2001, 293, 317). And although radio networks often avoided controversial topics such as birth control (for more on this see Ruth Brindze's 1937 book about the prevalence of radio censorship, *Not to Be Broadcast*), a look at the programming schedules of the 1920s and 1930s shows that Margaret Sanger did get on the air and talk about family planning, and the Birth Control League, despite being censored by NBC in 1930, found individual affiliates to broadcast their educational talk on the subject.

During the mid-1920s, members of the Lucy Stone League got the opportunity to discuss why women should be allowed to keep their own name when they married. The League of Women Voters, which was on the air from radio's earliest days, gave reliable and nonpartisan information about all of the important issues that listeners might encounter at the ballot box. The National Women's Party offered a series of talks about what women had achieved during the 1920s and what still needed to be done. Feminists such as Carrie Chapman Catt gave several talks, helping listeners to feel more personally connected to another newsmaker they had only been able to read about before radio. Granted, these occasional talks did not mean the women became as famous as Jessica Dragonette or Gracie Allen, but at least when an issue came up that affected women, there were usually stations that broadcast opinions by the women themselves, and people who wanted to listen could do so and make up their own minds. Most important, once women got the vote, female politicians were able to take their message directly to the voters. Perhaps the first to do so was Oklahoma's Alice Robertson, who gave a talk over KDKA as early as 1921, but throughout the decades of the 1920s and 1930s, when women campaigned for office, they increasingly took to the airwaves, just as the men did. One program, aired by WRC in Washington, DC, in March 1926 featured two women members of Congress defending their particular political party: Representative Edith Nourse Rogers of Massachusetts told why she was a Republican, and Representative Mary T. Norton of New Jersey discussed why she was a Democrat. Given that women had little political power before 1920, it must have made proponents of women's suffrage very gratified when they could not only have a say in the elections but also turn on the radio and hear the candidates they supported.

One other way that radio has an impact was in creating what Parry-Giles and Blair (2002) term the "rhetorical first lady." Where presidents had been out making speeches since the earliest days of our country, the role of the first lady was much more private until radio came along. In addition, when first ladies began speaking over the airwaves, attitudes and expectations gradually shifted. Historically, first ladies had been seen occasionally, especially at a formal state dinner, but if they had an opinion on a political matter, they rarely expressed it in public. Calvin Coolidge spoke on the radio a number of times during the 1920s, yet although his wife was a fan of radio and told reporters so, she refused to speak on the air (Kaiser, 1929, 13). Thus, when Eleanor Roosevelt took the then-controversial step of using radio to express her opinions, she created a precedent:

> First ladies are now expected to promote their own cause, regularly inhabiting the East Wing of the White House … As a visible voice for women, certain first ladies [have] facilitated the transformation of women's issues into national issues, evidencing the rhetorical power of the post and the public visibility of first ladies on important deliberative matters. (Parry-Giles & Blair, 2002, 586–587)

It is difficult to condense into one chapter everything that happened to women in the first two decades of broadcasting. Some women owned their own station, starting with Marie Zimmerman in Vinton, Iowa, in 1922. Some became famous preachers on the radio, as Aimee Semple McPherson did (and she, too, owned her own station, KFSG in Los Angeles). Women doctors, lawyers, members of Congress, scientists, child psychologists, and home economists showed the diversity of women's roles. Women's place in society was debated on a number of shows. When a traditionalist such as Henry R. Carey wrote in 1929 that feminism would always fail because it is ordained that "man must achieve, and woman [must] encourage achievement" (p. 743), he was writing the same year in which there were eight female members of Congress, seven of whom had recently spoken on radio about the legislation they hoped to support during the next term. The issues would continue to change, but even during more conservative times, radio would provide a forum where women could express themselves while giving the audience a chance to consider the opinions they had just heard.

Political theorist Jurgen Habermas once wrote, "The world fashioned by the mass media is a public sphere in appearance only" (p. 171). But for the millions of people nationwide who came to rely upon it, radio had some of the qualities of a public sphere. Radio made audience members feel that they were a part of a shared experience, listening to and enjoying their favorite shows, talking with friends about what they had heard, writing applause cards to the stars they loved, reading radio magazines, even sitting in the studio audience to watch a program taking place. In addition, although debates about the effects of media continue, it cannot be denied that owing to radio, women as musicians, as actresses, as businesswomen, as politicians, and, above all, as thinking human beings went from staying entirely within the domestic sphere to at least having a chance to make themselves heard in the public sphere. I can only wonder what Belva Lockwood would have thought about it all. Somehow, I think she would be very pleased.

References

Allen, Ida Bailey. (1930). Home-Makers Club Is a Magnet. *Radio Digest*, 24 (3, January), 74, 126.

———. (1930). Radio. *Radio Home-Makers Magazine*, 2 (27, March 31), 1.

Auerbach, Jonathan. (1999). McKinley at Home: How Early American Cinema Made News. *American Quarterly*, 51 (4, December), 797–832.

Ballinger, Willis J. (1932). Spinster Factories: Why I Would Not Send a Daughter to College. *Forum and Century*, May.

Both Parties Plan Campaign by Radio. (1922). *New York Times*, April 1, 7.

Brainard, Bertha. (1928). Radio. In Doris E. Fleischman (Ed.), *Careers for Women* (pp. 399–405). New York: Garden City Publishing.

Carey, Henry R. (1929). Career or Maternity? The Dilemma of the College Girl. *North American Review*, 228 (6, December), 737–744.

Douglas, Susan. (1992). Audio Outlaws: Radio and Phonograph Enthusiasts. In John L. Wright (Ed.), *Possible Dreams: Enthusiasm for Technology in America* (pp. 45–59). Detroit: Henry Ford Museum.

Dudderidge, Mary. (1912). Embattled Housewives. *Independent*, 73 (3339, November 28), 1230–1235.

Dunning, John. (1998). *On the Air: The Encyclopedia of Old Time Radio*. New York: Oxford University Press.

Eskew, Garnett L. (1930). Former Boss of Amos and Andy: Judith Waller of WMAQ. *Radio Digest*, 25 (4, August), 57, 90.

Ethel Waters Gets Contract. (1933). *Chicago Defender*, September 23, 5.

Field, Louise Maunsell. (1932). Our Lady Presidents. *North American Review*, 234 (4, October), 365–371.

Fraser, C. Gerald. (1980). Jessica Dragonette, Singer, Dies. *New York Times*, March 20, B15.

Greene, Lloyd. (1922). Throngs Attend Fine Radio Show. *Boston Globe*, May 4, 6.

Gurman, Joseph & Myron Slager. (1932). *Radio Roundup: Intimate Glimpses of the Radio Stars*. Boston: Lothrop, Lee, & Shepard.

Habermas, Jurgen. (1985). The Theory of Communication. Boston: Beacon Press.

Hartford Girl Only Woman Wireless Operator in Connecticut—Made Complete Apparatus Herself. (1915). *Hartford Courant*, January 12, 11.

Hillis, Mrs. Newell Dwight. (1910). Some Failures of American Women. *Outlook*, July 10, 8.

Hilmes, Michele. (1997). *Radio Voices: American Broadcasting 1922–1952*. Minneapolis: University of Minnesota Press.

Kaiser, Florence V. (1929). The First Lady Eludes Radio. *New York Times*, February 24, Section X, 13.

Lewis, Mrs. Stanley. (1923). Preparing Girls for the Business of Marriage. *The Herald of Gospel Liberty*, 4 October, 943.

Lockwood, Belva A. (1888). The Present Phase of the Woman Question. *Cosmopolitan*, 5 (6, October), 467–470.

———. (1893). Women in Politics. *American Journal of Politics*, April, 385–387.

———. Miss Powell's Radio Class to Take Tests Under U.S. Examiner. (1917). *Hartford Courant*, June 4, 7.

Mix, Jennie Irene. (1924a). Are Women Undesirable Over the Radio? *Radio Broadcast*, 5 (4, August), 333–335.

———. (1924b). For and Against the Woman Radio Speaker. *Radio Broadcast*, 5 (5, September), 391–395.

Morton, Robert A. (1909). Amateur Wireless Telegraph Stations of Greater Boston: Hundreds of Boys Are Busy Picking Messages out of the Air. *Boston Globe*, March 28, SM3.

Mrs. Julian Heath Dies of Heart Disease. (1932). *New York Times*, November 19, 15.

One of the Young Lady Operators. *QST*, April 1917, p. 70.

Parry-Giles, Shawn J. & Diana M. Blair. (2002). The Rise of the Rhetorical First Lady: Politics, Gender Ideology, and Women's Voice, 1789–2002. *Rhetoric & Public Affairs*, 5 (4, Winter), 565–599.

Patnode, Randall. (2003). "What These People Need Is Radio": New Technology, the Press, and Otherness in 1920s America. *Technology and Culture*, 44 (2, April), 285–305.

Pursell, Carroll. (1992). The Long Summer of Boy Engineering. In John L. Wright (Ed.), *Possible Dreams: Enthusiasm for Technology in America* (pp. 35–43). Detroit: Henry Ford Museum.

Radio for Women. (1925). *Literary Digest*, November 28, 20.

Radio Opens New Field to Women. (1922) *Christian Science Monitor*, June 30, 11.

Randall, Eunice. (1964). Hair Ribbon on a Radio Tower. *Yankee Magazine*, April, 111–112.

Rider, J.F. (1928). Why Is a Radio Soprano Unpopular. *Scientific American*, October, 334–337.

Seaver, Barry William. (2001). Rebecca Browning Rankin Uses Radio to Promote the Municipal Reference Library of the City of New York and the Civic Education of Its Citizens. *Libraries & Culture*, 36 (2, Spring), 289–328.

Senator New Talks by Radio to Voters 600 Miles Away. (1922). *New York Times*, March 31, 1–2.

Squier, Susan Merrill. (2003). *Communities of the Air: Radio Century, Radio Culture*. Durham, NC: Duke University Press.

St John, Jacqueline D. (1978). Sex Role Stereotyping in Early Broadcasting. *Frontiers: A Journal of Women Studies*, 3 (3, Autumn), 31–38.

Thomas, Robert McG., Jr. (1996). Anne Hummert, 91, Dies; Creator of Soap Operas. *New York Times*, July 21, 27.

Wells, H.G. (1924). Sex Discord Increasing? *Current Opinion*, November 1, 625.

West, Robert. (1934). *So-o-o-o You're Going on the Air*. New York: Rodin Publishing.

Wilson, Sarah. (2004). Gertrude Stein and the Radio. *Modernism/Modernity*, 11 (2, April), 261–278.

A Woman Director's View. (1929). *Christian Science Monitor*, January 9, 6.

Women Can Go to College by Radio. (1923). *New York Times*, July 13, 17.

Women Need Vocal Art to Speak to Mr. Mike. (1927). *Radio World*, May 21, 1927, 16.

6. *The Howl That Could Not Be Silenced: The Rise of Queer Radio*

Phylis Johnson

You know what was largely responsible for that guy's [Matthew Shepard's] death? Those two guys who killed him did not go out looking for a homo- sexual to kill that night. They were shooting pool. He went to the bar. He left with two guys he thought he was gonna have sex with. He got murdered. How many women has that happened to? How many women have left bars thinking they were gon- na get some action with some guy who raped and murdered and tortured and murdered them? Far more women than homosexual men have ended up dead that way, I would guess. Is that a hate crime against women? I think so but they specifically picked the woman who was willing to leave for sex. If Matthew hadn't been willing to leave for sex, he might still be alive. That certainly doesn't make him responsible for his own death but when you put yourself into a situation of going off to have anonymous sex with people you meet at a bar, what kind of person is gonna leave with you? Usually scum ... This was a terrible tragedy but it's also one that might have been avoided if he had simply gone home with his friends instead of thinking he was gonna get a little.

—*Transcript, Dr. Laura Radio Show (1999)*

In 2000, the battle lines were drawn for what was referred to as a cultural war in America (Buchanan, 1999; *Dr. Laura*, 2000). The supporters of talk radio host Dr. Laura Schlessinger, the grand mistress of morality, protested outside Procter & Gamble headquarters with signs that read "MATT IN HELL" and "GOD HATES FAGS" ("Video," 2000) after the company with- drew its advertising support for the fall 2000 debut of the Dr. Laura TV show. Dr. Laura's radio commentary regarding the 1998 death of Matthew Shepard had not gone unforgotten as she prepared to launch into television. Moreover, she had continued to blast the gay and lesbian community with controversial statements on her highly rated radio show. Anti-Schlessinger protesters caught the lens of the news cameras in San Francisco, Chicago, Boston, Dallas, Atlanta, St. Louis, Phoenix, Seattle, Las Vegas, Washington,

DC, and New York City. Subsequently, SkyTel, Geico Insurance, Xerox, Toys "R" Us and other radio sponsors pulled their ads from Dr. Laura's television show after being inundated with complaint letters (Coalition, 2000). In the midst of this controversy, rumors emerged with regard to Schlessinger as a possible running mate for Reform Party presidential candidate Pat Buchanan (*Dr. Laura*, 2000).

Schlessinger's radio show continues to wage war against immorality, and it has earned her a top spot among the hot talkers in the ratings. Not unlike Howard Stern's listeners, even those who hate Dr. Laura tune in to hear what she will say next. The Shepard controversy prompted the regulatory arm of the Canadian media to investigate the appropriateness of Dr. Laura's radio show in light of the country's policy on human rights and, first and foremost, her misrepresentation as a "doctor":

> The Councils are left with the uneasy sense that there is an understandable cumulative effect of Schlessinger's positions on so many matters which concern the gay and lesbian communities. The result of this perspective may well be that, while she does not herself advocate any of the homophobic hostility or, worse, brutality, which can be found in criminal corners of society, from her powerfully influential platform behind a very popular microphone, Schlessinger may well fertilize the ground for other less well-balanced elements, by her cumulative position, to take such aggressive steps. With the power emanating from that microphone goes the responsibility for the consequences of the utterances. (Canadian Broadcast Standards Council/Ontario Regional Council, 2000, 15)

In a statement released in May 2000, the Canadian Broadcast Standards Council ruled that the approximately one million of Dr. Laura's listeners across the 450 Canadian TV and radio stations must be warned of her "abusively discriminatory" comments on homosexuality in a public announcement during prime-time hours (Canadian Radio Ethics Council Blast Dr. Laura, 2000). In the United States, the marketplace, rather than the Federal Communications Commission (FCC) or the National Association of Broadcasters (NAB), has often determined the consequences for such broadcast abuses. This chapter examines the rise of Queer Radio amidst what has been deemed a cultural war by those struggling to find a voice across American airwaves as well as those opposed to any advances in that regard. This chapter delves into the rise of gay and lesbian radio, follows its successes and failures through the years, and considers the impact of its new advocate, corporate radio, on programming toward the queer community.

Can You Hear Me Now?

Over the past decade, a number of scholars have discussed how television has shaped the image of the queer community (Fejes & Petrich, 1993;

Gross, 1983; Hoy, 1991; Kielwasser & Wolf, 1992; Moritz, 1992). In contrast, one would be hard pressed to find an equivalent literature base devoted to queer radio culture. The history of gay and lesbian radio is one that is far from complete, for many short-lived (although significant) contributions continue to surface. Many of these stories remain in the closet, so to speak, and stored away in boxes and the memories of some of the early producers at various noncommercial stations in the United States.

Johnson and Keith (2001) attempted to chronicle the annals of queer radio and television in their book *Queer Airwaves*, Armonnk, NY,p.114 relying on station records and interviews with many of the leading lesbian/gay/bisexual/transgender (LGBT) producers in America. By the late 1950s, it became evident that the gay community was seeking outlets for civil rights issues that directly and indirectly would influence their lifestyles and image in the United States. San Francisco's KPFA-FM aired a two-hour documentary that invited lawyers, physicians, and criminologists into a discussion with the mother of a gay man and with Harold L. Call, editor of the leading gay rights magazine, the *Mattachine Review*. The magazine was the mouthpiece for the Mattachine Society, the first gay rights organization in the United States. "The Homosexual in America" aired in 1962 on WBAI-FM. It was a 60-minute program based on the conservative views of a panel of psychiatrists. Immediately, activists responded in protest, calling for airtime on the station to debunk the gay stereotypes raised during the show. WBAI-FM granted some of the protesters access to the airwaves, and the resulting discussion ended with a group of listeners filing a complaint with the FCC that was readily dismissed. Several Pacifica stations broadcast poetry and discussion shows during this era. In the late 1960s, the FCC demanded that Allen Ginsberg's poem "Howl," with its homosexual overtones, no longer be aired on Pacifica radio station KPFA-FM (Johnson & Keith, 2001). FCC's James Quello told Ginsberg it was a simple matter of deleting a few controversial passages (Morgan & Peters, 2006). He wanted Ginsberg to eliminate the very words that would ring in freedom for the gay rights movement. By the close of the 1960s, it had become impossible to quiet the growing frustration and anger within the queer community. On June 27, 1969, a surge of energy emerged on to the streets of New York City; it was "a resistance that rapidly spilled out into the Greenwich Village streets and grew into three nights of riotous rebellion" (Johnson & Keith, 2001). What began as "a routine police raid on [a] Greenwich Village bar that served transvestites turned violent after patrons decided not to run away from the police." The Stonewall Inn caught the attention of the police because it had routinely "ignored a state law against selling alcohol to homosexuals [and it] had become the social center for drag queens, gays, and lesbians in New York City" (pp. 10–11). The police conducted more and more frequent raids at the bar until the patrons found they had little recourse but to stand their ground. The Stonewall

Rebellion is often considered within the queer community as marking the start of its modern-day civil rights movement. This incident encouraged a new freedom across radio. Over the next two decades, queer radio stations emerged over public airwaves, with dedicated volunteers hosting and producing programs across the United States. Shows came and went as gay producers ran out of time and funds. In the 1970s, National Public Radio affiliates such as WXPN-FM created sophisticated and well-produced programs that featured music and information intended for queer audiences. During that decade, the liberal students running Georgetown University's WGTB-FM became tired of conservative music and politics and decided to take control of the programming, giving airtime to Vietnam War updates and the emerging queer culture—and "hosted guests like famed gay beat poet Allen Ginsberg" (Friends, 2007, 65). By the Reagan years, and with the fear of AIDS rampant, gay protesters fought harder to voice their opinions against a backdrop of diminishing civil liberties across the public radio airwaves. For the most part, commercial radio veered away from queer programming through the 1980s, and such programming remained nestled on the public airwaves.

This Way Out

Radio is a personal medium that creates a sense of community and privacy simultaneously, so listeners can share their thoughts with others in a safe community of anonymity. Adam Clayton Powell III (1993) applauds radio for its ability to provide listeners with "a shared identity and community" (p. 73). Some would suggest that radio has the "same benefits face-to-face relations" (Snow, 1983, 120). When *This Way Out* was launched in April 1988, it reached out to an untapped community hungry for news and information relevant to their lifestyles and interests. Radio seemed the medium of choice because it had "potential as a modern community's tribal drum—accessible even to those most deeply hidden in the closet" (*This Way Out*, 1993). The programs contained author interviews, humor, poetry, music from openly queer singers, and AIDS updates. Soon nearly 70 public radio affiliates aired the weekly program. Host Greg Gordon (1993) noted, at the time, that commercial radio stations had not provided a sustainable forum for queer programming. He knew then, as now, that his 30-minute program of news and features would likely be relegated to noncommercial stations, regardless of its quality. A typical program rundown reads like this:

RUNDOWN for Program #942, distributed 04/17/06
Right-wing Republican "False Promises" to African Americans are revealed,
A gay Irish patriot falls from human rights champion to shameful traitor,

Nigeria considers jailing GLBT supporters, initial Italian election results bode well for queers,
Dutch deportation of Iranian refugees is delayed,
A Polish "Stonewall" fails to save a Warsaw gay club,
Lesbigays are eliminated from Kentucky's bias ban.

This Way Out, in fact, continues today as a leading international lesbian and gay radio magazine show that is now nearly 20 years old and boasts an estimated audience of more than 400,000. The program is produced in Los Angeles and airs on more than 100 local stations throughout the world. It is distributed on Public Radio Satellite and Pacifica Radio's KU satellite in North America and on other satellite services across Europe, South America, the Middle East, Africa, Asia, and Australia. *This Way Out* is also available online at *PlanetOut Radio* and *Out America* and is broadcast on the shortwave station Radio for Peace International. According to the distribution list, 75% of the stations that broadcast *This Way Out* are public and community, and the rest are commercial outlets, mostly FMs. The leading U.S. states in terms of airing the program are California, Colorado, Pennsylvania, and New York, and the show is most likely to be heard on Tuesday evenings and during prominent daytime slots on Wednesdays and Sundays.

Host/producer Greg Gordon, associate producer Lucia Chappelle, and their team of reporters and producers have won numerous awards from the early days, including from the Gay and Lesbian Alliance Against Defamation (GLAAD); Parents, Families, and Friends of Lesbians and Gays (PFLAG); the Gay and Lesbian Press Association; and the National Federation of Community Broadcasters.

The Gay 1990s

Market researchers began to understand the powerful dynamics of the gay and lesbian community, and innovative partnerships with community organizations and businesses emerged as a result. In the 1990s, prominent noncommercial stations that aired gay and lesbian programming could be found scattered across the United States—no longer relegated to only major metropolitan cities: Amherst, Massachusetts; Duluth, Minnesota; Columbia, Missouri; Cincinnati, Ohio; Portland, Oregon; and other cities began to respond to the call for new voices. During this time, gay producers complained that they could not get their programs aired outside the public radio sector, for most commercial station managers and program directors were fearful of offending their advertisers or listeners (Boehlert, 1992). The record industry began to shift its support toward the gay and lesbian community, with Epic, Warner Brothers, and East West among record labels willing to support the Gay Games and Stonewall 25 Civil Rights March in June 1994 (McCormack, 1994). These companies were "activating long-term plans to factor the gay and lesbian community into the marketing schemes of future projects" (Flick, 1994, 1).

Much of the rationale behind the support had to do with market projections of the audience as one of the fastest growing in the United States (Davis, 1993). The *Wall Street Journal* touted a "dream market" that was "in the majority college graduates, and made more than 20,000 more than the national average" (Summer, 1992, 37). Marketing research began to break down the stereotypical assumptions about this once ignored audience. Overlooked Opinions of Chicago, for example, indicated that gays and lesbians were more likely to work in science and engineering than in social services, and 40% more were "employed in finance and insurance than in entertainment and the arts; and ten times as many work in computers as in fashion" (Stewart, 1991, 43). This emerging portrait of a viable audience began to persuade advertisers to seek ways to identify needs and wants. However, many radio stations were still struggling with the idea of advertising contraceptives or feminine hygiene products over the airwaves, with much less concern about the antics of Howard Stern, Laura Schlessinger, Rush Limbaugh, and a host of shockers who spewed epithets, intentionally or unintentionally, toward gays and lesbians.

In the 1990s, a few commercial outlets experimented with gay and lesbian programming. Although many of the efforts were short-lived, they paved the way for others. In Miami, a three-hour call-in talk show on Saturday nights began in fall 1992. WFTL-AM's Charlie Bado became a controversial icon in the market, saying that "he's pissed off as many gays as straight [listeners]," and his "Super Queer" moniker became his battle cry (Boehlert, 1992, 64). Nearly half of his sponsors were straight-owned businesses. Another Miami station, WVCG-AM, began to air the news magazine show *AlterNet* on Saturday afternoons. Both programs lasted only about nine months. In Washington, DC, WWRC-AM cancelled a short-lived program called *Ten Percent Radio* that same year. The three-hour show aired Sunday nights, beginning at 7 p.m., and included a mix of straight and gay-oriented businesses (Bloomquist, 1994).

Boston's *One in Ten* (2007) made its debut during this time. The show was more than three-hours long, and its magazine-type programming featured a call-in segment. It aired on WFNX-FM on Monday nights, and it developed a strong college audience, with advertisers being mostly restaurants and record stores. Cleveland Talk Radio WHF-FM aired *The Gay '90s* on Friday nights, beginning at 9 p.m. The two-hour show moved to Mondays and stayed as a popular forum in the community and among advertisers. In Chicago, WNUA-FM and WKQK-FM aired *Aware Talk Radio*, a health program that initially focused on HIV issues, on Sundays, beginning in 1992, and two years later *Lesbigay Radio* debuted on WCBR-FM in North Chicago (Nidetz, 1994).

One in Ten and *Lesbigay Radio* remain two of the longest-running advocates for queer community issues, and both programs have earned numerous awards over the years. *Lesbigay Radio* now airs on The Voice of Chicago's LGBT Community WCKG 105.9 FM. Co-host Amy Matheny is recognized as "the lesbian voice of Windy City Radio" (Lesbigay Radio, 2007). She is a senior account manager for the Windy City Media Group, which creates "multi-media campaigns in the LGBT community for corporations such as Anheuser Busch, Future Brands, American Airlines, IBM, LaSalle Bank, Subaru, Broadway In Chicago and many major arts organizations" (2007). The Windy City Media Group has published a weekly newspaper for the LGBT community since 1985. Matheny also co-hosted the syndicated *Aware Talk Radio* from 2001 to 2003, and the program—under the leadership of founder, executive producer, and host Chris DeChant—has thrived as a significant health forum within the LGBT community.

The *One in Ten* mission has matured over the years, and, in addition to entertainment features, it delves into "issues facing the gay and lesbian community including discrimination against gays in the armed services; the fight for recognition of same sex unions; and issues particular to gay youth" (WFNX-FM). It continues to air on WFNX-FM and commonly features reporters from leading newspapers and magazines, such as *Time*, *The New York Times*, *Rolling Stone*, *Entertainment Weekly*, *Salon.com*, *OUT*, *Genre*, and *Entertainment Weekly*.

Hey, Hey, Hey—It's KGAY

It was within this environment that the KGAY Radio Network was launched in Colorado Springs. KGAY was the most ambitious radio project of the 20th century. Its goal was to serve North America with gay and lesbian programming 24 hours a day, 7 days a week, via satellite (Johnson, Hoy, & Ziegler, 1995/1996). A terrestrial station, KGAY-AM, in Colorado Springs became the company's base of operations, and it owned a repeater station in Denver. The network launched on November 28, 1992, with 65 hours of news and talk shows targeted to its queer audiences, and it offered more than 100 hours of progressive rock, alternative, and dance music (Colorado Gay, 1993). Clay Henderson and Will Guthrie, the founders, had dabbled previously as producers of a gay radio show in Denver and had discussed the idea nearly two years before the plans were laid. The network began to operate soon after the passage of Amendment Two by 53% of Colorado voters (which would be later struck by the U.S. Supreme

Court). The amendment was crafted to prevent legal efforts to protect the civil rights of gay and lesbians, or to counter discriminatory challenges made on the basis of sexual orientation:

> No Protected Status Based on Homosexual, Lesbian, or Bisexual Orientation. Neither the State of Colorado, through any of its branches or departments, nor any of its agencies, political subdivisions, municipalities or school districts, shall enact, adopt or enforce any statute, regulation, ordinance or policy whereby homosexual, lesbian or bisexual orientation, conduct, practices or relationships shall constitute or otherwise be the basis of or entitle any person or class of persons to have or claim any minority status, quota preferences, protected status or claim of discrimination. This Section of the Constitution shall be in all respects self-executing. *Romer v. Evans*, 517 U.S. 620 (1996)

KGAY suddenly became the voice of the gay community, locally and internationally. A few hotspots of listening were Denver, Atlanta, Corpus Christi, and Indianapolis. Listener letters were sent in from small towns in North Dakota, Montana, Minnesota, Tennessee, Arizona, Illinois, and New York. Many of its supporters were nongay listeners who called into the station (Colorado Gay Radio, 1993). The AM station did not have the resources to support the larger radio enterprise, as management would need to wait patiently for the satellite (and cable) audience and advertisers to build over time. The City of Austin, at one point, offered its support to KGAY Radio Network by helping to arrange a partnership with Austin Cablevision (Herdon, 1993). A number of Austin listeners supported the station, but there was not enough advertising revenue to fund the project (Nathaniel, 1993).

Dan Radcliff, general manager, noted, "We were basically operating on an absolute shoestring" (1994, 14). One year later, the network went off the air. The satellite operation was not aiming for rural audiences, but that is exactly who began to listen. The KGAY Network offered a unique source of information and music for those living in isolated areas. It had a staff of volunteer disc jockeys who aired music that they thought would target their gay and lesbian listeners. Management's goal had been to provide a queer point of view in "commentary and selection" (*This Way Out*, 1993). Radcliff (1994), in retrospect, believed that KGAY should have focused on adding more talk radio programs to offer targeted listeners a truly alternative source of information. In fact, among it offerings was *This Way Out*. The experiment provided a valuable lesson for gay and lesbian producers, and many since then have considered the Web as a safe way to test their programs. KGAY's vision and efforts became the inspiration for subsequent producers, and especially for corporate radio's queer initiatives of the 21st century.

The State of 21st-Century Queer Radio

In the United Kingdom, gay radio came out across the airwaves in 1993 (BBC, 1993). By the turn of the century, British Broadcasting Corporation (BBC) producers had a newfound freedom to express themselves uniquely through queer talk and music programs. As the new century approached, U.S. commercial radio struggled with some birth pangs dealing with LGBT programming, especially on the commercial side of the dial. In 1998, Charles Raymond Bouley Jr. (a.k.a. Karel) and his co-host Andrew Howard became the first openly gay couple in the United States to host a drive-time show on a commercial station. The duo received their break after spending the previous year together on the very influential, but short-lived, gay radio service Triangle Broadcasting. Their program title, *Good Morning Gay America*, boldly announced the couple's arrival. From there, they were hired on Los Angeles' KFI-AM. The program ended nearly two years later owing to some waning ratings, primarily as a result of Howard's illness and eventual death and Bouley's controversial opinions on politics and the state of gay America. Bouley (2004), a columnist for leading gay publications, published a compilation of his essays, excerpts from many of which were featured on his radio show and Web site. His show airs on weekends on KGO-AM, San Francisco.

Bouley's efforts definitely made a strong statement to commercial radio owners that there was a market for queer programming. They also provided encouragement for LGBT producers, who struggled to be heard outside of noncommercial venues. However, other producers felt comfortable with their small niche market audiences. In essence, within the United States, volunteer community stations led in airing queer programming in the 20th century, and many of these efforts remain healthy in terms of audience numbers. One instance is East Village Radio, which is located in a storefront studio on 21st Avenue in Manhattan. It serves its local downtown culture and offers live streams and podcasts of its programming, including those targeted to queer audiences. Another community station that has regularly featured LGBT programming is KFAI-FM, a volunteer station in St. Paul-Minneapolis.

Atlanta had become particularly and increasingly queer-friendly across the radio dial. *Alternative Talk* is produced by Atlanta's WRFG-FM, 89.3 FM, and it airs WRFG 89.3 FM on Friday afternoon at 5 p.m. The program is targeted toward Atlanta's African American lesbigay audience. On Tuesdays, the station airs *Lambda Radio* at 6 p.m. for the larger gay community. The radio stations there, as elsewhere, typically have had a difficult time locating and supporting locally relevant LGBT programming, simply because it costs money (although it is *relatively* inexpensive) and takes time to produce these radio shows. *Outright Radio* became the obvious choice for affiliate station

WABE-FM and one of the most successful shows in the United States of the present decade, airing for several years in Atlanta among other cities. It began in 1998 as "experimental radio pieces" (Liddle, 2004) and developed into a program. One of its producers, David Gilmore, applauded the "courage" of WABE-FM's management in airing the show, with its frank style; he explained that radio is a strong, inexpensive storytelling medium, so it was "the obvious choice" for the show's "personal narratives, interviews and documentary pieces" (Liddle, 2004). One 60-minute show, for example, included segments on topics from gay pride and health issues to lifestyle pieces, such as "the experiences of one lesbian couple in a pre-natal yoga class" (Liddle, 2004). That same show featured a segment on the "proliferation of the rainbow flag" across America. Other shows have highlighted coming out stories of men and women in the military. Another featured the often neglected stories of queer Latinos. Gilmore, in an open letter to his audience and sponsors, detailed the station's successes and struggles:

> When PRI picked us up for distribution in 2000, there was no other network-syndicated gay and lesbian radio program in the US. When we go off the air, there will be none, once again. And why, you might ask, are we going off the air? Well, the primary reason is that there is simply little money available to independent producers … As the show gained national attention winning radio's top awards, we landed a big grant from the CPB. In the end, we found that managing the grant was more work than it was worth. (A Farewell Letter, 2005)

Gilmore and his small staff worked unceasingly to find a home for *Outright Radio*, but there were no takers:

> When the high tech industry collapsed in California where we were based, the funding streams ran dry. So, I lobbied unsuccessfully to get the show adopted by a radio station, but, considering that the "bottom line" is the paramount concern of most radio stations these days, a wacky little show that came with a network contract and a cache of awards and loyal affiliates simply wasn't enough. Everyone we approached raved about *Outright Radio*, but wasn't willing to become a station partner. (A Farewell Letter, 2005)

The affiliate list had grown to nearly 100 stations in small and large markets across the United States. *Outright* had won several awards, including four from the National Lesbian and Gay Journalists Association and three from the National Federation of Community Broadcasters, and it had picked up the well-respected Edward R. Murrow award (Liddle, 2004). Other programs continue to sustain audience and funding. One such program is *IMRU*, a news magazine for the LGBT community in Southern California, which is hosted by KPFK-FM 90.7. Long-running *Amazon Country* and *Q-Zine* remain relevant to their queer audiences in Philadelphia and are broadcast on WXPN 88.5 FM late night Sundays. Across the United States, from Albany to Tampa, Denver to Dallas, and Arizona to Los Angeles, several public radio stations have developed long-standing relationships with the LGBT community.

Radio with a Commercial Twist

In 2007, the nationally syndicated gay radio program *Radio with a Twist* was bumped two hours, from 10 p.m. to midnight, on Washington, DC, contemporary hit station WIHT-FM Hot 99.5, when management decided to air a Christian call-in program in its time slot. The program's ratings initially fluctuated, and it finished in 11th place in the spring ratings: "the station decided in July to bump *Twist* to its later time slot" (Lynsen, 2007, 19). Only months later, management discovered that the program had been ranked first by Arbitron among 18- to 34-year-olds, "but the summer score wasn't known until October". The program is produced by Wilderness, Twist's production company, whose president is Matt Farber. Farber stated, "We've gotten a lot of e-mails and calls to *Twist* from disappointed listeners that can't hear it as easily ... for a lot of people it was such an important connection" (personal correspondence). Furthermore, the program attempted to be inclusive of a wider audience beyond its target base. Farber pointed out, "The idea here is it's a program that's authentic for the LGBT community and inclusive" (personal correspondence). "And, if anything, it's not something for just a gay audience. It's something for the gay audience and straight audience to equally enjoy" (personal correspondence).

One listener, a 20-year-old, commented, "I liked *Twist* because it was a pop culture show that related to the gay community." He added that the station "did little to support the show" when it first aired at its earlier time slot: "First they did nothing for advertising to the gay community, or larger pop culture community, so as to maintain a consistent listener base" (personal correspondence). He also noted that the station "did nothing to promote their programming over streaming radio" (personal corrersppondence)

The program is available via AOL and several large markets across the United States. *Twist* can be heard on Sunday nights at 9–11 p.m. on Q100 FM in Atlanta, as well as on New York City's WPLJ-FM, Los Angeles' KBIG, Alice 97.3 in San Francisco, The Mix in Dallas, Houston, and Springfield (Massachusetts), Kiss 106.1 in Seattle, KLUC-FM in Las Vegas, Coast FM 93.3 in Providence, Radio Now in Indianapolis, KOB-FM in Albuquerque, 95 SX in Charleston (South Carolina), and Energy 101.5 in Calgary (Alberta). Dallas listeners can hear the show Friday nights at midnight, and other stations, in addition to WIHT, broadcast the show in prime weekend time slots.

In the 21st century, the LGBT audience demands relevant programming targeted to its needs and interests. A handful of programs remain viable across commercial and public radio airwaves, with commercial radio even less likely to sustain a show that might initially flounder in its ratings. What KGAY radio attempted in the 1990s is now a reality. Sirius Satellite Radio offers one channel exclusive to queer programming. Sirius Out Q airs news, information, and entertainment for the gay and lesbian community. Sirius's Q programming is also free online. It has a Web presence that highlights the top Q hits and personality lineup. The Larry Flick morning show has a woman sidekick on its team. Other than that, all of the radio hosts are men. Its satellite counterpart in the United Kingdom is Gaydar Radio, which delivers similar programming 24 hours a day and is live in the evenings.

The Pride of Corporate Radio

> Pride Radio: An Idea so big that we had to give it to you in High Definition
> Finally Hers and Hers Radio.
>
> —Dallas in Drag

Corporate radio had the benefit of assessing the strengths and weaknesses of the queer market, keeping an eye on gay programming successes and failures on commercial radio over the past two decades. Clear Channel Radio Inc., unlike most independent producers, has the resources and airspace to promote queer radio, which is becoming more than a market niche. Gay programming had already proven itself, with high ratings in large markets across the United States. The problem was that independent producers did not have the time, money, or staff to remain a consistent force in the marketplace. In March 2007, Clear Channel Radio launched Pride Radio out of Dallas-Ft. Worth. Pride Radio Dallas (2007) is heard as a subcarrier to KHKD-FM, which is one of more than 300 multicasting stations in the United States, since High Definition's on-air arrival in Detroit in May 2005. Pride Radio can be heard online or on KHKS (KISS) 106.1 HD Channel 2. Clear Channel Dallas has provided a strong promotional budget, backed by an experienced marketing team. It targets 18- to 34-year-old LGBTs with Top 40, dance, and what is called "gay anthems including original mixes and remixes from Madonna, Donna Summer, Justin Timberlake, Gwen Stefani, Janet Jackson and more" (New Radio, 2007). The station is concerned foremost with its local audience and has plans for a strong community agenda over the air and on the streets (Durnan, 2006). The station combines local news and happenings with community service and relevant conversation:

> PRIDE Radio celebrates all things pop culture and entertainment with syndicated show "Ryan and Caroline." The show blends music, entertainment news, celebrity gossip from the notorious Perez Hilton, fashion tips from celebrity stylist

Phillip Bloch, movie reviews, travel, style & health, live entertainment and more. The show has been dubbed radio's "Will and Grace." (New Radio, 2007)

Operations Manager Pat McMahon explains,

We've always been appreciative of the support that the gay community of North Texas has lent our radio stations through the years. Now with the launch of PrideRadioDFW.com we have an opportunity to give these listeners a unique brand that targets their specific tastes and interests. (New Radio, 2007).

Clear Channel has since launched several high-definition, locally driven Pride Radio subcarrier stations, besides Dallas's KHKS, all with a strong community presence: WKSS-FM, Hartford, Connecticut; KPTT-FM, Denver, Colorado; WHYI-FM, Miami, Florida; KXXM-FM, San Antonio, Texas; KBIG-FM, Los Angeles, California; KIOI-FM, San Francisco, California; WYYY-FM, Syracuse, New York; KPEK-FM, Albuquerque, New Mexico; and WKSC-FM, Chicago, Illinois (Clear Channel's, 2007; Pride, 2007).

Chicago seemed a particularly appropriate site to launch Pride Radio, with the market having one of the largest gay and lesbian audiences in the United States (Pride Radio, 2006; WKSC-FM, 2006). The success of LesBiGay radio and other ventures in Chicago paved the way for these larger commercial efforts. The station features upbeat dance music, with less emphasis on news programming, like its host station, Contemporary Hit WKSC-FM. In San Francisco, beyond Pride Radio on KIOI-FM's HD2 channel, Clear Channel launched Queer Channel on KQKE-AM, a liberal talk station, in August 2006. The live radio program airs on Sunday nights at 10 p.m. The two-hour show focuses on celebrity features and community information. The content and format were created by LGBT employees at the Clear Channel's Bay Area operation, who proposed the idea to management.

Internet Connections

Gay radio has been increasing, and often thriving, across the Internet for more than a decade (Gay Radio Waves, 2007). Radio Gay International Network, founded on June 1, 2002, is an online radio station that provides daily programming and interactive opportunities for listeners to communicate with each other. PNN Gay Radio began in 1997 and serves the LGBT audience as an online radio station that features personalities and dance music programming for the LGBT community.

GayInternetRadioLive.com is promoted as America's Dance Channel, another online radio station but with a promotional twist. Personalities make appearances at national queer venues and events. *Everyman's Gay Radio* streams love ballads for men, along with its dance, house, and club music. Bear Radio Network is strictly a music service that hosts a diversity of music from alternative to techno. Beyond the United States, online queer stations and music services include ManCandy (United Kingdom and Canada), Energize (United Kingdom), AGRadio and Radio Zonica (Argentina), Stads (Netherlands), the FG Web network of online stations (France), Circuito and Vibe (Brazil), Radio Mitos (Chile), Gay FM (Germany), Gay Dee Gay (Italy), Energize (United Kingdom), Queer FM (Australia), and Russian Gay Radio (Gay Radio Waves, 2007). Another notable station is located online out of Stockholm: Sweden's 95.3 FM Gay Radio. In fact, terrestrial stations are finding it critically necessary to have an interactive Web presence, complete with music, relevant news, and a calendar of events (Gay Radio Waves, 2007). Some community members, with varying success, seek low-cost ways to make a difference locally to the community of LGBT listeners. In September 2005, community-licensed Chorley FM was launched as an LGBT station in Manchester, England, with a target audience of 15- to 25-year-olds (Gay Radio Station, 2005). A growing number entrepreneurs—gay and straight—attempt to make a profit in the marketplace, targeting younger and older demographics, while serving the increasing demand for relevant queer programming, whether that be defined as information or entertainment.

Canada's "first mainstream, commercial station" for gay and lesbian listeners was launched as Proud FM at 103.9 on April 2007. The station, owned by Rainbow Media Group, Inc., can be heard in Toronto and across the Internet. Well-known native personalities Ken Kostick and Mary Jo Eustace from a national Canadian television cooking show *What's For Dinner?* host the morning show, which is aptly called *What's For Breakfast?* (Proud FM, 2007). The station features contemporary Top 40 and hits through the 1970s. The project has been underway for more than a decade and remains controversial owing to a number of factors, including questions about "just how much of the station's staff—from management to producers to hosts—actually represent and hail from the gay and lesbian community (Gay, Lesbian, 2007).

Conclusion

The progress of queer radio has been riven with struggles from within the LGBT community, as well as from the outside. When gay programmers reached out for financial support, very few station managers were able or willing to provide it or even the appropriate airtime or time slot to develop an audience. The pioneers of gay radio spent countless hours and resources to provide listeners access to issues and programming not typically available via mainstream commercial or sometimes public radio stations. What might appear as a sudden emergence of queer programming on the dial for many listeners has been a steady evolution for nearly a half-century. Corporate radio appears likely to benefit from the observations of seasoned LGBT programmers within its company ranks as well as the efforts of the early entrepreneurs and independent producers. Whether this new corporate version of LGBT radio will sufficiently address its audience's needs and interests has yet to be determined. Initially, Clear Channel Radio appears to understand the significance of developing a community presence within each of its targeted markets for its corporate brand of Pride Radio. KGAY radio learned all too late that its editorial content was perhaps more important than its music playlist during its attempt to define its audience.

References

BBC Program Explores the Rise and Fall of "Gay Radio." (2007, February 10). Retrieved from http://www.connexion.org/newsstory.cfm?id=8311&returnurl=news.cfm, May 16, 2007.

Bloomquist, R. (1994). Format Feverishly Springs Forward. *Radio & Records*, March 18, 41.

Boehlert, E. (1992). Gay Radio Comes Out Commercially. *Billboard*, 104 (50), 64, 66.

Bouley, C.R. (2004). *You Can't Say That*. New York: Alyson Books.

Buchanan, P.J. (1999). Why We Can't Quit the Culture War. *The American Cause*. Retrieved from http://www.buchanan.org/pa-99-0219—.html, May 18, 2007.

Canadian Broadcast Standards Council/Ontario Regional Council. (2000, February 15). The Dr. Laura Schlessinger Show. CBSC Decisions 98/990808–, 1003 and 1137 (pp. 1–17) .

Canadian Radio Ethics Council Blast Dr. Laura. (2000). RadioDigest.com, May 11. Retrieved from http://www.wiredstrategies.com/ stopdrlaura/news/fromus/may/000509can.htm, May 18, 2007.

Clear Channel's Gay and Lesbian Programming Catching On in New Markets. (2007). *San Antonio Business Journal*, January 22. Retrieved from http://sanantonio.bizjournals.com/sanantonio/stories/ 2007/01/22/daily7.html?jst=b_ln_hl, May 16, 2007.

Coalition Against Hate. (2000). Laura's Radio Advertisers. Stopdrlaura.com, July 15. Retrieved from http://www.stopdrlaura.com, May 18, 2007.

Colorado Gay Radio. (1993). *Progressive*, 57 (2), 16.

Davis, R.A. (1993). Sky's the Limit for Tour Operators. *Advertising Age*, January, 36.

Dr. Laura Radio Show. (1999, April 16). Transcript. Retrieved from http://www.wiredstrategies.com/ stopdrlaura/news/fromus/ may/000509can.htm, May 18, 2007.

Durnan, K. (2006). Pride Radio Launches in Dallas. *Dallas Morning News*, March 7.

Dr. Laura As Buchanan's VP? (2000). *U.S. World & News Report*, June 13. Retrieved from http://uspolitics.about.com/library/weekly/aa061300a.htm, June 13, 2000.

A Farewell Letter. (2005). Web site. Retrieved from http://www.outrightradio.org, May 14, 2007.

Fejes, F. & K. Petrich. (1993). Invisibility, Homophobia and Heterosexism: Lesbians, Gays, and the Media. *Critical Studies in Mass Communication*, 10 (4), 395–422.

Flick, L. (1994). Labels Broaden Social Perspective. *Billboard*, 1 (June 18), 99.

Friends Radio. (2007). Rainbow History. Retrieved from http://www.rainbowhistory.org/archives.htm, May 16, 2007.

Gay, Lesbian-Targeted Station Hits Toronto Radio Dial. (2007). *CBC Arts*, April 16. Retrieved from http://www.cbc.ca/arts/media/story/2007/04/16/radio-proudfm.html, May 5, 2007.

Gay Radio Station. (2005). Gay.Com, UK and Ireland, September 22. Retrieved from http://uk.gay.com/headlines/9057, May 5, 2007.

Gay Radio Waves. (2007). Web site. Retrieved from http://www.gayradiowaves.com, May 16, 2007.

Ginsberg v. New York. (1968). 390 U.S. 629.

Gordon, G. (1993). Personal communication. *This Way Out*, October. Los Angeles, CA: Overnight Productions.

Gross, L. (1983). The Cultivation of Intolerance: Television, Blacks, and Gays. In G. Melischek, K. E. Rosenagren, & J. Strappers (Eds.), *Cultural Indicators: An International Symposium*. Vienna: Austrian Academy of Science.

Herdon, J. (1993). KGAY Offers an Alternative. *Austin American Statesman*, July 1, 17.

Hoy, C.T. (1991). An Historical Look at Male Homosexual Characters on Network Entertainment Programs. Masters thesis, Southern Illinois University, Carbondale, IL.

Johnson, P., C. Hoy, & D. Ziegler. (1995/1996). A Case Study of KGAY: The Rise and Fall of the First "Gay & Lesbian" Radio Network. *Journal of Radio Studies*, 3, 162–181.

_____ & Keith, Michael C. (2001). Queer Airwaves: The Story of Gay and Lesbian Broadcasting. Armonk, NY: M.E. Sharpe.

Kielwasser, A.P. & M.C. Wolf. (1992). Mainstream Television, Adolescent Homosexuality and Significant Silence. *Critical Studies in Mass Communication*, 9 (4), 350–374.

Kiss FM. (2007). Web site. Retrieved from http://www.1061kissfm.com/main.html, May 16, 2007.

Lesbigay Radio. (2007). Web site. Retrieved from http://www.windycityqueercast.com, May 14, 2007.

Letter. (2007). Pride Radio Dallas. Retrieved from http://www.prideradiodfw.com/pages/pride/letter2.html, May 16, 2007.

Liddle, K. (2004). Atlanta Radio Station Carries Gay Show. *Southern Voice*, June 11. Retrieved from http://www.sovo.com/2004/6-11–/arts/radio/radio.cfm, May 16, 2007.

Lynsen, Joshua. (2007). D.C. Radio Station Bumps Gay Program. *Washington Blade*, January 5. Retrieved from http://www.washblade.com/2007/15–/news/localnews/radio.cfm, May 5, 2007.

McCormack, T. (1994). Bring Gay Music Out of the Closet. *Billboard*, June 18, 4.

Morgan, B. & N.J. Peters. (2006). *Howl on Trial: The Battle for Free Expression*. San Francisco, CA: City Lights Publishers.

Moritz, M. J. (1992). The Fall of Our Discontent: The Battle over Gays on TV. In D. Shimkin, H. Stolerman, & H. O'Connor (Eds.), *State of the Art: Issues in Contemporary Mass Communication* (pp. 262–267). New York: St. Martin's Press.

Nathaniel, N. (1993). Gay Radio Station Gets Airtime. *Daily Texan*, 2.

New Radio Station Targets DFW's Gay and Lesbian Community. (2007). Pegasus News Wire, March 2. Retrieved from http://www.pegasusnews.com/ news/2007/mar/02/new-radio-station-targets-dfws-gay-and-lesbian-com, May 16, 2007.

Nidetz, S. (1994). "Lesbigay Radio" Is Breaking New Talk Show Ground. *Chicago Tribune*, May 22, 5.

One in Ten. (2007). Web site. Retrieved from http://www.wfnx.com/1/jocksshows/jock.asp?id=30, May 14, 2007.

Pride Is First Breakout Hit from Clear Channel Radio's Format Lab. (2007). Clear Channel Radio Press Release, January 1. Retrieved from http://www.clearchannel.com/Radio/PressRelease.aspx?PressReleaseID=1874, May 16, 2007.

Pride Radio Comes to Chicago. (2006). Clear Channel Radio Press Release, June 16. Retrieved from http://www.clearchannel.com/adio/PressRelease.aspx?PressReleaseID=1674, May 17, 2007.

Pride Radio Dallas. (2007). Web site. Retrieved from http://www.prideradiodfw.com/pages/pride, May 16, 2007.

Proud FM. (2007). Web site. Retrieved from http://www.cbc.ca/arts/media/story/2007/04/16/radio-proudfm.html, May 17, 2007.

Queer Channel Radio Show to Debut in Bay Area. (2006). *Radio Ink*, August 1. Retrieved from http://www.radioink.com/HeadlineEntry. asp?hid=129716&pt=todaysnews, May 16, 2007.

Radcliff, D. (1994). Personal communication, July 6. Colorado Springs, CO: KGAY Radio Network.

Radio with a Twist. (2007). Web site. Retrieved from http://www.radiowithatwist.com/home, May 16, 2007.

Romer v. Evans. (1996). 517 U.S. 620.

Snow, R.P. (1983). *Creating Media Culture*. Beverly Hills, CA: Sage.

Stewart, T.A. (1991). Gay in Corporate America. *Fortune*, December 16, 43–56.

Summer, B. (1992). A Niche Market Comes of Age. *Publisher Weekly*, 239 (29), 36–40.

This Way Out. (1993). Promotional flyer. Los Angeles, CA: Overnight Productions.

———. (2007). Web site. Retrieved from http://www.qrd.org/qrd/www/media/radio/thiswayout, May 6, 2007.

WKSC-FM Chicago's HD2 Side Channel Is All about Gay Pride. (2006). *Radio Ink*, June 16. Retrieved from http://www.radioink.com/headlineentry.asp?hid=134011&pt=inkheadlines, May 16, 2007.

7. Underground Radio: A Voice from the Purple Haze

Larry Miller

How did "underground/alternative" commercial FM radio get to be that way? It had to do with the times. By the mid-1960s, the notion of programming rock music for adults from stereo albums on FM was an idea whose time had come. Rock albums had begun to outsell singles, but most of the music on those albums was not being heard on the radio. Both the music and the lyrics had gotten a lot more mature and sophisticated, but AM radio had not followed the trend. For every half-dozen teenybopper bubblegum hits, you might hear one reasonably interesting song on a typical Top 40 AM station.

But the simple idea of programming music with a little more depth from albums was not new. Looking back on the evolution of radio formats in the 1950s, we tend to focus on the most popular format: Top 40. We forget that other music formats had also emerged during the late 1940s and early 1950s.

When television finally came into its own, radio had to scramble to find new programming. The existing radio shows—comedy, drama, adventure, variety—all went over to the new medium, leaving radio stations in search of new and different programming. The concept of playing music from recordings presented by "disc jockeys" dated back to the late 1930s, with shows like the *Make-Believe Ballroom*. However, they were adjuncts to the popular and much more widely listened-to network shows. The disc jockey was relegated to smaller independent radio outlets that did not have the budget or access to network or syndicated programs.

The record show finally was elevated to primary status in the late 1940s and early 1950s and became the mainstay of radio broadcasting. Some syndicated programming held on through most of the 1950s, but music formats ruled. However, it was not all Alan Freed or Wolfman Jack; by the end of the 1950s, other music formats were firmly in place, such as big band, beautiful music, mainstream (non-rock) pop music, plus country and western, rhythm and blues, jazz, and classical music. Many of these formats did more than just play the hits; they created a broader range of variety by going to deeper album cuts, long before FM album rock radio.

The idea of playing rock music from albums as an alternative to the tightly formatted Top 40 was a natural development. Many of the jocks who were instrumental in developing this style of programming on FM were people like me who already had experience in some of these other music formats. The idea of playing music in sets evolved from the way many jazz shows presented their music. Others came to FM from Top 40 with an eagerness finally to get to play more than just the most popular hit singles.

So Why and Where "Alternative"?

It was largely a matter of time and place. KMPX, the first full-time FM rock station, began in San Francisco during the so-called Summer of Love, the peak of the countercultural revolution. If the first FM station to take an alternative approach to music programming had developed in another city, such as Los Angeles, New York, or Chicago, the resulting format probably would have been similar. Even in the midlands, in areas that were not as involved in this counterculture, there would have been a distinctively alternative flavor to the mix. It should be said that it is entirely possible that a politically neutral mainstream approach to playing album-based rock music might have evolved during that same period, but the odds were against it happening. In the culture clash between the hip and the square, for that brief moment in time the hip won.

San Francisco was considered by many to be the hippest city in America, with a long history of alternative culture. It enjoyed a well-earned reputation as a city where anything goes. It had always been a magnet for creativity for artists, writers, poets, musicians, actors, and more. The city had enjoyed a wide spectrum of activity in all the arts—theater, music, and literature. San Francisco had been uniquely multicultural, welcoming Asian, Latino, and a wave of other new Americans. Irish, Italians, and other Europeans found a home there as well. By the end of the 19th century, the city had established itself as a melting pot of trade, commerce, the arts, and political activism. Social leftists, the movements for equal rights and pacifism, and an open acceptance of the gay counterculture all added to the city's unique history. It did not hurt that the city was a beautiful place with amazing scenery, fine old Victorian-style buildings, and those cable car hills.

It was only natural that a city with a live-and-let-live culture would be a magnet for the so-called beatniks during the 1950s. With Lawrence Ferlinghetti's City Lights bookstore as the central gathering point, the North

Beach area became widely known as one of the important focal points of this new alternative culture. From the corner of Columbus and Broadway in the late 1950s and early 1960s within easy walking distance one could find great Italian and Mexican food, Chinatown, the Hungry i and the Purple Onion, several jazz clubs, coffeehouses, saloons of every kind, and even the infamous drag show at Finnochio's. It was a great place and a perfect time to be there.

All of this history carried over into the 1960s, and the city became a gathering place for a new generation of post-beat writers, artists, and musicians. It was also the focal point for experimentation in music, the visual arts (such as light shows and poster art), and the psychedelic subculture.

Beatniks Out to Make It Rich

In 1965 and 1966, I had been doing a show titled *Promenade* at a classical–fine arts FM station (WDTM) in Detroit. It was free-form radio, with more than just folk music. It was a predecessor to FM underground/alternative radio in many ways. The first half-hour of the two-hour daily show was always devoted to a specific theme or narrative, which usually was mostly folk music but also might include comedy and spoken word, cabaret, or just about anything else that would tell a story. The rest of the show was what might accurately be called a progressive folk music show.

Classical–fine arts stations, such as WFMT in Chicago, WCLV in Cleveland, WCRB in Boston, and WDTM in Detroit, had a long-standing tradition of a Saturday night show devoted to creating entertaining and enlightening narratives, often a comedic parody of current events. *Promenade* was a direct descendant of those groundbreaking Saturday night shows. I was lucky enough to be in the right place at the right time to host *Promenade*. I brought my personal experience as a folkie, along with whatever else I had figured out about life and the universe, to the show.

When folk music started to go electric, there were mixed reactions. As the daily show was surrounded by classical music on either side, what little electrification crept in had to be handled just right, or the phones would light up. However, on Saturday afternoons, I was able to get a lot more electric, given the eclectic nature of weekend programming at the station.

I learned some important lessons about music programming during those *Promenade* years. I steadfastly refused to pander to pop music tastes. I deliberately aimed high. Rather than aim for a small percentage of the general audience, I aimed for and got a much higher percentage of my target audience—the hip underground counterculture. I knew I could fill any hip folk-rock venue in Detroit (from a coffeehouse or bar to a concert hall) with an interview, a few spins of the performer's album or tape, and some good words. I had discovered, quite by accident, the difference between lowest and highest common denominator programming. This concept followed me to KMPX in San Francisco in 1967 and eventually became a prime ingredient in establishing the first commercial underground/alternative FM, which led to "Progressive Rock" radio.

Another startling realization was that we did not have to follow audiences—they could be led. I started doing requests on the Saturday *Promenade* show. The first time I opened up the phone lines, the results were somewhat mixed. For every "hip" request, there was another for some lightweight pop such as "Lemon Tree" by Trini Lopez, or some other such stuff. I did a bit of creative editing of the request list and wound up playing what I thought was best—Dylan, Baez, the Fariñas, Tom Rush, Buffy St. Marie, Dave Van Ronk, Jim, and Jean—even the more radical Kweskin Jug Band or the Holy Modal Rounders. I played all the best and hippest stuff I could get my hands on and then announced to my audience that this was the music that got the most requests. The next week, the requests were much more in line with what I had presented as the most popular music, and within a couple of weeks the pop music fans either went away or were converted.

When Gordon McLendon bought WDTM in the fall of 1966 and changed the call letters and format, I headed for San Francisco. I had been playing in a folk-rock band called the Southbound Freeway for most of that year and had dreams of joining the hip music scene out west as a guitar picker. Fortunately, when that did not work out, I had a fallback strategy—radio.

Kilo Mother Pot Xray

Initially, KMPX was a beautiful music station, but it had failed to find its audience and had become a foreign-language station. It had been an early pioneer in FM stereo—the MPX stood for multiplex. So the station stayed alive, as many AM stations have more recently done, by broadcasting brokered-time ethnic programs. In a multicultural, cosmopolitan city such as San Francisco, that could include Spanish, Italian, and Chinese language programs. Several deejays board operated [operated] the foreign shows and then filled in the empty spaces between brokered programming with music. The musical segments had little real direction but tended to feature popular rock music of the day. There also was, for some unknown reason, an all-night music show. I took over the all-night show in February 1967 and moved it in a whole new direction.

When I landed the all-night show on KMPX, it was a natural progression to follow the folk-rock fusion of *Promenade*, and for six hours a night, six nights a week, I did free-form folk-rock radio.

Initially, the other deejays (Bob Postle and Irv Jackson) and I did not editorialize all that much. We were mainly into the music, which conveyed the messages for us. It seemed more effective to play a set of antiwar songs than to do an antiwar rant.

Although there were no scheduled newscasts on the station, it was inevitable that the music and commentary reflected current events—the civil rights struggle, the general movement to "ban the bomb," and the antiwar movement among them. Our programming also reflected other social and political trends such as the legalization of marijuana and other psychedelic "soft" drugs, an open attitude toward sexual relations, and other progressive antiestablishment issues.

Break the Rules and Win the Game

What was it that made this new kind of radio different? How was it that this wild card was able to trump mainstream AM radio in such a short time? The key was content. Many of the musicians in the incredibly productive early 1960s environment were part of the folk scene, which was not only essential in sustaining traditional musical values but also carried with it a strong and deeply rooted political subtext.

By 1966, rock music had come of age. The turning point in the evolution of rock music in the 1960s was when Bob Dylan met the Beatles, joint in hand, and they fed each other's heads. Dylan came away with the realization that he could set his poems to electric music rather than the traditional unamplified guitar. The Beatles were given to understand that they could move beyond teenybopper love songs and experiment with emotionally and politically profound and poetic lyrics for a more mature audience.

The results were earthshaking. Dylan went electric at the 1965 Newport folk festival and then released his first step toward realizing a true fusion of folk and rock, *Bringing It All Back Home.* In 1966, he toured with the Band and released *Highway 61 Revisited,* his first all-electric album. This he followed with the capstone of his evolution during the 1960s, *Blonde on Blonde.* A few of the songs on these albums made it to Top 40 radio—"Like a Rolling Stone" got airplay—but most of the music went pretty much unheard unless fans bought and listened to the albums.

As other folkies followed the example of Bob Dylan by going electric, they often continued to incorporate a progressive political subtext into their music. Buffalo Springfield's "For What It's Worth" was one outstanding example, along with several political songs by groups such as the Byrds and Barry McGuire's Top 40 hit "Eve of Destruction."

The Beatles fostered this movement into what would become known as progressive rock with their series of albums *Rubber Soul, Revolver,* and their masterpiece, *Sgt. Pepper.* All across the United States and in England, an inspired and unruly mob of creative musicians jumped at the chance to do something new.

While there was certainly plenty of popular music around that was politically neutral, the folk-rock fusion gave early FM rock radio its direction. The folk music scene of the early 1960s had evolved from interpreting traditional folk songs to contemporary songs composed in a traditional style, to protest music, and then to folk-rock. As folk went electric, many of these influences became part of folk-rock. Trade in your old five-string banjo for an electric guitar, find a bass player and a drummer, and you were all set.

Some bands, such as the Loving Spoonful or the Youngbloods, took music from traditional artists, such as the Kweskin Jug Band or Holy Modal Rounders, and electrified it. Others, such as the Byrds, took more overtly political music from singer-songwriters such as Bob Dylan or Pete Seeger and put it to a rock and roll beat.

Dylan had been part of a folk protest movement, along with Phil Ochs, Tom Paxton, and Mark Spoelstra, who had been strongly influenced by the protest folk songs of Pete Seeger and the Weavers and Woody Guthrie. Very personalized romantic songs represented another category that emerged from the folk scene, as performed by Eric Anderson, Judy Collins, and Joan Baez, for example. Young white urban folkies had revitalized traditional folk and country blues only to be trumped by Paul Butterfield, with Mike Bloomfield playing good loud Chicago-style electric blues. Literary folkies had their role to play, making new music with an emphasis on the lyric as much more sophisticated post-beat poetry (just listen to the words and music of not only Bob Dylan but also Donovan or Richard and Mimi Fariña). All of these influences went into the melting pot of folk-rock. The leading artists of the British invasion soon followed suit. However, at the end of 1966, radio was still behind the curve, as they say today.

The Summer of Love

As noted, KMPX was on the air in San Francisco at the full blossoming of the hip counterculture and the Summer of Love, and in that respect timing was everything. The counterculture of the late 1960s was not something that could be defined as just one thing or idea—it was a holistic construct, a mix of music, art, literature, film, style, clothing, and politics. Given the civil rights struggle, the leftover ban the bomb movement, the growing dissent over the war in Vietnam, and an increasing discontent with the status quo, it was not entirely surprising that FM radio would be left-leaning, activist, underground, and alternative.

We not only played the best of the new emerging music but added the special flavor of the time and the place. When the *Berkeley Barb* published a tongue-in-cheek article on how to get high by smoking banana peels, we played *Mellow Yellow* and went along with the gag. When Paul Krassner of the *Realist* came to town to check things out, we had him as a guest on the overnight show. When we saw that the improv comedy group the Committee, who were right up the hill in North Beach, were the hottest and funniest new thing in town, we got Howard Hesseman and several others from the troupe involved with the station.

Tom Donahue brought his connections with him as our new program director, and we got tapes of *Sgt. Pepper* in advance of the official release. Bob McClay had a connection to the latest in British rock, and we were playing Hendrix, Cream, Traffic, and the Who's latest albums before anybody.

I got to interview Jerry Garcia and Bob Weir on the evening of the release of their first album. Late at night, I also got to interview Cream and Jimi Hendrix, as well as most of the San Francisco bands. When we needed some promotional art, we went to Mouse and Kelly and came up with the classic "Family Radio" poster. We were written about in the *S.F. Oracle* and in the first issues of *Rolling Stone*. When the Monterey Pop festival happened in June 1967, the station was well represented, and we took back what we had experienced to our radio shows. We were there at the Fillmore and Avalon, the Matrix, and the New Orleans House in Berkeley. I designed my own handbill for the all-night "folk-Rock" radio show on KMPX and took it to Marty Balin's father Joe Buchwald to get it printed. We introduced Dr. Hip-pocrates (Gene Schoenfeld) to the world with good medical advice for those in need. When Steve Miller did his first album, *Children of the Future,* the built-in segues were inspired by my all-night show on KMPX.

Our engineer at KMPX rigged up a color organ to project bright colors on the DayGlo-covered wall opposite the announce booth, with mind-boggling results. "The ball scores? There certainly are a lot of those tonight."

We were innovators not just in having chick engineers, but in eventually turning those women loose on the air with their own shows, at a time when most radio was all male.

In the San Francisco music scene during the mid-1960s, the bands that emerged as the first wave of purveyors of "psychedelic" music tended to be less political. They were having too much fun. The exception was a Berkeley-based band called Country Joe and the Fish, who managed to merge having fun with raising political consciousness.

"Country" Joe McDonald was typical of the folk singers of the early 1960s, but he tended to lean toward a more political form of the music. While eventually creating psychedelic masterpieces such as 1966's "Electric Music for the Mind and Body," he still was true to his activist leftist roots, eventually becoming best known for his anti-Vietnam anthem

"I-Feel-Like-I'm-Fixin'-to-Die Rag." He was as much influenced by Woody Guthrie as he was by good time jug band music.

Other bands in the area were less overtly political, although Jefferson Airplane's "White Rabbit" can certainly be seen as a counterculture song, with its allusion to psychedelic drugs and strong political undercurrent. Eventually, with the album *Volunteers*, they too became leading purveyors of antiestablishment political rock.

We Are the People Your Mother Warned You About

For that matter, any music that accurately (or inaccurately) conveyed the hippy counterculture message was at the core of FM alternative radio in the late 1960s. However, a lot of it was not only about political issues. An alternative lifestyle also included an open-minded attitude about experimenting with drugs.

Eventually, FM deejays got to the point where we were playing so many obvious pro-drug songs that in 1971 the Nixon regime's official hatchet man, Spiro Agnew, went on the attack against FM radio. Although technically they could not bust FM stations for playing songs such as "Magic Carpet Ride" or "One Toke Over the Line," the FCC, under Nixon's strong urging, had other ways of putting us on notice. We understood that when the FCC took a look at program and transmitter logs, technical operations, or other issues (such as obscenity), we would be subjected to additional scrutiny.

Where there was a will, there was usually a way. When the authorities found that they could not bust Detroit political activist John Sinclair for his politics, they busted him for possession of marijuana. This appeared to be fairly typical of the government's attempts to keep the counterculture in check, and as Steven Stills pointed out in song, "paranoia strikes deep."

All this pressure did not stop underground/alternative FM from being subversive in every other way it could. We not only played dope songs but also broadcast pertinent and useful information (on drug hotlines, for example) to our counterculture brethren. They served to talk people down from bad trips, deal with overdoses and related health and safety concerns, and also warn against such government attempts at quashing pot smoking as poisoning Mexican marijuana with paraquat.

With great glee, underground radio also played comedy cuts by the Firesign Theater, the Congress of Wonders, the Conception Corporation, the Committee, Monty Python, the National Lampoon, and most especially Cheech and Chong.

Moreover, we fell back on the classics from earlier standup comics, such as Lenny Bruce and Dick Gregory. We especially enjoyed playing Ronny

Graham's bit, "Harry the Hipster," from the "Take Five" review, in which he instructs a classroom on the correct way to smoke a joint. Lord Buckley's routine about how the smoking of a magic vine saved Jonah from the whale ("The whale say, 'Jonah, what in the world is you *smokin'* down there?") was another favorite. Add to that John Brent and Del Close's "How to Speak Hip." FM radio was unquestionably subversive, cool, and fun.

Die, Top 40 ... Die!

It is rare in the history of American pop music that the best is played the most often. As a kid, I had grown up listening to the kind of personality jocks (in the late 1940s and 1950s) who clearly were committed to playing the best music they could on the basis not only of what was popular and selling but also of their personal knowledge and musical tastes. Most of us who wound up doing alternative FM rock in the late 1960s were actually echoing what we had loved about radio when we were young. In the late 1950s and into the 1960s, owing to the movement to formularize the Top 40 format for better ratings (remember the lowest common denominators), the good old days of personality radio had died. We, the FM outlaws, brought it back.

The basic approach was almost too simple and quite obvious. Albums began to outsell singles. Stereo was replacing mono. There was clearly an audience developing for new rock music, ranging from folk-rock fusion to psychedelic to the British invasion. Rock had come of age. Top 40 radio played pop singles in monaural. We played music from albums in stereo. We also played for what would eventually become the hottest target demographic in radio—men and women from 18 to 34 years old.

As the adage goes, before you try to break the rules, you need to know what the rules are. AM Top 40 radio was programmed one song at a time, often with a commercial in between. At underground stations, we would squeeze a dozen or more songs in an hour, with a corresponding number of spots. We did music in 15- to 20-minute sets with a group of commercials presented three times an hour. We maintained a one-to-one ratio between songs and spots, but as the music was often longer, we wound up playing an average of eight to ten songs an hour, with a corresponding number of spots.

What we did not realize at the time was that we had accidentally stumbled onto one of the keys for getting good ratings. To rack up as many continuous quarter hours as possible, it is essential to try to sweep your audience past the quarter-hour points, usually by putting a piece of hot popular music on the air at that point. By doing three 20-minute sets an hour, we automatically swept our audiences past those points and started getting monster ratings. Those listeners with the Arbitron diaries were swept along with the rest, and the results shook the entire broadcasting industry.

Break-the-rules radio also made it a point to do the opposite of Top 40—our arch-opponent and programming nemesis. At every opportunity, we poked fun at what we saw as obsolete radio. If they ID'd the station with jingles, we avoided them, except as parodies. ("WABX-Big Deal!"—as sung badly by the staff.) Some of the FM stations even prohibited cheesy-sounding overproduced commercials from ad agencies, preferring to do them live or produce them in their own style. At WABX in Detroit, we got the agency for Ford to let us recut a set of Mustang spots with great results.

If the Top 40 jocks yelled like idiots, we talked one-on-one with our listeners in a laid-back, natural style. One of my favorite jocks while I was at high school in Hawaii and doing some of my first radio shows was a guy named Bill Anderson. He could put himself right in the room with you, be your new best friend. (He eventually changed his name to Adam West and went on to fame as TV's Batman!)

They had phony air names, often attached to the time slot by hot programmers such as Bill Drake. We used our real names or, at most, hip-sounding nicknames. Charles Laquidera resisted the temptation to use an air name such as "Charlie Lake" and went on to become a legend on Boston's WBCN under his real name.

Within the format guidelines generally adopted by most stations, each jock had a lot of elbowroom to exercise his or her personal musical tastes. I liked folk-rock, while another jock on the same station preferred soul and another liked to get jazzy from time to time. Tying sets together with a theme or narrative concept was a double-edged sword. For instance, you could do a "rain" set, but after the third song, it might get to be predictable and potentially boring. Admittedly, we could be notoriously self-indulgent. Although some of us could be truly creative in the fine art of "spontaneity" (spontaneous continuity), others relied on segue books. Some on-air people with music backgrounds like myself could create segues in the same key that carried listeners along musically. While this kind of radio created a lot of listener loyalty, it also eventually contributed to underground's downfall. After all, you could only do the killer A-minor segue from "Babe I'm Gonna Leave You" into "While My Guitar Gently Weeps" so many times before it got worn out.

I Read the News Today—Oh Boy!

Commercial underground radio stations also took an alternative approach to news and information programming, but they were not the first to do so. The legendary Pacifica group of radio stations blazed that trail. Founded in 1946 by pacifist Lewis Hill and a group of fellow conscientious objectors, the Pacifica Foundation launched its first radio station (KPFA-FM in Berkeley, California) three years later.

Having established the tradition of alternative progressive news, the Pacifica stations were an influence on the emerging underground/alternative FM radio movement and pioneer stations such as KMPX. The rise of FM rock radio as a divergent listening option quite naturally meant an evolution in the way news and information were presented. However, presentation varied from station to station.

Some FM stations, such as KMPX and WABX in Detroit, did not have a firm commitment to a set number of minutes of news in the station's license. In fact, in the early days at KMPX, we did not even come close to any kind of regularly scheduled newscasts. When we let our listeners know about what was happening in the world, it usually was in the form of deejay rap between record cuts.

In 1968 at WABX in Detroit, we had a lot of leeway and responded to the need for news (as part of our community service mission) by hiring the editor of an established Detroit alternative newspaper, *Fifth Estate*. Harvey Ovshinsky took to the airwaves like a duck to water and began to produce timely and topical news features that entertained as well as informed. Metro Media stations, such as KSAN in San Francisco, KMET in Los Angeles, and WNEW in New York, also had license commitments to news and responded with innovation as well. At KSAN, Scoop Nisker became a legend for signing off his news reports with "That's' the news. If you don't like it, go make your own." It worked so well that when the Symbionese Liberation Army wanted to contact the media and talk about Patty Hearst, they sent the tape to KSAN.

Underground/alternative FM radio offered a genuine counterculture approach to news and information between 1968 and 1972. We took our inspiration from alternative newspapers such as the *Fifth Estate* in Detroit; the *Berkeley Barb* and *San Francisco Oracle*; *Village Voice* and *East Village Other* in New York; and the *Los Angeles Free Press*. Others alternative presses influencing underground radio around the country included the *Chicago Seed*; *Old Mole* in Cambridge, Massachusetts; Denver's *Straight Creek Journal*; the *Quicksilver Times* in Washington; *Rising Up Angry* in Chicago; *Xanadu* in St. Louis; *Kudzu* in Jackson, Mississippi; *Off Our Backs* (a feminist paper); and *Prairie Fire* (the Weather Underground's organ). In their heyday back in 1969, there were more than 500 alternative papers, boasting millions of readers, underground radio deejays among them. We brought their radical words and ideas into the studio in the form of newscasts (often more extemporized than formal) and editorials. The papers linked up through information-sharing networks, foremost among them Underground Press Syndicate (UPS) and Liberation News Service (LNS).

Culture Clash

I was doing the afternoon drive-time show at KLOS in Los Angeles in 1971. As an ABC station, it aired news every hour on the quarter hour, and we had to meet the network feed. The results were often disastrous. After we had spent most of the hour trying to be as groovy as possible, at a quarter after the hour, the Voice of Doom (as we disparagingly perceived it) came blasting on with the latest body count. Free-form deejays, including me, J.J. Jackson, Andy Beaubien, and Tim Powell, had a hard time getting the music to time out right to hit the news on schedule. If we were late, we had to bail out in the middle of a piece of music, gritting our collective teeth. If we were short, we'd find something to fill with. Jefferson Airplane to the rescue—Jorma Kaukonen's great little guitar piece "Embryonic Journey" timed out at 1:53 and was a perfect way to fill the time and segue into the news. After a while (sorry, Jorma), many of our listeners thought that it was the official ABC Radio news theme.

Clashes with the corporate culture were not infrequent. One evening in early July 1971, I ran into the national promo man for Elektra records at the Whiskey A-Go-Go. Over the din, he yelled in my ear that Jim Morrison was dead. It took a few minutes for this dreadful news to sink in, but I then arranged for him to come on my show and break the news. The next afternoon, we aired a brief announcement on KLOS, followed by "When the Music's Over."

All well and good, except for one little error on my part. In the same building with KLOS, the ABC FM station, was KABC AM, and the ABC radio newsroom for the West Coast. When the ABC news guys heard what we had aired without telling them about it first, they went ballistic. I was thinking like a free spirit on alternative FM radio and had failed to understand the corporate mentality that was beginning its move on my style of radio.

Goodnight, and May You All Find a Little Pot at the End of Your Rainbow

By the mid-1970s, the lines were becoming more clearly drawn. Just as the music and style of underground presentation were beginning to morph into the much more tightly formatted album-oriented-rock (AOR), the counterculture was being co-opted as well. It is a familiar pattern of cause and effect. What begins as alternative culture out on the fringes bumps into the mainstream and then gets subsumed (or consumed) by it.

The big, loud, guitar-based bands eventually became corporate arena rock. The underground press became *Rolling Stone* magazine. The intimate and personal singer-songwriter music of the folk-rock era became bland pop music called "soft rock." Bankers started wearing paisley ties and sideburns. "Groovy" became a meaningless cliché of the teenybopper bubblegum set, a long way from its jazz roots as slang for being high on drugs (the needle is in the groove ...).

A generation that discovered it had been lied to about certain drugs, such as marijuana, assumed it had been lied to about other drugs as well and got hooked on heroin, speed, and coke.

Radio formats became less and less alternative and free-form. The age of experimentation was over, and the tighter playlist won the day. ABC's *Rock 'n' Stereo* issued memos declaring "no more sound-alike sets." The strategy was that whatever song you are now playing, the next song should be something entirely different. Thus, "Whole Lotta Love" segues into "Midnight Train to Georgia." Head to head with free-form, creative radio (à la Jim Ladd). And guess who won? Tight playlist radio.

Deejays who had become "communicasters" kept their jobs. Those who relied on the informal/improvisational approach were often left behind as corporate's version of alternative radio became just another means of peddling spots.

Top 40 finally made a comeback, having been nearly obliterated by FM progressive rock radio. It slipped (or slithered) back into the public mainstream disguised as the latest fad in pop culture—disco. Former rockers such as the Rolling Stones and Rod Stewart had apparently succumbed to the beast and sold out, recording disco-flavored hits aimed at the new Top 40 radio formats.

In the 1980s and 1990s, on-air personalities possessing real presence and style were replaced by liner card readers cookie-cut from the same old pop radio mold. As the original personality rock jocks of the 1950s had been replaced by the generic Top 40 voices in the early 1960s, so the innovators of the FM revolution were replaced.

Certainly, the cultural upheaval of the 1960s was transforming on a number of levels and, in large part, sparked the emergence of commercial underground radio. Many creative radio people who might otherwise have been marginalized by mainstream pop culture got a chance to change how radio was done. Irreverent TV shows such as the Smothers brothers opened the door for *Laugh-in* and *Saturday Night Live*. Film censorship outlived the old Hayes office rules and opened the door to a whole new level of creativity and free expression. The counterculture fostered a new generation of post-beat writers, such as Thomas Pynchon, Tom Robbins, Ken Kesey, Richard Brautigan, and Robert Stone.

Despite the odds, alternative radio would somehow survive, albeit in a somewhat altered form. Free-form/alternative radio has remained alive at college and community stations, and at groups such as Pacifica. NPR and PRI continue to provide programming through music and news that add to the depth and breadth of our culture. Meanwhile, Air America has made a valiant, if not financially successful, attempt at providing an option to dominate conservative talk radio, while populist media activists, such as Robert McChesney and Bill Moyers, have initiated a battle against corporatization of the airwaves, something they rightfully view as undemocratic.

The new and emerging (and converging) audio technologies provide even more alternative listening outlets. People can stream homemade radio shows from the Internet, post radical outlaw video on YouTube, and influence mainstream politics, economics, and culture through the Blogosphere, so the spirit of revolution fanned to some degree by underground radio lives on, and we are all better off for it, at least in the opinion of this old hippie deejay.

References

Armstrong, David. (1981). *Triumph to Arms: Alternative Media in America*. Boston: South End Press.

Carson, David A. (2005). *Grit, Noise, and Revolutions: The Birth of Detroit Rock 'n' Roll*. Detroit, MI: Regional.

Douglas, Susan, J. (2004). *Listening In: Radio and the American Imagination*. Minneapolis: University Minnesota Press.

Fisher, Marc. (2007). *Something in the Air: Radio, Rock, and the Revolution That Shaped a Generation*. New York: Random House.

Fong-Torres, Ben. (1999). *Not Fade Away: A Backstage Pass to 20 Years of Rock & Roll*. San Francisco, CA: Backbeat Books.

———. (2001). *The Hits Just Keep on Coming: The History of Top 40 Radio*. San Francisco: Backbeat Books.

Friedlander, Paul. (1996). *Rock and Roll: A Social History*. San Francisco: Westview Press.

Gillett, Charlie. (1996). *The Sound of the City: The Rise of Rock and Roll*. New York: De Capo Press.

Glessing, Robert J. (1971). *The Underground Press in America*. Bloomington: Indiana University Press.

Hamilton, Neil A. (1997). *The ABC-CLIO Companion to the 1960s Counterculture in America*. Oxford: ABC-CLIO.

Keith, Michael C. (1997). *Voices in the Purple Haze: Underground Radio and the Sixties*. Westport, CT: Praeger.

———. (2000). *Talking Radio: An Oral History of American Radio in the Television Age*. Armonk, NY: M.E. Sharpe.

———. (2001). *Sounds in the Dark: All-Night Radio in American Life*. Ames: Iowa State University Press.

———. (2007). *The Radio Station: Broadcast, Internet, and Satellite*. Boston: Focal Press.

Krieger, Susan. (1979). *Hip Capitalism*. San Francisco: Sage.

Passman, Arnold. (1971). *The Deejays: How the Tribal Chieftains of Radio Got to Where They're At*. New York: Macmillan.

Perry, Charles. (2005). *The Haight-Ashbury: A History*. New York: Wenner Books.

Selvin, Joel. (1996). *San Francisco: The Musical History Tour*. San Francisco: Chronicle Books.

Walker, Jesse. (2001). *Rebels on the Air: An Alternative History of American Radio*. New York: New York University Press.

Part 2 Pulpits, Politics, and Public Interests

This microphone is not an ordinary instrument, for it looks out on vistas wide indeed.

—Norman Corwin

8. Speaking of God, Listening for Grace: Christian Radio and Its Audiences

Tona J. Hangen

Religious groups in America began jostling for a voice on the pervasive medium of radio from its earliest years. By 1924, a church or religious organization held 1 out of every 14 station licenses; the number of stations operated by religious groups climbed quickly from 29 in 1924 to 71 in 1925. In that year churches or other religious organizations controlled 10% of the more than 600 radio stations in the United States (Martin, 1988, 1711; Schultze, 1988, 291; Sweet, 1993, 56). Religious programs could also be heard on secular stations and on the emerging radio networks in the late 1920s and early 1930s, where sustaining-time programs included the Jewish *Message of Israel*, *Catholic Hour* and other Catholic programs, and the NBC mainline Protestant standby the *National Radio Pulpit*, which served up decorous ecumenical fare from the likes of New York modernist church leaders Dr. S. Parkes Cadman, the Reverend Ralph Sockman, and Harry Emerson Fosdick (Erickson, 1992; Miller, 1985). Religious broadcasters hoping to use the airwaves to enlarge the boundaries of the emerging evangelical network, or to air the doctrines of the newly hatched fundamentalist movement, found themselves denied access to these sustaining-time handouts and quickly developed various commercial strategies for buying and holding on to airtime for their distinctive "gospel" message, music, and patterns of worship.

After the Radio Act of 1934, airing religious programming was one of the ways that stations could fulfill their mandate to broadcast "in the public interest, convenience, and necessity." During the golden age of radio, the Federal Communications Commission (FCC) gave priority to sustaining-time programs when evaluating a station's religious programming, but that policy ended in 1960, which resulted in the near-total loss of free airtime for noncommercial religious broadcasters. Many ecumenical, mainline Protestant, Catholic, and Jewish programs had often been aired on sustaining time and relied on the goodwill of stations. Concerned with their profit margins, which were narrower in the television age, radio stations came to see religious programming as a steady source of income rather than as a donation in the name of social responsibility. Commercial religious broadcasters (who were mainly evangelical) kept their foothold in radio into the second half of the 20th century, owing in large part to the donations of devoted listeners.

Long before television, Christian evangelicals created a thriving media industry from the efforts of many independent broadcasters—an industry that is still very evident on radio today. At first, the broadcasts of theologically conservative Protestants might have nurtured the faith of far-flung or geographically and culturally isolated listeners—farm folks without a local church, for example. However, audience research from the 1930s and 1940s, when considered alongside fan correspondence to some of the major gospel radio programs of the period, suggests that radio accomplished much more for its audiences.

Bankrolling the Religious Radio Industry

Indeed, the habitual tuning in of regular listeners and their faithful donations to radio ministries to keep them on the air represent a key piece of the story of religious radio. Religious radio might have been a passing fad of the experimental years of early broadcasting without its loyal listeners. Instead, commercial religious broadcasting became a mainstay of American broadcasting, always remaining a genre apart and above all persisting on the air.

Religious radio permitted some changes in the devotional practices of ordinary Americans, who might now worship wherever a radio could be installed or eavesdrop on the religious practices of others without being seen to do so. Media messages—and perhaps particularly religious messages—are always subject to reinterpretation by their consumers. The growth of a vital industry purveying religious messages, objects, and ideas can be explained only by understanding its appeal to the millions who listened. Media and cultural historians Jesus Martin-Barbero, Stewart Hoover, and Frederic Jameson remind us that audiences make the meaning, that unintended messages are always possible, and that interpreting the mass media is a process of negotiation and historical contextualization (Hoover, 1988; Jameson, 1979; Martin-Barbero, 1993). Recognizing the power of "alternative readings" of cultural texts, Mark Hulsether has argued that "postmodern cultural theory highlights how the residual power of religious traditions can be expressed and contested—not merely defeated and trivialized—within a society that communicates through commercial mass media" (Hulsether, 1992, 75).

In other words, knowing the content of religious broadcasting is not enough. Looking at the narratives constructed through mass media is only the starting point for understanding the role that these media, and particularly radio, have played in building identity and constructing cultural boundaries. The next step is to explore the agency exercised by the audiences for religious radio and the social frameworks within which listeners read radio as a cultural text (Long, 1994). Very seldom can we access ways the media served as a bulwark against the co-optations and degradations it simultaneously effected. The story of religious radio broadcasting is one way to get at that other story. Mass media, after all, channeled messages that were conservative (orienting, placing) as well as transformative (disorienting, displacing). Typically radio services have been seen as a way to avoid attending church; an example that comes to mind is an Aberdeen, South Dakota, listener who sat through Sunday night radio programs "until time to take up the collection when we got busy elsewhere" (Nelson, 1996, 112). However, radio also made it possible to *begin* going to church or to rethink entirely what church was and where worship could take place.

The persistence and growth of evangelical radio during radio's golden age also provides a good measure of the strength of religious conservatism during this period. Christian radio nourished, legitimated, and enlarged the boundaries of evangelical Protestantism throughout the 20th century. The relationship of gospel broadcasters to their audiences was a close one; broadcasters depended on voluntary contributions to pay for increasingly expensive airtime, and listeners depended on radio evangelists to provide familiar and reassuring programming. By 1948, more than 1,600 fundamentalist programs were being aired each week, but, by and large, conservative programs did not receive free or sustaining-time airtime from stations (Hangen, 2002, 17). One study concluded that while Baptist, Gospel Tabernacle, and Holiness/Pentecostal broadcasters bought two-thirds of their airtime in the 1940s and 1950s, more mainstream denominations such as Methodists and Presbyterians purchased a mere third, and 70% of Roman Catholic airtime was free (Finke & Stark, 1992; Voskuil, 1990). Evangelical broadcasting achieved remarkable prosperity despite receiving almost no free airtime. Evangelical radio buttressed the fundamentalist movement, helped give it institutional and tangible, audible form, and helped bankroll its growth and entrance into politics in the second half of the century.

Religious radio not only proved important for evangelicals but also had a profound effect on the medium itself. In particular, radio evangelism was part of the national identity forged by radio—many of these broadcasts went overseas or were part of the fare of high-powered Mexican border blaster stations—and of the ambient sound of 20th-century American life. Its echoes were heard in the spread of gospel music through radio venues such as the *National Barn Dance*, the Hillbilly Boys and the *Grand Ole Opry*;

in the call-and-response rhetoric of civil rights leaders, which brought the sound of revival preaching (and its nascent liberation theology) to the wider culture; and in musical genres as varied and popular as bluegrass, rhythm and blues, and country (Grundy, 1995; Ward, 1994).

Identifying Listeners

Who was listening in the golden age? Two surveys reported in the National Association of Evangelicals' periodical in 1946 suggested that small-town and rural households were more likely to listen to religious radio that year. A survey of 47 counties in Kentucky and southern Indiana, conducted for CBS radio station WHAS, found that religious programming took second place only to hillbilly music in popularity for residents in towns with populations under 2,500 (Religious Programs Popular in Kentucky, 1946). This finding followed that of the U.S. Department of Agriculture (USDA), which reported in a nationwide radio survey that programs of hymns and sermons, followed closely by news and discussions of farm problems, were preferred by farm and small-town listeners. People who preferred religious radio made up a smaller proportion of the audiences in cities (Farmers Prefer Religious Radio, 1946).

Yet (perhaps paradoxically) each radio evangelist who managed to build nationwide audiences for his or her programs—Paul Rader, A.A. Allen, Aimee Semple McPherson, Walter Maier, and Charles Fuller, to name a few—did so from an urban base of support. Even the surveys just cited, if read another way, demonstrate no particular regional enclave for religious broadcasting: farms were dispersed widely across the nation at mid-century, and small towns were everywhere. And indeed, conceivably the numbers of listeners in mid-size towns and cities were greater than those in small towns, although the audience share was smaller when considered as a proportion of the population. I would contend that audiences for evangelical radio were neither urban nor rural but rather defined along theological and behavioral boundary lines of belief and practice. Sociological boundaries, then, may be far more useful than geographic ones for identifying likely listeners to religious programming. Similarly, Ernest Sandeen contends that millenarianism, one of the two fountainheads of early 20th-century fundamentalism, was first an urban movement that became dispersed throughout the country through summer Bible conferences and other Christian gatherings. Millenarianism and its close cousin, dispensationalism, did not hold sway only in the rural South or Midwest in those years. As Sandeen argued, "their conference retreats to the lakeside, the seaside or the countryside were no more a reflection of an agrarian mentality than are fresh-air camps for ghetto children" (Sandeen, 1970, 163). What I am here suggesting about religious radio audiences makes all the more logical the findings of later 20th-century sociologists that American evangelicals are remarkably representative of the communities in which they live, rather than being clustered together in easily identifiable locales or regions of the country (Ammerman, 1987; Budziszewski, 2006; Smith, 2000).

The uncoupling of revival religion from American regional culture, and its dispersal among the general population, is a trend permitted and accelerated by the mass medium of radio. One way to snap a freeze-frame of this dynamic moving image is to delve into letters from religious program listeners. Although frustratingly partial as a source of information about the body of listeners, fan mail nonetheless offers tantalizing glimpses of the transformation of American culture (and American religions) made possible by radio and adds vivid qualitative detail to quantitative research.

"I have felt I should write and tell you how and why I love the radio hour," wrote Mrs. Vivian Blamey of Craig, Colorado, to Charles and Grace Fuller in 1937. "I also feel that though I am miles from a Church I have a very real and very busy pastor who still has time for me and comes into my home each Sunday evening." She added, "And that you do understand and do know the neads [*sic*] of our heart" (Blamey, 1937). Was Mrs. Blamey talking about the heart's needs of her own immediate household, or was she using "our" in some broader sense of some unseen community to which she felt she belonged? Given the importance of pastors in the lives of conservative Protestants, what might it mean that she thought of Fuller (someone she had never met) as her personal pastor?

Mrs. Blamey's letter captured the enthusiasm with which many Christians embraced radio. Thousands felt, as did Mrs. Blamey, that they were participants in radio ministries, and indeed they were, since religious broadcasters outside the Protestant mainline utterly depended on the nickels and dimes, year after year, of ordinary folks who listened and donated. Evangelical radio was a *vox populi* in every sense of the term, vicariously expressing the views, concerns, and beliefs of those who provided its financial and institutional support. The worldview and folk religion of the voiceless sponsors permeated every broadcast. Religious radio, then, also served as a meeting place, a shared and sacred space that fulfilled the desire for personal connection. Unlike the mass experience of a large-scale meeting, radio was intimate, conversational—the medium was the first to speak to people in their homes. Just as evangelicals believed the Word of God could speak to individual hearts, radio preaching was experienced simultaneously by thousands as a direct personal conversation.

Hearing Voices and Hallowing Spaces

American evangelicalism, since 19th-century camp meetings, relied on aural rather than highly visual worship styles; it involved the relationship between hearing and feeling, rather than between seeing and feeling. In Protestant evangelicalism, the ears were the channel to the heart. God "spoke" to converts rather than being incarnate in visual symbols. Therefore, evangelical religion made a smooth transition to radio. The rhetoric of preaching, the cadence of familiar gospel hymns, and even—in the case of Sister Aimee Semple McPherson's Thursday night show on KFSG Los Angeles—the splash of converts being immersed in baptism all needed only a microphone to be heard and experienced by people not physically present.

Nearly all evangelicals couched their stories of sacred encounter using ideas of speech and hearing. Radio pioneer Paul Rader's experiences represent the typical story. He remembered as a teenager being terrified to preach in his father's Methodist pulpit one Sunday. He spent the night before fasting and praying, even right up to the moments before the meeting was scheduled to begin, until "His voice came to me" (Rader, n.d.). On the occasion of Rader's reconversion as an adult,

> for the first time since my boyhood days, *I heard that old Voice.* I cannot tell you what it is, but you will know it when you hear it. His sheep know His voice and hear His voice, thank God, and He whispered like He used to when I was a boy and said as plain as could be, "*Now you think you have got something. If you will drop it all and follow Me I will lead you into the Truth and give you a message.*" (Tucker, 1918, 79).

This common conception among many people of faith of the literalness, even the *physicality*, of the voice of God prepared them to understand the radio in similar ways, with its disembodied voice, unseen mode of transmission, and a "receiver" tuned to contain God's truths. "Hearing voices" from the ether was no longer—in popular parlance—the fantastic imagination of the religious zealot or the insane, but in the 1920s became an everyday American reality. This idea reached its popular pinnacle in 1950, with MGM's release of William Wellmann's dramatic film *The Next Voice You Hear*, in which God startled a California suburb by speaking through the radio. However, by then the rest of the United States was merely confirming what religious broadcasters and their devoted audiences had been experiencing for a generation. As a listener to Rader's programming wrote from Sheboygan, Michigan, in 1926,

> It seems as if my heavenly Father speaks to me through you. I am a lonely old lady, living all alone, but *Jesus is with me,* I know ... My husband is dead, and I have had to travel life's path alone, but *I know* my Saviour has been with me,

and He has seemed nearer since I've been listening to your messages over WHT. (Hi-Ways and Bi-Ways, 1926a)

Likewise, the quintessential moment in an evangelistic meeting, the altar call, was just as effective on radio—if not more so, because of radio's illusion that the listener is being spoken to directly. Another of Rader's listeners offered this example in 1926:

> I listened to your sermon and I heard you extend the call. It seems that all at once I was trembling and the tears streamed down my face. I called my wife, and we sat together listening to the choir singing "Lord, I'm coming home" and heard you call for sinners to come forward. Finally I heard you say, "Come On, Big Boy." Now this is a name I go by sometimes and it seemed as though you were talking to me personally. I ... made a vow to serve the Lord. I am asking for your prayers. (Hi-Ways and Bi-Ways, 1926c, 36)

This man's demonstrative moment came at home, which raises the issue of how radio penetrated and redefined private devotion at home. But radio could also offer new ways of performing evangelical faith in the public square. Some radio evangelists literally took the place of preachers at the pulpit. An Ohio man, after hearing Paul Rader's broadcasts on Chicago's WHT, decided to use a radio set to "start Sunday evening meetings in churches that are disbanded, that have no Sunday school, or preaching" (Hi-Ways and Bi-Ways, 1926a, 31). Another Rader listener, from Ransom, Illinois, loaned his set to a local church so that "a good crowd may hear it" on Sunday evenings and participate in a service complete with a collection plate: "I will try and get some 'jack' from the audience to send you, to help lift the burden" (Hi-Ways and Bi-Ways, 1926b, 53). At least one evangelist made this a deliberate part of his ministry: E. Howard Cadle, an Indianapolis fundamentalist, started a program of "mountain church work" to expand the listenership for his Cadle Tabernacle services over Cincinnati station WLW in the late 1930s. Cadle bought radios in bulk, then installed them on the pulpits of small churches in remote Appalachian communities, billing himself as an unfailing "new circuit rider" and in the process transforming himself from "another anonymous radio voice into a familiar preacher with a personal connection to churches all over the Midwest and South" (Cadle, 1941; Cadle of Indianapolis Streamlines Evangelism, 1939; Cash and Cadle, 1939; Hi-Ways and Bi-Ways, 1926a; Slutz, 1995). In 1937, a pastor of a Christian and Missionary Alliance church surprised his Lincoln, Nebraska, congregation by bringing out a radio after the Sunday evening service and tuning in to the *Old Fashioned Revival Hour* (Branham, 1937). Those who put radios on otherwise vacant pulpits, or who enhanced their services with this novel device, widened the circle of possibilities for that sacred position at the head of the congregation. Instead of a human being, the authoritative source of the Word could include what amounted to a faceless electronic box, yet one imbued with all the veneration and respect accorded to a physical pastor.

The world outside the church could also be marked by hallowed air-space as evangelicals explored ways mediated religion became part of their own witnessing practices. One enthusiastic owner of a Jonesboro, Arkansas, drugstore played the *Old Fashioned Revival Hour* over the store's sound system whenever it aired (Letter on Court Square, 1955). Instead of keeping a small radio set behind the counter for his own enjoyment, this man could advertise his religious convictions along with the tooth powder and root beet floats, to the delight or dismay of the town's residents.

Radios, unlike other common household appliances, functioned as symbolic centers of the home and even the site of devotional religious objects and rituals. A Roseland, Louisiana, woman described to Charles Fuller the use she had made of the space around her radio:

> I have received the folder of the "Tabernacle in the Wilderness," and am much pleased with it. I have used scotch tape and fastened it to a piece of stiff paper and hung it over my radio and under your picture, so when your broadcast comes on each Sun[day] over station WJBO in Baton Rouge, La., I can see your "likeness." (Bradley, 1954)

In other words, in some religious households radios could become altars—complete with icons—around which the family gathered for religious instruction, worship, and prayer. Although at this remove it cannot be known for certain whether people interacted with radio programs as they did with church services in their faith traditions, or whether they might have exhibited less (or more) responsiveness while listening, many were not passive recipients in the least.

One man remembered listening to Charles Fuller's *Old Fashioned Revival Hour* in the 1930s as a boy on a farm 20 miles outside Traverse City, Michigan. "I can still remember how Grandpa and Grandma, Mom and Dad used to pull their chairs close to the radio so as not to miss a word and join the singing. I can still hear the 'Amens' and the 'Preach it Brother' with which they punctuated the sermon as you preached," he wrote to Fuller in 1954 (Way, 1954). The extended family gathering suggested private devotional behavior, but the verbal outbursts evoked a church meeting—again, blurring the boundaries between what was private and what was public in radio evangelism. Presumably, the words of praise and encouragement spoken by the listening adults in this boy's family were intended for one another, to reinforce beliefs held in common among them, and to mark key ideas for the impressionable children in the family. Many people apparently sang aloud too, like Mrs. Ernina Clayton of Split Rock, Wyoming, who requested a songbook in 1935 "so that I can turn to the song, and at least be with you in the spirit any way" (Clayton, 1935). "Preach it Brother" and similar variants spoken aloud may have been thought to carry spiritually to the actual radio preacher, but such responses, including singing along, certainly served the people at hand, legitimating the preacher's words to the folks assembled at the radio receiver and contributing to the socialization of children and newer (or potential) converts.

Another key form of interaction with radio evangelism was prayer. Letters almost never failed to mention that the writer prayed for the radio broadcaster. Historians should not underestimate the meaning for religious conservatives of this effort on their part. It is tempting to dismiss the importance that people of faith attached to their "prayer lists," but for them it represented focused attention, a powerful form of direct action toward their goals. A woman from rural Missouri wrote to Paul Rader in 1928,

> We live out in the country, but we don't get lonesome on Sunday nights—that wonderful band and music we get from your station! Last night, when you were giving the invitation, I sat by the Radio and wept for joy and prayed for souls. (A Radio Message from the Cathedral of the Air, 1928).

"I never cease to pray for your Wonderful! Wonderful! Work for our Blessed Saviour at a time when every true Christian needs to stand up and be counted," wrote a Colorado woman to the Fullers at the *Old Fashioned Revival Hour* in 1948 (Cooper, 1948). Her prayers, she felt, represented support for crucial causes when such support mattered, but also "registered" her in the cosmic census of "true Christians." As another *Revival Hour* supporter put it, prayer turned the key to open other kinds of supportive responses, too: "when I prayed for your services to be always on the air, some thing says to me that action goes with prayer so I am sacrificing another dollar" (Oldridge, 1937). Evangelicals devoted themselves to praying for radio broadcasting, just as they surely prayed for many other movements in which they perceived God at work. Remarkably, even one man who could no longer *listen* to religion radio—who had no access at all to its message—continued to pray. "I am stone deaf, and have not heard you for over ten years," he wrote, "but I have prayed daily for you and your work" (Travis, 1950).

For Protestants of all stripes, prayers were not rote recitations or mere ornaments to worship. They were the daily bread of spiritual life, utilitarian, the paramount tool humans possessed to communicate with God. Prayers were the means of receiving God's grace, forgiveness, and counsel, and, in the minds of evangelicals, prayers were one of the most powerful means available to make things happen—hence the thousands of "Prayer Warriors" recruited by Charles Fuller. Similarly, Sister Aimee Semple McPherson built a prayer tower at Angelus Temple in Los Angeles and staffed it around the clock with continually praying volunteers (*Foursquare Firsts*, 1973). Carl McIntire, radio broadcaster and tireless advocate of fundamentalist separatism, counted many "prayer helpers" among his radio audience (Echoes from Our Radio Audience, 1936). Focused prayer groups were an important feature of Billy Graham's Evangelistic Association, one of the most successful and financially trusted media ministries, and the association's practice of soliciting prayer for religious media outreach continues to this day. James Dobson's Web site for the *Focus on the Family* ministry invites users to sign up to pray for the program, providing a list of current prayer concerns so that the prayers might be properly oriented (Family, 2007). When they turn their prayers to radio broadcasting—and then see it grow and flourish—believers see their prayers answered, their supranatural abilities confirmed, their chosenness reaffirmed.

Some early evangelical programming, taking a cue from the spontaneity of live meetings, encouraged live audience phone calls during the program. Call-in shows, of course, have since become a staple of religious and talk programming of all kinds, but in the 1920s, when radio fundamentalists first took to the air, the format was completely novel. Chicago's Paul Rader employed 25 operators to handle the calls for his *Request Hour*, in which the Chicago Gospel Tabernacle musical staff took live requests for hymns, sometimes audibly scrambling through big notebooks of lyrics and tunes. Sister Aimee kept a phone under her red velvet chair on the dais of Angelus Temple, to receive relays from callers to her broadcasts (Ormiston, 1924).

In their letters to radio evangelists, many listeners sought feedback, some signs that their correspondence was received and appreciated. "Please *don't* mention my name or letter very much, only say, you heard from a friend in Wyoming so that I may know you received my letter," requested Mrs. Ernina Clayton to the Fullers (Clayton, 1935). Statements like this one speak to the literature on parasocial behavior, in which some members of the mass media audience have been shown to develop an "intimate, friend-like" relationship with media personas. Most of the research in this area has been done for television performers and their fans; sociologists in the 1950s first began to notice that the conversational, intimate modes of address on the air could elicit in some viewers an interpersonal response out of proportion to the actual contact between a television character and the audience member (Giles, 2002; Horton & Wohl, 1956). Robert Orsi (1998), too, has written of the intense identification of mid-century Catholic women with St. Jude, as a benevolent and predictable person in their lives. More recent research on talk radio suggests that listeners find their favorite hosts to be "credible relational partners" (Rubin, 2000). Regular listeners to religious radio programs could develop parasocial relationships with the evangelists—who often directly addressed the audience, expressed benevolent concern for the small details of the listener's life, and invited personal connections in a variety of ways. Like all serial broadcasts, the regularity and predictability of religious radio encouraged listeners to tune in again, to trust the speaker, to organize the day or week around the program, and to experience that listening as a participation in a genuine relationship.

Radio evangelists became pastors and counselors in occasional two-way encounters with their listeners. One woman from Camus, Washington, began her 1935 letter by stressing that she and her husband were faithful listeners to the *Old Fashioned Revival Hour*—establishing the basis, in other words, for assuming a personal relationship. "Now I am going to ask you for a little personal help which I wish you would answer by letter if not too inconvenient for you," she asked, and proceeded to pour out her heart in a series of questions about how to pray to a God who seemed hopelessly remote (Stebbins, 1935). In contrast to God, Reverend Fuller was accessible, and this letter reflects her confidence that he cared about her concerns and he would be able to answer her needs.

"I may not have the opportunity to meet you personally, but I will meet you in Glory," wrote a Texas woman to the Fullers, then added in a hastily scrawled postscript to her 1954 letter, "Bro. Fuller, Please pray for my husband. He is driving a beer truck and temptations are many" (Eaker, 1954). Perhaps her own prayers, she felt, needed additional strength; she turned to someone she expected never to meet for her most intimate and pressing of problems. In the case of Paul Rader, who had a large local audience, face-to-face connections could be made. Chicago Gospel Tabernacle workers visited homes and hospitals in outreach as they responded to specific listeners' letters for help (Eskridge, 1985, 125). Even among the Fullers' national audience, folks might attend the recording studio as they would plan a visit to their relatives. A woman from Ontario, who felt "as if I were writing to my cousin or aunt," relayed her itinerary for an upcoming trip to the West coast, to see "my youngest brother and oldest sister in Portland, and Harvey my husband has two sisters in Alberta, and want to see you folks, if nothing prevents us" (Unsigned author from Leamington, 1942).

Connecting Listeners

Religious radio, then, inspired all kinds of audience interactions, from simple singing along and spoken responses to the creation of perceived personal relationships with the personalities heard on the air. All of this was enhanced, of course, by the underlying topic of every evangelical broadcast: how to develop a personal relationship with a caring but unseen God, to whom one might appeal at any time for solutions to life's troubles. Further, evangelicals themselves were the connective tissue for religious media, as crossover listeners to multiple programs. Religious broadcasters of all affiliations recognized this. Charles Macfarland of the Federal Council of Churches wrote in a 1929 memo,

> Judging by the thousands upon thousands of letters that come, the radio congregations are not denominational. The people do not listen as Methodists, Baptists, etc. Brethren, believe me, we are facing a new situation here and one that can only be met unitedly and cooperatively. We can't reach ... listeners denominationally. (Macfarland, 1929)

In 1942, a representative of the Synagogue Council of America admitted "other denominations do listen in. We know from mail which comes in response to the Jewish religious broadcasts that our radio audience includes as many Christians as Jews" (Goldstein, 1942). And a 1948 telephone survey of 1,500 residents of Waco, Texas, found that Sunday-morning worship broadcasts attracted "a high percentage of people with similar denominational backgrounds but do not limit themselves to members of a particular church" (Radio Survey Shows Religion Is Popular, 1948). Letters to the *Old Fashioned Revival Hour* alluded to other radio evangelists, including the Bible Institute of Los Angeles (BIOLA) radio station, Dr. Walter Maier's *Lutheran Hour* (a production of the fundamentalist Lutheran Church Missouri Synod), Paul Myers's (a.k.a. "First Mate Bob's") *Haven of Rest*, and Billy Graham's *Hour of Decision*. Evangelical periodicals— which sometimes seemed to agree on little else—reprinted news and broadcast times for a wide range of conservative Christian radio programs. The patchwork purchasing of independent religious broadcasters surely helped this process along; by the late 1940s few evangelists could sponsor, as had Paul Rader or Sister Aimee in the 1920s, all-day programming from the lips of a single charismatic evangelist. Stations specializing in selling airtime to religious groups fielded a variety of programs, from which listeners picked and chose with varying levels of discrimination. "Hear your favorite religious programs on KFEL every Sunday," advertised one Denver station in 1944. KFEL's lineup opened with M.R. DeHaan's *Radio Bible Class* and then offered eleven different religious programs, from the *Voice of Prophecy* to the *Light and Life Hour* (KFEL schedule, n.d.). In her study of the Dust Bowl–era diary of a Kansas farm wife, Pamela Riney-Kehrberg found that radio was a "central organizing element" in the life of the diarist, Martha Friesen. Lacking electricity, Friesen's family worked to keep the radio batteries recharged and bitterly noted the days when dust storms interfered with reception. Friesen listened not only to R.R. Brown's weekly *Radio Chapel Service* from Omaha but also regularly took in the broadcasts from Unity Village in Kansas City and wrote to them for tracts. She even sent away for the text of an address by the Catholic Father Vincent McCauley, from the Mutual network's ecumenical *Faith in Our Time* series, and kept it tucked in her diary (Riney-Kehrberg,

1994). One letter to Charles Fuller from an enthusiastic California dial-twister in the late 1950s mentioned no fewer than seven separate radio ministries she felt were "worthy of Christian support" and to which she listened frequently (Fairbank, 1958). In their study of the religious media audience in New Haven, Connecticut, in the early 1950s, Parker, Barry, and Smythe found that *Old Fashioned Revival Hour* listeners were also regular viewers of the television programs of Billy Graham and Catholic bishop Fulton Sheen. New Haven's audience seemed remarkably ecumenical: the researchers found that nearly a third of those listening to or watching Protestant radio and television programs were Roman Catholics, while Protestants made up 14% of the audience for Catholic programs (Parker, Barry, & Smythe, 1955, 207, 356).

Religious broadcasting, then, forged a series of connections: between listeners and preachers, among listeners, and among disparate denominational groups. It may be contended that the shared experience of consuming a mass-media production is shallow connection indeed, but, in fact, the kinds of links that evangelical ministries and their listeners forged in radio's golden age represented something deeper than mere consumption. Audiences sought active involvement rather than passive reception, and religious radio audiences generated out of their participation new levels of interconnectedness, and new definitions of their community and its role in society. The growth of these connections may have been inchoate and unconscious, at least at first, but evangelicals were laying the foundation for their more conscious and visible organization—and its heavy reliance on mass media—later in the century. When the time came for evangelicals to act in overtly politicized ways in the broader culture, their decades-long involvement in broadcast media had already socialized ordinary believers to consider themselves connected to a broader movement and to be comfortable with mediated religion. Like the stylus slipping into the groove of a record, the seemingly insignificant connections made by religious radio listeners amplified their influence into a strong—though never a singular—voice.

Through conversions, reconversion, and the nurture of the faithful, radio enlarged the audience for its own message, operating as an important—and now, nearly ubiquitous—form of religious marketing. Radio was the modern, pop-culture missionary that could reach people where actual missionaries could or dare not go: naval vessels, taverns, death row cells, houses of prostitution, across the Southern color line, into the homes of the upstanding members of competing denominations, the car radios of late night truckers, and transistors on the beach. Its reach captured the imagination of evangelicals committed to fulfilling the biblical prophecy that the entire world must be evangelized before Christ's return. Believers have been, and indeed still are, motivated to donate funds in the hopes that a ministry on radio, television, or the Internet might reach the sinner who might never darken a church's door. As evangelists of radio's golden age rarely failed to point out, they were able to preach at a single sitting to more people than Billy Sunday or Dwight Moody reached in an entire lifetime of pavement pounding. To them, the radio as a "new witnessing medium" offered clear evidence not of the entrepreneurial streak in American Protestantism but of the divine hand of God, rolling forward his plans (Rader, 1938, 79).

Religious radio did far more than reach the unchurched, however. It also preached to the choir. The sermons, hymns, testifying, and other forms of oral worship operated for regular listeners in a way similar to mass-produced devotional art or religious popular literature, so that the act of being a consumer of these religious programs acknowledged and celebrated the broader community, taking a seat at a vast communion table. Maintaining a sense of belonging took on heightened importance in the middle decades of the 20th century, when for a variety of reasons Americans became increasingly mobile. From the 1920s forward, migration rates into cities accelerated, and communities across the nation were disrupted and reshaped by the Depression and World War II (Jackson, 1985; Kirby, 1987). In the past forty years, the expansion of both legal and illegal immigration into the United States has made multicultural communities out of every previously isolated corner of the nation. Evangelicals separated from their roots could retain their religious identity, or claim a new one, by relying on the radio to keep them tethered to the faith. As Paul Rader's program manager Floyd Johnson recognized as early as 1925, a church service via radio was "a vast ethereal cathedral, the dimensions of which are unknown … [and] anywhere where the receiving sets are in operation, one may find a pew and thoroughly enjoy the services" (Johnson, 1925). Since radio could reach millions simultaneously, it could offer a sense of participation in an imagined movement of innumerable others who might also be listening.

Religious Radio Legacies

Radio was also the catalyst for the organization of several important religious media advocacy groups—the National Association of Evangelicals and the National Religious Broadcasters in particular—that later proved critical to the development of the political activities of the religious right. Radio laid the foundation for televangelism in the 1970s and 1980s, which not only increased the visibility of evangelicals in the public sphere but also pointed the spotlight squarely onto the unseemly fundraising techniques, intolerant discourse, and seedy private lives of some prominent media evangelists. In addition, although new ways of delivering religious messages have proliferated in recent years, including Internet radio and video, satellite, and podcasting, traditional antenna-and-tower radio programming remains an important part of the media landscape of American religion.

Jumping ahead to today, the number of radio stations in America has been increasing each year (even while corporate consolidation reduces the number of station *owners* annually), nearly every American uses radio, and audiences remain large (Saxe, 2000). Religious radio is a growing market. Between 2000 and 2005, the number of stations in the United States increased by 4% to more than 13,000, and in the same years the percentage of religious-format radio stations grew by 14%. Arbitron defines the "religious" category as including not only religious talk shows (such as inspirational, magazine-format, and Bible study) but also stations with contemporary Christian music (CCM) and gospel music formats, and, taken as a whole, that "religious" segment of the radio market is on par with country music broadcasting and close behind news/talk format stations. The Barna Group reported in 2005 that 46% of all U.S. adults listened to a Christian radio broadcast monthly, which included 28% of the non-Christians in their survey (Powers, 2005). Two-thirds of the audience for Christian radio is female (Kennedy, 1997). Audiences for religious radio have grown 38% since 1998. In 2004, the fifth-largest radio owner was the American Family Association, which owned the Christian radio group American Family Radio (StateoftheNewsMedia.org, 2004). Salem Communications is one of the largest players in the religious radio industry, with a Christian station in 23 of the nation's top 25 radio markets in 2007 (Trammel, 2007).

Some of the early radio pioneers are still on the air, plugging away quietly, like the Moody Bible Institute station WMBI or the weekly *Music and the Spoken Word* from the Mormon Tabernacle of the Church of Jesus Christ of Latter-day Saints, which recently celebrated more than 75 years on the air. Dr. James Dobson's daily advice program, *Focus on the Family*, is the highest-rated national religious program, with an audience of perhaps 1.5 million listeners on more than 3,000 stations in the United States (however, international audiences are just as important to many of these broadcasters: *Focus on the Family* is also broadcast in 160 countries, with an estimated listening audience worldwide of 200 million, according to Dobson's organization). Other big-name religious radio broadcasters include Charles Swindoll, Charles Stanley, and Beverly LaHaye. Radio remains a safe place for conservative Christian religious and political viewpoints. "When conservatives talk about media bias, they are not talking about radio. It is a conservative bastion," concluded a recent conference session of the MIT Communications Forum on evangelicals and the media (Peverill-Conti, 2007). Yet Internet, digital, and satellite radio offer new opportunities for niche narrowcasters to develop a media presence for less mainstream religious groups, who are seldom heard on the FM and AM dials. The proliferation of non-Christian religious media voices (Radio Islam, Dharma Radio, Jewish World Radio, and Bhajan Kirtan, to name just a few) illustrates both America's vibrant religious pluralism and its diversifying media universe in the 21st century, providing ample opportunities for further study of religious radio and its audiences.

Note

Sections of this chapter are excerpted from the author's book *Redeeming the Dial: Radio, Religion, and Popular Culture in America*, with permission from the University of North Carolina Press.

References

Ammerman, N. (1987). *Bible Believers: Fundamentalists in a Modern World*. New Brunswick, NJ: Rutgers University Press.

Blamey, M.V.J. (1937). Letter to Charles Fuller. Unpublished correspondence. Fuller Theological Seminary.

Bradley, M.E. (1954). Letter to Mr. Fuller. Unpublished correspondence. Fuller Theological Seminary.

Branham, M. a. M.G.E. (1937). Letter to Rev. Charles E. Fuller. Unpublished correspondence. Fuller Theological Seminary.

Budziszewski, J. (2006). *Evangelicals in the Public Square*. Grand Rapids, MI: Baker Academic.

Cadle, H. (1941). *Flying Preacher: One Night Revivals*. Indianapolis, IN: Cadle Tabernacle.

Cadle of Indianapolis Streamlines Evangelism with Radio, Airplane, Glass-Fronted Baptismal Tank. (1939). *Life*, 6, 73–77.

Cash and Cadle. (1939). *Time*, 33, 39.

Clayton, M.E. (1935). Letter to Charles Fuller. Unpublished correspondence. Fuller Theological Seminary.

Cooper, L.S. (1948). Letter to Rev. Chas E. Fuller. Unpublished correspondence. Fuller Theological Seminary.

Eaker, M. a. M.A. (1954). Letter to Mr. and Mrs. Fuller. Unpublished correspondence. Fuller Theological Seminary.

Echoes from Our Radio Audience. (1936). *Christian Beacon*, 27 (February), 5.

Erickson, H. (1992). *Religious Radio and Television in the United States, 1921–1991: Programs and Personalities*. Jefferson, NC: McFarland.

Eskridge, L.K. (1985). *Only Believe: Paul Radio and the Chicago Gospel Tabernacle, 1922–1933*. College Park: University of Maryland.

Fairbank, E. (1958). Letter to Rev. Fuller. Unpublished correspondence. Fuller Theological Seminary.

Family, F. o. t (2007). Retrieved from http://www.family.org/prayer, May 5, 2007.

Farmers Prefer Religious Radio. (1946). *United Evangelical Action*, March 1, 13.

Finke, R. & R. Stark. (1992). *The Churching of America: Winners and Losers in Our Religious Economy*. New Brunswick, NJ: Rutgers University Press.

Foursquare Firsts. (1973). Los Angeles: International Church of the Foursquare Gospel.

Giles, D. (2002). Parasocial Interaction: A Review of the Literature and a Model for Future Research. *Media Psychology*, 4 (3), 279–305.

Goldstein, I. (1942). Responsibilities and Opportunities of Religious Broadcasting. In J. H. MacLatchy (Ed.), *Education on the Air: Thirteenth Yearbook of the Institute for Education by Radio* (pp. 232–233). Columbus: Ohio State University Press.

Grundy, P. (1995). "We Always Tried to Be Good People": Respectability, Crazy Water Crystals, and Hillbilly Music on the Air, 1933–1935. *Journal of American History*, 81 (March), 1591–1620.

Hangen, T. (2002). *Redeeming the Dial: Radio, Religion, and Popular Culture in America*. Chapel Hill: University of North Carolina Press.

Hi-Ways and By-Ways. (1926a). *National Radio Chapel Announcer*, February, 27.

———. (1926b). *National Radio Chapel Announcer*, March, 29.

———. (1926c). *National Radio Chapel Announcer*, May.

Hoover, S.M. (1988). *Mass Media Religion: The Social Sources of the Electronic Church*. Newbury Park, CA: Sage.

Horton, D. & R.R. Wohl. (1956). Mass Communication and Para-Social Interactions: Observations on Intimacy at a Distance. *Psychiatry*, 19 (August), 215–229.

Hulsether, M. (1992). Evangelical Popular Religion As a Source for North American Liberation Theology? Insights from Postmodern Popular Culture Theory. *American Studies*, 33 (2), 63–81.

Jackson, K.T. (1985). *Crabgrass Frontier: The Suburbanization of the United States*. New York: Oxford University Press.

Jameson, F. (1979). Reification and Utopia in Mass Culture. *Social Text*, 1 (December), 130–148.

Johnson, F.B. (1925). The National Radio Chapel: What It Is. *National Radio Chapel Announcer*, December, 4.

Kennedy, J.W. (1997). Women Broadcasters Make Inroads, Slowly. *Christianity Today*, March 3, 66–67.

KFEL schedule, entry in Scrapbook 3, fall 1945–1954. (n.d.). Fuller Theological Seminary.

Kirby, J.T. (1987). *Rural Worlds Lost: The American South 1920–1960*. Baton Rouge: Louisiana State University Press.

Letter on Court Square (Jonesboro, AK) Drug Store letterhead. (1955). Unpublished correspondence. Fuller Theological Seminary.

Long, E. (1994). Textual Interpretation As Collective Action. In J. Cruz & J. Lewis (Eds.), *Viewing, Reading, Listening: Audiences and Cultural Reception* (pp. 181–211). Boulder, CO: Westview Press.

Macfarland, C. S. (1929). A Memorandum from Charles S. Macfarland to the Members of the Conference on Religious Publicity. Unpublished memorandum. National Council of Churches.

Martin-Barbero, J. (1993). *Communication, Culture and Hegemony: From the Media to Mediations* (E.F. a. R.A. White, Trans.). Newbury Park, CA: Sage.

Martin, W. (Ed.). (1988). *Encyclopedia of the American Religious Experience: Studies of Traditions and Movements*, volume 3. New York: Charles Scribner's Sons.

Miller, R.M. (1985). *Harry Emerson Fosdick: Preacher, Pastor, Prophet*. New York: Oxford University Press.

Nelson, P.M. (1996). *The Prairie Winnows Out Its Own: The West River Country of South Dakota in the Years of Depression and Dust*. Iowa City: University of Iowa Press.

Oldridge, M. (1937). Letter to Mr. and Mrs. Charles Fuller. Unpublished correspondence. Fuller Theological Seminary.

Ormiston, K.G. (1924). Listening In: Radio K.F.S.G. *Bridal Call Foursquare*, October, 30.

Orsi, R.A. (1998). *Thank You, St. Jude: Women's Devotion to the Patron Saint of Hopeless Causes*. New Haven, CT: Yale University Press.

Parker, C.E., D.W. Barry, & D.W. Smythe. (1955). *The Television-Radio Audience and Religion*. New York: Harper.

Peverill-Conti, G. (2007, 6 April). MIT Communications Forums—April 5—Evangelicals and the Media. Retrieved from http://www.ucredible.com/OTR/2007/04/06, May 23, 2007.

Powers, B. (2005). Nearly Half of All Americans Listen to Christian Radio. *National Religious Broadcasters*, March 23.

Rader, P. (1938). *Life's Greatest Adventure*. London: Victory Press.

———. (n.d.). *Paul Rader's Stories of His Early Life: Interspersed by Spiritual Messages of Priceless Value*. Chicago, IL: Chicago Gospel Tabernacle.

A Radio Message from the Cathedral of the Air. (1928). *World-Wide Christian Courier*, January, 8.

Radio Survey Shows Religion Is Popular. (1948). *United Evangelical Action*, September 1, 16.

Religious Programs Popular in Kentucky. (1946). *United Evangelical Action*, August 1, 11.

Riney-Kehrberg, P. (1994). *Rural Women and the Radio*. Paper presented at the Social Science History Association.

Rubin, A.M. (2000). Impact of Motivation, Attraction and Parasocial Interaction on Talk Radio Listening. *Journal of Broadcasting and Electronic Media*, 44 (4), 635–654.

Sandeen, E. (1970). *The Roots of Fundamentalism: British and American Millenarianism, 1800–1930*. Chicago: University of Chicago Press.

Saxe, F. (2000). Study Finds Fewer Radio Owners Since 1996. *Billboard*, 112 (September 30), 1–7.

Schultze, Q. J. (1988). Evangelical Radio and the Rise of the Electronic Church, 1921–1948. *Journal of Broadcasting and Electronic Media*, 32 (Summer), 289–306.

Slutz, T. (1995). Selling Christ: E. Howard Cadle's Big Business for God. Unpublished paper.

Smith, C. (2000). *Christian America? What Evangelicals Really Want*. Berkeley: University of California Press.

StateoftheNewsMedia.org. (2004). State of the News Media Report, 2004. Retrieved from http://www.stateofthenewsmedia.org/2004/narrative_radio_audience. asp?cat=3&media=8, 28 April 2007.

Stebbins, M.A.W. (1935). Letter to Charles Fuller. Unpublished correspondence. Fuller Theological Seminary.

Sweet, L.I. (1993). Communication and Change in American Religious History: A Historiographical Probe. In L.I. Sweet (Ed.), *Communication and Change in American Religious History* (pp. 1–90). Grand Rapids, MI: Eerdmans.

Trammel, M. (2007). Making Airwaves. *Christianity Today*, February.

Travis, C.C. (1950). Letter to Dr. Charles Fuller. Unpublished correspondence. Fuller Theological Seminary.

Tucker, W.L. (1918). *The Redemption of Paul Rader*. New York: The Book Stall.

Unsigned author from Leamington, O. (1942). Letter to Charles Fuller. Fuller Theological Seminary.

Voskuil, D. (1990). The Power of the Air: Evangelicals and the Rise of Religious Broadcasting. In Q.J. Schultze (Ed.), *American Evangelicals and the Mass Media: Perspectives on the Relationship between American Evangelicals and the Mass Media* (pp. 69–95). Grand Rapids, MI: Academie Books.

Ward, M., Sr. (1994). *Air of Salvation: The Story of Christian Broadcasting*. Grand Rapids, MI: Baker Book House.

Way, F. (1954). Letter to Charles Fuller. Unpublished correspondence. Fuller Theological Seminary.

9. Broadcasting Unionism: Labor and FM Radio in Postwar America

ELIZABETH FONES-WOLF

On June 24, 1948, the leading officers of the United Automobile Workers (UAW) union rode in a quiet motorcade to a vacant lot in the northwest section of Detroit where they broke ground for the autoworkers' new non-profit FM radio station, WDET. At the ceremony, they promised that a "new deal" in radio was coming to the motor city (Electrons, 1948, 12). This new deal represented labor's chance to stake a claim in the broadcasting industry. Across the nation, corporate interests had ruled the airwaves, using radio to promote their political and economic ideology while restricting the voices of unions and other minority groups. By the mid-1940s, labor had succeeded in overcoming some of the barriers to access, but unions still chafed at censorship and denial of airtime. The UAW hoped that WDET would carry labor's unfiltered voice directly to the public, enabling unions to contest business more effectively for the loyalty of the working class. However, the autoworkers also promised that the entire community would benefit from labor broadcasting. Instead of the dismal offerings of commercial stations, WDET promised high-quality programming, exceptional variety, and a forum for all groups and classes to participate in free speech and discussion unparalleled in the history of radio. It was to be a community station that emphasized the "real needs and interests of the people" (Electrons, 1948, 13).

WDET was one of five FM stations launched by the UAW and the International Ladies' Garment Workers' Union (ILGWU) in the late 1940s. Unionists expected these stations to serve as a model for a new kind of socially progressive, culturally uplifting, nonprofit, community-oriented broadcasting. By focusing on economic, social, and political issues mostly ignored by mainstream radio, labor broadcasting would educate and mobilize listeners, thereby improving the lives of millions of Americans. Just as organized labor had "forged an industrial democracy in the plant," labor stations would "create a kind of electronic democracy in radio" (Electrons, 1948, 13). The union experiment with FM, however, was short-lived. By the end of 1952, all the stations had returned their licenses to the Federal Communications Commission (FCC) and were off the air, the victims in part of the larger problems facing FM radio in finding an audience during the 1950s and of hostility toward organized labor. While discouraged by the failure of their stations, unions did not turn their backs on broadcasting, although they significantly narrowed their vision. In the 1950s, unions developed a considerable local and national media presence on commercial AM stations, but never again were they an important force in the movement to reform broadcasting. Labor's FM stations represent yet another road not taken in the quest for a more democratic broadcasting system.

Early Labor Radio

The mass media, beginning with newspapers and then movies, radio, and television, has always been a critical area of conflict between business and organized labor in the United States. Generally, a corporate-controlled media has projected a negative image of unions as greedy, corrupt, violent and un-American. Newspapers, for instance, tended to turn a cold shoulder to unions, burying labor news in the back pages or ignoring it altogether. When the mainstream press did cover a labor story, such as a strike or other dramatic industrial conflict, it inevitably cast unions in an unflattering light (Puette, 1992).

The rise of radio shook the foundations of the American media system. Broadcasting offered minority voices such as labor a chance to contest corporate control of the media. From its inception in the 1920s, radio exerted a powerful influence on American society. It transcended spatial boundaries, blurring the private domestic and public sphere and reshaping American culture and politics (Douglas, 1999). Excited about its possibilities, in the early 1920s, hundreds of small stations, many operated by churches, universities, and other nonprofit groups interested in public service, took to the air (McChesney, 1993). A few union leaders in the 1920s also recognized radio's unique power. The most significant result of this early interest was the establishment in the mid-1920s of a small, listener-supported, labor-owned station in Chicago, WCFL, and of a Socialist-owned station WEVD in New York City, which had close ties to labor (Godfried, 1997).[1] By the end of the decade, however, once business realized that there were profits to be made in radio advertising, the medium rapidly became commercialized. A new regulatory regime reallocated frequencies and power assignments, benefiting the larger commercial stations to the detriment of the smaller nonprofit stations, most of which were ultimately forced off the air. By the

1930s, the network-dominated, advertising-driven broadcasting system was in place, and critics were already complaining about drivel on the air and the medium's failure to serve the public interest (McChesney, 1993).

Having experimented with broadcasting in the 1920s, unions soon recognized its incisive power. During the 1930s, a resurgent labor movement spurred on by a crop of youthful labor leaders associated with the newly formed Congress of Industrial Organizations (CIO) sought more fully to exploit the possibilities inherent in this new medium. They understood that radio, which reached directly into the comfort of workers' homes and thus bypassed employer intimidation, could serve effectively as a tool for organizing and union building and as a means of constructing an oppositional community within the working class. Unionists took to the air, sponsoring an array of programs on smaller, local, non-network stations that helped fuel the massive upsurge of organized labor in Depression-era America (Fones-Wolf, 2000).

However, there were significant barriers to labor's access to the air and to its freedom to speak its mind. The networks and most larger stations refused to sell time to unions, deeming their programming too controversial. While they also avoided selling airtime for some of the most partisan business programs, they welcomed shows such as Henry Ford's *Ford Sunday Evening Hour*, which preached the virtues of American capitalism and ignored the antilabor diatribes of business-sponsored commentators (Fones-Wolf, 1999). When labor could secure airtime, stations routinely censored union scripts. An irate R.J. Thomas, president of the UAW, asked why radio stations gave "free rein to notorious demagogues and unscrupulous foes of our union and the CIO," while the autoworkers had "difficulty in purchasing an adequate amount of time from the larger stations" (United Automobile Workers, 1940, 50). During World War II, the CIO launched a multipronged campaign to open the airwaves to labor and with the help of sympathetic elements of the FCC began to puncture the barriers to labor broadcasting. Nevertheless, in the late 1940s, radio stations in some communities continued to censor unions or exclude them from the air (Fones-Wolf, 2000).

Labor and Postwar Media Reform

In the postwar period, labor joined a chorus of voices that argued radio was controlled by advertisers. They blamed weak-kneed broadcasters for tasteless and often dishonest commercials and charged that most programming, which advertisers shaped to their own special interest, was mediocre (Wang, 2002). Critics worried about the dangers of media monopoly and about big business's tremendous influence over what Americans heard about national and world issues. Unionists also linked radio's problems to the patterns of ownership in the broadcasting industry. According to the CIO, a relatively small group of manufacturers, bankers, and newspaper chains owned the vast majority of the most powerful stations. It was no coincidence that newspapers denounced labor during strikes and that unions struggled for access to the airwaves (Free Press, 1947; Money behind the Headlines, 1947).

One approach to improving broadcasting was greater regulation, a tack taken by the FCC, which in 1946 issued a report, *Public Service Responsibility of Broadcast Licensees*, known more popularly as the Blue Book. It was a groundbreaking document that pushed broadcasters to take seriously their public service responsibilities by giving airtime to nonprofit educational, civic, religious, agricultural, and labor organizations. The FCC also championed the concept of localism. To reduce network control over broadcasting and provide an opportunity for community participation in radio, it called for stations to emphasize live local programming (Hillard & Keith, 2005).

More oversight might improve the existing AM broadcasting system, but for groups such as organized labor a more effective solution was ownership of their own stations. After World War II, the emergence of FM broadcasting, which offered more channels and better sound quality than AM, provided a second chance to create a more democratic and diverse broadcasting medium. This new system could potentially break the monopoly control of advertisers and networks over radio and open station ownership to previously excluded groups such as labor (Mosco, 1979). In 1944, the CIO warned that unless labor took speedy action to get in on the ground floor, FM broadcasting "will become monopolized by the same interests that now control AM broadcasting and the daily press" (Congress of Industrial Organization, 1944, 238). It urged that three-fourths of the new FM channels be reserved for veterans, farm, cooperative, labor, and citizens groups and that higher standards of public service be established for all broadcasters (Fones-Wolf, 2000). The possibilities of FM broadcasting quickly caught the imagination of organized labor, and many unionists flirted with the idea of operating their own media outlet. By the end of 1945, 19 unions and groups with labor connections had filed applications for FM stations (Riesel, 1945).

Labor's FM Goals

Ultimately, most of the FM licenses went to existing AM stations or to newspaper interests. However, for a short while, in a small number of communities, labor was able to reach the public through its own stations. By mid-1949, the ILGWU and the UAW had five FM stations on the air. They joined WCFL, the Chicago Federation of Labor's AM station, and WCFM, a Washington, DC, cooperative FM station, in an informal liberal-labor network that shared some programming. The ILGWU stations were located in New York City, Chattanooga, Tennessee, and Los Angeles and the UAW stations in Detroit and Cleveland (Union Network, 1949). By building a station in Chattanooga, the garment workers hoped to strengthen labor's presence in the South (Novik, 1985). The other cities contained high concentrations of garment or auto workers. Indeed almost three-fourths of the UAW's membership lived in the reception area of the union's Cleveland (WCUO) and Detroit (WDET) stations. Operating at 52,000 watts, WDET was one of the most powerful FM stations in the country, reaching towns within a 60-mile radius of Detroit (United Automobile Workers, 1949, 1950).

A deep commitment to education and political action drew the ILGWU and the UAW to FM radio. Both unions historically pursued sweeping, innovative social agendas that reached far beyond the workshop confines. Radio seemed the perfect medium to send labor's message out on the streets and into people's homes. To the ILGWU, operating FM stations was a natural extension of its ongoing educational and political activity (Tyler, 1995). It offered an array of recreational, social, and cultural activities designed to make unionism a way of life. Similarly, the UAW was a strong advocate of education and was a politically engaged, socially active institution that fought not only for better contracts to benefit members but also for social and political reforms designed to improve the lives of all Americans (Boyle, 1995).

UAW president Walter Reuther believed that if labor was to counteract powerful corporate forces, unions needed to reach the public with labor's message. He believed that the UAW could make its Detroit station, WDET, "a powerful instrument for propaganda free news." According to Reuther, the importance of impartial coverage could not be overestimated, especially "in a city like Detroit where the daily newspapers consistently distort the news."[2] Similarly, the ILGWU's New York City station symbolically took the call letters WFDR. At its opening, ILGWU president David Dubinsky promised that the station would be a voice not only for labor but also for progressive politics (FDR's Genius, 1949). Indeed labor's FM stations would provide an outlet for liberal voices that had been silenced by the commercial media. Unions intended to create a "new kind of democracy on the air" by cutting through the "iron curtains" that hid the "inequalities and injustices" of the American economic and political system.[3] FM radio also offered an important means of communicating with the rank and file, helping to make "them disciplined trade unionists, militant social democrats, and racial egalitarians" (Lichtenstein, 1995, 300).

Labor's FM stations were designed to give the community a radio voice. Reuther believed that FM radio provided a unique opportunity for unions to serve the community while advancing labor's political and economic goals. Indeed, Reuther regularly argued that what was good "for the community as a whole is good for the union and its members."[4] Labor's FM stations, which would operate on a nonprofit basis without excessive commercialization, planned to open the air to all groups, races, and religions. Although the stations aimed to support themselves by selling some advertising, the unions promised that at least 50% of the programming would be noncommercial (Labor in Radio, 1947). The ILGWU intended to make WFDR "the most articulate town meeting hall, the outstanding music hall, the most attractive cultural center in the community" (Umhey, 1945, 11). Similarly, WDET wanted to be the "people's station, where all the problems, social, political, economic—which affect labor and the community generally can be talked about openly and honestly."[5] To ensure that its stations were receptive to the needs of the community, the UAW established advisory boards of community, religious, and minority leaders to help develop broadcasting policies and programming (WDET-FM, 1948).[6]

Morris Novik, who served as radio consultant to both the ILGWU and the UAW, helped in large part to shape programming for labor's FM stations. Many of Novik's ideas came from his experience as program director during the 1930s of the Socialist Party's New York City station, WEVD, and of New York City's community station, WNYC (Godfried, 2001; FM, 1948). He would later become one of the leaders in educational radio and television. Novik worked closely with all the labor FM stations, providing advice on programming, technical issues, hiring personnel, and marketing. Like most radio reformers, he was disgusted with the excessive commercialism of American broadcasting and with the failure of radio to provide public service to the community. Novik endorsed the goals of the FCC's Blue Book and believed that FM gave labor the opportunity to show how a local station could effectively serve the public interest. He urged labor-owned stations to avoid serving as special peddlers for organized labor, advising unions instead to operate as community stations that featured serious music and unbiased news, promoted local talent, and most importantly developed a wide range of public service programming (Novik interview, 1985; Novik, 1950b).[7]

Labor Programming

Labor's FM stations emphasized cultural and educational programming and avoided the types of programs that radio critics considered the worst examples of advertising excess and poor taste, especially soap operas, mystery shows, and children's adventure stories.[8] Instead, the stations carried quality children's programs and "intelligent discussion" of community and national problems as well as music and the news (Electrons, 1948, 12). The music varied, but most of the stations broadcast more classical and semiclassical than popular music. With a bit of initial trepidation about the size of the potential audience for classical music, WCUO offered a symphony program nightly. However, its misgivings were soon dispelled by letters and phone calls from hundreds of listeners, and *This Is Music* became one of the most popular classical programs in Cleveland.[9]

Although the focus was on highbrow culture, labor's FM stations also sought to represent the authentic expressions of the people. The ILGWU's stations in New York and Los Angles, for example, mixed in jazz and folk music with programs featuring the symphony, ballet, and opera. The ILGWU's Chattanooga station carried classical music but also embraced its Southern roots with gospel shows, hillbilly, and country music.[10] Local programming was a priority, and labor stations provided a platform for broadcasting the work of local musicians and small theater groups (Novik, 1950b; Along Radio Row, 1949).

Union FM stations provided a platform for liberal and labor voices that were often ignored by the commercial media. WFDR and the two UAW stations, for instance, broadcast *A Liberal Look at the News*, a daily evening program developed by Morris Novik. It featured commentary on national and international events by prominent liberals including Robert Nathan, a progressive economist who helped shape the CIO's postwar economic policy, John Carmody, a former New Dealer, and John Herling, Washington correspondent of the International Labor News Service (Laboring Voice, 1949). Former California congresswoman and prominent Democratic liberal Helen Gahagan Douglas, who was red-baited during the 1946 election by Richard Nixon, provided the ILGWU's Los Angeles station with reports on the Washington political scene. Beginning in January 1950, all the labor stations broadcast the *Washington Report*, which featured journalists Joseph C. Harsh and Marquis Childs, both of whom had impeccable liberal credentials (ILGWU Stations, 1950).[11]

Local labor commentators also put a liberal spin on their news analysis, presenting labor's perspective on local and national questions and shedding light on issues overlooked by the mainstream press. In Detroit, WDET carried the *Voice of the CIO*, a Sunday afternoon program with labor editor Ted Olgar. During early 1950, Olgar exposed inequities in the tax laws, advocating plugging loopholes that allowed rich companies to avoid 500 million dollars each year in taxes and publicizing the CIO's program for an excess profits tax on corporations and higher income tax exemptions for low-income families. He also took Michigan Republicans to task for undermining efforts to improve the state's unemployment compensations law and admonished Congress for passing a "toothless, spineless" Fair Employment Practices bill that had no provision for enforcement but instead relied on ineffective voluntary compliance. Declaring the congressional debate on the Fair Employment Practices Commission (FEPC) "a shameful exhibition,"

Olgar urged that "all distinctions between men in America—based on race, color or creed—must disappear." The labor commentator regularly defended the welfare state, noting that business leaders who equated social security and public housing with communism ignored government benefi-cence to corporations in the form of subsidies and tax breaks.[12]

Guy Nunn's daily news and commentary program over WDET was the most popular of the FM labor news shows. Nunn's commentary took con-servatives and business to task in a hard-hitting, caustic style and regularly exposed the biases of the commercial press. In a typical swipe at the Detroit media, which the UAW viewed as mouthpieces for the auto industry, Nunn charged that the Detroit *Free Press* editorials were so poisonous against labor that their sale "should be made illegal unless accompanied by a stomach pump" (UAW Newscaster, 1949, 10). In June 1950, he observed that *Free Press* regularly rose up "in fearless wrath and indignation" at the supposed cheat-ing by "some sick and aged welfare recipient" but earnestly defended the "streamlined extortion practiced by big-time advertisers."[13] Like Olgar, Nunn was a staunch advocate of civil rights. Frustrated with moderate congressio-nal Democrats who failed to support civil rights legislation, he observed that unlike Dixiecrats, these politicians did not "scream their heads off against civil rights" but did little to advance the cause. As Nunn saw it, on issues as important as fair employment and lynching, "a sin of omission is as great as any other." He warned that labor considered it "high time that some of Mr. Truman's old but not so reliable wheel-horses were put out to pasture."[14]

Public service was a top priority for labor's FM stations. As one reviewer observed, the audience of "KFMV, WDET and WCUO must take Gilbert and Sullivan, Beethoven and an occasional play with generous sprinklings of the American Cancer Society, health programs, [and] the U.N. Story."[15] Among the UAW's Detroit station's public service offerings were *You and Your Health*, a show produced in cooperation with the city's health department, and *WDET Roundtable*, a weekly half-hour discussion program devoted to cur-rent local legislative, social, and economic issues. City officials and commu-nity representatives tackled issues ranging from schools to taxes, recreation, housing, and smoke abatement. *Great Books on the Air* featured "ordinary everyday" people, including prisoners broadcasting from the Detroit House of Correction and a group from the tuberculosis ward at the Dearborn Vet-erans' Hospital, tackling the classics from Plato to Aristotle and Sophocles. Beyond regularly scheduled programming, the station stepped up to the bat to aid the community during times of crisis. For instance, at the height of Detroit's infantile paralysis epidemic, WDET produced a series of special programs with the city's health authorities to counteract parents' hysteria and allay the fears of the community.[16]

WFDR's public service programs included *Civil Defense Reporter*, a weekly roundup of civil defense news, *The Power in Your Purse*, a consumer co-op program (WFDR Goes on Air, 1950), and *Skidmore Scans the Books*, a Sunday afternoon book discussion program featuring professors at Skidmore College. A *Variety* reviewer found the Skidmore program, which was also broadcast by the labor stations in Chattanooga and Cleveland, "listenable and literate" and not "too highbrow" (Skidmore, 1950). Intent on addressing civic issues affecting the lives of listeners, in December 1949 WFDR responded to a municipal water crisis with a special Wednesday night program with city officials and on-the-scenes reports explaining why water was scarce (Water Crisis, 1949). The ILGWU's Chattanooga outlet was the first radio station in the city to take its microphones into City Hall to broadcast public hearings on community problems (Novik, 1950a).

Labor's FM stations openly engaged in controversial issues. Among WDET's special programs in 1949 was a forum on "What Should Michigan Do about the Sex Deviate?" It also provided coverage of an American Civil Liberties Union conference considering whether Communists' civil rights were being violated, while WCUO in Cleveland aired a dramatic show titled *Daddy, Am I White?*, billed as the "true experience of a Negro in war and peace" (Novik, 1950a, 45).[17] In sharp contrast to commercial stations, labor stations broadcast much of their public interest programming in prime evening hours, reversing the practice of most broadcasters, who gave their best times to programs that were "shoddy but salable" (On the Air, 1949).

Also unlike commercial stations, union broadcasters reflected the diversity of American society. For instance, foreign-language programming that had been abandoned by commercial stations found a new home at WDET (WDET, 1949). Mainstream radio also largely ignored African Americans in both hiring and programming policies (Savage, 1999; Ward, 2004). These were inequities that labor's FM stations sought to ameliorate (For Better Listening, 1946). Dedicated to combating racial discrimination, WDET was the first Detroit station to appoint African Americans to its professional staff, placing Jerry Hemphill, a composer and music instructor, in charge of musical programming and making Bob Gill staff director. In addition, WDET featured black deejay Ernie Durham, who spun jazz and popular music weekdays in the early afternoon.[18] Other union-owned stations also promoted black on-air talent. Recognizing that the Los Angeles African American community had "no radio voice," the ILGWU station broadcast the Joe Adams Show, featuring a black disc jockey. The garment workers' station in Chattanooga aired a show spotlighting African American teens that earned immediate attention from an appreciative black community. Station manager Joe Siegel reported that "Negroes stop me on the street and thank me because the station carried the program."[19]

Union stations often addressed racial issues that local broadcasters ignored or deemed too controversial. The ILGWU's Chattanooga station,

WVUN, supported the campaign to overturn the poll tax, broadcasting the plea of the "man in the street" to be allowed to register and vote (Novik, 1950a; FM, 1948). Fighting racism was a top priority for the UAW's Detroit station. Located in a city where racial tensions were constant and formidable, WDET aimed to promote interracial understanding and to advance the cause of civil rights. Programs such as *Community Clinic*, a roundtable discussion moderated by members of the Detroit Mayor's Interracial Committee, endeavored to combat discrimination and bigotry. Each Monday evening, members of the Mayor's committee and special guests from the community wrestled with contentious civil rights issues such as employment discrimination, segregation in housing, and the relationship between the police and minorities.[20]

WDET paid special attention to housing, which was a particularly controversial racial issue in Detroit. In March 1950, for instance, it was the only Detroit station to broadcast a two-hour Detroit Common Council hearing on re-zoning a neighborhood to prevent the construction of a union-backed cooperative housing project that was committed to racial integration. Crowded galleries at the hearing reflected the intense community interest in the issue. WDET's broadcast enabled listeners to hear civic, labor, and religious leaders defend "interracial living" as well as neighborhood property owners deny that their objections to the development were based in racial prejudice.[21]

Bolstering Unionism

Labor's FM stations also shone the spotlight on union activities. Programs such as WDET's *Inside the UAW Political Action Committee* and KFMV's *This is Labor and Labor and You* kept members aware of union activities and developments (KFMV's First Year, 1949). WDET's weekly program *Brother Chairman* visited a different local each week, introducing the listeners to officers who discussed the local's history and activities. The UAW's magazine *Ammunition* claimed that when "some of the people start to talk on this program, you can almost hear the foreman coming up behind you in the shop, it brings your shop experiences so close to you" (Turn It On, 1950, 10). Larger locals, such as Ford Local 600 and Dodge Main Local 212, spoke directly to members through their own programs. These shows, produced, written, and performed by rank-and-file members, served as an outlet for workers' self-expression.[22] As Jerry Sherman of Local 3 saw it, part of WDET's mission was to serve as an "extension of the actual voices of honest-to-God, rank-and-file trade union people!" Indeed, like later community stations, labor stations encouraged the participation of listeners. Paul Morris, WDET's publicist, urged listeners to join the UAW choral group, which performed regularly on the station. No professional training was required. "All you need," he declared, "[is] an old rusty windpipe and the will to warble. That's no reflection on the caliber of the group," Morris hastily added . To encourage rank-and-file participation, the UAW offered classes in broadcasting techniques. Young talent, including musicians, composers, and singers, such as those in the choral group, gained valuable training through the union stations.[23]

Unlike the mainstream media, workers could count on equitable treatment from labor's FM stations. WFDR's May 1951 broadcast *Strike in Danville*, for instance, provided the public with an unbiased account of a bitter two-month strike against the Dan River Mills that involved 12,000 cotton mill workers. In sharp contrast to the media's typical coverage of labor conflict, the ILGWU program allowed union leaders and strikers themselves to speak as well as management spokespeople. *Variety* praised the broadcast as "sharp and gripping ... adult radio at its best" (Strike in Danville, 1951).

WDET provided even more direct support to the workers during labor conflict. Detroit's three daily papers sided with management during the 1949 Ford strike and the 1950 Chrysler strike. As a result, autoworkers relied on WDET for coverage of their side of the dispute. The UAW FM station was on the picket lines from the start, recording spontaneous comments from the marchers. It went into union halls and interviewed local officers, committeemen, and soup kitchen operators, giving the public a "true picture of what actually goes on inside a local hall during a strike" (WDET-FM, 1949). A sound truck fitted with an FM tuner broadcast Guy Nunn's evening news commentary, which included progress reports on the strike, to the men and women on the picket lines.[24] Emil Mazey recalled that "these broadcasts were terrific morale builders," for "every picket knew that his story was being beamed to thousands of listeners in southeastern Michigan." During the Chrysler strike, Guy Nunn added a special series of weekday afternoon programs to his regular evening broadcast. Hundreds of Chrysler workers gathered in their local union halls to hear Nunn's latest strike news as well as interviews with striking union members. Special bulletins provided information about union meetings and about how to obtain strike assistance from local community service committees. To help boost morale, every Saturday night WDET broadcast amateur night programs, featuring songs, music, and comedy performed by Chrysler strikers and their families (WDET Stages, 1950).[25] While the station was certainly sympathetic to strikers, unlike the mainstream media, it strove to be evenhanded in its coverage of the controversy. During both the Ford and Chrysler strikes, it offered time to the corporations. When the companies refused to speak for themselves, the station prided itself in presenting management's case with "scrupulous detail."[26]

The UAW and the ILGWU both actively promoted their stations. Like many FM outlets in the early 1950s, labor stations struggled to find an audience. One difficulty was the shortage of inexpensive FM receivers, which the unions tried to address by offering low-cost FM converters to their members and by making arrangements with dealers for discounts on new sets (Zenith Set, 1950). To increase the audience, they attached cards with the station's schedules to new FM receivers in local stores, ran listener contests, placed banners on city buses, and plastered posters in union halls. Mildred Jeffrey, head of the UAW Radio Department, urged local officers to encourage members to buy receivers, pointing out that the success of the UAW's program was "in direct proportion to the number of conscientious loyal members."[27]

The desire to draw union listeners and to boost audience size led to differences over the stations' programming philosophies. Novik urged that labor's FM stations define themselves primarily as community stations that emphasized high-quality programming and that they should avoid being too closely identified with their union sponsors. Although classical music and public service certainly remained signature elements of all the labor stations' programming, Novik made a stronger imprint on the ILGWU's stations, especially in New York and Los Angeles, than on the UAW stations. UAW president Walter Reuther, who took an active interest in the operation of the WDET and WCUO, wanted them to project a strong public identification with the autoworkers. He also desired more distinctly labor programs that advocated the economic and political goals of the UAW as well as popular programming attractive to working-class listeners. Mildred Jeffrey agreed that while "we want to make both stations community-minded in their general orientation ... in the final analysis we are not going to make WDET a success unless we build up first of all a loyal and devoted group of listeners among UAW and organized labor."[28]

As a result, WDET and WCUO began to emphasize their ties to labor, broadcasting announcements such as "This is Station WDET-FM, owned and operated by a million members of the UAW-CIO" and expanding their union-oriented programming. They also scheduled more popular music, ranging from Dixieland to light classical, and more sports and worked harder to involve members. Detroit began live broadcasts of the *Fight of the Week* (WDET to Air, 1950) and the Cleveland station aired high school football games (Cleveland Hears, 1949) and amateur radio shows featuring members and their families.[29] Seeking to attract autoworkers' children with lighter programming, WDET created *Teen Tempo*. A group of teenagers with aid from the station staff produced the show, which was broadcast on Saturday mornings. The program included music, a teen book of the week, high school notes, and appearances by visiting show business celebrities. Early guests included Bob Hope, musician Spike Jones, singer Lena Horne, and President Truman's daughter, Margaret. Seeking to broaden its audience, the ILGWU's Chattanooga station reached out to religiously minded workers with broadcasts of revival meetings, including one led by a nine-year-old preacher.[30]

Many listeners appreciated WDET's broadcasts of classical music and enjoyed the educational programming. For Charles Adrian, WDET was a "breath of *fresh air.*" C.J. Major of Wyandotte, Michigan, enjoyed the radio concerts, observing that it was "gratifying ... that at least one station in this area tries to satisfy the tastes of true music lovers." Another listener found the station to be a "bright spot in the generally dismal and depressing condition" of Detroit radio.[31] Others reported that they regularly listened to Guy Nunn for the "true slant of the news." One Detroit couple tuned into WDET religiously. For them, the evening symphony hour was "very precious and a wonderful antidote after a dull day at work." Moreover, the "speeches and treatment of economic problems" were "gems." Marion H. Bemis, assistant director of the Citizens' Housing and Planning Council of Detroit, particularly enjoyed the symphony hour and the *Great Books* roundtable discussion. She urged station manager Ben Hoberman to stand firm against any pressure to popularize the station's programming. The station did more than preach to the choir. Bemis reported that one of her workers who was "exceedingly antiunion" regularly listened to WDET. "Perhaps," she hoped "you are making some converts whether you know it or not."[32]

Accolades and Problems

Labor's FM stations quickly won numerous accolades. A Southern California listeners' group praised KFMV's programming, and in March 1951 the Los Angeles city council passed a resolution commending the union for operating KFMV in the public interest.[33] In 1950, KFMV and WFDR earned awards in Billboard's annual radio promotion competition, with WFDR being recognized for innovations in FM programming (KFMW, WFDR, 1950). That year KFMV was nominated for a Peabody Radio Award (Novik, 1950a), and WDET won a *Variety* Show Management award, one of radio's top industry honors. The station's strong commitment to civil rights particularly impressed *Variety* (Postwar-Station, 1950). Finally, during 1951, WFDR won one of media's most coveted citations, the Page One Award of the Newspaper Guild of New York as well as a *Variety* award. The guild award cited the station for consistently championing "liberalism and labor's rights" and "for its responsibility to the public" (WFDR, 1951). *Variety* applauded WFDR for recognizing that many New Yorkers were tired of soap operas and whodunits and wanted programming "produced with intelligence and imagination for adult minds" (WFDR, 1951).

Despite the acclaim won by union stations, labor's experiment with FM was short-lived. By the spring of 1952, financial losses had forced all of the stations off the air, leaving a void unfilled by mainstream radio. *Justice*, the ILGWU's newspaper, observed that in a medium "swamped with commercialism," WFDR had provided an "auditory oasis for the intelligent listener" (WFDR Signs Off, 1952). Secretary-treasurer Emil Mazey regretted Detroit was losing the only station that "had the courage to air consistently controversial issues and present differing viewpoints" on such critical issues as labor struggles, civil rights, housing, and race relations.[34] Daniel Strassberg of New York City was shocked when he learned of WFDR's impending closing and mourned the loss of the city's "only progressive radio voice" (Strassberg, 1952). Similarly, the discontinuation of WDET brought sadness to a Detroit machinist. He wrote that "it is one of the best stations in the area and we need more like it." For Chattanooga station manager Joe Seigel, the closing of his station struck a critical blow at efforts to promote liberalism and labor in the South. He observed that "this city desperately needs a liberal outlet" and predicted that the station's demise "will be bad for the union and unionism."[35]

Labor's FM quest was a victim of the radio industry's refusal to promote FM, the manufacturers' unwillingness to promote low-cost AM-FM receivers, and increasing competition from television (International Ladies' Garment Workers' Union, 1950, 1953).[36] In some cities, newspapers refused to publish FM station broadcasting schedules. Despite an aggressive UAW campaign to encourage workers and others to purchase FM sets, in the early 1950s FM ownership among auto workers was still "woefully small."[37] It would be more than a decade before a large FM audience materialized. In March 1952, radio analyst Saul Carson regretfully observed that "there was hope in FM a few years ago. That's gone now" (Carson, 1952, 23). Labor stations' format, with its stress on classical music and public interest programming, may have also hindered the formation of a substantial audience. Surveys showed that most listeners were professionals, intellectuals, and other members of the middle class (WFDR Skirts Axe, 1952). The ILGWU and the UAW had trouble justifying continued investment in a medium that was missing an important part of their target audience.[38]

Finally, animosity and suspicion toward unions hurt some of the labor stations. In Detroit, the school board rejected WDET's proposal to broadcast high school football games, which the station hoped would increase audiences. Guy Nunn concluded that there was "little question that CIO prejudice went into the decision."[39] Although the stations were nonprofit, the unions had expected to sell enough advertising to help pay station expenses. Station staff searched high and low for advertisers to help cover operational costs. Trading on workers' consumer power, they targeted local merchants who wanted labor's good will as well as labor's business. WDET also sought sponsorship from larger firms with which the UAW had union contracts. Union stations, however, had great difficulty finding sponsors, mostly because of the small FM audience. There was also a reluctance among many advertisers to be associated with union-owned stations, especially in times of labor conflict. In May 1949, during the Ford strike, for instance, several merchants who were considering sponsoring programs backed out, fearful that it would appear that they were endorsing the strike. After almost a year on the air, it had become clear to Mildred Jeffrey that advertisers "both large and small" were suspicious that WDET would be a "CIO propaganda outlet" and thus withheld their business.[40]

Beyond FM

By the spring of 1952, labor's venture into FM broadcasting had ended. The Chicago Federation of Labor's AM station, WCFL, was the only union station still broadcasting. It, however, was increasingly operated like a conventional commercial station and was in the process of slowly deemphasizing its labor connection (Godfried, 1997). The union voice, however, did not disappear from broadcasting. Despite the failure of labor's experiment with FM, organized labor remained committed in the 1950s to using the mass media to reach its members and the public. In the postwar years, local labor programs sprang up in communities across the nation. By the early 1950s, Michigan alone had 16 weekly local CIO radio shows. Unions also developed a significant nationwide voice over network radio. Listeners commonly heard union leaders spar with their corporate counterparts on the networks' public affairs and news programs on both radio and television. In an effort to build an even larger audience, the AFL and the CIO began buying network airtime, sponsoring daily evening radio broadcasts that reached millions of Americans (Fones-Wolf, 2000). By the late 1960s, however, as the labor movement settled into a somnolent complacency, unionists discontinued much of their broadcasting activities.

For a brief period after World War II, unions were at the forefront of a now largely forgotten campaign for a more democratic media. Organized labor established ambitious goals for its FM radio stations, which they hoped would serve as a model for a new type of nonprofit, culturally uplifting, public service–oriented broadcasting. For a time, these stations produced some of the most innovative programming on the air. By emphasizing the community interest, the ILGWU and the UAW challenged America's commercial broadcasting system, which stressed profits over public service. This commitment to the community placed these unions at the forefront of an effort to democratize broadcasting. Ambitious unionists, however, had perhaps too lofty expectations about their ability to change American broadcasting and perhaps not enough understanding of the many barriers that they would face.

Notes

1. At the same time, labor's only station, the lower-powered WCFL, faced a desperate struggle for survival in a hostile political climate, which resulted in it becoming increasingly commercialized over the years (Godfried, 1997).
2. Walter P. Reuther to Sir and Brother, April 18, 1949, Paul E. Miley to Sirs and Brothers, Aug. 5, 1947, both in box 14, Mildred Jeffrey Papers (hereafter Jeffrey Papers), Archives of Labor and Urban Affairs (hereafter ALUA), Wayne State University, Detroit, MI.
3. Notes on WDET-FM, ca. June 1948, box 11, Jeffrey Papers; Reuther to Sir and Brother, April 18, 1949, box 14, Jeffrey Papers.
4. "Six Non-Profit Davids and the Commercial Goliath: Labor Hits the Air As the Networks Hit the Skids," ca. May 1950, box 11, Jeffrey Papers.
5. Untitled flyer on "Community Clinic," ca. Feb. 1949, box 15, Jeffrey Papers.
6. Walter Reuther to all Local Unions in the WDET Reception Area, June 10, 1949, box 146, Walter Reuther Papers, ALUA; Mildred Jeffrey to Hardy Merril, Dec. 3, 1948, box 14, Jeffrey Papers; Notes on WDET-FM, ca. July 1948, box 11, Jeffrey Papers.
7. UAW Executive Board Minutes, March 1–6, 1948, box 5, ALUA; Morris Novik, "Radio," box 1, Morris Novik Papers, Broadcast Pioneers Library, University of Maryland, College Park, MD; M.S. Novik, "Do We Need a New National Policy for Radio and Television: Labor's View," Twentieth Institute for Education by Radio, Ohio State University, May 4, 1950, box 8, Jeffrey Papers.
8. In many ways the labor station's programming was similar to that of KPFA, Pacifica's first station, which went on the air in 1949 and is commonly viewed as one of the nation's first community stations. Pacifica's historian, Matthew Lasar (2000), has described KPFA's programming as "hybrid highbrow," which included classical music, folk jazz, contemporary poetry and drama, and public service–oriented lectures and discussions.
9. Labor's F.M. Radio Stations, n.d., box 10, Jeffrey Papers.
10. Pat Peterman report, ca. Nov. 1950, box 8, Jeffrey Papers; KFMV Sept. 1950 Program Schedule, box 41, Joe Siegel to Frederick Umhey, Nov. 18, 1948, March 16, 1949, box 47, Frederick F. Umhey Papers (hereafter Umhey Papers), Kheel Center for Labor-Management Documentation and Archives, Cornell University, Ithaca, NY (hereafter KCLMDA).
11. Report on the Progress of KFMV since Opening, n.d., box 3, Morris Novik Papers, George Meany Memorial Archives, Silver Spring, MD.
12. "WCUO Publicity: Programs of Interest to Every Union Member," n.d., box 14, Jeffrey Papers; *Voice of the CIO*, scripts, Feb. 12, 19, 26, March 12, box 1, UAW Radio Department Papers, 1984 Acc., ALUA.
13. News Release, "How Clean Is the Commercial Press," ca. June 15, 1950, box 147, Walter Reuther Papers, ALUA.
14. *Labor Views the News* Script, undated, ca. May 1950, box 7, Jeffrey Papers.
15. Pat Peterman report, ca. Nov. 1950, box 8, Jeffrey Papers.
16. WDET News, Jan. 16, 1950, and Ben Hoberman to Emil Mazey, Dec. 31, 1949, both in box 9, UAW Public Relations Department Papers, ALUA; Byron E. Farwell to Ben Hoberman, April 22, 1949, box 1, UAW Radio Department Records, 1984 Acc., ALUA.
17. Ben Hoberman to Emil Mazey, Dec. 31, 1949, box 9, UAW Public Relations Department Papers.

18. "Six Non-Profit Davids and the Commercial Goliath"; undated *Pittsburgh Courier* clipping, box 9, UAW Public Relations Department Papers; Ben Hoberman to Emil Mazey, Sept. 6, 1949, box 22, UAW Research Department Papers, ALUA.

19. Cliff Gill to M.S. Novik, Feb. 17, 1949, box 41, Umhey Papers; Ben Hoberman to Emil Mazey, Sept. 6, 1949, box 22, UAW Research Department Papers, ALUA; Joe Siegel to Frederick Umhey, March 27, 1949, box 49, Umhey Papers.

20. Mildred Jeffrey to Hardy Merril, Dec. 3, 1948, box 14, Jeffrey Papers; "Civic and Community Programs Heard Exclusively on WDET in 1949," n.d., box 11, Jeffrey Papers.

21. While the advocates of the co-op development won this hearing, they ultimately failed to overcome the neighbor association's intense opposition to the building of the housing project. "Detroit Labor Station Airs Controversial City Council Housing Hearing," n.d., box 1, UAW Radio Department Papers, 1984 Acc., ALUA.

22. "Best in Radio," flyer, n.d., box 147, Reuther Papers; Ben Hoberman to Morris Novik, May 11, 1949, box 6, UAW Radio Department Papers; WDET News, Feb. 15, 1952, box 53, UAW Secretary-Treasurer Emil Mazey General Files, ALUA.

23. Jerry Sherman to Millie Jeffrey et al., Feb. 19, 1951, box 16, Jeffrey Papers; WDET News, Dec. 12, 1949, box 9, UAW Public Relations Department Records; Press Release, March 26, 1952, box 53, UAW Secretary-Treasurer Emil Mazey General Files, ALUA.

24. "Six Non-Profit Davids and the Commercial Goliath"; "FM Sound" truck flyer, n.d., box 16, Jeffrey Papers.

25. WDET News, Feb. 9, 1950, box 9, UAW Radio Department Records.

26. WDET News, Jan. 25, 1950, box 13, Jeffrey Papers; "Six Non-Profit Davids and the Commercial Goliath."

27. Al Rightley to Local Union Presidents in WDET Reception Area, Jan. 20, 1950, box 21, UAW Local 212 Papers, ALUA; FM Ownership in Detroit and Prospects for Its Growth, n.d., box 11, Jeffrey Papers; Joe Siegel to Frederick Umhey, Jan. 30, 1950, box 49, Umhey Papers; Mildred Jeffrey and J.A. Rightley to International Representatives and Local Union Presidents in WDET Reception Area, Jan. 28, 1950, box 32, Michigan AFL-CIO Papers, ALUA.

28. Minutes, Annual Membership Meeting of the UAW-CIO Broadcasting Corporation of Michigan, Jan. 24, 1950, box 10; Mildred Jeffrey to Emil Mazey, Feb. 25, 1949, box 14, Jeffrey Papers.

29. Emil Mazey to Walter P. Reuther, Sept. 21, 1949, box 9, UAW Public Relations Department Papers, ALUA; Mildred Jeffrey to Emil Mazey, Feb. 25, 1949, box 14, Jeffrey Papers; Announcing Amateur Radio Show, n.d., box 14, Jeffrey Papers; "WDET-FM Presents Fight of the Week," flyer, n.d., box 147, Reuther Papers.

30. WDET News: Bob Hope Guests First WDET "Teen Tempo Show," n.d., box 1, UAW Radio Department Papers, 1984 Acc., ALUA; Joe Siegel to Frederick Umhey, June 10, 1949, box 49, Umhey Papers.

31. Charles Adrian to Program Director, WDET, March 23, 1950, box 5, Jeffrey Papers; Sample of Listeners' Reaction to WDET, April 14, 1949, box 1, UAW Radio Department Papers, 1984 Acc., ALUA; WDET News, Praise from Listeners, Oct. 8, 1949, box 9, UAW Public Relations Department Papers.

32. Typical Listener Comments Taken from Letters Received by WDET, ca. 1950, box 146, Reuther Papers; Marion H. Bemis to Ben Hoberman, Oct. 5, 1949, box 9, UAW Public Relations Department Papers.

33. Maxwell Fox to Frederick Umhey, Dec. 5, 1949, box 44, Cliff Gill to Frederick Umhey, March 9, 1951, box 40, Clara S. Logan to David Dubinsky, Feb. 28, 1941, box 39, all in Umhey Papers.
34. Press Release, March 26, 1952, box 53, UAW Secretary-Treasurer Emil Mazey Papers.
35. "Regrets Passing of FM Station," clipping, April 10, 1952, box 14, Jeffrey Papers; Joe Seigel to Frederick Umhey, Aug. 24, 1950, box 49, Umhey Papers.
36. Minutes of the Second Quarterly Meeting, box 12, Umhey Papers.
37. WDET News, Nov. 4, 1949, box 13, Jeffrey Papers; Joseph L. Rauh to T.J. Slowie, March 18, 1952, box 13, Jeffrey Papers .
38. Analysis of Public Symphony Hour Listeners According to Occupational Groups, n.d., box 14, Jeffrey Papers.
39. In some ways, the FM stations' financial struggles were similar to those of WCFL, which attempted to solve its fiscal stress by reducing labor programming and adopting a more commercial orientation. Godfried, *WCFL*, chapters 9 and 10; Labor's F.M. Radio Stations, box 10, Jeffrey Papers; Guy Nunn to Mildred Jeffrey, Aug. 30, 1950, box 11, Jeffrey Papers.
40. Jeffrey to Ken Robinson, Oct. 18, 1950, box 11, Jeffrey Papers; Ben Hoberman to Morris Novik, May 24, 1949, box 6, UAW Radio Department Papers, 1984 Acc., ALUA; Joe Siegel to Frederick Umhey, April 1, 1948, box 49, Umhey Papers; Mildred Jeffrey to Bob Miller, Nov. 23, 1949, box 4, Jeffrey Papers.

References

Along Radio Row. (1949). *New York Times*, June 12, X9.

Boyle, K. (1995). *The UAW and the Heydey of American Liberalism, 1945–1968*. Ithaca, NY: Cornell University Press.

Carson, S. (1952). On the Air. *New Republic*, 126 (12, March 24), 22–23.

Cleveland Hears Football Games. (1949). *United Automobile Worker*, October, 10.

Congress of Industrial Organizations (1944). *Proceedings of Seventh Constitutional Convention of the Congress of Industrial Organizations*. n.p.: CIO.

Douglas, S. (1999). *Listening In: Radio and the American Imagination, from Amos'n' Andy and Edward R. Murrow to Wolfman Jack and Howard Stern*. New York: Random House.

The Electrons Are Organizing. (1948). *Ammunition*, 6 (7, July), 12–13.

FDR's Genius Extolled As WFDR Goes on Air. (1949). *Justice*, July 1, 1–3.

FM Stations. (1948). *Fortune*, 38 (12, December), 200–201.

Fones-Wolf, E. (2000). Promoting a Labor Perspective in the American Mass Media: Unions and Radio in the CIO Era, 1936–1956. *Media, Culture & Society*, 22 (3), 285–307.

For Better Listening. (1946). *Ammunition*, 4 (7, July), 19.

"Free Press" for the Rich. (1947). *CIO News*, February 17, 5.

Godfried, N. (1997). *WCFL: Chicago's Voice of Labor, 1926–78*. Urbana: University of Illinois Press.

———. (2001). Struggling over Politics and Culture: Organized Labor and Radio Station WEVD during the 1930s. *Labor History*, 42, 347–369.

Hillard, R.L. & Michael Keith. (2005). *The Quieted Voice: The Rise and Demise of Localism in American Radio*. Carbondale: Southern Illinois Press.

ILGWU Stations Carry Kaiser-Frazier Newscast. (1950). *Justice*, February 1, 3.

International Ladies' Garment Workers' Union. (1950). *Report of the General Executive Board to the Twenty-Seventh Convention*. New York: ABCO Press.

———. (1953). *Report of the Proceedings of the Twenty-Eighth Convention*. New York: ABCO Press.

Jeffrey, M. (1999). Interview with author, Detroit, Michigan, June 2.

KFMV's First Year Rolls Up Record for Labor "Exclusives." (1949). *Justice*, December 1, 10.

Labor and FM. (1946). *Tide*, 20 (5, March 8), 66–68.

KFMW, WFDR Win Awards in Annual Billboard Contest. (1950). *Justice*, March 1, 1–2.

Labor in Radio. (1947). *New York Times*, April 13, X9.

Laboring Voice. (1949). *Time*, 53 (25, June 27), 24–25.

Lasar, M. (2000). *Pacifica Radio: The Rise of an Alternative Network*. Philadelphia, PA: Temple University Press.

Lichtenstein, N. (1995). *The Most Dangerous Man in Detroit: Walter Reuther and the Fate of American Labor*. Ithaca, NY: Cornell University Press.

McChesney, R (1993). *Telecommunications, Mass Media, & Democracy: The Battle for The Control of U.S. Broadcasting, 1928–1935*. New York: Oxford University Press.

Money Behind the Headlines. (1947). *CIO News*, February 24, 7.

Mosco, V. (1979). *Broadcasting in the United States: Innovative Challenges and Organizational Control*. Norwood, NJ: Ablex Press.

Novik, M.S. (1950a). Radio's Labor Pains. *Variety*, July 26, 45.

———. (1950b). Radio Must Serve. *American Federationist*, 57 (10, October), 25–26.

———. (1985). Interview: Oral History. Kheel Center for Labor-Management Documentation and Archives, Cornell University, Ithaca, NY.

On the Air: WFDR. (1949). *New Republic*, 121 (1, July 4), 20–21.

Postwar-Station Showmanship. (1950). *Variety*, May 24, 25.

Puette, W. (1992). *Through Jaundiced Eyes: How the Media View Organized Labor*. Ithaca, NY: ILR Press.

Radio Music Head. (1948). *Pittsburgh Courier*, December 18, 21Riesel, V. (1945). Labor Is Big Business. *American Mercury*, 61 (264, December), 728–734.

Savage, B. (1999). *Broadcasting Freedom: Radio, War, and the Politics of Race*. Chapel Hill: University of North Carolina Press.

Skidmore Scans the Books. (1950). *Variety*, January 25, 46.

Strassberg, D. (1952). To the Radio-Televison Editor. *New York Times*, February 17, X11.

Strike in Danville. (1951). *Variety*, May 16, 28.

Turn It On. (1950). *Ammunition*, 8 (5, May), 10.

Tyler, G. (1995). *Look for the Union Label: A History of the International Ladies' Garment Workers' Union*. Armonk, NY: M.E. Sharpe.

UAW Newscaster Gets Wide Audience with Vivid, Forthright Commentary. (1949). *United Automobile Worker*, May, 10.

Umhey, F. Radio Stations Run by Labor. (1945). *American Federationist*, 45 (5, December), 10–12.

Union Network (1947). *Business Week*, December 17 (954), 92–93.

United Automobile Workers of America. (1940). *Report of R.J. Thomas, President, UAWA*. Detroit, MI: United Automobile Workers of America.

———. (1949). *Report of the President*. Detroit, MI: United Automobile Workers of America.

———. (1950). *Report of the President*. Detroit, MI: United Automobile Workers of America.

Wang. J. (2002). "The Case of the Radio-Active Housewife": Relocating Radio in the
    Age of Television. In M. Hilmes (Ed.), *Radio Reader: Essays in the Cultural History of
    Radio*. New York: Routledge.
Ward, B. (2004). *Radio and the Struggle for Civil Rights in the South*. Gainesville: University
    of Florida Press.
Water Crisis. (1949). *Variety*, December 28, 26.
WDET, Auto Workers' Station Bows. (1949). *Billboard*, February 19, 14.
WDET-FM. (1948). *Ammunition*, 6 (11, November), 32.
WDET-FM on the Air. (1949). *Michigan CIO News*, May 19, 26.
WDET Stages Chrysler Amateur Shows. (1950). *United Automobile Worker*, April, 10.
WDET to Air Boxing Shows. (1950). *Michigan CIO News*, October 19, 7.
WFDR Awarded Page 1 Oscar for "Liberal Stand." (1951). *Justice*, April 1, 1, 5.
WFDR Goes on Air. (1950). *Justice*, October 1, 3.
WFDR on the Air. (1951). *Justice*, June 1, 10.
WFDR Signs Off. (1952). *Justice*, February 15, 12.
WFDR Skirts Axe; To Stick It Another Year. (1952). *Variety*, January 9, 26.
Zenith Set, By Vim Is WFDR Selection. (1950). *Justice*, April 15, 1, 3.

10. The Public's Radio: All Things on the Dial

Corey Flintoff

After nearly four decades of struggle and a remarkable degree of success, public radio is facing challenges—and not just to its existence but to its very definition. Broadcasters are wondering whether their medium can continue to be either radio or public, at least as Americans have come to know it. Those questions are driven by new forms of competition, new technologies, changes in revenue flow, and an uncertain political climate. Public radio's strength on the airwaves is threatened by radio-like media that operate from different platforms: the Internet, portable download players such as the iPod, and satellite radio. As public broadcasters establish themselves on these platforms, they risk losing some of the local community-service collaboration and identification that comes with having to ask for voluntary contributions from listeners.

To survive, the system will have to call on its history—one of creative adaptation to technology, innovation in funding models, and the development of strong grassroots political support.

Don't Call It Radio

The challenge facing public radio is exemplified by a name change. Over the past few years, National Public Radio (NPR) has made a conscious shift in its branding strategy, identifying itself more and more as "NPR" and de-emphasizing the "radio" part of its name. That brings the network in line with other media companies that traditionally go by their initials, from CBS to CNN, but it also reflects a desire to be known for a more diverse product. Just as KFC now offers a wider variety of fare than Kentucky Fried Chicken once did, NPR wants it known that it offers more than radio. NPR CEO Ken Stern stresses that the network is now a "comprehensive media company."

NPR and other broadcasters in the public sector, such as Public Radio International (PRI), American Public Media (APM), and the Pacifica Foundation want the public to understand that they have a presence on the Web, in podcasting, and on satellite. Even the name of the public radio product has changed; what used to be described as "programming" is now known as "content," in part to reflect the fact that much of the material on the Web is not in the discrete, highly individualized blocks of time known as radio shows but consists of ever-changing text, photographs, and video (NPR News, 2007). NPR's leadership has stressed that it wants to give the company's Web presence as much emphasis as is now given to the flagship radio programs *Morning Edition* and *All Things Considered*.

Public radio in the United States has enjoyed remarkable success with its core offerings, magazine-style radio programs that combine sound-rich news and feature stories with interviews and analysis. From its beginnings in 1970, NPR has grown from a small, ill-funded alternative radio source to a mainstream broadcaster that attracts more than 26 million listeners a week. As commercial radio—and media overall—lost market share, NPR's audience doubled over the period from 2000 to 2005 (NPR Annual Report, 2005). The company's programming airs on more than 850 stations, and it had a 2007 financial year operating budget of approximately $144 million (Steinberg, 2006). PRI counts stations that air its programming as affiliates and reaches nearly 800 of them (History of PRI, 2007). The smallest of the networks, Pacifica, distributes its programs to nearly 100 affiliates (Pacifica, 2007).

Why meddle with such a successful formula? NPR executives point out that public radio fundraising remained relatively flat from 2004 to 2007, with little prospect for growth (Stern, 2007). Just as worrisome is that recruitment of new listeners from younger demographics appears to be falling off. Public radio used to be able to count on a steady flow of new listeners as college-educated young people graduated from commercial music radio to the public stations. Consumers were already habituated to listening to radio. Some of them simply graduated to public radio as they moved on to responsible jobs, marriages, mortgages, children, and greater civic engagement. But today's youth are more likely to listen to music that they download from the Internet or exchange with their peers. Aside from whatever programs they may have been forced to listen to while strapped into their car seats, they may bypass the traditional radio listening experience altogether (Lindsay, 2007). These two problems, waning funding and aging listenership, are driving public radio broadcasters to seek new avenues for growth.

U.S. public radio has always been a response to civic needs, bolstered by new broadcasting trends and technologies. The first public network in the United States was Pacifica, an organization of five community radio stations stretching from Berkeley, California, to New York City. The first Pacifica station, KPFA, was established in 1949 by World War II–era pacifists as a forum for leftist progressive views, and it became a model for radio funded by community memberships (Lasar, 2000; Walker, 2004).

Commercial radio was also transforming itself during this era, creating a bigger niche for educational and community stations. In the late 1940s and early 1950s commercial radio had begun to come under pressure from television, which was attracting audiences with video versions of successful radio fare, from soap operas and sports to news, variety, and quiz shows. To survive, radio broadcasters took advantage of improvements in recording technology, including audiotape and long-playing vinyl records, to evolve new formats (Sterling & Kittross, 2002). The 1950s saw the rise of radio stations that played the best-selling (usually Top 40) songs from various genres, from rock and rhythm and blues to country and classical (Radio Formats, 2007). The arrangement, which provided discrete segments of the audience to advertisers and boosted sales for record companies, turned out to be immensely profitable. To make room for more advertising and more music, commercial radio companies began reducing their news and public affairs programming to the bare minimum required by the Federal Communications Commission (FCC). In 1981, the FCC dropped its licensing guidelines for non-entertainment programming altogether. Even though big networks such as CBS radio continued to produce a strong news lineup, executives acknowledged that stations were not using much of it (Fox, 1992). By the mid-1960s, the availability of commercial news and information programming had dwindled to the point that educational broadcasters were able to convince Congress that it would be in the public interest to promote a viable noncommercial broadcasting alternative. In late 1967, President Lyndon B. Johnson signed the Public Broadcasting Act, which established the Corporation for Public Broadcasting (CPB) to foster public radio and television. The act specified that public broadcasters would be "a source of alternative telecommunications services for all the citizens of the nation" (U.S. Congress, 1967).

The Act did not provide much in the way of funding, and it took major grants from the Ford Foundation, CBS, the Communications Workers of America, and other groups to set the organization on its feet. By 1969, CPB was able to convene a group of educational broadcasters to discuss what kind of programming its projected new radio network should produce. Helping to lead the discussion was a young radio station manager from Buffalo who had written a thought-provoking essay called "Public Radio: Some Essential Ingredients." Bill Siemering wrote that public radio should be "on the frontier of the contemporary and help create new tastes … It must also supply the basic nutrients to save the life of the public from information starvation" (Collins, 1993, 24). Siemering came on board with the new NPR as its first program director, and his vision helped shape the network's first program, *All Things Considered*, launched in 1971 (Siemering, 1970). Siemering combined a variety of influences into his conception for the program; as a schoolboy in Wisconsin, he had grown up listening to cooperative extension information and educational programs on WHA in Madison. As a college student, he went to work for the station. He went on to become manager of WBFO, the student station of the State University of New York in Buffalo, where he learned to adapt the cooperative extension model to an urban environment (Collins, 1993, 18). Siemering says he was also influenced by hearing programs of the Canadian Broadcasting Corporation (CBC) from across the border (Siemering, 2002).

The first broadcast of *All Things Considered* foreshadowed what would become a highly successful formula. It ranged from the sound of a massive antiwar demonstration in Washington, DC, gathered live on the streets in the hours before the program, to a soft-spoken interview with a young heroin addict (Collins, 1993, 25). Siemering had a hand in other innovations as well, including the decision to make Susan Stamberg a host of the program. Stamberg was the first woman to host a national news program, and she did it at a time when many station managers complained that a woman could not sound "professional" or "authoritative" enough to hold an audience's attention (Stamberg, 1982).

The political climate in the late 1960s was right for public radio, as one of the elements in President Johnson's "Great Society" program, and the technological climate was favorable too, because FM radio was rapidly gaining in popularity. Before the medium became popular, FM licenses were easier for many universities and community groups to obtain, so many newer stations gained the technology as they joined the system (Schardt, 1996). In 1979, FM first overtook AM as the most-listened-to form of radio in the United States (Sterling & Kittross, 2002). FM's audio quality was much better than that of AM, and that made it effective for the kind of material that public radio was trying to broadcast: sound-rich, multilayered news and feature programming, classical music and jazz. Listeners to FM were better able to appreciate the subtleties of ambient sound in the background of many public radio pieces. Distribution, of course, was still a problem. Most stations received *All Things Considered* over a telephone line, so that no matter how good the production quality, the listening experience was still limited by the carrying capacity of the wire. The technological step that finally brought the nuances of public radio production to FM listeners came in 1979–1980, when CPB funded the public radio satellite system. The first of its kind in the United States, it is still managed by NPR, and it now distributes programming to more than 800 radio stations. The system is available to all public broadcasters, including APM, Pacifica, and PRI (PRSS, 2007; Collins, 1993, 30).

The other technical innovation that favored public radio's emerging style was the introduction of the audiocassette tape recorder. Philips had introduced the first audiocassettes to the United States in 1964, but the era of high-fidelity audiocassette recording really begin in 1971, the year *All Things Considered* was born. That same year, Advent Corporation introduced the first compact tape recorder that combined Dolby B noise reduction with chromium dioxide tape (CrO_2) (Phillips, 2002). Sony and Marantz soon brought out light-weight cassette recording machines, which made it much easier for radio reporters to operate in the field. A photograph used in NPR's publicity at the time shows science correspondent Ira Flatow in Antarctica, bundled up against the cold, extending a microphone toward a curious penguin. Combined with innovations in multitrack studio recording and mixing, the light-weight field recorder was the innovation that came to define public radio's sound.

Still, the network was ill-funded, receiving only 10% of the money doled out each year by the CPB. The rest went to public television, which was a far costlier proposition. NPR grew slowly until 1977, when journalist, public relations executive, and Democratic political operative Frank Mankiewicz took over as president. Mankiewicz was appalled to find NPR "the best kept secret in journalism." When he was being interviewed for the job, he told the network's board that his priority would be "to do whatever [is] necessary so that people like me have heard of NPR" (Collins, 1993, 38; Lindsay, 2007, 78). Mankiewicz had the political experience to know that lawmakers would be more inclined to support public radio if Congress were given a starring role on the public airwaves. He brought the network national attention by winning the right to broadcast live from the Senate floor during debate over passage of the 1972 Panama Canal Treaty (Collins, 1993, 35; Lindsay, 2007, 78).

Mankiewicz also brought his political savvy to bear in the fight for a bigger portion of CPB funding. Using NPR's greater visibility and credibility, he was able to double radio's portion (to approximately 20%) of public broadcasting's funding pie. The additional money was used to expand the network's news department and hire more reporters, editors, and producers (Collins, 1993, 35).

Despite the success of *All Things Considered*, NPR needed to have a program in the morning if it was to become a major broadcast presence. Morning "drive time" was when commercial radio listening was at its height, so the potential market was enormous (Lindsay, 2007, 78). Mankiewicz raised the money to develop a morning radio show that would have the journalistic scope of *All Things Considered* but be tailored to the needs of an audience that was just starting its day. *Morning Edition*, the eventual result, went on the air in November 1979. *Morning Edition* was far more than just a clone of *All Things Considered*; it was designed to have a stronger host presence than the network's evening program. That host, Bob Edwards, covered many news stories by interviewing newsmakers himself, whereas *All Things Considered* would have a reporter create a produced piece. Edwards expressed his own dry sense of humor by highlighting strange bits of Americana that appeared in the news each day. He held weekly conversations with the colorful former sportscaster Red Barber, a feature that became one of the program's most popular elements (Edwards, 1993). During five years on *All Things Considered* as a co-host with Susan Stamberg, Edwards had cultivated a low-key persona that fit with psychologists' appraisals of what listeners wanted in the morning. The consultants (hired by Frank Mankiewicz during the show's development) said listeners wanted to ease into their day with security, a sense that while all might not be right with the world, it would be bearable (Collins, 1993, 45). Edwards's persona provided that reassurance so successfully that he remained the program's only host for nearly 25 years (Lindsay, 2007, 162).

Morning Edition was innovative in another important respect: the way it was designed for use by NPR's member stations. The program was produced in discrete modules with lengths that remained the same, day after day. That gave public radio stations the ability to maintain their own morning presence by dropping certain national segments and replacing them with local news, weather, and traffic. Some *All Things Considered* producers saw the new product as choppy, lacking the flow from one item to another that kept evening listeners tuned in. However, audience research showed that the modular structure was far more in keeping with the way consumers use radio in the morning. They listen for relatively short periods, sandwiched in between showers, children's breakfasts, and the morning commute (Collins, 1993, 43).

Frank Mankiewicz also foresaw that NPR could not continue to rely on government funding. The model adopted by the Public Broadcasting Act of 1967 was never intended to become state-sponsored radio along the lines of the British Broadcasting Corporation (BBC), the CBC, or the broadcast agencies of much of Western Europe. The British state broadcasting company was chartered in 1927, and Britain's commercial broadcasting developed only years later, and in its shadow. In the United States, on the other hand, commercial radio grew the fastest, and educational stations didn't manage to secure a reserved set of radio frequencies for themselves until 1941 (Schardt, 1996; Sterling & Kittross, 2002). By 1967, commercial broadcasters were wary enough about supporting an alternative radio source (albeit one that took much of the public service programming off their shoulders; Sterling & Kittross, 2002); they had no interest at all in funding a potential rival.

Although Mankiewicz succeeded in increasing radio's share of the government funding pie, it was clear that political opposition would always keep Congress from being a secure source. The first example of that had come early in the network's history, in 1972, when President Richard Nixon vetoed a public radio funding bill. The second came in 1981, when President Reagan's transition team called for the elimination of CPB within two years, claiming that public radio and television were hotbeds of leftist bias (Barsamian, 1995; McCauley, 2002, 68). So Mankiewicz began developing corporate and foundation support. Sponsors were acknowledged with discreet "donor" messages that gave their names and businesses but were supposed to stop short of anything encouraging listeners to buy a product or service (Lindsay, 2007, 78).

One thing at which Mankiewicz did *not* succeed, however, was controlling NPR spending. In 1983, NPR underwent a financial crisis when accountants belatedly found out that the organization was millions of dollars in debt. After increasing its staffing by 14% the year before, the network had to let more than 100 people go. Mankiewicz tried to salvage the situation by spending more money on commercial ventures that he hoped would put NPR on the road to financial independence, but none of these projects bore fruit quickly enough (Collins, 1993, 67; Lindsay, 2007, 78). Mankiewicz departed in 1984, and CPB brought in managers and financial advisors to sort out the network's finances. About a third of NPR's member stations agreed to take part in an unprecedented effort to raise money directly for the network. *All Things Considered* did a fundraising version of the program that solicited money directly from listeners for the "Drive to Survive." It raised approximately $2.5 million in just three days. Over the course of tense negotiations, CPB agreed to a loan package that would keep the NPR's core programs afloat, but at the price of increased financial scrutiny (Collins, 1993, 73–76).

The tension between NPR and CPB eventually led to a fundamental change in public radio funding policy. Because the two entities could not agree on how to use some additional money provided by Congress, CPB created a Radio Fund that was open to grant applications from anyone in the public radio system. The move took away NPR's monopoly on federal money allocated for public radio. Ultimately, NPR agreed to take the change even further. Instead of going to NPR, CPB funding would go directly to public radio stations, which were then able to spend it on any programming they chose. The change created a buffer between NPR and the federal funding agency, but it also gave member stations important purse-string control over the network. In addition, it opened public radio to an era of increased competition (Schardt, 1996).

Soon the first public radio rival appeared on the horizon. Bill Kling, who had built Minnesota Public Radio into a strong statewide network, was looking for national distribution of a popular program called *A Prairie Home Companion*. The show was the creation of Garrison Keillor, a radio personality and *New Yorker* writer who borrowed the name from the Prairie Home

Cemetery in Moorhead, Minnesota. It had a previous existence as a morning program on Minnesota Public Radio, but Keillor says he got the idea for a live radio variety show after doing research for an article on the *Grand Ole Opry*. However, Keillor went far beyond the musical acts and comedy skits of the Nashville show by introducing the element of storytelling. One of the most popular features of the program was Keillor's weekly monologue, "The News from Lake Wobegon." He told lengthy, seemingly rambling stories about a fictional Minnesota town that drew on his upbringing in a fundamentalist Christian church in Anoka, Minnesota (Wroe, 2004). His cadences ranged from those of a sermonizing preacher to those of a barroom yarn spinner, and he had the knack of bringing every digression around to the main thread of the story for a satisfying ending. Kling offered the program to NPR, which turned it down. Frank Mankiewicz later said that he found the style of the show patronizing to the heartland people it was supposed to be representing (Lindsay, 2007, 78). Kling then banded together with three big-city public stations, WBUR in Boston, WNYC in New York, and KUSC in Los Angeles, to establish a new distribution network, American Public Radio (APR).

In addition to carrying *A Prairie Home Companion*, the network developed the popular business program *Marketplace* in 1989. The concept for the program came from Jim Russell, a former executive producer at NPR. APR asked Russell to critique *Business Update*, a program produced for public radio under an arrangement with CBS. He reported that solid though it was, the show sounded too much like CBS and not enough like the thoughtful, more conversational style that had become a signature of public radio. Russell agreed to produce a show that sounded "smart, literate, and witty," that took its subject seriously, but not itself (Marketplace, 2007).

In 1994, APR changed its name to PRI, a bid to emphasize its working relations with the BBC. The collaboration went further two years later, when PRI joined with the BBC and WGBH in Boston to create a new magazine program focused on foreign news for an American audience (PRI, 2007). That program, *The World*, competes strongly with NPR for foreign news coverage. In the same year, 1996, PRI also began distributing a program that was to become enormously influential, and, like *A Prairie Home Companion*, had been turned down by NPR. It was *This American Life*, the creation of a former NPR staffer named Ira Glass. Glass had started his radio career at the age of 19, as an intern at NPR's Washington headquarters. He worked his way through virtually every job at the network, moving up to reporter and then interim host of the NPR talk show *Talk of the Nation*. When he was not picked as the program's permanent host, Glass moved on, establishing himself in Chicago with a show that was also literate and witty, drawing on a storytelling style that was an edgier, more urbane version of Garrison Keillor's (*This American Life*, 2007). Glass had analyzed storytelling in the oral tradition and noted that it tended to fall into a pattern of a short anecdote, followed by a moment of reflection on the action, followed by another anecdote. He developed a technique of interviewing that elicited that pattern and enhanced it with editing that followed the same rhythm (Abel & Glass, 1999). Each week's program has a theme, loosely examined in stories and essays that are described as "like movies for radio." By 2007, *This American Life* had built a weekly audience of 1.7 million and was carried on more than 500 stations (*This American Life*, 2007).

While competition flourished, NPR steadily regained its footing. The new CPB funding formula, with money flowing to stations rather than to the network meant that NPR had to offer programs that would attract audiences for the member stations. It meant the network would produce more mainstream news and fewer of the quirky, alternative features that endeared NPR to loyal but smaller audiences in the past. The tempo of NPR programs quickened, with more news, and especially more business and foreign reporting, to counter the inroads made by programs such as *Marketplace* and *The World*.

Network staffers got a morale boost in 1985 when the financial crisis had abated enough to allow NPR to produce a new program, *Weekend Edition Saturday*, with Scott Simon. The program gave the network a foothold with a weekend audience that had not been served by much in the way of public radio news. *Weekend Edition Saturday* was so successful that, two years later, NPR was emboldened to add a Sunday version with Susan Stamberg as host (Collins, 1993, 92).

The strength of NPR's revival began to be tested by foreign stories that demanded solid, ongoing coverage rather than a quick visit by a correspondent. In 1989, the network's reporters covered the Tiananmen Square uprising in China and the fall of the Berlin Wall. That coverage laid the groundwork for an even bigger undertaking: the 1991 Gulf War. Cadi Simon, then the network's foreign editor, said, "The coverage of the Gulf War did not happen in a void. It came out of a network that was established, a mind-set that we had come into" (Collins, 1993, 99).

NPR sent many of its top reporters to cover the first war in Iraq, including Deborah Amos, John Burnett, Neal Conan, John Hockenberry, Deborah Wang, and John Ydstie (Collins, 1993). Radio reporters, armed with nothing but a tape recorder, microphone, and notebook, had some notable advantages in the vast, confused battle space. They were often more mobile than television crews and yet could bring sound that had more impact than print reporting.

Neal Conan was among a group of correspondents captured by Iraqi forces in Kuwait and taken north to Baghdad, where they were held for several days (Phillips, 2006). The network's reporting on the war and its aftermath—the burning of oilfields in Kuwait and the Kurdish refugee crisis in northern Iraq—showed that NPR could compete with the television networks and with 24-hour cable news. The coverage and public interest in the war brought a surge of new listeners to NPR news programs, reinforcing the network's trend toward harder news and more mainstream story choices. The network's round-the-clock coverage also strengthened the weekend news magazines, *Weekend All Things Considered*, *Weekend Edition Saturday*, and *Weekend Edition Sunday*.

At the same time, NPR was establishing itself as a reliable source of national political, legal, and social issue coverage. NPR's senior legal affairs correspondent, Nina Totenberg, enhanced the network's reputation with her reporting on the Supreme Court. In 1987, Supreme Court nominee Douglas Ginsburg removed himself from consideration after Totenberg broke the story that he had smoked marijuana while teaching at Harvard Law School in 1970s. In 1991, the Senate Judiciary Committee reopened confirmation hearings for another nominee, Clarence Thomas, after Totenberg reported allegations of sexual harassment against him. She anchored NPR's gavel-to-gavel coverage of the contentious hearings, an effort that won NPR a Peabody award (Phillips, 2006).

Although the financial crisis of 1983 led to the demise of many of NPR's arts and entertainment programs, they too underwent a gradual resurgence. In 1987, the network picked up *Car Talk*, a call-in show with Tom and Ray Magliozzi, who provided car repair advice and comedy to bemused callers. The program had been popular in Boston for about ten years before going national, where it became an immediate hit. NPR bills the program as the highest-rated, most financially successful public radio program in the nation, with a weekly audience of more than 2 million listeners.

Another of the network's most popular entertainment offerings is the news quiz show *Wait Wait ... Don't Tell Me*, which debuted in 1998. With playwright and actor Peter Sagal as its host, the show has a rotating panel of humorists who are challenged with questions about the lighter side of the news. NPR newscaster Carl Kasell is the program's judge and scorekeeper, acting as sidekick and comic foil for Sagal (NPR, 2007).

Criticism

Public radio has faced criticism for years about a perceived lack of diversity, both in its news coverage and in its reporting and editorial staff (Deggans, 2005). The situation is reflected in NPR's audience, which is approximately 53% male, overwhelmingly white, affluent, and highly educated. As of 2007, only approximately 10% of the network's listeners were African American or Hispanic. The network has attempted to improve diversity in its workplace with a program called the *Diversity Initiative*, which involves staff members and management in an ongoing dialogue about race, gender, and religious issues at work. Results of the initiative include the appointment of a diversity director to monitor progress around the company and an in-house mentoring program for staff members as they move to higher-level jobs. The network also sponsors a training program called Next Generation Radio, begun in 1999. This helps recruit and train NPR interns, and project director Doug Mitchell travels with his team to conduct week-long training programs in conjunction with the conferences of the main associations for minority journalists. Several ethnic news organizations sponsor a joint convention every five years called UNITY: Journalists of Color, at which the major public radio networks showcase their programs and recruit potential talent (Swanson, 2007).

NPR has also tried to increase diversity in its programming and reach out to minority groups (Swanson, 2007). In conjunction with a group of member stations known as the African American Public Radio Consortium, the network recruited black talk show personality Tavis Smiley to do a program in 2001. Smiley, who had worked at Black Entertainment Television, hosted the hour-long daily *Tavis Smiley Show* from January 2002 to December 2004, building a national audience of approximately 900,000. Eighty-seven stations picked up the show, including 18 that specifically target African American audiences. NPR research says the audience was 29% African American. Smiley left the show in a dispute over the amount of support the network would provide to produce and publicize it. He issued a statement saying that NPR was too slow to make the changes needed to reach a more diverse audience (Janssen, 2004).

Smiley kept the television talk show that he had developed on the Public Broadcasting Service (PBS), and he eventually returned to public radio with a two-hour version of the *Tavis Smiley Show* show that is broadcast not by NPR but by its rival, PRI.

NPR replaced the *Tavis Smiley Show* with *News & Notes*, now hosted by writer and correspondent Farai Chideya, who is based at NPR's West Coast production facility in Culver City, California. The show aims to take national and international news, the "mainstream story," and examine it in a context and perspective of interest to African Americans. The network also started a minority-interest talk show, *Tell Me More*, with former ABC correspondent Michel Martin. The program's mission includes bringing "fresh voices and perspectives to public radio."

In addition to acquiring the weekly *Tavis Smiley Show*, PRI has sought to distribute a mix of multicultural programs, including *National Native News*, a five-minute daily newscast that has been on the air since 1987. The program is carried by more than 100 stations throughout the United States and in Canada (*National Native News*, 2007).

Over the years, NPR has been accused of bias, and particularly of favoring the left in its reporting. In 2003, President George W. Bush appointed

Kenneth Tomlinson, a former head of Voice of America, to be chairman of the CPB. Tomlinson launched a campaign to bring conservative programming to public radio and television and rid them of what he perceived to be liberal bias. He commissioned secret reviews of talk shows on PBS and NPR in an effort to analyze the political leanings of their guests. Tomlinson resigned in November 2005 after a CPB inspector general's report questioned his spending and management style (Farhi, 2005).

Not everyone accepts the notion that NPR tilts toward liberal ideas. Fairness and Accuracy in Reporting (FAIR), which identifies itself as a progressive media watchdog group, has published studies of NPR programming in which it says that the network's guest lists are "elitist" and lack diversity. One study, reported in May 2004, found that NPR sources were overwhelmingly white, male, and Republican, that corporate sources tended to be used more often than labor ones, and that women made up only 21% of the sources used. Although the report acknowledged that NPR has more diversity of voices and more depth than most commercial media, it concluded that the network has become more establishment oriented and more conservative (Rendall & Hart, 2005).

Jeffrey Dvorkin, NPR's ombudsman at the time, responded that there was some merit in FAIR's assessment, but he countered with a similar study conducted by the network. He questioned FAIR's characterizations of some of NPR's sources as liberal or conservative (e.g., FAIR identifies the Brookings Institution as a "centrist" organization, when many observers see it as solidly liberal).

Accusations of bias also extend to NPR's foreign coverage, especially its reporting on Israel and its role in the Middle East. The Committee for Accuracy in Middle East Reporting in America (CAMERA) monitors U.S. media for what it perceives to be bias against Israel. CAMERA has repeatedly charged that NPR misrepresents facts, blames Israel for the failure of the Mideast peace process, and downplays threats that Israel faces from terrorism and anti-Semitism. In 2002, CAMERA supported boycotts against some NPR stations to protest the network's coverage. One station, WBUR in Boston, reported a loss of more than $1 million worth of underwriting and donations (Janssen, 2002a).

Around the same time, FAIR complained that NPR was promoting a pro-Israeli position, and similar charges were made on a pro-Palestinian Web site, "The Electronic Intifada." NPR's then ombudsman Jeffrey Dvorkin acknowledged that the network needed to be "more nimble" about correcting errors, but he said NPR should be willing to face any loss of income caused by boycotts rather that sacrifice its journalistic integrity (Janssen, 2002b).

The criticism did spur change at NPR. The network's senior vice president for programming, Jay Kernis, reported to the board that the Foreign Desk was devoting more resources to Middle East coverage. News managers wrote an in-house guide to fair coverage of the story and set up a process to review the coverage periodically. Still, the process has done little to dampen criticism. CAMERA published a lengthy critique of an NPR series on the anniversary of the Six-Day War in June 2007 (Levin, 2007).

Funding a New Era

As the United States enters the digital age, public radio finds itself with essentially the same challenges it faced at its inception: adapting to the new technologies, developing new funding models, and maintaining political support.

Public radio has been working hard to find an Internet model that will make it a leader among online news and entertainment providers while generating advertising and other revenue to make up for potential declines at the station level. The system's current revenue model presents a fundamental problem: local stations produce much of the revenue for the entire system, including listener memberships as well as grants from CPB, private foundations, and corporations. The stations support NPR by providing between 50% and 60% of its income in the form of membership dues and fees for use of the network's programming. Most of the remaining network's revenue comes directly from donors, which also include foundations and corporations (NPR Annual Report, 2005). Because of this funding regime, all the public networks have had to be very careful about soliciting money that might conflict with fundraising by the individual stations (Lindsay, 2007, 160). The 1983 "Drive to Survive" was a one-time effort, and for good reason: stations cannot allow the networks to bypass them by soliciting directly from listeners or to poach on major funders in their backyards.

NPR received a significant infusion of direct funding in late 2003, in the form of a $236-million grant from the estate of Joan B. Kroc, the widow of the founder of the McDonald's hamburger chain. Most of the money went to NPR's endowment, but it enabled the network to expand its newsgathering with a three-year, $15-million effort to hire and train new reporters and editors (NPR News, 2007).

The funding issue has been a significant problem as the networks and the stations establish an Internet presence: if NPR offers its full array of content on the Web, then listeners would presumably have less motivation to listen to or support their local stations. For the first decade or so of public radio's presence on the Web, the two interests were less divergent because listeners used the Internet in different ways. Until the advent of the iPod for instance, it was difficult to use media downloads at some of the prime radio listening times, commuting to and from work. Now it is possible to play your iPod through a car radio. Many listeners also preferred having their content programmed for them by the radio stations. It can be difficult and time consuming to find and download program elements that suit a listener's interests. Now services such as Last.fm, Pandora.com, and Slacker.com can program to your specific tastes, by taking your favorite songs and introducing new music in the same style or music that's been selected by other members with similar tastes (Hamilton, 2007). Radio managers can foresee a time when terrestrial broadcast radio, whether commercial or public, will serve a smaller and smaller audience.

There is, of course, no technical reason why public radio cannot adopt these and similar technologies. The public networks and their member stations are already important players in podcasting. NPR began podcasting in summer 2005 (Glaser, 2005). By 2007, it was the leading podcaster among media organizations, offering a directory of nearly 400 titles. Podcasts of music programs were upgraded from 64K monaural to 128K stereo. Among the year's newest products were a full-program podcast of the interview show *Fresh Air with Terry Gross* from WHYY in Philadelphia and a video podcast of the music program *Morning Becomes Eclectic* from KCRW in Santa Monica, California. Titles from the public radio system, such as *This American Life* and the *Car Talk Call of the Week*, routinely appear among the "most downloaded" on iTunes and other services. NPR and the member stations are looking at models for sharing revenue from short ads on podcasts (Glaser, 2005).

Public radio is working to resolve conflicts between stations and the networks, to make its Internet efforts profitable, and to make its various products easier for consumers to find and use. In 1997, stakeholders began a new association to address ways to "harness the power of the Internet and other media platforms for the benefit of public broadcasters." That group, now known as the Integrated Media Association, has focused on ways to derive revenue from the new media forms and ways to measure how the system's products are used (IMA Web site, 2007). PBS, NPR, and PRI all have seats on the association's board.

In 2005, the IMA's Mark Fuerst wrote a commentary in the industry trade paper *Current* in which he noted that members of the public radio system had probably spent $50 million on Internet activities and said they had very little to show for it. He pointed out that almost every public radio system, station, and program had its own Web site but that most were little more than online brochures. Research, he said, suggested that only approximately 10% of listeners used public radio Web sites and that their visits were short and infrequent. Fuerst challenged the system to try something new, and he suggested that Major League Baseball might offer a model. Major league team owners created a composite site, using resources from every team to make a Web destination that could offer far more than any single team. Users who entered the site from a Boston Red Sox Internet address see Red Sox pictures and information, but they can also move easily around the rest of the site. Fuerst's proposal was for public radio to create a similar composite, with shared servers and database and a single, skilled management (Fuerst, 2007).

NPR has explored similar ideas in 2006 by sponsoring a system-wide planning project called New Realities. The exercise involved bringing from 30 to 60 station leaders together for two-day meetings at locations around the country and engaging them in the discussion of how to thrive in the new media environment. The result was a Blueprint for Growth, which laid the groundwork for three "initiatives" and five "expeditions." The initiatives called for stations and networks to share expertise and resources in a Newsroom of the Future, to set up an infrastructure for distributing digital content, and "to raise Big Money collaboratively." The last initiative proposes to examine how the system can unite around projects that will attract funding from major donors. The "expeditions," somewhat less-defined goals, would include setting goals, principles, and performance standards for public radio collaboration and finding ways to build multimedia experiences around "topics of strong public interest" (Davis Rehm, 2006; Janssen, 2006a). Consultant Robert Peterson, who led the New Realities project, said the ultimate goal is for the public radio system to be viewed and used as a "trusted space" where listeners and their communities can rally around shared concerns (Janssen, 2006b).

The New Realities process seeks innovative responses to the challenges that public radio has faced from its very beginnings. It calls for creative adaptation to technology, including effective ways to integrate the Internet, podcasting, and other platforms into the service of public radio's mission. It looks for innovation in funding models that will not abandon the voluntary, community-building spirit of individual donations and station memberships. In addition, it envisions doing all of that in the framework of ever-stronger grassroots political support (Davis Rehm, 2006).

As the Blueprint for Growth suggests, it will mean changing a system culture that has often been fragmented and internally competitive to face far bigger challenges from without.

References

Abel, J. & I. Glass (1999). *Radio: An Illustrated Guide*. Chicago, IL: WBEZ Alliance.
Barsamian, D. (1995). The Right-Wing Attack on Public Broadcasting. *Public Eye*. Retrieved from http://www.publiceye.org/eyes/medi_pow.html, June 30, 2007.
Bruno, A. (2006). Web Radio Starts to Cast a Wide Net. *Billboard*, 118 (April 29), 17.
Collins, M. (1993). *National Public Radio: The Cast of Characters*. Washington, DC: Seven Locks Press.
Davis Rehm, D. (2006). NPR's Blueprint for Growth. *Current*, July 7. Retrieved from http://www.current.org/pbpb/npr/NPRBlueprintForGrowthJuly06.pdf, June 23, 2007.

Deggans, E. (2005). NPR's White Noise. *St. Petersburg Times*, April 3.

Edwards, B. (1993). *Fridays with Red: A Radio Friendship*. New York: Simon & Schuster.

Farhi, P. (2005). Kenneth Tomlinson Quits Public Broadcasting Board. *Washington Post*, November 4, C01.

Fox, N. (1992). Public Radio's Air Wars. *Columbia Journalism Review*. Retrieved from http://backissues.cjrarchives.org/year/92/1/publicradio.asp, June 23, 2007.

Fuerst, M. (2005). For Our Second Decade on the Web: Step Up to Baseball's Lead. *Current*, February 21. Retrieved from http://www.current.org/web/web0603fuerst. shtml, June 27, 2007.

Glaser, M. (2005). Will NPR's Podcasts Birth a New Business Model for Public Radio? *USC Annenberg Online Journalism Review*, November 11. Retrieved from http://www. ojr.org/ojr/stories/051129glaser, June 30, 2007.

Hamilton, A. (2007). Learning to Love Radio Again. *Time*, 169 (June 11), 24.

History of PRI. (2007). PRI fact sheet. Retrieved from http://www.pri.org/inside_pri. html, June 26, 2007.

Holahan, C. (2006). What Podcasting Revolution? *Business Week Online*, November 28. Retrieved from http://www.businessweek.com/technology/content/nov2006/ tc20061127_441486.htm?chan=search, June 9, 2007.

IMA Web site (2007). About IMA: Our Mission. Retrieved from http://www.integrated-media.org/nav.cfm?cat=16&subcat=76&subsub=141, June 30, 2007.

Janssen, M. (2002a). NPR Mideast Correspondent Broke Ban on Speaker Fees. *Current*, March 11. Retrieved from http://www.current.org/news/news0205mideast.html, June 18, 2007.

———. (2002b). NPR's Pro-Israel Critics Punish WBUR. *Current*. Retrieved from http:// www.current.org/news/news0210wbur.html, June 23, 2007.

———. (2006a). Smiley Quits, Faults NPR on Diversity. *Current*. Retrieved from http:// www.current.org/news/news0423smiley.shtml, June 23, 2007.

———. (2006b). NPR Rallies System to Jointly Build "Trusted Space": New Realities Process Yield Far-Reaching Plan to Fuse Newsrooms, Engage Audiences. *Current*. Retrieved from http://www.current.org/npr/npr0613blueprint.shtml, June 23, 2007.

Lasar, M. (2000). *Pacifica Radio: The Rise of an Alternative Network*. Philadelphia, PA: Temple University Press.

Levin, A. (2007). Six-Day War Series—Agenda-Driven and Biased. *Camera.org*. Retrieved from http://www.camera.org/index.asp?x_context=4&x_outlet=28&x_article=1332, June 19, 2007.

Lindsay, D. (2007). Has Success Spoiled NPR? *Washingtonian.com*, March 1. Retrieved from http://www.washingtonian.com/articles/mediapolitics/3603.html, June 30, 2007.

Marketplace. (2007). About/History. Retrieved from http://marketplace.publicradio. org/about/history.html, June 30, 2007.

NPR. (2007). NPR People. Retrieved from http://www.npr.org/templates/story/story. php?storyId=2101115, July 1, 2007.

NPR Annual Report. (2005). Retrieved from http://www.npr.org/about/ annualreports/2005_Annual_Report.pdf, June 28, 2007.

NPR News. (2007). The Expansion of NPR News. Retrieved from http://www.npr.org/ about/news.html, June 18, 2007.

Pacifica. (2007). About Pacifica. Retrieved from http://www.pacifica.org/about, June 30, 2007.

Phillips, L.A. (2006). *Public Radio: Behind the Voices*. New York: CDS Books.

Phillips, W. (2002). Henry Kloss: The Man Who Changed Audio and Video—Time and Time Again. *On Hifi*, February 15. Retrieved from http://www.onhifi.com/features/20020215.htm, June 18, 2007.

PRI. (2007). Inside PRI. Retrieved from http://www.pri.org/InPRI_FactSheet.html, June 30, 2007.

PRSS. (2007). What Is the PRSS? Retrieved from http://www.prss.org/about, July 1, 2007.

Radio Formats. (2007). Retrieved from http://radiostationworld.com/directory/Radio_Formats, June 30, 2007.

Rendall, S. & P. Hart. (2005). Time to Unplug the CPB: Replace Corrupt Board with Independent Trust. *FAIR: Fairness and Accuracy in Reporting*. Retrieved from http://www.fair.org/index.php?page=2671, June 29, 2007.

Schardt, S. (1996). Public Radio—A Short History. Retrieved from http://www.wsvh.org/pubradiohist.htm, June 20, 2007.

Siemering, W.H. (1970). National Public Radio Purposes. Retrieved from http://www.current.org/pbpb/documents/NPRpurposes.html, July 1, 2007.

———. (2002). Personal communication.

Stamberg, S. (1982). *Every Night at Five: Susan Stamberg's All Things Considered Book*. New York: Pantheon.

Steinberg, J. (2006). Money Changes Everything. *New York Times*, March 19.

Sterling, C. & J. Kittross. (2002). *Stay Tuned: A History of American Broadcasting*, 3rd edition. Lea's Communication Series. Mahwah, NJ: Laurence Erlbaum.

Stern, K. (2007). *Statement of Kenneth P. Stern, Chief Executive Officer National Public Radio before the Committee on House Appropriations Subcommittee on Labor, Health and Human Services, and Education, and Related Agencies*. Washington, DC: CQ Congressional Testimony.

Swanson, W. (2007). Diversity at NPR. Retrieved from http://www.npr.org/about/diversity, June 28, 2007.

This American Life. (2007). About the Radio Show. Retrieved from http://www.thislife.org/, June 30, 2007.

U.S. Congress. (1967). Public Broadcasting Act of 1967, As Amended. Retrieved from http://www.cpb.org/aboutpb/act/text.html, June 25, 2007.

Walker, J. (2004). *Rebels on the Air: An Alternative History of Radio in America*. New York: New York University Press.

Withersponn, J. & R. Kovitz. (2000). *A History of Public Broadcasting, with an update by R. Avery & A. Stavitsky*. Washington, DC: Current.

Wroe, N. (2004). Minnesota Zen Master. *Guardian Unlimited*, March 6. Retrieved from http://books.guardian.co.uk/departments/generalfiction/story/0,6000,1163066,00.html, July 1, 2007.

11. Indecency and Radio Programming, 1927 to 2000: A Reflection of Their Times

Louise Benjamin

When a recording of the famous 1937 appearance of Mae West in the Arch Oboler skit "Adam and Eve" is played for students in electronic media history classes, the reaction is both puzzled and amazed: They thought that was indecent!? Of course, West's sultry voice inflections as Eve convincing the snake or, in her words, the "palpitatin' python," to pick some of the forbidden fruit in the Garden of Eden are fairly innocuous when compared with contemporary radio fare. Today, the racy programming found on the airwaves would no doubt shock the more staid regulators and moralists of pre–World War II.

Explaining societal changes and cultural expectations and standards helps students (and others) understand how a nation's customs and practices affect what is on the air and how, in a pluralistic society, clashes occur over what is acceptable for a medium that all can easily access, including children. From radio's inception in the 1920s to the 21st century, American society's attitudes toward what material is appropriate for broadcast have adapted to the times and, some would argue, have coarsened with a loosening of cultural mores at the end of the 20th century. In looking at "radio culture" and concepts of indecency, this chapter reviews what was, and has been, acceptable in radio programming from the passage of the Radio Act of 1927 to the dawn of the 21st century. This review also shows how difficult it can be to develop a common understanding of what constitutes improper radio fare.

Indecent Radio Programming, 1927 to 1945

When the first law designed specifically to regulate broadcasting—the Radio Act of 1927—was passed, Congress included a prohibition against improper broadcast material: "No person within the jurisdiction of the United States shall utter any obscene, indecent, or profane language by means of radio communication." The Federal Radio Commission (FRC) was charged with implementing the clause, and in 1934 this same language was included in the Communications Act. In 1948 Congress moved the provision to the U.S. Criminal Code as Section 1464, but by then the Federal Communications Commission (FCC) had its own rules prohibiting the same type of content, and it continued to apply the law pertaining to prohibited utterances.

Although today's broadcasters have little to fear of FCC action in the area of profane language because courts in the 1950s said government had no prerogative in regulating blasphemous speech, that was not the situation in 1930. That year radio station KVEP in Portland, Oregon, broadcast the tirades of Robert Duncan, who had been defeated in a primary election for Congress. As a result of his rants, not only was Duncan fined and sentenced to six months in jail, but the station also lost its license. Consequently, this case is given in detail here as it presents a clear contrast to programming today.

After his defeat in Oregon's primary, Duncan used the airwaves to attack his opponents in ways the FRC said violated prohibitions against the broadcast of obscene, indecent, and profane language. Duncan accused his opponent for the Republican nomination, Congressional Representative Franklin Korell, of being a "degenerate" and a "sodomite." Because KVEP's signal blanketed all of Portland, his invectives reached about one-third of the state's population. In attacking Korell and others, Duncan used words and phrases such as "hell" and "by God." The FRC commissioners found his broadcast of May 9, 1930, particularly offensive. During it, Duncan said,

> Now, let us examine this man Korell himself. If Korell is really a man—which is a debatable proposition. Korell is a bachelor, and when he was asked why he didn't marry he says: "I don't care for women." What do you know about that? Isn't it a strange statement for a natural man to make? I don't think a natural man ever made that statement. It must be explained thoroughly, and in ways that I can understand, to free the man who says it from the charges of practicing the vices that caused the destruction of Sodom and Gomorrah. (FRC, 1930a, vol. 3, 155)

Duncan then charged Korell with fraternizing with Clarence Brazell, whom Duncan implied had been convicted on morals charges. He accused Korell of being "the roommate and bed-fellow" of Brazell for three years. Then Duncan called for all "natural men" to vote Korell out of office as a favor to the women in their lives. Duncan also threatened to broadcast the names of Korell's supporters.

In other attacks Duncan denigrated a newspaper editor, a member of the Portland school board, and businessmen, especially those associated with banks and chain stores. He used epithets such as "a dirty low-down puke," "you undiapered kid, you," "you yellow dog son-of-a-gun," "dirty, stinking, lying coward," "cock-eyed liar," and "half-brother of the skunk." He also vowed "by the living God" that he would shoot anyone trying to bully him and threatened to broadcast information about scandals that only he knew about (FRC, 1930a, vol. 3, 156–159).

In hearings the FRC stated that language broadcast over radio need not be taken in complete context if words and phrases in and of themselves could be deemed objectionable. FRC chair Ira Robinson noted that even a good, religious sermon containing inappropriate language would be deemed inexcusable over the airwaves. "The fact that there is good in it does not excuse the indecent part," he said (FRC, 1930a, vol. 3, 210). The FRC said its decision was consistent with the First Amendment because "this constitutional provision has never been construed to protect obnoxious and indecent language" (FRC, 1930b, vol. 2, 12–13).

The FRC refused to renew the station's license, saying its owner William Schaeffer should have prevented the broadcasts. Duncan was convicted and sentenced to six months in jail and required to pay a $500 fine for "knowingly, willfully and feloniously uttering obscene, indecent and profane language by means of radio communication." In appeal, the court found that Duncan violated the law's prohibition against profane language through using words such as "damn" and "by God." The court stated that while his "vulgar" rants were "extremely abusive and objectionable," they did not violate the law in terms of indecency and obscenity as they did not "deprave and corrupt morals" or stimulate "lewd or lascivious" actions (*Duncan v. U.S.*, 1931).

Although the language Duncan used was not indecent or obscene, the court said it was profane. Citing cases from the 1800s and early 1900s, the Ninth Federal Court of Appeals concluded,

> Under these decisions, the indictment having alleged that the language is profane, the defendant having referred to an individual as "damned," having used the expression "by God" irreverently, and having announced his intention to call down the curse of God upon certain individuals, was properly convicted of using profane language within the meaning of that term as used in the act of Congress prohibiting the use of profane language in radio broadcasting. (*Duncan v. U.S.*, 1931)

Of course, in today's environment the same language would not have resulted in Duncan's prosecution, and Schaeffer would not have lost the station's license. Today such a tirade would be considered quaint and, possibly, childish. But in the 1930s, cases such as this one made broadcasters more sensitive to public reaction to their programs.

In the 1930s churches and organized groups of mothers often led the assault against offensive radio programs, and broadcasters—not the FRC or its successor, the FCC—led the way in keeping material deemed unfit for entry into the home off the air. They became self-censors of their own programming for fear of offending the listening public. Songs and skits especially came under review as stations and networks sought to ward off any church or mothers' crusades against indecent radio programming (Benjamin, 2001, 142–145).

In March 1933, a group of New York mothers complained that radio programs were too bloodcurdling and disturbed their children's sleep. Other complaints were aimed at shows using poor grammar and presenting "trashy" love sentiments to junior-high school girls. Station and network censors banned some songs outright, and they demanded word changes in other melodies. For example, Cole Porter's "Love for Sale" was banned in 1932, and lyrics to others, such as "Forty-Second Street," were sanitized. By June 1933, humming often replaced words deemed inappropriate, and the following year orchestra leaders formed a committee to self-censor suggestive songs and song titles. Well-known orchestra leader Paul Whiteman spoke for this committee when he noted that its members were "trying to discourage off-color songs because, unlike stage shows where customers paid money to see the production, radio came into the home" (Benjamin, 2001, 144–145). For the most part, during the interwar and World War II years, network censors and advertisers who sponsored the shows were able to keep "blue material" off the air, whether it was song or skit (Benjamin, 2001, 142–145). The Mae West sketch mentioned at the beginning of this chapter was an anomaly and not the norm.

Post–World War II to Pacifica

The postwar years brought profound change to American radio programming. With the advent of television, radio moved to programming primarily for local audiences and often turned to music and deejay patter to entertain audiences. As local ratings grew in importance for radio station owners and as societal mores changed in the 1950s and 1960s, concerns over what was inappropriate for radio audiences adjusted to suit the times. In addition, the Supreme Court finally provided legal definitions for the terms "obscenity" and "indecency," albeit—with one important exception—for cases that involved media other than broadcast.

In 1957, the Supreme Court defined obscenity in *Roth v. U.S.* as material "utterly without redeeming social importance" (modified to "social value" in the 1966 "*Fanny Hill*" case) where, "to the average person, applying contemporary community standards, the dominant theme of the material taken as a whole appeals to the prurient interest." (*Roth v. U.S.*, 1957) Then, in 1973 the *Miller v. California* case changed several aspects of this definition. First, with reference to the work, the Court said it still had to be considered "as a whole" and judged by its effect on average persons, not on the most susceptible. But "contemporary community standards" did not have to be standards "of the nation as a whole." Second, *Miller* dropped the "social value" test, substituting a requirement that an obscene work "lack serious literary, artistic, political, or scientific value." Third, the Court stated Congress and state legislatures should pass precise laws, describing exactly what kind of sexual content was prohibited. Thus, the definition of obscenity as applied since 1973 is as follows:

> A work is obscene if, to the average person applying contemporary community standards, the dominant theme of the material taken as a whole appeals to the prurient interest in sex, depicts or describes sexual content in a patently offensive way (as explicitly defined by law), and lacks serious literary, artistic, political or scientific value (*Miller v. California*, 1973).

As no case of broadcast obscenity has reached the Supreme Court, the FCC has adapted whatever definition of obscenity was then current to cases involving alleged broadcast obscenity or indecency, even though these definitions come from cases involving print and motion pictures. Because broadcasting differs from print and film, the FCC modified its standards to the medium and differentiated between what constituted broadcast obscenity and broadcast indecency. Until 1973 it applied a modified *Roth* standard, and a modified *Miller* standard was utilized in post-1973 situations.

In a rare broadcast obscenity case decided in 1973 before the *Miller* decision, the FCC decided that the "topless radio" talk show format for stations popular in the early 1970s was obscene. This time was one of "liberation" for women, and the term came from the controversial practice of some women abandoning their bikini tops. Hosts of "topless radio" encouraged their callers, who were usually women, to discuss their sexual fantasies and practices on air. Complaints against such programs aired by Sonderling Broadcasting's WGLD-FM in Cleveland, Ohio, especially one titled *Femme Forum*, resulted in the FCC's declaration that the programs were obscene under the *Roth* standards. The FCC noted that "if discussions in the titillating and pandering fashion (broadcast on the station) do not constitute broadcast obscenity within the meaning of 18 USC 1464, we do not perceive what does or could." Furthermore, the FCC stated, "We have no doubt the explicit material set out above is patently offensive to contemporary community standards for broadcast matter" (Sonderling, 1973). Critics claimed the FCC did not take into account works as a whole and applied its own standards rather than those of average persons in the local community. The FCC countered that audience members could join programs at any given time so it could not apply the criterion of "as a whole" to broadcasts and added that appropriate community standards were those for broadcast, not print, media.

After *Miller* the FCC changed its definition of broadcast obscenity in a 1975 case involving a then student-run station owned by the University of Pennsylvania, WXPN. This case is largely forgotten today because the *Pacifica* decision came a few years later, but it provides an excellent backdrop to *Pacifica* in illustrating what the FCC considered obscene in the mid-1970s. The station carried *The Vegetable Report*, a call-in program with exceedingly descriptive discussions and descriptions of sexual matters. The FCC cited examples it said violated its rules against broadcasting obscene or indecent programming (FCC Reports, 1975).

In one situation a male announcer discussed oral sex with a female caller, and words such as "pussy" and "motherfucker" were used by both parties. The female caller, with the encouragement of the male host, told him how she wanted to be treated: "Suck out my ass. Get a straw and strip it to the bone and suck out that motherfucker." In another example a male caller told the male host about a toy doll available in a local adult store: "Not only has she got a mouth and a cunt, but she's got an asshole, too." In what the FCC cited as a particularly offensive exchange, a male announcer encouraged a female caller to take her toddler son to bed with her, to teach him "to beat off" and "to say 'fuck'" because it was "good" to do so and to "give him all the physical attention you can give him now, so he won't be starved for it and go out raping later." The male announcer even asked her, "When was the last time you blew him?" The FCC ruled the program "obscene" (FCC Reports, 1975). Again critics said the FCC did not consider the broadcasts as a whole and added that the FCC had neglected to apply community standards correctly, but the FCC's decision held.

Although these cases applied definitions of obscenity used in print cases to broadcasting, the FCC was far more likely to receive complaints about broadcast indecency and, consequently, modified its use of obscenity definitions to broadcast indecency complaints. The pre-*Miller* case involved a taped interview of Jerry Garcia of the rock group the Grateful Dead on Temple University's WUHY in 1970. During the interview Garcia peppered his comments with "gratuitous expletives," according to the FCC decision. Garcia was known to begin many of his sentences with "shit, man ..." and to use the f-word liberally throughout his comments. The FCC quoted him as saying phrases such as "that kind of shit," "it sucks it right fuckin' out of ya, man," and "political change is so fuckin' slow" in the taped conversation WUHY aired. Such sexual and excretory references should have been edited out of the recorded interview, the FCC stated, as the words themselves were patently offensive according to contemporary community standards for the broadcast media. To complaints that it had failed to consider the work as a whole, the FCC responded that the concept "as a whole" could not be applied to a broadcast as listeners could tune in at any time, not just at the show's beginning. Thus, WUHY became the first station to be fined for airing indecent material, and the FCC hoped the station would appeal, as it wanted a test case to force the courts to define what the term "indecent" meant for broadcast media. However, because the station paid the nominal $100 fine, the commission had to wait a few more years to get its test case (FCC, 1970).

From Pacifica *to the Millennium*

That test case—the *Pacifica* or "seven dirty words" case—supplies the post-*Miller* definition of indecency for the broadcast media still used at the beginning of the 21st century. The case began one afternoon in 1973 in New York City when Pacifica-owned WBAI aired a cut from a George Carlin comedy album as part of a series on contemporary English-language usage. Originally part of Carlin's nightclub act, the humorous monologue contained the "seven dirty words" that, according to the monologue, "will curve your spine, grow hair on your hands": shit, piss, fuck, cunt, tits, cocksucker, and motherfucker. A man (who headed the state of Florida's division of the national Morality in Media [MIM] organization) and his 15-year-old son heard the 2 p.m. broadcast, and the father complained to the FCC that such material should not be carried during the times of day when young people were likely to be in the audience. It was the only complaint the FCC received on the broadcast. Because the commission had been under pressure from Congress to clean up the airwaves, the FCC reviewed the monologue and agreed that it was indecent and patently offensive for the broadcast media. The commission placed a warning in WBAI's file, and, on principle, Pacifica appealed. The appellate court reversed the FCC's ruling (*FCC v. Pacifica*, 1978).

The FCC appealed to the Supreme Court, which in 1978 reversed the lower court and authored the definition of indecency for the broadcast media that stands today. Because broadcasting has "a uniquely pervasive presence in the lives of all Americans," the FCC could regulate indecency.

> Patently offensive, indecent material presented over the airwaves confronts the citizen, not only in public, but also in the privacy of the home, where the individual's right to be left alone plainly outweighs the First Amendment rights of an intruder ... broadcasting is uniquely accessible to children, even those too young to read ... Pacifica's broadcast could have enlarged a child's vocabulary in an instant ... The ease with which children may obtain access to broadcast material ... amply justifies special treatment of indecent broadcasting. (*FCC v. Pacifica*, 1978)

The commission now had not only its ruling on jurisdiction over indecency cases but also a definition of indecency specific to broadcasting to apply.

Over the next three decades the FCC's implementation of the *Pacifica* case varied from including context of speech and innuendo in the words themselves to focusing on only the seven dirty words, especially if they were used at times when children might be in the audience. Immediately after *Pacifica*, the FCC said that it would go only after broadcasters who used the precise seven words during times children were likely to be in the audience and only when they were used repeatedly, as Carlin had done in his monologue. By the mid-1980s the commission stated that in general it would refer complaints about broadcast indecency to the U.S. attorneys for prosecution under the U.S. Criminal Code, but pressure soon mounted on the FCC to become more forceful in enforcing upon broadcasters its own standards regarding indecency.

By 1986 the religious right and other right-wing groups began pressuring the FCC to clean up the airwaves by applying a more open interpretation of *Pacifica* that expanded beyond the seven dirty words alone. The National Federation for Decency (NFD) and MIM led the charge and picketed the FCC's offices in Washington, DC. In addition, the organizations mounted a campaign to produce numerous complaints from their members and others against so-called obscene or indecent programming. In April 1987, the FCC issued several indecency decisions and a public notice of inquiry indicating it planned to take a new direction in enforcing *Pacifica*. In essence, the commission stated it was returning to a "pure" *Pacifica* definition of indecency. No longer would just the words alone be the FCC's concern; innuendo and context would play significant roles (Hilliard & Keith, 2003, 36–42).

In addition, the "safe harbor"—those times broadcasters could carry otherwise questionable material as children were not likely be in the audience—might be eliminated. A footnote to a case in November, though, indicated the FCC did not consider children to be audience members after midnight. Since the text indicated the commission believed children were in the audience as early as 6 a.m., broadcasters concluded they had a safe harbor from midnight until 6 a.m. for more adult material that was indecent but not obscene. However, this six-hour window was much too long for right-wing groups, which pressured Congress to direct the FCC to create a total ban on indecent programming. The FCC did so in 1990, and its decision was quickly challenged in the courts. In less than one year, the U.S. Court of Appeals found the 24-hour ban overbroad and told the FCC to revive a safe harbor for more adult fare (Hilliard & Keith, 2003, 36–42).

In the early 1990s, the number of hours comprising the safe harbor fluctuated, and once it was abolished completely, albeit briefly, allowing any questionable program to be aired at any time. Although 6 a.m. ended the harbor, over the next few years, various times were set as its beginning—8 p.m., 10 p.m., and midnight. Finally, the issue reached the Supreme Court in 1996, and the Court refused to hear challenges to two appellate court decisions upholding the FCC's power to set safe harbor provisions enacted to further the state's interest in protecting children (Hilliard & Keith, 2003, 41–42).

The safe harbor concept, however, did not preclude the evolution of the daytime and early evening "shock jocks" and their continuing presence into the 21st century. Beginning in the 1980s regular programming emphasizing sexual themes began growing, and, with the expansion, complaints about the content also rose. Of the shock jocks, Howard Stern was among the most notorious, so this chapter concentrates briefly on his exploits as an example of late 20th-century programming. During the 1980s and 1990s and into the 21st century, Stern's banter resulted in fines against Infinity Broadcasting, which syndicated and aired his morning show. Beginning in 1987 Stern became a primary target of FCC fines and rule making for his "specific references to masturbation, ejaculation, breast and penis size, sexual intercourse, oral-genital contact, sodomy, bestiality, menstruation, and testicles" (*Infinity Broadcasting Corporation of Pennsylvania*, 1987).

The FCC cited six examples of indecent exchanges between Stern and others appearing on his programs:

#1—STERN: God, my testicles are down on the floor. Boy, Susan, you could really have a party with these. I'm telling you, honey.

RAY: Use them like Bocce balls.

#2—STERN: Let me tell you something, honey. Those homos you are with are all limp.

RAY: Yeah. You've never even had a real man.

#3—SUSAN: No. I was in a park in New Rochelle, NY.

STERN: In a park in New Rochelle? On your knees?

SUSAN: No, no.

RAY: And squeezing someone's testicles, probably.

#4—STERN (to a caller):
I'd ask your penis size and stuff like that, but I really don't care.

#5—STERN (in a discussion about lesbians):
I mean, to go around porking other girls with vibrating rubber products and they want the whole world to come to a standstill.

#6—STERN: Have you ever had sex with an animal?

CALLER: No.

STERN: Well, don't knock it. I was sodomized by Lambchop, you
                know the puppet [children's program host] Shari Lewis
                holds? Baaaah. That's where I was thinking that Shari
                Lewis instead of like sodomizing all the people at the
                academy to get that shot on the Emmys, she could've
                had Lambchop do it (*Infinity Broadcasting Corporation of
                Pennsylvania*, 1987).

These examples illustrate a broadening of the indecency applications the
FCC adopted immediately after *Pacifica*, and their implementation pleased
the right-wing groups pushing for even more stringent application of prohibitions against on-air indecency.

Over the next few years the FCC kept leveling fines against Infinity for
carrying Stern's ever popular program, and by 1994 they totaled more than
$1.7 million. Infinity appealed the fines, but in many ways such penalties
seemed to be a cost of doing business as the Stern morning show was a ratings winner. In 1995, the corporation decided to settle the fines with the
FCC, but this resolution did not end Stern's outrageous banter and on-air
behavior. Stern's highly rated, but admittedly raucous and raunchy, programs remained on broadcast radio until 2007, with stations carrying his
program paying the increased fines (Hilliard & Keith, 2003, 77–88). In the
spring of 2007, Stern was fired for making vulgar, but not indecent, dis-
paraging remarks about the NCAA champion Rutgers University women's
basketball team. As of this writing, Stern has promised to revive his program
on satellite radio.

Conclusion

As illustrated by examples in this chapter, society's expectations over the years
greatly affect radio programming and what is considered acceptable for air.
Epithets such as "hell," "damn," and "by God" that were interpreted as indecent or profane in an earlier generation are acceptable today. Coarser discussion of sexual matters and bodily functions undreamed of in days past are
readily offered to a more willing public as entertainment. Time and change
in social attitudes have influenced what listeners receive. Concepts of indecency that once prohibited any mention of sex are no more. Restrictions,
whether governmental or self-imposed by broadcasters, no longer hold, and
ratings seem to rule, as in the case of Howard Stern.

With the exception of the *Pacifica* case, the regulatory bodies overseeing
radio have had to rely on cases involving print media for definitions of indecency. Lack of clear definitions of indecency for broadcasting has caused
the FCC to vacillate over the years in how it decides indecency cases. In its

application of the limits it has developed under *Pacifica*, the FCC has been inconsistent as to what actually constitutes indecency—only the specific words that Carlin used, the context in which they occur, or extensions of that use to include innuendo. In addition, the FCC has varied times of day when indecency regulations apply—before midnight and after 6 a.m., during morning drive time, or 24/7.

Broadcasters are frustrated by such variations and the apparent unpredictability in determining what might be acceptable when they consider airing questionable material in an environment of ever fragmenting audiences drawn to not only radio but also other media such as television and the Internet. Determining whether broadcast material is indecent is based on seemingly elusive grounds—what could be indecent in one context or time period is not, in another. But as troublesome as attempting to control inappropriate material is, under pressure from Congress or special interest groups, regulators will continue reviewing material deemed unacceptable, improper, or offensive, and broadcasters will continue trying to deduce from the regulators' pronouncements how far they can push the envelope of taste in broadcast programming.

References

Benjamin, L. (2001). *Freedom of the Air and the Public Interest: First Amendment Rights in Broadcasting to 1935*. Carbondale: Southern Illinois University Press.

Duncan v. U.S. (1931). 48 F.2d 128.

FCC. (1970). *NAL against Eastern Educational Radio (WUHY-FM)*. 24 RR2nd 408.

FCC Reports. (1975). *In Notice of Apparent Liability to the University of Pennsylvania (WXPN-FM), December 18*. FCC 75–1405.

FCC v. Pacifica. (1978). 438 U.S. 726.

FRC. (1930a). Hearings in Re Application of William Schaeffer, Docket No. 837, National Archives Record Group 173, Box 116, FCC Docket Section 837, volumes 2 and 3.

———. (1930b). Statement of Facts and Grounds for Decision No. 5228, National Archives Record Group 173, Box 116, FCC Docket Section 837, volumes 2 and 3.

Hilliard, R. & M. Keith. (2003). *Dirty Discourse: Sex and Indecency in American Radio*. Ames: Iowa State University Press.

Infinity Broadcasting Corporation of Pennsylvania. (1987). 2 FCC Rcd 2705.

Miller v. California. (1973). 413 U.S. 15.

Roth v. U.S. (1957). 354 U.S. 476.

Sonderling Broadcasting. (1973). 27 RR2nd 285.

12. Band of Hate: Rancor on the Radio

Robert L. Hilliard

In the late 1990s two radio broadcasting veterans—the editor of this book, Michael C. Keith, and I—were listening to a small radio station based in Rhode Island and, despite our assumed familiarity with all forms of radio programming, were shocked by what we heard. We were especially disturbed because, like most everyone else, we adhered to the stereotype of the northeast and especially New England as bastions of tolerance and proponents of civil rights and liberties.

Here, in our own backyard of what many people in the country would call liberal dedication, we heard words of hate. Not only words of hate but thinly veiled calls for violence against people of color, especially African Americans, Jews, homosexuals, immigrants, different ethnic groups, Catholics, physicians who provided abortions, and anyone who might not fall under the rubric of white Protestant Aryan American.

In addition, the rhetoric did not stop there. White Protestant Aryans who did not agree with a proposed Racial Holy War against these other groups were labeled "whiggers" (a combination of two words, one pejorative, the other not) and traitors and would be among the first to be eliminated when the anticipated Armageddon came.

Was this an aberration, misplaced ugly humor, the ravings of a demented mind? Was there a possibility that more programs and more stations promulgated this kind of hatred? We decided to investigate. What we found went beyond shock.

Hundreds of domestic radio stations throughout the country and a number of shortwave stations were carrying such programs, prepared by and usually presented on the air by hate groups in the United States. The more we looked, the more we found, and not only on radio but sometimes on cable television as well and, at the beginning of what would be phenomenal growth during the ensuing decade, on the recently developed Internet. We were so overwhelmed by what we found and so disturbed by the cacophony of hate, violence, and fear that these radio programs were imposing on our democracy that we ended up writing a book about it: *Waves of Rancor: Tuning in the Radical Right*.

The Hate Mongers

Who were these hate mongers who had introduced a new and significant component into our radio culture, or—depending on one's beliefs—had perverted our radio culture. What were their goals, what were they saying, and what impact did it have on the people of America?

The principal producers and distributors of hate programs were and are those organizations associated with the radical right: neo-Nazis, skinheads, the Ku Klux Klan (KKK), white supremacists, Holocaust deniers, survivalists, antienvironmentalists, conspiracy theorists, the Christian Identity, black separatists, and similar groups with antiprogressive hate agendas. Their basic orientations are racist, anti-Semitic, and homophobic. Associated with a, but generally labeled, as the Patriot Movement are the nongovernmental armed militias. The Southern Poverty Law Center noted in its Spring, 2007, *Intelligence Report* that 844 hate groups were operating in the United States, an increase of 40% since 2000 (Potok, 2007). Although their individual structures and goals may differ to greater or lesser degrees, they have some fundamental beliefs and purposes in common.

The Targets

For most, though not all, of the radical right hate groups, the overriding aim is protecting and enhancing their versions of a white Aryan Christian society. Under the rubric of anti-Semitic Christian Identity coupled with white supremacy and self-styled patriot designation, they are preparing for a racial holy war in which they plan to destroy all those who do not fit into their category of superior beings. Their principal targets are (1) people of color—most especially, in the United States, African Americans, but, with the increasing concern over immigration in the new century, other races are included as part of their anti-immigrant phobia; (2) Jews; and (3) homosexuals. Their media programs, including radio, not only denigrate these groups but also frequently advocate hate and even violence toward them. Interestingly, some of these groups designate as their primary target those they call "whiggers"—an obvious combination of two oft-used labels. These are white Aryan Christians who do not agree with them that people of color, Jews, and homosexuals should be eliminated, who are considered the worst of all—race traitors—and who would be the first to die after the hate groups win the expected racial holy war.

Another key target is the government—ranging from federal to state to local. This is especially true for those groups that adopt conspiracy theory beliefs. One of the fundamental facets of such beliefs and the subject of many of their media programs is that the U.S. federal government is a pawn of the United Nations (UN), which in turn is a pawn of Jewish bankers in Tel Aviv bent on destroying the white Christian race through the establishment of a new world order. The epithet they use to describe the U.S. establishment in Washington is ZOG: Zionist Occupied Government. Part of this belief is that the UN is flying black helicopters over many parts of the country spying on these groups, especially the armed patriot organizations, in preparation for disarming them and "mongrelizing" the white race with nonwhite troops from Africa and Asia, who, they claim, are currently training at secret bases in the United States. Their strong opposition to any form of gun control—consistent with the efforts of many moderate, nonradical right-wing groups such as the National Rifle Association—is based on their need for the freedom to arm themselves for what they see as the coming white versus nonwhite Armageddon.

A number of other targets appear from time to time in some of their programs, including Catholics, advocates of free choice in regard to abortion (they seem to object less to abortions among people of color than among whites, who, they say, must procreate to avoid destruction of that race), Muslims and Arab Americans (especially since the 9-11 attacks on the World Trade Center and the Pentagon), and immigrants, as noted above.

A New Medium

In the new century, the use of radio for messages of hate has diminished in favor of the Internet. The Internet, they have found, is less costly, anonymous, and safer for them (radio stations, easily located, were occasionally picketed or threatened by those objecting to the hate programs); it can reach not only a region but the entire country and even the world instantaneously. The Internet not only spreads their messages but also, as an interactive medium, makes it easier for them to recruit members. The number of hate sites varies from year to year because these sites frequently go on and off, but in the first decade of the 21st century some estimates indicate that there may be as many as 2,000 hate Web sites operating in the United States in any given year, and as many as 20,000 worldwide.

Although the Internet has become the medium of choice for hate groups, radio still plays an important role. Some studies have indicated that there may be some 150 domestic radio stations throughout the country that carry one or more programs prepared by hate groups. That does not include talk show hosts who may from time to time, and some much more frequently, spew hate against the target groups. Many people, when discussing hate radio, will almost automatically mention Rush Limbaugh.

Limbaugh is not part of the radical right; compared with that extreme he is quite moderate. In fact, some on the radical right have advocated that Limbaugh be "eliminated" because they believe he is too moderate and therefore a traitor to their cause. (That studies of Limbaugh's programs show that he very frequently presents false information to his listeners is another matter—and one not substantively related to this chapter.)

An Old Medium

Use of radio for hate purposes is not new; in fact, it is almost as old as the medium itself. In the 1920s, shortly after regular radio broadcasting began, a number of people with special agendas saw the new medium as a means of instantaneously reaching more people with their messages. Ben Gross (1954), an early radio critic, wrote, "Tailors, preachers, loan sharks, swamis, and physical culture men, merchants, nostrum dispensers, and frenzied advocates of odd ideas—who combine primitive theology with hatred of chain stores, indulged in a saturnalia of 'free speech'" (p. 68).

One finds individual charlatans rather than organized hate groups spewing hate over the air in the radio's early days. Perhaps the best known and nationally most successful was a Catholic priest, Father Charles E. Coughlin. Beginning his broadcasts in 1926 from his Detroit parish, Coughlin eventually ended up being carried by CBS. In another few years he became the country's most popular radio personality; in a 1933 national poll, he was designated the "most useful citizen of the United States" (Dolan, 1996, 20). Coughlin pioneered the radical right approach to the use of the media that continued to be the benchmark into the 21st century. He "had broken down the barriers between political opinion molding and celebrity. By fusing his talent and training in the thespian arts with an entirely new medium of communication [he] transformed radio broadcasting, and thereby public discourse, in American society" (Warren, 1996, 37).

Coughlin's style was similar to that of televangelists of a later period. He targeted minority groups in an attempt to capitalize on the overt or latent hate of his listeners and sought monetary support for his broadcasts. He received millions of dollars in donations. The rise of fascism in Europe gave him further fuel, and his admiration for Mussolini in Italy and Hitler in Germany was profuse. He called the American president, Franklin D. Roosevelt, a Communist for opposing fascism. He used the frustrations of many Americans during the 1930s economic depression to turn them against Jews, labor unions, immigrants, and racial minorities. He blamed the Jews for all the problems in the world. Much like most radical right-wing groups today, he advocated an "America whose people would control the economy and preserve their Christian values" (Kazin, 1995, 37).

Coughlin developed an approach that has since been copied by many right-wing media commentators, including most effectively by Rush Limbaugh. He got his listeners' attention with dramatic half-truths or outright falsehoods. He emphasized what was titillating and even outrageous to appeal to the fears, concerns, and prejudices of his listeners, all the while steering them toward his political beliefs. When America entered World War II, Coughlin's star began to fade. Although he supported Hitler and Mussolini, the vast majority of Americans supported the United States against the Nazis, and CBS dropped his program. He established a syndicated network, but soon the affiliate stations also dropped him. In his heyday, however, he had an enormous influence, particularly in exacerbating anti-Semitism in America, and his radio rhetoric has had a lasting effect on the United States.

Hate radio continued to be principally an individual endeavor for several decades. For example, during then late 1940s through most of the 1950s—the McCarthy era in America, when it was claimed America was riddled with communist conspiracies—individual radio commentators, including powerful journalists such as Walter Winchell and Fulton Lewis Jr., excoriated and labeled as "red" anyone they believed disagreed with McCarthyist beliefs and policies. Although, over a half-century later, as this is written, some commentators subscribe to President George W. Bush's implication that anyone disagreeing with his war policies is aiding terrorists, the accusations are not as strident or as blatant. In the McCarthy era few commentators (with notable exceptions such as Edward R. Murrow) were willing to publicly disagree with McCarthy for fear of being blacklisted.

As early radio "shock jocks" added more and more political commentary to their repertoires, the intensity of hate appeared to increase concomitantly. I recall appearing as a guest in 1953 on the *Joe Pyne Show* (Pyne was a popular right-wing talk show host at the time, with a "go gargle with razor blades" type of humor). That was the day Julius and Ethel Rosenberg were executed. Pyne reduced his guests and audience to laughter because "we finally burned [those] Commies," regretting that electrocution was too good for them, and gleefully referring to "roasting the Rosenbergs" throughout the program. Pyne was the model for many later political talk show hosts.

During the 1960s the civil rights movement in America (and, to a lesser extent, the women's equal rights movement during the 1970s) stimulated hate radio commentators. As a matter of continuing practice, particularly in the South, many radio stations were racist not only in their hiring practices but also in their programming, even where the majority in their listening area were African American. Individuals and groups attempting to challenge the status quo were attacked as enemies of society, with radio commentators advocating hate and violence.

As the use of radio by radical right hate mongers—individuals and groups—grew, their orientation took two major paths: some were ranters and ravers, many affiliated with groups dedicated to violence, such as the KKK; others were soft-spoken intellectuals, who aimed their rhetoric to those in the middle, rather than preaching principally to those who already agreed with them.

Several factors contributed to the rise of hate groups and their increasing use of the media in the latter part of the 20th century. The proliferation of media distribution outlets—more radio and television stations, the growth of cable, and the incipient Internet—made it possible to obtain more airtime and to reach more people, not only influencing more people but also recruiting more people to any given cause or organization. The demise of the Fairness Doctrine—which had provided for comparable time to respond if only one side of a controversial issue in the station's community was represented, until a Fairness Act was vetoed by President Ronald Reagan in 1987 following a court ruling stating that the FCC's Fairness Doctrine was not mandatory—made it easier for stations to provide time, gratis or paid, to hate groups without fear of having to provide response time.

Uncle Sam's Role

In addition, the U.S. government's use of excessive force at the Weaver family compound at Ruby Ridge, Idaho, in 1992 and at the Branch Davidian compound at Waco, Texas, the following year served as rallying cries for the conspiracy theorists and spurred instant growth of antigovernment groups and their increased use of the media, especially radio, at a time preceding widespread use of the Internet. For example, some estimates indicate that as many as 400 new armed militia groups were formed in the two years following Waco and Ruby Ridge.

Individual political shock jocks may not necessarily be affiliated with a hate group, and media programs and personalities representing hate groups may differ in emphasis and intensity, but generally the messages are similar. Chip Berlet, a leading researcher on hate groups, described the general orientation of these organizations as a reflection of the principles of the Christian Identity movement: white power, Aryan supremacy, African American inferiority, anticommunism, patriotic jingoism, wariness government and law officials, conviction that Jews and Communists control the media, and certainty that their survival depends on their being armed for a holy war (Hate Groups Are Increasing, 1998, A-7).

Over the years individual political shock jocks have by and large been better known than the on-air representatives of the hate groups, principally because they are usually syndicated nationally or regionally and are not labeled as spokespersons for the KKK or neo-Nazis or armed militias or other organizations. Although hate groups have access through ownership, owner-friendly support, or purchase of time, most radio stations do not—some for ethical reasons and some for public relations reasons—provide access for hate-labeled groups.

Most listeners today think of talk radio as principally presented on FM stations, and many of the popular personalities are on that popular distribution service. However, many are on AM stations, especially because at night the AM signal reflects off the ionosphere and reaches further than does the FM signal. In addition, hate groups make as full use as they can of shortwave radio stations, which carry much of the radio programming of the Christian right and the armed militias. Many shortwave stations are operated by individuals. These stations are licensed for the sole purpose of using their higher power to broadcast overseas. U.S. regulations prohibit the licensees of shortwave stations to broadcast material aimed at domestic audiences. However, anyone can obtain a shortwave receiver and pick up shortwave signals, and until the advent of the Internet, it was clear that the radical right was making extensive use of shortwave radio to influence and recruit a domestic audience: One purchased the hate materials, books, and other goods they advertised from a U.S. address.

The Players

Some of the key far-right political talk hosts over the years have concentrated on molding minds; others have attempted to stimulate violence. Others have combined the two approaches. It is important to note that the most influential political radio personalities' consistent and sometimes outrageous misstatements do not overtly advocate violence. He is not in the far-right category. Among those who are considered on the cusp is convicted Watergate conspirator G. Gordon Liddy. Liddy once advocated the assassination of a journalist who was highly critical of him. Very popular among government-phobic conspiracy theorists such as armed militias, Liddy once described how to shoot a federal agent whom one considered threatening. As federal agents usually wear bullet-proof vests, Liddy advised shooting them in the groin, because "they cannot move their hips fast enough and you'll probably get a femoral artery and you'll knock them down at any rate" (Berger, 1995, C-1). He also advocated that his audience prepare for such encounters with target practice—using as targets cardboard figures of Bill and Hillary Clinton (Petrozzello, 1995, 26).

Another example of the individual radio hate host is Bob Grant, for years on New York's WABC and then WOR. His program was described as a "Ku Klux Klan rally of the airwaves—cruel, racist, with hints of violence" (Cohen and Solomon, 1994, 138). He called African Americans "savages" and "subhumanoids" and expressed his wish that the police had machine-gunned the marchers at a New York Gay Pride parade (Hilliard & Keith, 1999, 138).

Some of the hate radio personalities made the transition from local stations to national exposure on television. One of these is Sean Hannity, who at this writing is part of a popular right-wing political commentary duo on a Fox cable new outlet. Critics have noted that he made his initial reputation by "race baiting" and "gay bashing." Reportedly, one of his favorite radio personalities when he was growing up was Bob Grant (Hilliard & Keith, 1999, 141).

Few hate jocks are on mainstream radio stations in the early 21st century, as the Internet has become their medium of choice in the new century—although, as noted earlier, it is estimated that some 150 radio stations still carry one or more hate programs. The new controversial personalities who ostensibly go to extremes appear to do so deliberately to gain audience attention and personal notoriety rather than to proselytize. Howard Stern, for example, consistently airs sexist material and occasionally racist material, although it is clear that his goal is not to forward the particular sexist agenda of a given survivalist group or the racist agenda of white supremacist organizations. The same is true for the sexist approach of much of the work of shock jocks Opie and Anthony. In addition, Don Imus is not representing conspiracy theorists when he attacks the government or the KKK when he makes racist comments.

Yet, the prejudice and hate nevertheless come across to their listeners. Because they are so popular on mainstream radio, they are sometimes penalized for comments that are relatively mild compared with those of consciously hate-dispensing personalities. For example, in 2007 Don Imus was fired from his radio job for using the term "nappy-headed hos" to describe the women members of a college basketball team. And in the same year Opie and Anthony were in trouble—again—for airing a crude sexist segment of a homeless man talking about how he would like to rape Condoleeza Rice, Laura Bush, and Queen Elizabeth. They were suspended from their radio jobs, a fairly frequent occurrence for them.

More in keeping with the traditional hate hosts in the new century is Michael Savage, whose nationally syndicated radio show, *The Savage Nation*, consistently contains messages of hate toward gays, lesbians, liberals, people of color, people of Middle Eastern heritage, Muslims, and women. This contemporary hate program has prompted some citizen groups to call for reinstatement of the Fairness Doctrine by the FCC—to no avail.

Many of the extremist personalities in radio history have overtly reflected the views of specific hate organizations. Perhaps the best known is David Duke, an erudite and convincing speaker who is a former KKK leader. His charisma and rhetoric almost got him elected governor of Louisiana and, in another campaign, U.S. senator. He supported Klan beliefs and policies for many years over the radio and in the new media age has become a television and Internet personality and one of the world's leading Holocaust deniers. One of the effective radio representatives of the neo-Nazi movement in America was Tom Valentine, who presented one of the longest-running shortwave radio shows, *Radio Free America*. His principal backer was the neo-Nazi Liberty Lobby. The program added satellite and Internet distribution. Valentine also represented the conspiracy theorists' beliefs, and his program was once described as "Radio Paranoia" (Flynn in Hilliard & Keith, 1999, 225).

One of the most effective radio representatives of the conspiracy theorists and armed militias, particularly in regard to antigovernment and anti–gun control beliefs and actions, has been Chuck Baker. He has encouraged listeners to stockpile arms and ammunition, join armed militias, form guerilla cells, and take their guns and march on Washington to shoot members of Congress. (One of his listeners did go to Washington and attempted to shoot up the White House, and several others shot out traffic control cameras that they believed were being used to spy on antigovernment groups to confiscate their weapons; Hilliard & Keith, 1999, 228–229.)

The National Alliance

Arguably the most effective neo-Nazi use of radio has been that of the National Alliance, for years considered the largest and best organized of America's Nazi groups. Its longtime radio program *Dissident Voices* overtly preached hate and violence. Its late director Dr. William Pierce was known for his neo-Nazi, anti-Semitic views and was described as "the white supremacist movement's undisputed master of propaganda" (*Intelligence Report*, 1996). His radio shows covered topics such as the destruction of American life through "diversity," the subversion of American universities through the introduction of nonwhite curriculum materials, and the use of the Holocaust fantasy by Jews to extort money. A recurring sentiment surfaced frequently in this shoes:

> all the homosexuals, race mixers and hard case collaborators in the country who have gone too far to be re-educated can be rounded up, packed into 10,000 or so railroad cattle cars, and eventually double-timed into an abandoned coal mine. (Olson, n.d.)

Pierce's novel *The Turner Diaries* was widely distributed in print and was read on *Dissident Voices*, reaching and influencing many in its hate for the federal government. The novel tells how true patriots fought back against the Jewish-controlled, antiwhite government through a detailed plan that resulted in the bombing of a federal building. It is not a coincidence that one of the National Alliance's strongest supporters, an avid listener to

Dissident Voices and a member of the nongovernmental Michigan armed militia, Timothy McVeigh, followed virtually the same plan and methods as outlined in *The Turner Diaries* when he bombed the Murrah Federal Building in Oklahoma City. It is reported that even when he was on death row the radio in his prison cell was tuned to *Dissident Voices*.

Another strong voice from the National Alliance on *Dissident Voices* was Alfred Strom's. A direct quote from one of his programs sums up the kinds of goals and rhetoric he used, which reflect those of so many other hate purveyors. He condemned

> [t]he Jewish leadership and their anti-American agenda ... the Jewish kingpins of international finance who control the major news media in the United States ... telling us we must bring unlimited numbers of non-White immigrants into our country ... telling us that any speech or action which tends to preserve our unique genetic and cultural heritage is "racism" and must be outlawed ... telling us that interracial sex and homosexuality, perversions which our ancestors have condemned and punished as crimes for millennia, are just "personal lifestyle choices" and must be tolerated and even promoted ... telling us that we must give up our hard-won national independence and freedom and become part of a global tyranny which they call the New World Order ... telling us that we give up our right to own effective firearms, and leave their BATF, their FBI, their UN armies, and their poets in the ghettos as the only ones with guns.

He states that the Jews are nonwhites whose race and religion are as destructive "as an arrow aimed at America's heart ... this overwhelming preponderance of Jews in anti-American and anti-White activities is a biological rather than a political phenomenon" (Hilliard & Keith, 1999, 169).

Racism is not neglected by American *Dissident Voices*. In another radio broadcast Strom said,

> Every January the media go into a kind of almost spastic frenzy of adulation for the so-called "Reverend Dr. Martin Luther King, Jr." ... he is not a legitimate reverend, he is not a bona fide Ph.D., and his name isn't really "Martin Luther King, Jr." What's left? Just a sexual degenerate, an America-hating Communist, and a criminal betrayer of even the interests of his own people. (Strom, 1994)

In addition, in another broadcast, the intelligence of blacks was cited as being quantitatively and qualitatively inferior to that of whites; blacks were said to differ from whites in their "essential nature" and not to have the ability to deal with abstract concepts because key portions of their brains are less developed than in whites (The Roots of Civilization, 1993).

Even as time progressed and *Dissident Voices* was less and less heard on terrestrial radio and more and more on Internet radio, the same basic messages continued. In mid-2000s, ADV featured a new principal radio voice, Erich Gliebe. Here are some of the things he broadcast on the Internet for downloading in 2007: Muslims, in alliance with Jews, are the single greatest threat to Europe; for our survival, we have to be guided by the man who dared more, believed more strongly, and fought with superhuman strength for the realization of a folkish German state and a purer Europe; the Jews with their group paranoia have created a self-fulfilling prophecy—they are indeed persecuted—not because of irrational anti-Semitism but because of the inevitable reactions to their own behavior; all-white cities will have better schools, pride and quality will replace greed, neighborhoods will be family-like, and the economy will be stable; the Holocaust lie is used to browbeat our people into submission and the Holocaust lie must be destroyed; the National Alliance demands the freedoms to enjoy white government, white neighborhoods, white schools, and white workplaces and to live in our own white world with white values (http://www.natvan.com/internet-radio).

The "Patriots"

The patriot movement, represented principally by the armed militias, like the neo-Nazis, has made significant use of radio. Mark Koernke, a member of a Michigan militia, has been one of their most effective representatives. So extreme was he that even some far-right stations threw him off the air. He urged citizens to arm themselves and provided directions on how to make and use weapons—for example, from gasoline cans and matches—for use in urban centers. Extreme-right survivalists have used radio for messages that are sometimes similar to those of the militias in their support of conspiracy theory and the need to acquire and use weapons. Kurt Saxon is considered to be a founder of survivalism but has accused militias of not understanding the principles of self-reliance and self-defense. His personal slogan can be a mantra for many other conspiracy theorists who support the survivalist movement: "A pistol for the bedroom—A shotgun over the door—A 30.06 for reaching out—You don't need any more."

Radio talk host Chuck Harder was once described as the "King of Conspiracy Theorists, who pound for pound engenders more listener loyalty than any talk show host in America" (Freivogel, 1995). He is especially effective because he does not use the usual stereotypical far-right language. For example, he noted that Bill Cosby's son was killed by a Russian immigrant, implying that it was the result of what he considered our too liberal immigration policy. He also implied that the killing of the son of Time-Warner chair Gerald Levin by a rapper was a result of Levin's own promotion and distribution of rap music. He also warned the public that the Armageddon between blacks and whites and the fight against the new world order would take place in this new-millennium century (Hilliard & Keith, 1999, 205).

The New Century

Today, as previously noted, the Internet has become the medium of choice for hate radio programs. However, hate can be heard every day and every night on traditional terrestrial radio stations. Talk shows that are not deliberately oriented to spread hate, either by individual hate jocks or by sponsoring hate groups, frequently present virtually the same messages. One of the reasons is that almost all talk shows are right-wing oriented—from conservative right to radical right. Many of them are syndicated. Few talk shows can be described as liberal. In fact, until the advent of the Air America radio network in the mid-2000s, not a single liberal talk show was syndicated, compared with the dozens of syndicated conservative/right-wing talk shows. Why is there such an imbalance? Historically and especially since the elimination of virtually all anti-monopoly rules in the Telecommunications Act of 1996, almost all media—radio and television—have been owned by conservatives. Consolidation of radio by large conglomerates has dramatically reduced diversity and virtually eliminated localism, resulting in programming that deliberately or by accommodation reflects the conservative views of the radio station owners (Hilliard & Keith, 2005).

Because a talk radio station or program or personality is not overtly identified with a hate group or as a hate monger does not mean that it does not disseminate hate materials. Steve Randall, senior analyst with the media watchdog organization Fairness and Accuracy in Reporting (FAIR), stated that "talk radio can be one of the most divisive mediums in the nation" (Olsen, 2003). For example, a talk show host on station KGEZ in northwest Montana attacked local environmentalists and conservationists as being linked to Al Qaeda. They were blamed for deteriorating economic conditions in the area and called "Green Nazis" and "The Fourth Reich." Their names and some of their addresses were broadcast. The result: Cars were vandalized, phone threats—including warnings of being killed—were received, property was defaced. Similar effects have resulted from anti-gay rhetoric on radio stations in the Northeast, anti-Arab rhetoric in the Midwest, and anti-Latino rhetoric in the Southwest (Olsen, 2003). Political scientist David Barker tracked the voting records of talk show listeners for three consecutive elections and found a clear correlation between what they heard on talk shows and their political behavior (Olsen, 2003).

Probably the definitive listing of Internet hate sites is Raymond A. Franklin's semiannual Hate Directory. For the first, in 2007, he included radio under the heading "Racist Internet Radio Broadcasts." The contents of these programs go beyond racism and include the panoply of targets, beliefs, and goals presented thus far in this chapter. They are reflected in a sampling of these sites (Franklin, 2007).

- Aryan Nations Radio (with program titles such as *By Yahweh's Design, Judgment Day Perspective, Unfair and Unbalanced,* and *Voice of Christian Israel*)
- Blood and Honour Radio
- European Brotherhood Radio
- KKK Radio
- Aryan Front Radio
- Mice Trap Radio (subtitled Radio White)
- National Socialist Workers Radio, with a program titled *National Socialist Workers Survival of the Fittest* (the Nazi party name and goal)
- Scriptures for America (operated by Pete Peters, arguably the country's most dedicated and vicious homophobe)
- Storm Front Radio (operated by the first and most successful Internet hate site, with programs featuring David Duke)
- Turner Radio Network (with programs titled *Insurgent Radio, The HoloHoax, Yahweh's Truth*)
- White Nationalist Radio
- White Power Radio
- White Pride Radio (emanating from the Brotherhood of Klans)

Countering the Hate

Although there are many hate organizations, there are relatively few organizations whose principal orientation is fighting the hate. Among the best known are the Southern Poverty Law Center, various branches of the Anti-Defamation League, and the Simon Wiesenthal Center. Anti-hate organizations using media or concentrating on countering hate media, including radio, are even fewer. One of the best known is Radio for Peace International (RFPI). For years, it operated a shortwave radio station in Costa Rica, dedicating the content of its programming to social justice, human rights, women's rights, and environmental protection. It frequently countered some of the rhetoric of hate radio directly. Attacks on the station included bombing, cutting off its power, and personal assaults on its operators. In 2003 it was evicted from its studios. It not only survived but expanded its coverage with the establishment of an Internet radio station, Global Community Radio.

FAIR, mentioned above, has as one of its major goals the challenging of hate radio. It not only exposes hate but also urges the public to join in by listening to talk shows, documenting hate talk, informing others of the content, calling in to a given program to counter the hate statements, offer assistance to anti-hate organizations, and organize and build opposition that will overtly challenge hate content in the media.

Another, more recently formed group is Stop Hate Radio, which states, "Hate destroys. Hate kills. Hate corrodes. Hate radio has got to go." It advocates boycotts of sponsors of stations that carry hate programs as a means of removing them from the air. It rejects First Amendment considerations by saying that "Hate Radio is NOT free speech" (Stop Hate Radio, 2007). StopHateRadio.com and TakeBackTheMedia.com express frustration with a plethora of so-called conservative talk shows that frequently are "nothing more than platforms for hate speech" (www.tampabaycoalition.com/no2hate).

However, radio hate speech has created a dilemma for those opposed to it. Does the harm caused by hate radio warrant an abrogation of its perceived First Amendment rights by removing it or censoring it? Are there any other means for stopping the cancer of hate from spreading and destroying a democratic society? In *Waves of Rancor: Tuning in the Radical Right*, Michael C. Keith and I stated that much of the hate speech we encountered went beyond cruel viciousness; it fomented violence that could maim and even kill designated groups and individuals. Yet, no matter how abhorrent we found it, we found even more abhorrent any censorship—which, given the political winds of a given time, could be used to stifle not only the extremists' speech but anyone's, including one's own speech. We may abhor the flagrant hate we hear and see on radio and television, in films and in books, on cable and on the Internet. But tolerance is the price we must pay for freedom. It is not too large a price (Hilliard & Keith, 2007, 160–161).

References

Berger, Kevin. (1995). Shortwave Rightists Make Liddy & Co. Seem Moderate. *San Francisco Examiner*, May 1, 48.

Cohen, Jeff & Norman Solomon. (1994). Spotlight Finally Shines on White Hate Radio. *Media Beat*, November 3, 43.

Dolan, J.P. (1996). Hate Radio (review of *Radio Priest: Charles Coughlin, the Father of Hate Radio* by Donald Warren). *New York Times*, August 25, Section 7, 17.

Flynn, Adrienne. (1999). Radio Show's Ties a Shock for Salmon; Program Linked to Neo-Nazis. In Robert Hilliard & Michael Keith (Eds.), *Waves of Rancor: Tuning in the Radical Right*. New York: M.E. Sharpe.

Franklin, Raymond A. (2007). Hate Directory. http://www.bcpl.net~rfrankli/hatedir.htm January 15.

Freivogel, William. (1995). King of Conspiracy Theorists. *Houston Chronicle*, May 14, 17.

Gross, Ben. (1954). *I Looked and I Listened*. New York: Random House.

Hate Groups Are Increasing in the U.S. (1998). *St. Louis Post-Dispatch*, March 4, 51.

Hilliard, Robert & Michael Keith. (1999). *Waves of Rancor: Tuning in the Radical Right*. New York: M.E. Sharpe.

———. (2005). *The Quieted Voice: The Rise and Demise of Localism in Radio*. Carbondale: Southern Illinois University Press.

————. (2007). *Dirty Discourse: Sex and Indecency in Broadcasting*, 2nd edition. Malden, MA: Blackwell Publishing.

Intelligence Report. (1996, May). Southern Poverty Law Center. Birmingham, Alabama Montogomery, AL.

Kazin, Michael. (1995). The First Radio Populist: A Lesson from the 1930s. *Tikkun*, January-February.

Olsen, Ken. (2003). Does Talk Radio Incite Hate? April 25. Retrieved from http://www.tolerance.org/news/article.

Olson, Rochelle. (n.d.). [Turner Diaries] Author Urges All to Think About Supremacist Stand. Associated Press.

Petrozzello, Donna. (1995). Emotions Run High at Talk Radio Convention. G. Gordon Liddy Wins Freedom of Speech Award. *Broadcasting & Cable*, July 3, 27.

Potok, Mark. (2007). The Infection of Hate (Editorial). *Intelligence Report*, Spring.

The Roots of Civilization. ADV broadcast, May 29, 1993.

Stop Hate Radio. (2007). Retrieved from http://www.hartwilliams.com/stophate, May 17, 2007.

Strom, Kevin Alfred. (1994). The Beast As Saint: The Truth about "Martin Luther King, Jr." ADV broadcast, January 15.

Warren, Donald. (1996). *Radio Priest: Charles Coughlin, the Father of Hate Radio.* New York: Free Press.

13. Talk Nation: Turn Down Your Radio

PETER LAUFER

Talk radio is pornographic. There is something perverse about lonely misfits and amateur information distorters waiting on hold for an hour and more just for the opportunity to be abused by a loudmouthed so-called host, a host often equipped with no discernible credentials other than fast-paced patter. This bizarre behavior exhibited by the callers—waiting patiently to get on the air and provide free programming material for commercial radio stations—is mirrored by the voyeuristic passive response of the millions and millions of Americans who eavesdrop on the superficial conversations of talk radio: the listeners.

"Turn down your radio!" the talk show barkers demand. "Turn down your radio!" they tell the endless callers who jam the phone circuits and wait on hold for their Warholian moment on the air, a fleeting moment to engage the host. The playing field is never level. "I'm running out of time" is the cavalier explanation from the host for cutting the caller off in mid-thought, mid-sentence. The nastier hosts just slam the telephone with a litany of complaints about the caller.

Talk radio is a carnival—an amusement show. Fancy parades as fact. Uninformed opinion is championed as thoughtful commentary. Groundless innuendo gets the same respect as investigative journalism. Hate is heralded as a valid response to problems. Besides these negatives, talk radio too often is a noisy waste of time; it is usually just a bunch malcontents yelling at each other or a bunch of blowhards impressing each other.

Dislike it as I seem to, I keep returning to it. It is seductive. It is a growing power in our society. It is fun and easy and lucrative for those of us with radio skills and talents to perform. It can be dangerous. I am part of it. Its actors—both the stars and the journeymen (and women)—are my friends and colleagues. And periodically the players in this potent medium engage in thoughtful and entertaining discussion and debate important to society.

Too often, however, talk radio is an example of the degeneration of American popular culture. Nonetheless it must be taken seriously, because it is such a powerful influence. Even Americans who listen to talk radio cynically—the ones who call it base and uninformed—are subtly seduced by it.

The Potency of Talk Radio

The power of the talk show host to influence lives, to hurt feelings, to effect change, cannot be discounted—despite the lack of reasonable and established criteria for the job. I remember, with some pain, complaining fervently one night about the Los Angeles smog over KABC, where I hosted a talk show in the early 1970s.

"It doesn't bother me!" responded a caller enthusiastically.

I acted horrified, asking him why he wasn't bothered by the poison muddying the air. "Walk over to your window," I ordered, "open the shade and look out at that filthy horizon!"

"I can't," answered my caller, "I'm blind and a double amputee."

Was he toying with me, or was he really blind and without legs? Who knows for sure? One of the bizarre beauties of talk radio is the anonymity of the callers. But I believed him on some intuitive level; I believe him still.

"I just came home a day early from a business trip," the caller to one of my talk shows was speaking fast and crying, and it was clear to me that he wasn't making it up; his was a real crisis. "I walked into our bedroom and another man was in bed with my wife!"

Through his sobs he explained that he ran from the house to get his gun and then, before rushing back to shoot one or both of them, he decided to call me for advice; he was a regular listener to my show. We talked about his crisis, and his options. The call came in the late 1970s to KXRX in San Jose, a news and talk station on which I hosted a show called *Instant Gratification* in the late 1970s and early 1980s. It was minutes before four in the afternoon, when my show was scheduled to conclude for the day. I consulted with the news department and we delayed the start of the afternoon news while I continued our conversation, hoping to distract the poor fellow and keep him out of his house. Sure, I wanted to save lives, but it was compelling radio. I doubt any listener who tuned in during that call wanted to turn off the radio or change the station. Finally, when I viscerally concluded that he was no longer an immediate danger to his frolicking wife, I made a deal with him on the air. I broke my own rules never to meet with a caller and asked him to join me after the show at a bowling alley adjacent to the studios. We talked out his immediate passion for violence and he agreed to seek professional counseling. He called back several days later to announce that he no longer intended to shoot his wife and her lover.

Most talk radio hosts share similar experiences, some with less happy endings. From trivial consumer concerns to life and death crises, talk radio can be the most available institution of last resort that alienated citizens turn to for help.

Talk radio holds the potential to bring out the best and the worst in both the hosts and the audience. My files bulge with love and hate mail sent to me by my listeners. After hosting a talk show about immigration on KPFA in Berkeley in 2007, I received this typical example from a correspondent who identified himself as Mike North (the punctuation is his):

Hey dipshit,

Heard your ridiculous, typical leftist nonsense on the radio regarding the illegal invasion

Bravo dork, thank you for standing up for the corrupt American business climate that profits off their illegal slaves

Please do me a favor, don't act as if you're concerned with the lower echelon of the American worker, because everytime [sic] you act as if you do, your snobbish, elitist bullshit shows thru [sic]

The lower wage workers, actual American workers, are being displaced (and wages depressed) due to the never ending supply of "slaves", & apparently, you're all for it

What I'd like to see happen is illegal aliens (oh the horror of truthful verbiage) come & take jobs that elitist snobs like you do. Then I'd love to hear you spew your leftist bullshit, the "they're only doing jobs Americans won't do" rhetoric

If our country's future was [sic] in your hands, the hands of altruistic, anti-Western civilization white dorks like you, our country would be over in short order

I only wish I could debate you in person. You wouldn't be able to speak over me or shut me up, like you did with your radio callers

Now, before you brand me as a "racist" & "uneducated," I hold two BA's & a Masters. I'm also a musician who has friends of all ethnicity's [sic]

But I have something you don't, common sense. And I actually put the citizens of my country above the invaders (oh how racist of me)

Just admit it dork boy, you hate America & Americans. Your skin color repulses you. How progressive!

If you ever want to debate in person, just let me know. I eat leftist mommy's boys like you for lunch

M. North

Talk Radio Flexes Its Muscles

Long considered a troubled stepchild of so-called mainstream media and usually viewed with disdain by writers and broadcasters associated with more traditional outlets for their journalistic endeavors, talk radio finally demanded credibility and at least some limited respect after claiming credit for defeating attempts by Congress to grant itself a substantial pay raise. Although after the brou-ha-ha generated by a loose network of talk radio hosts in late 1988 and early 1989 finally subsided Congress proceeded to guarantee itself the extra money it wanted anyway, the talk radio industry chalked the stalled pay raise up as a victory and convinced itself and much of the listening audience that talk radio shows express the ultimate *vox populi* of modern America. "What's the third branch of government?" asks a civics teacher in a political cartoon of the time. "Talk radio!" shoots back a confident student.

The talk show hosts involved were ecstatic about the vote, but it was not the first time they perceived themselves powerbrokers. Three years before, at WRKO, Jerry Williams managed to generate enough negative public reaction to the Massachusetts law that mandated the use of automobile seat belts to get the law repealed. In 1987, in Nevada, Travus T. Hipp used KPTL to lobby the legislature to change the automobile insurance law. Instead of requiring each registered car to be insured, Nevadans could then insure themselves and be covered no matter what they drove.

The actual and perceived power of the talk hosts and their callers made traditional politicos nervous; a new institution was playing their game and changing the rules. Even the *Nation* magazine cranked out an anti-talk radio editorial—the journal expressing its worry that talk radio poses a potential danger to the republic. *Nation* credited President Clinton's inability to nullify the military ban on homosexuals and the Senate confirmation failures of his attorney general nominees Zoë Baird and Kimba Wood to talk radio. "Listeners were successfully mobilized to act on their blatant homophobia and only slightly displaced sexism," determined the *Nation*'s editors (*Nation*, 1995, 255–256). The magazine blamed the arrogance of a nonresponsive government and its corporate partners for creating the environment that led to the self-appointed saviors on talk radio. "But in instant referendums-by-radio there is always the capacity for bashing unpopular minorities," worried the *Nation*, before really lashing out at their broadcast competition. "The talk show demagogues are adept at manipulating anger and turning righteous resentment into fearful hatred of the oppressed. That, indeed, is a constant danger in any democratic system," the editors acknowledged, "but in more moderated forums—legislatures, town meetings, public hearings, op-ed pages—there is space and time for the development of coalitions, compromises and sometimes even common sense. Unmodulated majoritarianism can be as undemocratic as totalitarianism." The *Nation* did not call for censorship but blamed politicians for failing to engage the electorate in adequate dialogue on the issues of the day, thus creating an environment that allowed the "demagogues" of the airwaves to flourish and become empowered.

Who Are the Callers?

From my experience hosting and producing talk shows since 1966, I'm convinced that callers to talk shows are seeking companionship and entertainment more than information. They are lonely, stuck at home, or stuck in traffic. Many feel disenfranchised from society and they desire an opportunity to be heard; they are convinced they have something to say. A steady and growing number are members of some activist political organization—groups throughout the spectrum of ideas are fast learning how to manipulate talk radio—and wait interminably on hold for the chance to gain some free radio airtime. Some callers even seem quite average and normal and are successfully spurred to participate in a show by skillful hosts. Most are subject to restrictive screening by producers before they can get a chance to be on the air. And all are subject to the vagaries of the amount of time left in the show at the time they call. In no way should random callers to talk radio stations be presumed to represent ideas that constitute the feelings of a majority who choose to express themselves. Despite the seriousness with which many talk show hosts insist on taking themselves, the medium usually remains one primarily of entertainment, not journalism. At times, talk show hosts do practice journalism. Too often, though, the audience is confused and interprets the entertainment as journalism. Worse, skillful manipulators hide behind the guise of entertainment to shroud hate and lies—intentionally confusing the audience.

"If we keep blurring the distinctions and standards between news and entertainment," wrote then–CBS News anchor Dan Rather in a thoughtful and concerned letter to the *New York Times*, "we're all going to have to pay. And I respectfully submit the price is too high" (Rather, 1994, A-20).

The Host Is a God

"Fuckin' Howard, radio God!" Howard Stern quotes one of his listeners as saying after enjoying one of Stern's lascivious fantasies. The "radio God" reference is in Stern's book *Private Parts*, attributed to a listener who claims he masturbates to the accompaniment of Stern's show while commuting. Radio god is often the role talk show hosts place themselves in on the air. It is bizarre that so many listeners and callers bow and pray to that self-created role. "Thank you for taking my call!" They set up their encounter with subservience. "I'm a first-time caller, long-time listener" comes out like a chant to an almighty. While the talk show host uses the callers as free actors in the ongoing and extemporaneous radio play that constitutes a talk show, a dynamic is successfully created to convince the callers that the radio god is actually indulging the callers by allowing them the opportunity to fill some airtime between the advertisements, advertisements that the radio station needs to pay its bills and generate a profit. What the callers rarely realize is that most talk show hosts exist in abject fear that there will be no calls, a sign most feel means the show is a failure. While the callers wait for communion with the radio god, the host is praying for calls so that he or she is not forced into an hour-long monologue and an uncomfortable after-the-show meeting with the boss.

The town meeting analogy further breaks down because of the anonymity of talk radio. In a crossroads village governed by a town meeting, the citizens all know one another. Their children go to school together. What they say and do at the town meeting will follow and haunt them throughout the rest of their local lives—at work and play. Screaming and yelling, insults, and accusations rarely go unchallenged. Speeches with inadequate documentation rarely find acceptance. Follow-up conversations are easy to conduct and frequently occur. The people are interconnected; they must face the consequences of their town meeting actions. In the ether of talk radio, there is no worry about responsibility for speeches; there rarely are consequences.

Perhaps that creates a healthy outlet, perhaps not. However, it is no town meeting.

The Genesis of Talk Radio

The beginnings of interactive talk on the radio between the audience and the host are vague. Broadcasting consultant and researcher Willis Duff traces it to the 1930s and John J. Anthony's *The Goodwill Hour* advice show, aired over the Mutual Broadcasting System. "You have a friend and adviser in John J. Anthony," his announcer started each program, "and thousands are happier and more successful today because of John J. Anthony!" Anthony would simply paraphrase over the air his listeners' letters and telephone calls. Other listeners were in the studio and part of Anthony's trademark was to remind them not to touch the microphone and to use "no names, please" as they told him their deepest troubles. Eventually he joined the staff of what Duff identifies as the first 24-hour talk station in America, KLAC in Los Angeles. Duff was program director at the station from 1963 to 1967.

Alexander Woollcott started talking on the radio over New York's WOR in 1929, although without the interaction with the audience that characterized *The Goodwill Hour*. Woollcott announced that on his show he would "talk of people I've seen, plays I've attended, books I've just read, jokes I've just heard." He switched to the CBS network the next year, naming his show *The Town Crier*. He launched into each edition with the call, "Hear ye, hear ye. This is Woollcott speaking." As became the case with the telephone talk format, Woollcott's approach to broadcasting was to offer himself to the audience in a conversational manner. He was a radio acquaintance, not an authoritative voice talking at listeners.

Other radio historians trace the talk format back to the earlier 1920s. Kenneth S. Stern headed a study on hate in talk radio for the American Jewish Committee in New York and concluded that the first talk show was about farming, broadcast in 1921 over WBZ, then headquartered in Springfield, Massachusetts.

Talk radio and the first radio broadcasting developed concurrently according to Fitchburg (Massachusetts) State College assistant professor of communications and talk show scholar Wayne Munson. He studied the 1928–1929 schedules of the American radio networks for an example and found 21 programs he defines as talk radio. "Most of these programs were monologues," Munson determined, "experts talking at the audience rather than dialogue or audience participation shows" (Munson, 1993, 27). An exception Munson found was *The Voice of Experience,* an offering that ran from 1933 to 1940 on CBS, drawing attention to people in need of help. Audience participation took the form of listener contributions to host Dr. Marion Sayle Taylor's fund for what he called the "less fortunate."

Munson lists variety shows that took listener requests into consideration, game and quiz shows, and amateur shows all as progenitors of today's telephone talk show—along with interview and debate programs dealing current affairs and offering opportunities for participation from an audience listening in the radio studio. One of those early shows, *Vox Pop*, ran from 1938 to 1947 jumping from NBC to CBS to ABC. It first aired in 1935 under the title *Sidewalk Interviews* and featured street reporters interviewing passersby in encounters that sounded remarkably like a current radio talk show.

On a January 1936 edition, the questioners hailed what sounded like impromptu guests and engaged them with questions such as "What is the difference between lingering and loitering?" and "How wide is a half dollar?" and "Would you feel better if you knew nobody was listening to you right now?" Not all of the conversation was based on silly questions; political matters were mixed in with the funny responses and the resulting laughter from the studio audience. As is a telephone talk show on the radio, *Sidewalk Interviews* was captivating because of its spontaneity and because the interviewees really sounded as if they were examples of average men and women on the street—especially in the face of the polished questioning coming from the professional announcers.

"Contrast and incongruity are at the root of the humor," is Munson's review of *Vox Pop*.

The common folk become the slick interviewers' foils. Arcane or absurd questions surprise the people, thus magnifying their performance awkwardness and prompting their honest, emotional reactions. Sometimes their laughter breaks the formal frame of the interview situation; more often, the interviewee plays along, heightening the listener's sense of the absurd. (Munson, 1993, 32)

Programs all over the country contained precursors of telephone talk radio. Fueled by the Depression, Father Charles E. Coughlin harnessed millions of radio listeners who were captivated by his oral response to their needs. As his following grew, he strayed far from Catholic teachings to promoting fascism and, as World War II began, he was prevented from buying the radio airtime he needed to maintain his popularity.

Just after the war, Barry Gray hosted his WMCA show from a New York bar called *Chandler's*. Interviews with celebrities were a primary element of that program. From the mid-1950s into the 1960s Kenny Mayer talked on WBOS in Boston. A columnist for the *Boston Herald*, Mayer broadcast from his Brookline home and would pick up the telephone if it would ring, talk with the caller, and then relay the conversation to his radio audience. Larry Glick was an early practitioner of talk on the radio, using the telephone on his WBZ show in Boston as a device to connect with the audience by calling out to the city and talking with on duty policemen, customers at truck stops, waitresses in doughnut shops.

Wolfman Jack mixed talk radio techniques with music to hawk an endless array of products over the Mexican border blasters XERF and XERB and become a legend for American radio listeners growing up in the 1960s. "Who is dis onna Wolfman telephone?" he would howl at callers. "Speak up! You gotta mind tumor? How sweet are your little peaches? Stand on your head and howl! Bye!" (Crawford & Fowler, 2002, 271) is typical of the Wolfman's popular one-way exchanges with listeners.

Pacifica stations in New York and Berkeley broadcast variety shows in the 1960s that included what is now identified as talk radio. In New York, the Pacifica outlet WBAI showcased Bob Fass's Saturday night program *Radio Unnameable*. Aficionados of the program remember it in detail and fondly as a counterculture radio oasis.

"Fass used to say that what he was doing was running a giant switchboard," said one of his WBAI colleagues, Steve Post. "Fass would use his program and the telephone lines to put people in touch with one another" (Armstrong, 1981, 77). As was the case a few years later at KSAN, WBAI— and several so-called underground stations around America—did not simply report the news or observe the parade, the stations and their personnel participated in the breaking news. KSAN's first news director, Scoop Nisker, became famous for ending his newscasts with the stock line, "If you don't like the news, go out and make some of your own."

Joel A. Spivak was at KLAC in the early 1960s, as a disc jockey, playing recorded music. Soon after he was hired, the station added Joe Pyne as a show host. Pyne's aggressive and offensive form of telephone talk was a huge hit with the Los Angeles listeners and the station adjusted its format to all talk in 1963.

Spivak remembered Pyne as a mentor to learn from but not copy. "Pyne was a great showman, and we all tried to emulate him," he told me. After a while, things calmed down a little bit. Pyne didn't, but the rest of us did because we suddenly realized when you're talking about issues that are important to people, you have a public trust to be responsible about it. So it evolved from what was shock radio in 1963 into something a little bit more responsible—but still a heck of a lot of fun.

Spivak and I met in 1994 to talk about radio and those old days at KLAC brought a dreamy look to his eyes. "We owned that town," he said about Los Angeles in the early 1960s before I changed the subject to Joe Pyne.

"He was a master showman," he said again and again about Pyne. "He created a sensation. Forget about his right-wing politics. Forget about the fact that Joe wasn't a great intellect. He talked a language people understand." With fondness, Spivak recalled, "He could be devastating. Limbaugh is bright," he said about the man many radio students believe is the direct descendent of Pyne. "I would rather listen to Pyne. Limbaugh does the same show every day. You could never fully predict what position Pyne would take on anything." As an example, Spivak cites Pyne's decision to come out against the death penalty after he witnessed an execution.

"He didn't scream all that often," said Spivak about his teacher. "But he was very animated. It was like professional wrestling. People just loved to hear Pyne do battle. He would lacerate people, but he was funny. Pyne was really a phenomenon. One of those comes along once or twice a lifetime. He was way ahead of his time."

As for Pyne, one of his own memorable lines long outlived him: "I have no respect for anyone who would come on my show."

My first radio job was at one of the first radio stations to program interactive telephone talk shows 24-hours a day. It was 1966 and Metromedia had just bought the old Top-40 station KEWB, licensed to Oakland. "KEWB, channel 91, color radio!" was a jingle pounded into San Francisco Bay area teenage brains throughout the 1960s; most of us who heard it then can still sing it. The call letters were changed to KNEW and the station was converted to talk with a massive billboard campaign advertising it as "Radio Free Oakland." It was the sister station of Duff's Los Angeles talker KLAC, also owned by Metromedia. Both stations, along with several CBS-owned stations, talked through the late 1960s and into the 1970s before changing their formats. KLAC and KNEW went to country music (KNEW changed back to far right-wing talk in the 1990s). Most of the CBS stations slid toward an all news presentation.

In its prime, KNEW broadcast energy and excitement via its talk shows. Opinionated hosts challenged a nonstop assault of opinionated callers—and each other. Two of the KNEW stars fostered their disagreements with each other. Pat Michaels played the right-winger, Joe Dolan the liberal. Their on-the-air conflicts were developed by the station's promotion department, escalating at one dramatic—and well-attended—point, into a staged duel between the two set in a Golden Gate Park meadow. It was talk radio that refused to take itself too seriously.

Why Talk Radio Skews Right

Rush Limbaugh, Pat Buchanan, G. Gordon Liddy, and Oliver North are all recognizable in the popular culture as talk show hosts. Even former Ku Klux Klanner and presidential candidate David Duke has hosted radio talk show in Louisiana. Across America successful talk shows shout their right-wing message. Left wing programs trail as a miniscule minority. The preponderance of successful shows promulgating right-wing content helps debunk the continuing myth of a left-leaning media. Why most radio talk show skew right politically is not certain, but what we learned from the Pat Michaels-Joe Dolan days at KNEW is that a professional per-formance draws audiences no matter the politics of the host. Perhaps advertisers feel more comfortable with the usually pro-business attitude of the right-wing hosts and want them hawking their products, and it's hard to imagine that profit-oriented station licensees would find it com-fortable to cater to the proclivities of advertisers regarding the programs they sponsor.

A tennis show company, one can imagine for example, would probably rather have a talk show host selling its shoes who believes in unrestricted world trade than hear its commercials adjacent to Jim Hightower as the talk show populist draws attention to the company's factories in Asia and says working conditions there violate baseline health and safety standards and workers make in a day less than the minimum hourly wage in the United States.

Many radio station owners and operators—understandably—are more comfortable hiring hosts who embrace the business world with no ques-tions asked. "Can we find out what he's going to talk about in advance?" a radio station general manager I worked with as program director asked me about Hightower after Hightower attacked Nike for the third time. It was not that he disbelieved or disagreed with Hightower's position vis-à-vis the show company's Asian factory policies, or even that was upset about the effect the criticism might have on any business the radio sta-tion might do with Nike. He was worried that such direct challenges to Nike—or any company—potentially could instill fear in all advertisers, and make them afraid that they may be the next target. "Can we find out what he's going to talk about in advance?" implied that the radio station should consider preempting those Hightower shows that might offend paying clients.

Pat Buchanan's sometime co-host Barry Lynn agreed that commerce must affect talk show programming. "Most businesses are somewhat more comfortable being on a program that tends to be politically conservative. It's easy to sell a show where there is a conservative and a liberal because then you don't offend anyone in the audience, or maybe you offend everyone, but at least it's an equal opportunity offense and therefore it's easier to sell," he told me in 1993.

"But most local stations can't afford to put two people on the air. They're lucky to be able to afford to put one person on the air to fill up four hours. So I think there's a natural tendency if you're only going to have one side to have it be conservative simply because that's where the money may be."

The market-driven right-wingers rarely surprise managers and their clients with attacks on business. Yet controversial subject matter and shock styles—even coming from the political right—can scare away advertisers and even charities, and can result in consumers rejecting products associated with some of the more offensive hosts.

Early in 1994, the Florida State Citrus Commission decided endorsements from talk radio hosts could help increase orange juice sales. They signed up Dr. Dean Edell—the medical advice host—for a couple of hundred thousand dollars, paid half a million dollars to Larry King, and agreed to a million dollar fee for Rush Limbaugh.

The reaction was quick and loud. "It is totally unbelievable that the Citrus Commission could possibly be so insensitive as to choose a person of such extreme views to represent the chief product of this state and by inference the state itself," was the immediate institutional response from Florida's National Association for the Advancement of Colored People.

"The decision to buy time on Limbaugh's show was insulting, offensive and unwise," said the president of the Florida National Organization for Women Chapter, Siobhan McLaughlin. "There are broader audiences to reach," judged Florida Governor Lawton Chiles, "because our orange juice leaves a good taste with people and should be promoted on programs that represent good taste."

On his February 17, 1994 show, Limbaugh attacked his critics. "Just keep chugging the stuff," he told his audience, "that's the single best message you can send." He dismissed calls for boycotts as, "Childish and embarrassing."

G. Gordon Liddy offended St. Jude Children's Research Hospital in Memphis when he solicited photographs from women listeners wearing only underwear and carrying guns. "It's not the fault of the lump of iron that someone misuses it," he said when questioned about the message he was sending when so many children are in hospitals suffering from gunshot wounds. "That's like saying we can't show kids in station wagon commercials because a lot of kids get killed in station wagons," said Liddy. Liddy's idea was to pick his favorite photographs of the women-with-guns-pictures and produce a calendar, donating any profits to St. Jude. "Mr. Liddy is working totally independently," the hospital made clear its relationship to the bizarre project, "and has not contacted us."

Talk Radio and Advertising

But the spontaneous nature of talk radio in general and the notoriety for controversy achieved by some hosts keeps some important advertisers away. "Hartz Mountain has made a request that none of their network spots are to run in the Rush Limbaugh program on Mutual or NBC affiliates," wrote syndicator Westwood One Vice President of Station Relations George Barber to the network's affiliates in one of a series of letters designed to separate some clients from specific shows. "If you carry Rush Limbaugh, please do not air Hartz Mountain spots within the program," requests the July 27, 1993 Barber letter. It explains further, "We apologize for the inconvenience, but Hartz Mountain has made it very clear to us that they do not wish to be associated with this program."

Johnson & Johnson was even more concerned. It requested that advertisements for its "Clean 'n Clear" product not air during the Howard Stern Show, the Greaseman Show, and all other "talk programs of any type," according to another letter from Westwood One to its affiliated stations. "The advertisers have made it very clear to us that they do not wish to be associated with these types of programs."

Despite some advertisers' reticence to be affiliated with talk shows, some hosts continue to blur the traditional lines not just between news and entertainment, but also between editorial endorsements and commercial endorsements. Bruce Williams, who gained nationwide popularity for his financial advice was famous for sliding from his free recommendations for distraught callers to paid commercials broadcast using his trademark voice and an identical homespun ("Hey, Tiger!") delivery.

"Bruce is available to record spots for your clients," a letter from his office to affiliated stations made a straightforward pitch for extra business for Williams. I received one when I was program director at WRC in Washington, DC. "Over the past couple of years," continued the presentation, "Bruce Williams has been recording commercials for clients of local radio stations across the country. The response from these clients has been overwhelming. Simply put, they love having Bruce advertise their business or product, and they always report increased revenues!!"

Prices ranged from $600 to $2,000 in late 1993 for commercials that ran in one radio market for 13 weeks. The top figure represents products or services endorsed on the air during the commercial by Williams.

One fascinating aspect of the brochure describing Williams's availability and rates is the complete lack of any criteria that must be observed by a client (besides anteing up the $2,000) to receive the powerful Williams endorsement. "Radio is a commercial enterprise," Williams had explained his availability for a price for endorsements to *People* magazine for its October 9, 1989, issue. "If I thought endorsements were damaging, I wouldn't do them."

The Left Tries to Talk

In an effort to combat the perceived political muscle of right-wing talk shows after George W. Bush was selected president, well-funded attempts began in earnest to develop left-leaning national talk shows.

Democratic Party fundraisers collected money that was used to launch an entity called Democracy Radio, essentially an incubator designed to develop and promote talk show hosts who would broadcast shows supporting Democratic Party policies, candidates, and elected officials. I gave the keynote address to their first gathering at the Capitol, telling a roomful of hosts and host hopefuls who looked forward to being picked for support from the Party my theories of why right-wing content dominated talk radio. Democratic senators and representatives paraded into the gathering to say a few words of encouragement to the assembled throng. They repeated a disturbing talking point line, "We need an echo chamber," a phrase that made clear they wanted to control the content their supporters subsidized.

Ed Schultz was one of those in the audience whose show was chosen for success by Democracy Radio director Tom Athans. His program was eventually weaned from Democracy Radio funding and he went on the air across America with private backing, becoming one of the few successful nationwide left-leaning hosts, along with Thom Hartmann and Stephanie Miller.

Although Democracy Radio worked with political money, private investors launched Air America, banking on the star power of new-to-radio comedian Al Frankin for its initial success. The business plan for Air America created problems for the fledgling network from the time of its inception. The salary for Frankin was good news for him but it, along with high costs the company paid for other hosts and producers, helped create the network's continuing fiscal crises. Its insistence that stations run its entire programming schedule dissuaded some program directors from participating in its offerings. The decision to lease time from major market stations to air the network's schedule in important markets was flawed, especially because those stations available for lease often suffered from poor signal strength and dial positions. In addition, Air America was plagued by capitalization shortfalls and seemingly perpetual management upheavals.

Along with its internal problems, Air America was attacked and ridiculed relentlessly by its powerful right-wing competition. And some advertisers only added to the difficulties. A listener to the San Francisco-based talk show host Peter B. Collins leaked an ABC Radio Networks internal October 26, 2006 memo that listed advertisers who demanded that their commercials not be aired on stations during Air America programs. It was an all-star list of some 90 entities, from Allstate to Wrigley's, including Microsoft, Wal-Mart, and the U.S. Navy.

Collins, who self-syndicated his own left-leaning talk show to stations in California during the Air America start-up phase, told me in 2007 that he was not surprised to watch it founder:

> They tried to change the business model of commercial radio. There were few radio professionals involved with the development of Air America, and they though they could force the radio industry to adapt to their model. They required stations that wanted to carry Al Franken to also air their entire schedule, and program directors weren't willing to take the risk with an unproven line-up.

But worse then the failure of a company that seemed poised to change the talk radio paradigm was the fact that the Air America's stumbles fueled the right-wing propaganda that insisted left-wing talk radio inherently could not succeed in the marketplace because of its content. That propaganda was reinforced when some Clear Channel stations that had been experimenting with so-called progressive talk using Air America shows chose to abandon the format rather than seek alternative available independent programs such as Collins's show, or take the time and expense to develop their own talk talent. "Air America created expectations that they never lived up to and that caused some station managers to believe that the category of progressive talk is not viable," Collins said. "Personalities create great radio shows," he correctly noted, "the neophytes at Air America sadly never learned that."

A legendary iconoclast of the talk radio wars, Travus T. Hipp, who also started his talk career at Oakland's KNEW, observed the Air America errors from his hideaway in rural Nevada, where he continued to originate daily rants and raves that play on a handful of cult-like radio stations in the West.

"Air America failed for two reasons," he told me in 2007. "The founders and backers were radio groupies who always dreamed of having their own station and show; Mickey Roony and Judy Garland painting the barn and opening a musical revue comes to mind." Professional radio management was missing, said Hipp, and he also faulted Franken as a performer:

> Al Franken is not a radio personality, and over several years he proved unable to learn the skill set to become one. His voice is whining and his ad lib ability is slow. He often stepped on whatever his guest was trying to say. To be fair, few print purveyors make good on-air practitioners, due to their thought process being keyed to writing rather than speaking composed thoughts. Franken is a glowing example.

With such clear evidence that talk radio is no bastion of liberalism, how is the myth that the media leans left maintained? Barry Lynn believes the tactics are the same as those espoused in *Mein Kampf.* "It gets perpetrated successfully because it gets repeated so many times that people believe it," he told me.

> It's just like the study that said teachers were surveyed in the 1940s and the 1980s and in the 1940s they said that the big problems in schools were gum chewing, running in the hallways, and talking and that in the eighties it was suicide, rape, and assault of teachers. This was a completely fictitious set of non-surveys. The data didn't exist. It was all invented out of whole cloth. Yet it was repeated by Bill Bennett [the former Education Secretary and frequent Limbaugh guest], by Rush Limbaugh, by every conservative, religious, or cultural conservative in the country as if it were true until the *New York Times* exposed it as a complete myth. If you hear a lie enough times, you're going to start to believe it's true.

Talk radio allows those with access to the microphone the opportunity to repeat falsehoods repeatedly—either maliciously or inadvertently. The medium can be easily taken advantage of by outside manipulators. Plenty of talk show hosts repeated the school survey misinformation not because they knew it was false and wanted to mislead their audience, but because it made terrific talk show fuel and they simply did not bother to check the veracity of the material fed to them. Every day talk show hosts and radio stations are deluged by material, material that is rarely checked and often comes from sources with clear ulterior motives.

Radio talk shows, despite their popularity and the respect a select few have managed to develop over the years, usually play the same role as the supermarket tabloids. They offer frivolous entertainment, not credible news. The comparison breaks down however because, while the tabloids clearly refuse to take themselves too seriously (witness the plethora of Elvis and alien sightings in their pages), more and more radio talk show hosts are believing their own harangues. And worse, in part because of the built-in credibility that a voice on the radio carries in our culture, too many listeners in the audience believe the unsubstantiated and undocumented propaganda now blaring out of radios across the country 24 hours of every day.

A close listening of just an hour or less of most any talk show on the air in America proves two dangerous points.

The first egregious problem that becomes apparent is that the hosts repeatedly and regularly present information as facts and truths without bothering to rely on accepted journalistic devices for ascertaining that the information presented comes from reliable sources. Sometimes the host ignores the techniques of journalism because he or she is intent on spreading misinformation and disinformation. Rush Limbaugh's work is full of examples of such propaganda, and journalist David Remnick collected a litany of such abuses for a February 20, 1994 attack piece in the *Washington Post*. "Do you really think the situation in the schools would turn around if we threw more money at them? What would they do with it? Buy condoms with an even greater variety of colors and flavors?" Limbaugh's setup for his coming distortion is typically flip, perhaps even comical. But then comes the lie, in the guise of a news report. "We're spending enough money per classroom today," the authoritative voice over the air proclaims, "to provide chauffeured limousines to the teachers and the kids."

Most talk radio hosts continue to attempt to create an exemption for themselves, claiming that they need not engage in the basic rules and practices adopted by credible journalists because they are only entertainers. The second problem is worse: Some hosts are flat-out not interested in pursuing truth, but only seeks to take advantage of an opportunity to stir up the audience in hopes of generating increased ratings.

Irresponsible Talk Deconstructed

Hearing the nationwide successes of the Rush Limbaugh and other right-wing screamers encouraged struggling radio announcers from coast to coast to throw away their music and "go to the phones" beginning in the late 1980s. The result was an epidemic of fast-talking performers trying to woo listeners by spinning tales instead of records. I inherited one of those disc jockey-trained talk show hosts when I took over the programming duties at WRC in Washington, DC in 1993. Brian Wilson (not the Beach Boy) had been a successful disc jockey, earning high ratings for his quick ad-libbed one-liners at stations in Baltimore and New York. However, when he turned to the all-talk form of radio, he started presenting his prattle as news.

Shortly after six one morning, a manipulative and anonymous caller used Wilson's Washington talk show to suggest that the Clinton Administration was forbidding the military from working in uniform when at the White House. Whether the caller was intentionally spreading lies or simply confused was not clear. Since callers to talk shows are usually allowed to speak anonymously, determining motives for calls is all but impossible.

"Let's get out there and chat with Wanda," is how the episode began the morning of February 25, 1993, as Wilson introduced her to the airwaves. "Let's see what she's up to this morning. Hi, Wanda."

"What I called about," she was ready to get to work as soon as he put her on the air, "is that I was reading in the *Washingtonian* magazine last night, the new issue, and it says that the White House doesn't appreciate military men during duty hours wearing their uniforms to the White House." She paused, waiting for the response she expected.

"What?" said Wilson, sounding dumbfounded. "Run it by me again. The White House...." he paused this time.

Wanda reiterated, "They wish that the military would not wear their uniforms during duty hours when they come on business to the White House." Her terminology has switched from "doesn't appreciate" to "wish they would not."

The verb changes again as Wilson repeats Wanda's claim. "The White House does not want," he says back at her as a question, "military men wearing their uniforms when they visit the White House?"

"Right," says Wanda.

"On duty?" asks Wilson.

"Right"

"In other words," Wilson is still querying Wanda, "they want them to appear out of uniform while they're on duty when they approach the White House."

"Right, right, right," says Wanda, "Yes, that's what it says in the *Washingtonian*."

Wilson and his sidekick question Wanda for details. She tells them the Pentagon is upset, that the problem started when an officer was asked not to wear his uniform. She apparently is paraphrasing the article she read in the magazine. Her terminology is changing again from talking about what she read to speaking as if she has learned a fact.

"That's the mentality of this White House," says Wanda with disgust. "It's just unbelievable."

"First it's smoking, now it's uniforms," says Wilson.

"Yes," agrees Wanda.

"I'm telling you, it's unbelievable," says Wilson. "I appreciate the tip in the *Washingtonian* magazine. We ought to get a copy of that and see if we can trace that one down." He is correct. That is exactly what he should have done. But he didn't. Instead, he turns Wanda's telephone call into a news report. "That's rather phenomenal. You can't wear your uniform at the White House."

The charge was false, but it was accepted as fact by Wilson who then—acting outraged—invited the audience to react.

After his sidekick reads a newscast and the traffic reporter announces road conditions, Wilson takes a few listener calls on other subjects, he is back on the uniforms at the White House story, and he adds a new charge.

"Word in from our White House sources," he says authoritatively, "an individual," now he becomes conspiratorial, "that for obvious reasons cannot and would not go on the air." He pauses and proceeds to incite, "Along with the President's consideration of a ban on military uniforms at the White House, military aides have been instructed—and this," he emphasizes, "is purely a report exclusive to 'Mornings with Brian and Bob,' military aides have been instructed they must no longer salute the President." He repeats it for emphasis, "They must no longer salute the President."

"What?" yells the sidekick.

Wilson comes in with the punch line, "Because he doesn't know how to salute in return. And if any of you have seen him in those standard clips of him getting off the helicopter, there's the aide at the bottom, snapping to, you know, ripping off a nice crisp one, and there's our President giving this kind of....." He makes a groan and laughs and then reiterates the "news," and by this time the qualifying terms such as "allegedly" are being abandoned. The audience, of course, tunes in and out, and those just turning the program on are hearing Wilson identify the uniforms and salute issue that—so far—is based on nothing more than Wanda's call, as the latest example of President Clinton's "loathing for the military."

As an afterthought, he muses about the story that's fast becoming his prime focus of the morning, "I wonder if anyone can substantiate that. Maybe we can call over to the White House."

In fact, the radio station's news department made the call. Deputy White House press secretary Lorraine Voles was asked specifically whether there were any orders issued or under consideration in regard to saluting and uniforms. Her response to each question was an unequivocal, "No." Meanwhile the NBC radio network White House correspondent (WRC was an NBC affiliate and aired NBC News newscasts)—who was listening with amazement to the nonstory developing on the air—reported to his assignment editor with further confirmation that there were no such orders.

By just after seven that morning Wilson was informed that the story was false. It wasn't until half past seven that Wilson bothered to share the official information with his listeners. Predictably, in the meantime, the phones went wild. Callers were outraged, understandably accepting the story as true. After all, it had been repeated by the host and his sidekick as true, and listeners are conditioned by audio experiences going back to Edward R. Murrow and his staff of news professionals to give the benefit of the doubt to radio announcers presenting news.

"I'm just so livid about what I'm hearing," caller Angela checked in from Alexandria. "My husband is active duty. He happens to be in Somalia right now. I'm waiting for him to get home in about ten days. Do you have a list of who all I call? I'll call the White House to complain, if I can get through."

Calls continued from outraged listeners all morning, despite a mention during the 7:30 newscast that the White House "vehemently denied" both stories. Wilson interrupted the newscaster to mock the White House denial.

After the show I met with Wilson. He was excited about what he considered his success, a success he gauged on the great quantity of telephone calls he was able to generate from listeners upset about the uniform and saluting story. But the story was based on a falsehood, I pointed out. He expressed no remorse. On the contrary, Wilson was well pleased with the program, explaining his philosophy to me, "The purpose of the show is to strike nerve endings. As long as it gets attention, it's a success."

I objected that what he was generating was a fraud—entertainment posing as news.

"On my show," he explained, "I'm not relying on things factual. I have never had any design to build credibility." He seemed genuinely surprised and confused by my irritation and frustration with him. He told me he would air just about anything imaginable to develop interest in his show, including false news. "The show in and of itself is an entertainment entity," was his rationalization. "Credibility is never a question. You'd have to be dumber than a box of rocks not to get it," is how he dismissed any concern that he might be misleading anyone in the audience.

That morning he certainly misled Angela and a long list of other callers and listeners.

The producer on duty the morning, the no uniforms and no saluting misinformation was spread made it clear after the show how easy it is for a caller to manipulate a talk show. I asked her how, as call screener, she made the decision to allow the anonymous caller to announce on the air erroneous information unchallenged. "The guy who called did not sound like he had intent to give me bad information," Sheila Jaskot told me that same morning. She made reference to her previous job, screening calls for Bruce Williams at NBC's *Talknet*, saying she answered as many as 500 telephone calls there each night. "You're on the phones for years," she said about herself, "and you pick out the phonies. I don't know what it is, but you can pick it out by some small thing in their voice." With a positive attitude toward talk radio callers, and really the only attitude a call screener can adopt, she said, "I like to give people the benefit of the doubt." And with a realistic—if callous—look at the impossibility of checking the veracity of the claims of anonymous callers, she dismissed her responsibility to the audience casually, saying, "They'll believe what they want to believe."

Sometimes producers such as Jaskot can pick out the phonies with that vague technique, but certainly not always. Many skillful and calculating callers, seeking to manipulate a talk show for their own purposes, certainly develop the needed techniques to maneuver past the gatekeeper in the screener's booth.

Brian Wilson repeatedly explained to me that he operates in an intellectual and moral vacuum, simply as a performer. At another meeting—a couple of weeks after the Wanda call—came these easy words from him about his philosophy for working a talk show: "You want me to wear the white hat, I'll wear the white hat, you want me to wear the black hat, I'll wear the black hat. I can be pro-gun, I can be anti-gun on the radio, I just happen to be pro-gun personally. My personal feelings are one thing. What you do on the air is another. It's show biz!"

I'm Out of Time, Thanks for Calling!

In today's broadcast marketplace, news and news-like products are lucrative commodities. Hence their abundance.

Talk programming, no matter the contents—from the profane to just plain wrong—is protected from most government interference by the First Amendment, as well it should be. However, talk show audiences must be wary of this still-evolving new form of show business. It requires that listeners concerned with differentiating between fact and fancy learn how to sift through the growing clutter on the radio to determine which sounds coming out of the speaker need to be heard as entertainment or propaganda and which might be worthwhile to consider as reasonably accurate portrayals of people and places, events, and opinions.

References

Armstrong, David. (1981). *A Trumpet to Arms*. Los Angeles: J.P. Tarcher.
Crawford, Bill & Gene Fowler. (2002). *Border Radio*. Austin: University of Texas Press.
Munson, Wayne. (1993). *All Talk*. Philadelphia, PA: Temple University Press.
Nation (unsigned editorial). (1995). Vox Populi. *Nation*, 256 (8, March 1), 255–256.
Rather, Dan. (1994). When News and Entertainment Look Alike (Letter to the Editor). *New York Times*, March 8, A-20.

14. Political Waves: Radio and Politics, 1920–1940

DOUGLAS CRAIG

In October 1922, *The Wireless Age* argued that radio broadcasting, then only two years old, had created a new age of American citizenship and political debate. Radio would provide Americans with a new form of political communication that would bypass newspapers to create a direct bond between voters, candidates, and office holders. Henceforth,

> [n]o vital issue can be decided fairly in this country ... without the use of the radio telephone. Radio can carry into the home nothing more important than the truth about those vital issues to decide which is to determine the course of this greatest of countries. (George H. Clark Papers. Museum of American History, Washington DC, Series 14, Box 197)

The Wireless Age was not alone in its enthusiasm for the political possibilities of radio. The magazine's prediction that radio would transform American political life was widely shared by politicians, political commentators, and social analysts. Radio broadcasting offered the United States a technological solution to a problem that had bothered political theorists and practitioners since the earliest days of the republic: that of informing citizens, and creating consensus among them, across geographic expanse, demographic diversity, and partisan division. Soon, radio's boosters promised, all Americans would be able to hear their president and their congress debate the pressing issues of the day. As voters, they could make more informed choices on the basis of frequent radio broadcasts beamed into their homes at times best suited to attentive family listening. Politicians and candidates would also benefit from the radio age; no longer would they need to undertake physically demanding speaking tours to address their constituents, and no longer would they be hostage to the willingness of voters to leave their homes to attend rallies. Radio promised voters and candidates a universal medium of communication that would assist in creating a more informed and effective political system (Craig, 2000, 167–177).

The Statutory Context of Political Broadcasting

Before the passage of the Radio Act of 1927, broadcasters had no statutory or regulatory guidance for their treatment of political broadcasting and advertising. The Radio Act of 1912, passed long before broadcasting began, was necessarily silent on the issue. When federal lawmakers did legislate for political broadcasting in 1927, they opted for a provision that provided minimal regulation of political advertising, requiring equality of access without mandating equality of time among candidates for office. If a station chose to accept advertising from a candidate, it had to accept advertising from all his or her rivals in that contest, and it was specifically forbidden to censor such material. Section 18, which was reiterated almost verbatim as Section 315 of the Communications Act of 1934, did not require licensees to accept political advertising, nor did it require them to charge candidates the same rates as other advertisers.

The theory behind Sections 18 and 315 was a familiar one in American political culture: political advertising should occur within an open marketplace, ensuring equality of access but not of outcome. By refusing to require broadcasters to provide either free time or a set period for political advertising, legislators left key issues to be decided between buyers and sellers of political airtime. No effort was made to ensure that poorer candidates or parties could compete equally with better-off competitors, and no attempt was made to ensure uniformity across the nation. Sections 18 and 315 made no attempt to disturb the existing balance of power within American political culture whereby some parties and some candidates were far wealthier than others, and thus more able to take advantage of the opportunities presented by radio advertising (MacNeil, 1968, 281ff; Rorty, 1934, 12; Rose, 1940, 206; Smith, 1990, 348).

In keeping with the minimalist scope of Sections 18 and 315, neither the Federal Radio Commission (FRC) nor the Federal Communications Commission (FCC) showed great willingness to issue regulations fleshing out these statutory provisions. The FRC issued only one regulation concerning Section 18, a warning to licensees that violation would be sufficient grounds for license revocation, and the FCC issued only three technical rulings on matters concerning Section 315 of the Communications Act. Section 315 survived the interwar period untouched, and its regime for political broadcasting remained until Congress suspended its equal treatment provisions in 1960 so that broadcasters could exclude minor party candidates from the presidential debates of that year (Smith, 1990, 348).

Broadcasters' Policies on Political Programs and Advertising

By June 1924, the major broadcasting companies had developed a common policy on political broadcasting. AT&T, RCA, Westinghouse, and GEC executives agreed that their political broadcasting would be primarily limited to the two major parties, although requests from other parties would be dealt with on their merits. The companies also agreed that they would broadcast addresses only from "speakers of national prominence ... dealing with policies and candidacies of more than local interest" and that speakers would be asked, but not required, to submit their scripts before their broadcasts. The companies agreed that each would limit political programming to an hour per day, and all the companies agreed to negotiate only with national party committees (Owen D. Young Papers, Owen D. Young Library, St. Lawrence University, Canton, New York, File 11-14-50, Box 3; *The New York Times*, July 19, 1924, 1, July 29, 1924, 4). These policies, which overtly privileged national issues, the two major parties, and candidates for federal office, became the basis for all political broadcasting during the interwar period.

Three major developments in American broadcasting caused broadcasters to rethink their policies after 1925. The triumph of commercial broadcasting meant that airtime became a valuable commodity, to be apportioned between the competing demands of political and commercial advertisers. The second major development concerned the advent of the new national networks. The formation of NBC in 1926 and CBS in 1928 provided parties and candidates with highly attractive national forums, and the growing dominance of the networks over local and independent stations meant that the new chains had to deal with political programming very carefully. The third major development, the passage of the Radio Act of 1927, created a statutory framework for political advertising for the first time, forcing stations and networks to reassess their policies to comply with the law.

As part of its commitment to public service and civic education, NBC committed itself to broadcasting political programs and advertising. It also reaffirmed that it would cover nominating conventions without charge, but at other times would sell airtime at normal commercial rates to the national committees of both major parties (*The New York Times*, April 29, 1927, 14). This policy, however, had to be changed by 1928. The attractiveness of NBC to commercial advertisers meant that the network's sponsored time was quickly tied up in long-term contracts. It thus became increasingly important for the network to assure its commercial clients that their time would not be preempted by political speeches and advertisements. To this end NBC decided that it would accept political advertising only between the end of the nominating conventions and election day during presidential election years and that it would broadcast political programming at other times only when it could do so without prejudice to its commercial commitments (Owen D. Young to David Sarnoff and M.H. Aylesworth, October 16, 1934: Owen D. Young Papers, File 131/2675). The passage of the Radio Act and Section 18 in 1927 also forced NBC to include minor parties within its list of potential political advertisers, and to incorporate their conventions into its free programming.

The networks provided a donation to the two-party political system through their free coverage of Democratic and Republican nominating conventions, presidential nominees' notification ceremonies, election returns, and presidential inaugurations. Broadcasts of inaugurations became progressively more extensive and sophisticated, as both networks used the occasion to impress listeners with their technological prowess. CBS's coverage of Franklin D. Roosevelt's second inauguration in January 1937, for example, involved the use of a blimp, 26 broadcast points, two mobile transmitters, and a relay transmitter in the tip of the Washington Monument (Owen D. Young Papers, File 134, Folder 267Y).

NBC and CBS worked hard to ensure that their programming avoided overt partisanship. FDR's election to the presidency and the coming of the New Deal presented NBC and CBS with a number of new challenges to their policies on political programming. FDR and his New Dealers were strong believers in radio's ability to communicate government policies and to develop public support for them. The sense of national emergency arising from the banking crisis of 1932–1933, and the Depression in general, provided the rationale for many requests for airtime from the new administration. Although the president's fireside chats were the most famous use of radio during FDR's first term, most members of his cabinet took to the airwaves to reassure the public that the Democratic administration was working tirelessly toward economic recovery (Best, 1993, 8, 11–12; McCamy, 1939). At first, the Republicans, reeling from their repudiation in 1932, seemed to acquiesce in this flood of Democratic radio publicity. By 1935, however, the Grand Old Party had sufficiently recovered its composure to demand that it be given equal access to the airwaves to answer partisan administration speeches.

NBC and CBS, and many local stations, generally took the view that the president and members of Congress should be given access to the airwaves on request during nonelection periods without charge. Their policy was to treat such broadcasts as educational programming rather than partisan campaigning. Having classified such programming as educational and nonpartisan, the networks resisted Republican demands for equal time to rebut presidential or cabinet addresses, although they did try to ensure that Republican members of Congress and other party leaders received some access to their studios (Craig, 2000, 124–131).

The practical effect of these policies was to allow the administration's voices to predominate over radio between election campaigns. From the Republican perspective, it appeared that the networks' policy was a disguised subsidy to incumbent Democrats (Thomas Sabin to Richard J. Patterson, September 14, 1935: National Broadcasting Company Records, State Historical Society of Wisconsin, Madison, Box 41, Folder 4). FDR's fireside chats, and especially those that took overtly partisan positions, prompted a Republican demand for radio time in response. In August 1940, the National Association of Broadcasters (NAB) released a general policy on presidential addresses that equal time would be granted to rival candidates if the president used his radio speeches "as a vehicle for electioneering." The burden of proof, however, fell on the GOP, and the issue would be decided by each network (NAB Press Release, August 7, 1940: National Broadcasting Company Manuscript Collection, Library of Congress, Washington DC, File 337).

Stations and networks also faced awkward issues when candidates from minor and radical parties applied for radio time. The networks' free broadcasts of the major parties' nominating conventions encouraged others to demand similar treatment. This put the networks' frequent protestations of nonpartisanship and public service to severe test. In June 1928, the Workers' Party of America demanded that NBC provide its convention with the same gavel-to-gavel coverage that was to be given to the Democrats and Republicans. "After discussion," NBC President Merlin Aylesworth informed his board,

> I finally offered them the facilities of WEAF at eleven o'clock at night, for the purpose of summing up their platform and the speech of acceptance by their candidate for President. I adopted the same policy for the Socialist Party. (Aylesworth to Owen D. Young, June 2, 1928: Owen D. Young Papers, 11-14-50, Box 10)

When Jack Perilla of the New York State branch of the Communist Party of America (CPA) wrote to NBC in September 1930 to request airtime on WEAF to match that given to the major parties, network executives simply sat on his letter until it was too late to schedule any time. Nonpartisanship and civic duty had their limits (National Broadcasting Company Records, Box 4, File 96).

The coming of the Depression made the broadcasting of radical political groups even more sensitive for national networks and local stations. Some stations, put off by the requirement to accept advertising from all candidates, and fearing a backlash from their listeners over broadcasts from radical candidates, decided not to sell any time for political advertising (*The New York Times*, October 27, 1936, 10). Because of their greater prominence and their aspirations to further radio's civic work, the networks did not feel able to cut and run. After a great deal of soul searching, CBS aired a speech by Earl Browder, general secretary of the CPA, in March 1936. William Paley hailed this decision as a noble exercise in free speech and public service, but many of CBS's affiliates refused to carry the program. CBS was picketed by the National Americanization League and accused of treason by some members of Congress, who were not appeased by the network's decision to invite Republican Representative Hamilton Fish to give a vigorous rebuttal of communism a day after Browder's speech (*Literary Digest*, 121, 37; *The New York Times*, March 5, 1936, 16, March 6, 1936, 9).

Radio and Political Campaigning

The first politician to use radio for campaigning appears to have been New York City Mayor John F. Hylan during his reelection campaign in 1921. His opponent, Henry F. Curran, delivered a radio campaign speech on the following evening. Indicative of the primitive state of radio broadcasting at the time was the advance publicity given to Curran's speech. "His campaign managers did not know last night the exact hour of the speech tonight," the press reported, "but it probably will be late in the evening. They said they did not know just where Mr Curran would speak into the transmission apparatus, but that it would probably be at the home of some amateur operator who had the proper facilities for the transmission." Curran went on to defeat at the polls (*The New York Times*, November 7, 1921, 2, November 8, 1921, 1).

From these unpromising beginnings the progress of radio campaigning became closely connected with the development of the broadcasting industry itself. As more and more Americans bought radios, and as stations sprang up to broadcast to them, the technological preconditions for effective radio political campaigning matured during 1922 and 1923. By the end of 1923, a growing number of broadcasters, and especially those owned by GEC, Westinghouse, RCA, and AT&T, were in a position to offer politicians an increasingly competent and reliable broadcasting service.

Although the 1924 elections were the first federal campaigns to be conducted with the help of radio, they can scarcely be called true radio elections. Political organizations were too inexperienced with broadcasting, and too wedded to older publicity media, to conduct radio campaigns. The broadcasters themselves were also undecided as to how much of their facilities and time should be devoted to political information and campaigning. Despite early predictions that 1924 would see a deluge of radio electioneering, radio in fact played a relatively minor role in the contests of that year. It appears that the Democrats and Republicans spent $90,000 between them on radio publicity (*The New York Times*, August 1, 1924, 2).

The broadcasting industry matured rapidly after 1924, becoming commercialized, networked, and more formally regulated. Political strategists and candidates also developed their ideas as to how they could best use radio's potential. This confluence of industry development, statutory regulation, and campaign strategy meant that the Hoover-Smith contest of 1928 deserves the title of the first true radio campaign.

Both the Republican National Committee (RNC) and the Democratic National Committee (DNC) needed large war chests to capitalize fully on radio broadcasting's potential in 1928. The triumph of commercialism and the formation of NBC and CBS significantly increased the cost of radio airtime between 1924 and 1928. When John Davis ran against Calvin Coolidge in 1924, their campaigns had to pay only for technical costs; in 1928 the networks charged $10,000 per hour for their airtime (Jamieson, 1984, 25). Although national networking and the growth of the radio industry as a whole meant that the radio audience was far larger in 1928 than in 1924, political parties had to find much greater sums to reach it.

Indications of the new role of radio in campaign strategy, and of its much greater costs, were made plain in the campaign budgets prepared by the RNC and the DNC in 1928. On the Republican side, an overall campaign budget of $3.9 million was formulated toward the end of August. From this amount, $889,500 went to various publicity costs, including postage, books, pamphlets, buttons, and foreign-language publications. The total allocation for radio was $350,000, a sum significantly greater than the $250,000 devoted to the Speakers Bureau. In all, the RNC dedicated approximately 9% of its total budget, and slightly more than 17% of its total expenditures on publicity, to radio broadcasting. During the heat of the campaign, the RNC increased its radio budget to $500,000, but then cut it to approximately $400,000 in the middle of October, when Hoover's victory seemed assured (Herbert Hoover, Campaign and Transition Materials, Herbert Hoover Presidential Library, West Branch, Iowa, Box 162, Subject: "Republican National Committee"; Casey, 1935, 101).

The Democrats accorded even greater importance to radio in their early campaign budgets. The DNC originally budgeted for a total expenditure of more than $3.4 million in 1928, of which $600,000—or 17.5%—was set aside for radio. This appropriation was the single largest item of the entire campaign budget, slightly exceeding the entry of $540,000 for printed publicity and dwarfing those for candidates' travel ($100,000) and speakers ($75,000). Although later DNC budgets eased the radio appropriation back to $530,000, it remained as the single largest budgeted expense (Owen D. Young Papers, File 15–29, Box 3; *The New York Times*, September 1, 1928, 12). When the RNC made its final tallies at the end of the 1928 campaign it, too, found that its actual expenditure of nearly $436,000 on radio was the single largest element of its overall publicity and advertising expenditures of slightly more than $2 million (*The New York Times*, February 17, 1929, IX, 19). Between them, the RNC and the DNC pumped $1 million into the networks' and independent broadcasters' coffers between July and November 1928.

Campaign strategists in 1928 used radio not only to reach the whole electorate through broadcasts during peak listening times on the national networks but also to address targeted groups through what would later be termed "narrowcasting." The Democrats, worried about the weakness of Smith's support among female voters, made heavy use of morning radio to reach female voters at home. The RNC, confident that Hoover stood to benefit greatly from disaffected female Democrats, also made heavy use of morning radio (*The New York Times*, August 31, 1928, 4, September 14, 1928, 6, September 16, 1928, 7). Anxious to achieve maximum coverage without boring listeners, both parties introduced other innovations to political advertising. The Democrats presented programs that mixed politics with entertainment within 30-minute programs, devoting 10 minutes to speeches and the rest to entertainment by musicians, movie stars, and stage actors (*The New York Times*, September 9, 1928, 2; Jamieson, 1984, 36). The 1928 campaign also witnessed the birth of the "spot" advertisement, when both sides aired five-minute segments extolling their candidates on local stations.

The First Radio Presidents

As befitted the winner of the first true radio election, Herbert Hoover was a frequent radio performer during his troubled presidency. His nearly 80 broadcasts between March 1929 and November 1932 represented a radio presidential record that more than doubled Coolidge's total and even compared favorably to FDR's early years in the White House. NBC broadcast 34 Hoover speeches in 1931 and 28 FDR addresses in 1935 (National Broadcasting Company Records, Box 49, File 17). Although Louis Liebovich and others have argued that Hoover was not a radio president, this judgment is valid only when it is made ahistorically by comparing Hoover's radio skills to those of his successor. In the context of his own presidency, and in comparison with his predecessor, it is clear that Hoover made very significant use of the new medium and demonstrated a growing awareness of the role that radio might play to assist national economic recovery, and his own political fortunes, as the Depression wore on (Liebovich, 1994, 194).

Hoover's unprecedented use of radio, however, did not make him a broadcasting virtuoso. He tended to confuse quantity of broadcasts with quality of broadcasting. Although he had made the first radio address without a live audience in American presidential history during the 1928 campaign, Hoover did not carry that innovation into the White House. He also retained his dull and halting speaking style that made no allowances for broadcasting's special oratorical requirements. Hoover tended to pack his speeches with facts, figures, and complex arguments that seemed simultaneously not only to demand but also to discourage close listening. The United States found its first radio president in Herbert Hoover, but it met its first political radio virtuoso when FDR won the White House in 1932. Although FDR was the third president to use radio broadcasting to communicate with the electorate, historians of the presidency and the media are unanimous in their judgment that FDR was the first national leader to understand fully the requirements and potential of the medium (Best, 1993, 11; Braden & Brandenburg, 1955; Brandenburg & Braden, 1952; Buhite & Levy, 1992, xvii; Chase, 1942, 107; Ryan, 1988, 19–24 White, 1979, 94–118; Winfield, 1990, 107).

FDR and his advisers thought hard about radio and how best to use it. Quite apart from his good luck in possessing a voice that transmitted across radio clearly and melodiously—Mark Sullivan once remarked that FDR could "recite the Polish alphabet and it would be accepted as an eloquent plea for disarmament"—FDR took his broadcasting technique very seriously (Sullivan, quoted in Best, 1993, 11). After working through many drafts of a radio script with his writers, and at least one rehearsal, FDR spoke slowly, at an average of 95 words a minute, and took care to use the simplest and clearest possible language. To create a sense of immediacy in his radio speeches, FDR customarily referred to himself as "I" and his listeners as "you." He also attempted to unite his audience by the use of familiar expressions—"I have no expectation of making a hit every time I come to bat"—and by identifying a small group, such as "chiselers," or the European dictators, against whom he and his listeners had to struggle (Braden & Brandenburg, 1955; Buhite & Levy, 1992). Herbert Hoover was no doubt told of these radio techniques by his radio consultants, but FDR was the first president to listen.

Well aware of the strict scheduling inherent in network radio, FDR often divided his scripts into five-minute sections so that he could time his speech precisely. He scheduled most of his fireside chats on Sunday, Monday, and Tuesday evenings, when radio audiences were greatest and press coverage the following day most comprehensive. FDR kept his radio speeches short, usually 15 minutes, and tried to interfere as little as possible with the networks' commercial commitments. FDR was also careful not to overexpose himself on radio; he made only 16 fireside chats in the first two years of his presidency, and only 31 during his 12-year tenure. Despite, or perhaps because of, his reputation as a radio maestro, FDR spent less time on the airwaves during his first term than Herbert Hoover did in his (Craig, 2000, 156).

FDR's use of broadcasting reflected more than his proficiency with the mechanics and strategy of radio politics. The president's distrust of newspaper owners, editors, and columnists is well known, and he believed that radio had at last had given Democrats fairer access to national opinion. Radio also offered to the president unprecedented opportunity to originate that information himself. Well aware of his radio skills, FDR prided himself on his ability to mold public opinion through his broadcasts and to manage the flow of information from the White House to become, in Jackson Lears's phrase, "the master advertiser" of government and his administration (Lears, 1994, 243). "Five years of fierce discussion and debate, five years of information through the radio and the moving picture," FDR told a fireside chat audience in 1937, "have taken the whole nation to school in the nation's business" (White, 1979, 123).

Radio Campaigning, 1933–1940

FDR's first term was notable not only for its flood of New Deal publicity but also for the enormous popularity of two other radio political orators whose opposition to the president threatened to upset the new balance of power established by the election of 1932. Father Charles Coughlin of Detroit and Senator Huey Long of Louisiana emerged as FDR's only contemporary rivals for the title of the nation's most effective radio politician (Brinkley, 1983).

Both men used network radio to extend their influence far beyond their own fiefdoms. Father Coughlin, who began his radio sermons in 1926 to swell his dwindling congregations, received more mail than any other American, including the president, in 1934. Coughlin's radio sermons became increasingly political after 1929, attacking Hoover, the banks, and greedy industrialists for their inactivity in the face of the Depression. Under pressure from the Hoover administration, CBS banished Coughlin from its airwaves in 1931, forcing him to broadcast on a network of unaffiliated stations. The radio priest urged his listeners to vote for FDR in the 1932 election but, after a brief honeymoon, turned against the new president and the New Deal. He accused them of complicity with an international Jewish banking and gold cabal and its plans for the deliberate impoverishment of workers. FDR, he told his listeners, was "the dumbest man ever to occupy the White House" and an "anti-God" (Brinkley, 1983, 93–123; Coughlin, quoted in Brown, 1980, 203).

Huey Long also perfected his radio technique before his assassination in 1935. After working his way up through Louisiana's Democratic organization, Long served as governor for two years before winning election to the U.S. Senate in 1930. Long concentrated on using radio to create a personality cult and to publicize his "Share Our Wealth" plan (Merriam, 1949, 373). His position as a U.S. senator ensured him easy access to the national networks, and he used this national exposure to publicize his promise to every American family of a minimum annual income of $2,500, as well as a "household estate" of a car, a washing machine, and—not surprisingly—a radio, all paid for through confiscatory taxes on the rich (Brinkley, 1983, 72).

At the state and local level radio made more modest headway in political campaigns between 1933 and 1936. During the New York City mayoralty race in 1933, for example, NBC sold 16 time slots for a total of $7,331.20 to the four main candidates (National Broadcasting Company Records, Box 20, File 6). For most local and state races, it appears that radio remained as an occasional supplement to more traditional forms of campaigning. Election funds during the Depression were scarce, and candidates remained convinced that voters still expected more intimate contact with their office seekers. When U.S. Senator Robert LaFollette Jr. from Wisconsin sought reelection in 1934, for example, he relied heavily on speeches and personal appearances. During September and October LaFollette made only two paid broadcasts, for which he paid $56. His speaking schedule for the last week of the campaign called for 12 speeches and only 1 radio date at Station WISN in Madison (Robert M. LaFollette Jr. Papers, Library of Congress, Washington DC, Cont. C510, File: "1944 Campaign: Post-Primary").

Radio played a prominent, but still subordinate, role in the most celebrated state election campaign of the decade. When the novelist and socialist Upton Sinclair ran in 1934 for governor of California on the Democratic ticket, he campaigned on a platform of End Poverty in California (EPIC). Sinclair promised Californians a way out of the Depression through his plans to put the unemployed to work in idle factories and to give them ownership of what they produced. Sinclair's opposition undertook an intense and well-funded campaign against EPIC, using movies, newsreels, billboards, newspapers, and radio. The radio campaign against Sinclair, conducted by the Lord and Thomas advertising agency, focused on radio serials made specifically for the campaign. During the height of the battle, 35 actors made a series of programs, including *The Bennetts*, which followed a middle-class family's debates about the election and its eventual decision to vote against Sinclair in the interests of fiscal prudence and state pride. *Weary and Willy* portrayed two bums on their way to California to share in the largesse promised by EPIC. Anti-Sinclair radio programs ran almost every day during the campaign; in the final week some local stations ran 10 features a day against EPIC. Local stations ran spot advertisements as short as 35 words in a final radio blitz against Sinclair. In its heavy and well-financed use of visual and radio campaigning, and in its relentless negativism, the successful campaign against Sinclair in 1934 presaged later electioneering techniques. In the context of the early 1930s, however, the California race was an aberration. Very few local and state candidates and political organizations during this period could afford the high cost of the intensive newsreel and radio campaigns that had sunk Upton Sinclair (Mitchell, 1992).

As the Democrats planned their national election campaign in 1936, they made plain the relative importance of radio to other forms of campaigning. In an early DNC budget, $340,000 out of a total of $1.65 million was set aside for radio costs. This budget was submitted to the president, who increased the appropriation for radio to $500,000 within a new total of nearly $2.3 million. The DNC's radio spending, which reached $540,000 by the end of the campaign, thus represented nearly a quarter of the total national Democratic expenditures in 1936. This amount dwarfed the DNC's budget of $382,000 for printed publicity, $32,000 for speakers, and $15,000 for motion pictures (Franklin D. Roosevelt Papers, President's Secretary's File. Franklin D. Roosevelt Presidential Library, Hyde Park, New York, Box 129, File: "Democratic National Committee, 1932–43").

Once again, the two parties choreographed their nominating conventions to maximize their exposure and appeal to the listening audience. Nomination ceremonies for FDR and Republican candidate Alf Landon occurred during the evening, and the Republicans were careful to introduce their little-known candidate with carefully staged and timed applause (*The New York Times*, June 26, 1936, 13). Both sides shortened their program lengths to a maximum of 30 minutes, and the GOP began its radio campaign on August 1, nearly a month earlier than in 1932. The RNC and the DNC made heavy use of spot advertisements on local stations, and the Republicans imitated the anti-EPIC tactic of frequent repetition of 35-word announcements. The Women's Divisions of both national committees undertook intensive radio programs during the morning hours, and the GOP targeted foreign-language voters through non-English broadcasting on stations in 10 industrial cities of the Northeast and Midwest (Casey, 1935, 33).

For their part, Democratic strategists recognized that their chief radio weapon was FDR. Landon was generally perceived to be a poor radio performer, and few expected him to compete effectively against FDR on the airwaves (*The New York Times*, September 6, 1936, IX, 10). Republican dismay at the results of their total radio expenditures of nearly $1 million was profound; Landon won only 36.5% of the national vote and two states. For the third time in succession, the losing party had spent more on radio than the winner had.

The last of the interwar presidential campaigns witnessed further refinement of radio campaigning techniques. Although total campaign budgets for both the Democrats and the Republicans in 1940 were less than in 1936, radio expenditures increased markedly. Erik Barnouw estimated that the two major parties' national and state organizations spent $2.25 million on broadcasting, from their combined total expenditures of

$6.2 million (Barnouw, 1968, 144). This further entrenched broadcasting as the single largest expense of modern campaigning. Republicans and Democrats worked hard to coordinate an increasing number of nominally independent organizations created to sell their candidates to specific groups. The RNC, for example, maintained close connections with a large number of groups who chose not to work formally under the aegis of the Republican Party. Organizations such as the Associated Clubs for Willkie, the No Third Term Democrats, and the Commercial Democratic Business Men for Willkie all bought radio time on their own accounts from the national networks during 1940, at the same time cooperating with the RNC's overall publicity strategy. The RNC maintained oversight over radio scheduling for itself, the party's state organizations, and these independent groups to avoid overlapping and duplication (Mark Sullivan Papers. Hoover Institution Archives, Stanford University, Palo Alto, California, Box 35, File: "Presidential Election of 1940").

The Democrats also refined their earlier techniques of targeting specific audiences through radio. Women voters were again prime targets, and the Women's Division of the DNC, led by Dorothy McAllister, devised a series of one-minute spot advertisements for local stations across the Northeast, Midwest, and West. Each of the spots, containing about 130 words, featured a woman representing a specific occupation and region, and the Women's Division scripted them "in the first person, and wherever possible in the appropriate idiom of the individual represented" (National Committee of Independent Voters for Roosevelt and Wallace, 1940 Records, Franklin D. Roosevelt Presidential Library, Hyde Park, New York, Box 5, File: "Radio, Screen and Personal Appearances [1]"). During the 1940 campaign the Women's Division peppered its members with reminders of the importance of radio to Democratic victory. Radio Directors were sent advice on radio speaking and were encouraged to host "listening parties" to coincide with important Democratic broadcasts. Radio, Democratic women were told, "is God's gift to the Democratic party" (Democratic National Committee, Women's Division Collection Papers, Franklin D. Roosevelt Presidential Library, Hyde Park, New York, Box 283, File: "1940-Radio Publicity").

At the end of the 1940 campaign NBC reported that it had sold time to 23 organizations, of which 5 represented Democratic interests and 16 supported the GOP ticket. NBC also sold approximately $9,000 worth of time, or slightly more than 1% of its total political billings, to the Socialist Labor Party and to the CPA (NBC Interdepartmental Correspondence, 1940, Library of American Broadcasting Collection, University of Maryland, College Park, File 82). Because of smaller campaign budgets and the use of shorter programs on local stations, NBC devoted only 55 hours 55 minutes to political programming in 1940, a sharp drop from the 127 hours 15 minutes used in 1936. The network suffered a much smaller decline in its billings, from \$904,021 in 1936 to \$809,606 in 1940 (Craig, 2000, 165). As in 1928, 1932, and 1936, the losing party spent more on radio than did the winners.

The gross mismatch in 1936 between Republican spending on radio and their performance at the polls was not repeated so glaringly in 1940. Although the GOP still outspent the Democrats significantly on radio, Willkie's electoral performance was much more creditable than the hapless Landon's; he won 44.8% of the popular vote and 82 Electoral College votes. The Republicans had nevertheless failed again to translate large radio budgets into electoral majorities; the DNC, on the other hand, had proved to be highly skilled in using their more limited radio funds to maximum effect. The Democrats were in addition blessed by having "the best radio voice in the world" on their side and in the White House. Like Hoover before them, Republicans during the 1930s confused radio quantity with quality, whereas the Democrats seemed more able to transform listeners into voters. As the medium matured from technological wonder into everyday functionalism, both major parties learned that effective radio politics depended much more on careful targeting and effective content than on mere volume.

Radio and the Art of Political Oratory

At first, there was no doubt among political observers that the radio age would bring a new form of oratory to political discourse. Radio, Samuel Blythe declared in 1929, "has slain the political orator. He is out. The day of the spellbinder is over" (p. 9). The old form of oratory, in which speakers traversed the stage, waved their arms, and employed emotional rhetoric to engage and entertain their audiences, was now extinct. Radio required strict discipline from speakers, who were now required to remain behind their daises to deliver consistent voice volume into the microphone.

Radio politicians also had to submit to the discipline of a script. Pre-radio oratory favored those who could speak extemporaneously; speakers could then move around the stage and respond more directly to the emotions of the audience. Radio, however, worked on tight scheduling, and politicians had to time their speeches carefully. Doing so without a script, and without careful rehearsal, proved too difficult for most orators. *The Saturday Evening Post* claimed that radio had come to the rescue of speakers too unimaginative or too nervous to depart from their scripts. For such speakers, who had long been failures in the auditorium, radio was a "godsend ... he needs no personal appeal or magnetism" ("Spellbinding," n.d., in Alfred E. Smith Private Papers. New York State Archives, Albany, File 508). In addition, national politicians speaking over extensive networks used a script to avoid embarrassing or damaging misstatements. With the whole nation rather than a single audience listening, candidates and leaders needed to choose their words carefully (*The New York Times*, September 16, 1928, XII, 10).

Old-time political oratory was also perceived to be inconsistent with the essentially domestic nature of the radio audience. Politicians were frequently reminded during the first half of the 1920s that the radio audience differed markedly from political meetings and stump speeches. Speakers could no longer assume that their audiences were partisan enthusiasts who had taken the trouble to leave their homes to hear their hero speak. Oratory under those circumstances was largely preaching to the converted, and its primary function was to mobilize supporters to go forth and do battle. The radio audience, on the other hand, was a heterogeneous and fickle body of people whose places of residence, occupations, and party affiliations were diverse. It included the converted, the unconvinced, the apathetic, and the hostile, and politicians had to adjust their technique accordingly (Bliven, 1924, 155ff.; Dunlap, 1936, 76; *The New York Times*, July 20, 1924, IV, 1).

The confidence that radio listeners were not as susceptible to emotional appeals as were members of a physical audience stemmed from a faith in the insulating influence of the home. There, surrounded by family and possessions, the radio voter was a modern exemplar of the republican ideal, sovereign in his or her home and deliberative in his or her political judgment (Wolfe, 1969, 311). Without the visual pomp of the old torchlight parades, and without the pressures generated by a large crowd, radio politicians now needed to combine entertainment, education, and civility to appeal to potential voters listening in family groups. That commentators during the 1920s assumed that the radio audience was more rational than a crowd attested more to their faith in radio, and to their wishful thinking, than to the quality or depth of their research. Detailed audience surveys were almost unknown in the 1920s, leaving early commentators free to indulge in hopeful speculation (Goldsmith & Lescarboura, 1930, 200).

Despite the hopes of its enthusiasts, radio did not usher in a new form of campaigning to American politics. It was instead integrated into what Michael McGerr has called the advertising style of campaign, which first appeared during the tumultuous election of 1896. Election campaigns since the Civil War followed three stages of development, beginning with the "spectacular," or military, style between 1864 and 1880. The spectacular campaign, heavily influenced by the martial atmosphere and paraphernalia of the Civil War, witnessed heavy use of parades, rallies, and picnics. As memories of the Civil War faded, and in the face of declining partisanship and the salience of new issues in the 1880s such as civil service reform, tariff policy, and industry regulation, a new educational campaign style emerged. Rather than devoting their resources to mobilizing the faithful, political parties concentrated on wooing independent voters through massive speech and pamphlet campaigns designed to "educate" voters about issues and solutions to them (McGerr, 1986, 40, 69–70, 130). By the turn of the century, the educational campaign style had been eclipsed by a new way of electioneering. The McKinley-Bryan campaign of 1896, fought at the tail end of the populist era and during the Depression of 1893, ushered in a new campaign style that relied heavily on advertising. The advertising campaign model became the 20th-century norm, transforming voters into consumers and policies and politicians into competing commodities. Campaigning became less concerned with enlightening voters and more interested in selling them the rational and irrational virtues of competing sets of propositions and images (Westbrook, 1983, 171, 145).

Inherent in the advertising style is a heavy emphasis on candidates rather than platforms or parties, slogans rather than pamphleteering, and speech making rather than front porch campaigning. As new technology such as photography, lithography, electric signs, phonographs, sound trucks, movies, radio, and television emerged, campaign strategists integrated each into the massive selling effort of national political campaigns. Although radio did not invent the advertising campaign, it provided the means by which millions of potential voters could be sold candidates and platforms within a context of declining partisanship and competing demands on the public's attention. In doing so, radio also completed the eclipse, but not the eradication, of the educational style, which persisted in muted form alongside an increasing focus on the "personality" and image of candidates (Dinkin, 1989, 128ff.; McGerr, 1986, 177–81).

The impact of broadcasting on political discourse and campaigning highlights the dangers of categorizing campaign styles too rigidly and of overestimating the effect of the new medium on the ways that politicians and electors interacted. In practice, the differences between the educational and advertising styles were often subtle; the advertising style still "educated" voters, albeit more about candidates than policies, and radio was seen by contemporaries to be a vital new educative force in politics. Political campaigns during the golden age of radio were still marked by massive pamphleteering and mailing campaigns designed to make voters aware of real and imagined differences in party platforms and policies.

The triumph of candidate-based politics was also patchy during the interwar period. There is no doubt that radio brought to many voters a more immediate and personal conception of candidates than they had received from old advertising media such as pamphlets and posters. By bringing a form of personal campaigning into American homes, radio simultaneously relieved voters who sought a personal impression of candidates from the obligation of attending meetings and assisted those groups traditionally marginalized by the old stump speeches and meeting-hall campaigning, such as women and the elderly, to form their own impressions of those who sought their votes. Radio did not, however, either immediately or single-handedly revolutionize American politics into wholly candidate-based advertising campaigns. Potential voters during the radio age still seemed to yearn for visual and physical contact with candidates (*The New York Times*, March 9, 1924, IV, 9).

Radio broadcasting did not arrest the trend toward more public candidacies that had characterized campaigns, especially for the presidency, since the end of the 19th century. Presidential candidates until the late 1880s were generally neither seen nor heard by voters; personal appeals for votes and national speaking tours were thought to be undignified for candidates and demeaning to the office (McGerr, 1986, 36ff.). William Jennings Bryan in 1896 ushered in a new era of modern presidential campaigning by his frenetic speaking tours across the nation, but in the following two decades his precedent tended to be followed only by underfunded or desperate candidates, such as Theodore Roosevelt in 1912, James Cox in 1920, and Robert LaFollette Sr. in 1924 (*The New York Times*, March 9, 1924, 9). Most presidential aspirants steered a middle course between reticence and barnstorming; sitting presidents such as Taft in 1912, Wilson in 1916, and Coolidge in 1924 stayed close to the White House but engaged in set public appearances, whereas nonincumbents such as Hughes in 1916, Harding in 1920, and Hoover in 1928 attempted to become nationally known through a limited number of major speeches and numerous brief addresses either from their front porches or from the rear platforms of their campaign trains.

Radio assisted candidates to disseminate their speeches, but it did not remove the perceived necessity to press the flesh. In 1928, Al Smith not only made 12 major campaign speeches, all of which were broadcast, but also undertook several speaking tours during the campaign. Herbert Hoover, far better known nationally and less objectionable to provincial voters than Smith, still found it necessary to schedule large numbers of public appearances in front of live audiences from his campaign train (*The New York Times*, October 6, 1930, V, 10). Even FDR, acknowledged as the radio master of age and limited by his physical disability, made personal appearances in all four of his presidential campaigns. These occasions were covered by all media and were the centerpieces of the hybrid style of campaigning during the radio age. In 1936, for example, the president undertook a tour of western states by train, accompanied by 25 newspaper reporters, 8 photographers, 2 telegraph operators, and 5 radio announcers and technicians. Traditional campaign media subsided but did not disappear in the 1930s; in 1932, the DNC sent out 42 million printed articles and 10 million buttons to the electorate alongside its intensive radio campaign (Louis McHenry Howe Papers. Franklin D. Roosevelt Presidential Library, Hyde Park, New York, Box 55, File: "Dem. Nat'l. Convention 1932").

By the mid-1930s, it had become clear that radio had not replaced personal campaigning but had instead modified it to improve voters' abilities to make informed judgments about candidates. The age-old electoral imperative for politicians to be seen to be in touch with voters has proven to be remarkably resilient in the face of technological advances such as radio and television. The Brooklyn *Eagle* in 1924 described personal campaigning as "an implied compliment to the electorate in the physical effort involved in a 'swing around the country,' in the honest willingness to go to personal trouble and inconvenience to meet Mr and Mrs Voter in their home communities" (quoted in *Literary Digest*, 182, 11). Despite the feasibility of a radio front porch campaign, politicians in the radio age still felt constrained to pay voters this compliment. Radio, the first of the electronic media, created a hybrid campaign style that combined education with advertising, as well as a engendering a greater focus on candidates' personalities and style and front porch oratorical skills.

The mixed influence of radio on political campaigning during the interwar years is best illustrated by comparing the hopes for a new political style that were prevalent during the 1920s, when broadcasting was still new, with the more measured analyses of radio politics that emerged during the 1930s. Numerous articles in newspapers and popular magazines during broadcasting's first decade argued that radio was creating a new and better political culture. Apart from its supposedly chilling effect on "bunk" and old-style oratory, radio was thought to have changed the very nature of American politics. "Broadcasting is really a house-to-house canvasser," CBS president Andrew White told the press in 1928:

> It accompanies the candidates into the home—direct to the family circle. The members of the family now form their own political opinions… Today, mother may vote for Hoover and father for Smith, just because of impressions formed by listening in on the radio. (*The New York Times*, October 28, 1928, X, 16)

Others foresaw different results from the radio revolution. "As a row of houses goes down before a cyclone," Charles Willis declared in 1930, "the immemorial and apparently eternal institutions of campaigning are falling before the radio hurricane. No longer does the candidate kiss babies; no longer does he go to fairs and put himself on exhibition" (*The New York Times*, October 26, 1930, X, 10). After witnessing the two national parties' nominating conventions in 1928, *The Nation* remarked that radio had made the physical audience of delegates "relatively unimportant" compared with the broadcast audience, to whom proceedings were now primarily addressed. One writer declared during the 1928 presidential election that radio had proved itself to be "the greatest debunking influence that has come into American public life since the Declaration of Independence." Radio had created a modern equivalent of the town meetings of colonial New England, with the "only difference" being that modern listeners "cannot talk back" (*The Nation*, July 11, 1928, 127, 34; *The New York Times*, October 28, 1928, X, 16).

More skeptical evaluations of the extent of the radio revolution in politics appeared during the 1930s. Even in 1924, Robert and Helen Lynd, in their study of life and culture in Muncie, Indiana, questioned the idea that radio listening led inevitably to greater interest in political life. The inhabitants of Middletown seemed to use radio more for entertainment than for civic education, and the Lynds found no evidence of an upsurge in political interest or engagement in their community. Voter turnout in Muncie had declined from 86% in 1892 to 53% in 1916, and in 1924, despite the influence of radio, only 46% of eligible voters in Middletown bothered to cast a vote (Lynd & Lynd, 1956, 416).

Instead of pointing to the failure of radio to excite the electorate into political engagement, as they had done in the 1920s, those who questioned in the 1930s the assumption that broadcasting would automatically improve political life looked with alarm at the success on radio of Adolf Hitler, Huey Long, and Father Coughlin. Will Irwin typified this approach in his *Propaganda and the News*, published in 1936. Early radio enthusiasts, Irwin remembered, had promised that radio would lead to "less buncombe and more reason in political speaking." Radio had instead replaced one form of spellbinding with another; successful radio oratory eschewed the emotionalism of the old oratory and was "something akin to the pleasing conversation of the peddler dispensing brushes ... [but] when at its most vicious, it is exactly as meretricious as the rolling periods of the old spellbinder." Within five years of the advent of commercial radio and national networks, Irwin noted gloomily, Long and Coughlin "were broadcasting effective fairytales to millions of wishful thinkers" (Irwin, 1936, 249–50).

Other critics noted that the old rules and foibles of politics seemed remarkably resilient to the supposedly cleansing effect of radio broadcasting. In July 1932, Mark Sullivan noted in the New York *Tribune* that the recent Democratic convention, at which William McAdoo and the California delegation had dramatically shifted their votes to ensure FDR's nomination, had shown that traditional backroom politics was alive and well in the radio age (National Broadcasting Company Records, Box 8, File 64). Four years later, at the end of the Democrats' 1936 convention, *The New York Times* reported that many of the delegates went home disgruntled. The convention had been so geared toward the radio audience that many of the party faithful who had come to Philadelphia felt that they had served only "to supply scenery and sound effects so that the home audience can hear the animals roar" (*The New York Times*, June 28, 1936, 24).

In 1932, 12 years after the beginning of radio broadcasting, the two presidential candidates once again boarded campaign trains and made numerous speeches. Herbert Hoover, increasingly desperate, made 22 speeches in

15 hours during his train journey from Washington to California in a performance that rivaled those of Bryan in 1896 and Cox in 1920 for frenetic barnstorming (*The New York Times*, October 29, 1932, 14). Such spectacles, *The New York Times* admitted during the campaign,

> may indicate that we have been too hasty in assuming that the radio and talking pictures… have radically revolutionized our political campaigning. They have undoubtedly wrought a wondrous change in it, but have they destroyed the old human conviction that an actual personality is the most moving and vitalizing thing in the world—even in the world of politics? (*The New York Times*, September 26, 1932, 14)

The New York Times returned to its theme of the incomplete radio revolution as it anticipated the 1936 campaign. Under a headline declaring that "radio campaigning demands a technique of its own, but it has not changed the basic rules of the game," the *Times* assessed the effect of radio on political life as "uncertain." It had undoubtedly transformed Long and Coughlin into national figures, and it had perhaps increased public consciousness and knowledge of politics, although this latter claim had to be tempered by the fact that "the great political use of radio has coincided with a social crisis when the public, if ever, would be interested in its government." Yet the foundations of party politics—local organizations, patronage, money, and personal campaigning—had not crumbled before the microphone: "In national politics the radio has had less effect, despite all that has been said, than might be expected" (*The New York Times*, February 9, 1936, VIII, 3).

Some critics of radio politics argued that broadcasting had contributed to a dangerous inflation of campaign expenditures during the 1920s. Election funding had long been a contentious issue, fueled both by concerns that democracy should not be for sale and by the propensity of Republicans to raise far more money than the Democrats. In 1920, the last presidential and congressional elections of the pre-radio age, election expenditures ran to more than $10.3 million, divided almost 4 to 1 in favor of the GOP (Ray Lyman Wilbur Papers, Hoover Institution Archives, Stanford University, Palo Alto, California, Box 95, File: "Political - Misc.Corr. 1921–1927"). In 1928, as both parties took advantage of prosperity and the new national radio networks, concern about election funding again surfaced. Both sides spent freely, and contemporaries pointed to exploding radio budgets as the chief contributor to the two parties' combined election expenditure of more than $17 million. In 1860, *The New York Times* pointed out in 1928, committees supporting Abraham Lincoln and Stephen Douglas spent approximately $150,000; now the DNC alone contemplated spending more than $7 million on behalf of Al Smith. With both national committees spending between $50,000 and $60,000 for each national radio hookup, broadcasting costs had added a significant new element to the costs of modern campaigning (*The New York Times*, August 12, 1928, II, 1).

These fears do not appear to have been well founded. Although figures for campaign expenditures are notoriously imprecise, it is clear that total spending by the two major parties fluctuated through the 1920s for reasons other than radio. Total expenditures in 1924 were below those of 1920, mainly because of a collapse in Democratic fundraising in the wake of its disastrous convention. Total expenditures in 1928 did rebound to historically high levels, but they then subsided under the influence of the Depression (Overacker, 1932, 80). Expressed in terms of cost per vote, campaign expenditures were remarkably stable during the 1920s, despite the doubling of the potential electorate through female enfranchisement and new expenditures on radio. In 1968, Robert MacNeil estimated that the average cost per vote between 1912 and 1928 was between 19 and 20 cents. Given that average costs per vote jumped from 19 cents in 1956 to 32 cents in 1960 and 41 cents in 1964, MacNeil concluded that TV, and not radio, had caused campaign costs to inflate (MacNeil, 1968, 228). Louise Overacker in 1932 calculated that the RNC and DNC spent an average of 19 cents per vote in 1912, 20 cents in 1920, 15 cents in 1924, and 20 cents in 1928. Given that prices in 1928 were 40% higher than in 1912, Overacker concluded that the real cost per vote declined significantly during the first years of the radio age (Overacker, 1932, 80).

Conclusion

Between enthusiasm and skepticism lay a body of opinion that radio's effects on American political life were still uncertain. Radio "has not revolutionized politics," Samuel Blythe wrote in the *Saturday Evening Post* in 1929. "It hasn't changed politics one iota. But it has expanded politics, and, therefore, it is possible the revolution will come" (p. 9). Others were unsure about the long-term implications of the one-way nature of radio communication for political debate and education. "The radio has furnished us a conversational meeting ground," Eunice Fuller Barnard wrote in 1924. "But it has not yet allowed us to any extent to converse ... How far it can directly accelerate political progress until there is more mutuality, more free interchange... is still in doubt" (p. 93). The result of these developments was to reinforce skeptics' arguments that radio had not revolutionized American political culture but had rather been integrated into it. After 20 years of broadcasting, American voters had largely disappointed radio enthusiasts' dreams of a new age of political information, enlightenment, and engagement.

References

Barnard, Eunice Fuller. (1924). Radio Politics. *New Republic*, March 19, 93.

Barnouw, Erik. (1968). *A History of Broadcasting in the United States*, volume 2: *The Golden Web: 1933 to 1953*. New York: Oxford University Press.

Best, Gary Dean. (1993). *The Critical Press and the New Deal: The Press versus Presidential Power, 1933–1938*. Westport, CT: Praeger.

Bliven, Bruce. (1924). How Radio Is Remaking Our World. *Century Magazine*, 108, 147–154.

Blythe, Samuel G. (1929). Political Publicity. *Saturday Evening Post*, 201, 9.

Braden, Waldo W. & Ernest Bradenburg. (1955). Roosevelt's Fireside Chats. *Speech Monographs*, 22, 290–302.

Bradenburg, Earnest & Waldo W. Braden. (1952). FDR's Voice and Pronunciation. *Quarterly Journal of Speech*, 38, 23–30.

Brinkley, Alan. (1983). *Voices of Protest: Huey Long, Father Coughlin, and the Great Depression*. New York: Vintage Books.

Brown, James A. (1980). Selling Airtime for Controversy: NAB Self-Regulation and Father Coughlin. *Journal of Broadcasting*, 24, 199–224.

Buhite, Russell D. & David W. Levy. (1992). *FDR's Fireside Chats*. Norman: University of Oklahoma Press.

Casey, Ralph D. (1935). Party Campaign Propaganda. *Annals of the American Academy of Political and Social Sciences*, 179, 96–105.

Chase, Francis, Jr. (1942). *Sound and Fury: An Informal History of Broadcasting*. New York: Harper and Brothers.

Craig, Douglas B. (2000). *Fireside Politics: Radio and Political Culture in the United States, 1920–1940*. Baltimore and London: Johns Hopkins University Press.

Dinkin, Robert J. (1989). *Campaigning in America: A History of Election Practices*. New York: Greenwood.

Dunlap, Orrin E. (1936). *Talking on the Radio: A Practical Guide for Writing and Broadcasting a Speech*. New York: Greenberg.

Goldsmith, Alfred N. & Austin C. Lescarboura. (1930). *This Thing Called Broadcasting*. New York: Henry Holt and Co.

Irwin, Will. (1936). *Propaganda and the News: Or, What Makes You Think So?* New York: Whittlesey House.

Jamieson, Kathleen Hall. (1984). *Packaging the Presidency: A History and Criticism of Presidential Campaign Advertising*. New York: Oxford University Press.

Lears, Jackson. T.J. (1994). *Fables of Abundance: A Cultural History of Advertising in America*. New York: Basic Books.

Liebovich, Louis W. (1994). *Bylines in Despair: Herbert Hoover, the Great Depression, and the U.S. News Media*. Westport, CT: Praeger.

Lynd, Robert S. & Helen Merrell Lynd. (1956). *Middletown*. (First published 1927.) New York: Harcourt, Brace, and World.

MacNeil, Robert. (1968). *The People Machine*. New York: Harper & Row.

McCamy, James L. (1939). *Government Publicity: Its Practice in Federal Administration*. Chicago: University of Chicago Press.

McGerr, Michael E. (1986). *The Decline of Popular Politics: The American North, 1865–1928*. New York: Oxford University Press.

Merriam, Charles E. with H.F. Gosnel. (1949). *The American Party System: An Introduction to the Study of Political Parties in the United States*, 4th edition. New York: Macmillan.

Mitchell, Greg. (1992). *Campaign of the Century: Upton Sinclai's Race for Governor of California and the Birth of Media Politics*. New York: Random House.

Overacker, Louise. (1932). *Money in Elections*. New York: Macmillan.

Rorty, James. (1934). *Order on the Air!* New York: John Day.

Rose, C.B. (1940). *National Policy for Radio Broadcasting*. New York: Harper and Brothers.

Ryan, Halford D. (1988). *Franklin D. Roosevelt's Rhetorical Presidency*. New York: Greenwood.

Smith, F. Leslie. (1990). *Perspectives on Radio and Television*. New York: Harper and Row.

Westbrook, Robert B. (1983). Politics As Consumption. In Richard Wightman Fox & T.J. Jackson Lears (Eds.), *The Culture of Consumption: Critical Essays in American History, 1880–1980* (pp. 145–173). New York: Pantheon.

White, Graham J. (1979). *FDR and the Press*. Chicago: University of Chicago Press.

Winfield, Betty Houchin. (1990). *FDR and the News Media*. Urbana: University of Illinois Press.

Wolfe, G. Joseph. (1969). Some Reactions to the Advent of Campaigning by Radio. *Journal of Broadcasting*, 13, 304–314.

15. Community Renegades: Micro-radio and the Unlicensed Radio Movement

LAWRENCE C. SOLEY

When police beat Dewayne Readus during a 1983 scuffle at the John Hay Homes housing project in Springfield, Illinois, they were no more aware that their actions would lead to a large-scale revolt than were the Los Angeles cops who beat Rodney King eight years later. Unlike the revolt in Los Angeles, the one that started in Springfield was nonviolent, invisible, and international. It triggered the micro-radio revolt of the 1990s—an explosion of unlicensed, low-power radio stations that originated in, and broadcast to, neighborhoods across the United States and across the globe.

Dewayne Readus grew up in the John Hay Homes public housing project, a 600-unit complex of low-rise apartments for low-income families a short distance from President Abraham Lincoln's historic home. In the 1980s, the project was home to approximately 3,000 people, the vast majority of whom were African American. No commercial broadcasting stations were directed to Springfield's 15,000 African Americans, most of whom lived within a one-and-a-half-mile radius of the John Hay project.

In 1983, Readus, partially blinded by glaucoma as a child, was like many young African American men—unable to find a full-time or even a part-time job. To earn money, Readus became a disc jockey at project parties, spinning R&B discs and getting drunk. One of these parties turned into a brawl and the police were called. Readus was so severely beaten by police during the ensuing turmoil that he was completely blinded. After that, he became depressed and drank heavily (M. Kantako, personal communication, July 8, 1996).

After shaking his depression, Readus became interested in social activism and police accountability rather than parties and booze. In 1985, he helped organize the Tenants Rights Association (TRA), which demanded that Hay Homes authorities be accountable to project residents, rather than the other way around.

To improve TRA's outreach, Mike Townsend, a family friend and professor at Sangamon State University, now called the University of Illinois at Springfield, suggested that Readus start a neighborhood newspaper. Readus, who later changed his name to Mbanna Kantako (or "resisting warrior"), replied, "I'm blind, let's do radio. I don't get off on print that much" (M. Townsend, personal communication, July 8, 1996).

In addition to Kantako's blindness, there were other reasons the TRA needed to use radio. Kantako explains, "Studies show that 40 percent of black men are illiterate. Newspapers can't get them any information ... Besides, given technology today, using print is like using the pony express instead of air freight delivery" (quoted in Shields & Ogles, 1995).

At the next meeting of the TRA, members discussed "the most effective way of getting our message to the people," Kantako says. The group discussed the legality of operating an FM station without a license from the Federal Communications Commission (FCC). The TRA members weighed the legality of operating a transmitter, and concluded that the benefits outweighed the risks. "We were not even concerned about the FCC regulations. Clearly they were designed before blacks were allowed to hold their heads up," Kantako said about the decision. "And, obviously, being designed at that period of time, there was no consideration of what we as people might want to do" (LeBlanc, 1990).

Despite being illegal, the TRA decided to put an FM station on the air using money from a Catholic Church Campaign for Human Development grant. "We got the equipment ... for about $600 out of a catalog," says Kantako. They purchased a 1-watt Panaxis transmitter, assembled it themselves, adjusted it for 107.1 MHz so as not to interfere with existing stations, put up an antenna, and made their first broadcast on November 27, 1986, from the living room of Kantako's apartment.

The station was named for the association and given the call letters WTRA. At its inception, about a dozen Hay Homes residents worked on WTRA, whose signal was audible only within a mile-and-a-half of the transmitter. Nevertheless, the micro-power station reached most of Springfield's African American residents.

Initially, WTRA was on the air for just two nights per week, broadcasting live. In 1988, the station went to three nights per week, 12 hours per night (6 p.m. to 6 a.m.), carrying commentary, news reports, and music. The station also changed its name to Zoom Black Magic Liberation Radio to reflect its broader outlook, which was "to build community" and "raise the consciousness of the people" (M. Kantako, personal communication, July 8, 1996).

Around this time, Zoom Black Magic Liberation Radio started airing complaints about police brutality. The station also demanded that an independent police review board be established in Springfield. The predominantly white city council held a hearing on this issue and rejected the proposal.

The Springfield police chief contacted the FCC, claiming that he had received complaints about the station's use of profanity. Responding to the police chief's complaint, FCC agents visited the station on April 6, 1989, and determined that Kantako was operating without a license. He was ordered to stop broadcasting and slapped with a $750 fine.

Kantako shut the station down that day, but started it up again on April 17 during a press conference in which he demanded that the police arrest him for operating the station. When the police refused, Kantako went to the federal building in Springfield, where he asked to be arrested by U.S. marshals, who also refused. Because of these confrontations, Kantako decided to put the station on 24 hours a day, 7 days a week, which is how it operated until 2000, when the FCC finally seized the station's transmitter. It later reappeared on the Internet at http://www.humanrightsradio.net.

In 1989, the station was renamed Black Liberation Radio (BLR) to reflect its political outlook. It has since been called African Liberation Radio and Human Rights Radio, reflecting the changing perspective of Kantako and his associates. "We're learning as we go," said Kantako about the changes. "We named our original organization the name that we thought was a solution to our problems—the Tenant's Rights Association. We thought if we got tenant's rights—boom—everything would fall into place. We learned that wasn't the case" (Personal communication, July 8, 1996).

In March 1990, a federal court ordered Kantako to shut down his transmitter. Kantako ignored the order but did contact the San Francisco–based National Lawyers Guild Committee on Democratic Communications, formed in 1987 to explore "the applicability of traditional First Amendment concepts in the face of the worldwide monopolization of communication resources by commercial interests."

"I got an e-mail from Mike Townsend," said attorney Peter Franck, then co-chair with Sally Harms of the National Lawyers League Committee, about his first contact with BLR (Personal communication, March 5, 1997). "We felt what they were doing was very important. The choice was to either reform the existing media or start your own," said Franck, who doubts that the existing, corporate-controlled media can be reformed.

After discussing the case, the committee decided to take on Kantako's case. "We debated whether we should go to court affirmatively to try and get the ban on low-power radio ruled unconstitutional," said Franck, but "Mbanna wasn't very anxious to go to court. He didn't have much faith in the courts. And our feeling was that going in affirmatively makes it tougher to win than if we are defending him against a criminal charge or action." The brief was never filed on Kantako's behalf because the FCC backed away from the confrontation. Although the brief was not filed, it was not wasted—it was later revised and submitted on behalf of Free Radio Berkeley, an unlicensed station that challenged FCC licensing policies in 1993.

The first station inspired by Kantako's example and the second micro-power station to take to the air was BLR of Decatur. Like Springfield, which is 40 miles west, Decatur is a predominantly white city that dilutes minority representation through at-large elections, ties to business, and a police force that does not hesitate to use force against political dissidents, minorities, and union workers, as demonstrated during the Caterpillar, Bridgestone, and Staley strikes (Franklin, 1994; *Chicago Sun Times*, 1994).

Started by Napoleon Williams and Mildred Jones on August 20, 1990, BLR broadcast from a studio in the couple's small west-side home using a less than 1-watt Panaxis transmitter tuned to 107.3 MHz FM, a vacant frequency in the Decatur-Springfield radio market. The station was created to give Decatur's African American community uncensored access to the airwaves. A leaflet distributed in the African American community to announce its sign-on reported that BLR would give "a voice to those who have no voice of their own through the mass media" (BLR Leaflet, n.d.).

"We want[ed] total community involvement, so anybody can be on the air," Williams said about the station's philosophy in 1996. "If you have a problem with the judicial system, you don't have to call Napoleon Williams and ask him, 'What can you do?' You can come on and present your case to the people. There may be someone out there that will hear you, who has had the same problem and knows what to do." In Williams's view, radio should operate like public access channels on cable television, where interested groups and individuals can produce and air programs (Personal communication, July 9, 1996).

The FCC also visited this station, ordered Williams to stop broadcasting, and slapped him with a $17,500 fine. "I told them if I got $17,500, come and get it ... Hell, if I had $17,500, I'd have a better radio station than this," said Williams (Personal communication, July 9, 1996), who ignored the agency and continued to broadcast.

BLR never had a specific schedule during the week; only a few hours daily were devoted to scheduled programs. Most mornings, Williams did a show in which he discussed and reinterpreted news stories reported that day by the corporate press. "A lot of people don't buy the newspaper because they know Napoleon's going over it," said Jones about the show (M. Jones, personal communication, July 9, 1996).

After that, the station often played music, sometimes with Jones as disc jockey. On some nights, a live call-in show, *Hot Line*, was featured. Music programs by disc jockeys such as D.J. Ice also aired on weekdays. About the schedule, Williams said, "Throughout the day, you're going to find something you dislike and then, if you listen long enough, something you're going to like—that's guaranteed."

In May 1996, a commercial, album-oriented rock station in a nearby city signed onto 107.3 MHz, forcing BLR to change frequencies. Because he needed to shut down the station to alter its frequency, Williams decided it might be a good idea to install a new, more powerful transmitter at that time.

To buy a new transmitter, Williams conducted a one-day fundraiser over the air, asking listeners to drop $5 off on Saturday. Very late on Friday, Williams heard a knock on the door. When opened, there stood a local gang member who said, "I'm going to pay for 20 brothers right now," and handed Williams $100. During the next 24 hours, Williams was given more than $1,000, almost all of it in $5 donations.

The money was enough to buy a 15-watt transmitter, a new antenna, and even a meter to check the transmitter's output. The new transmitter allowed BLR to broadcast on 107.7 MHz to most of Decatur, rather than just its east or west sides.

The new transmitter was not in operation long, however. On January 9, 1997, the home of Williams and Jones was raided by the police, who had a search warrant allowing them to seize electronic equipment that could be used for "evesdropping" (Macon County, 1997). The allegations were not contained in the search warrant, but Williams allegedly taped his conversations with public officials without getting their permission, which is a felony in Illinois. (In most states, this taping is legal.) Rather than seizing tapes and tape recorders, the police seized every piece of broadcasting equipment in the house, suggesting that the raid was an attempt to force BLR off the air.

After news about the raid got out, BLR received help getting back on the air from many sources. Money, tapes, and tape recorders were brought to the station by supporters, and Stephen Dunifer, founder of Free Radio Berkeley, sent Williams a new transmitter. With this help, BLR was back on the air in a few weeks.

The Rebellion Spreads

Williams's belief that radio stations should function like public access channels, rather than as producers of pabulum and profits, was also held by Tom Reveille, who in 1991 started Radio Free Venice, California's first micropower station. "In my view, we have a media government. If you need information, you can only get it from the media....They have a stranglehold on information," Reveille said about the corporate media, which dominate the U.S. airwaves (Personal communication, December 27, 1996). "This is the only war in history, where one side gets all of its information from the other side."

Inspired by the example of Mbanna Kantako, Reveille decided to start an unlicensed station, where listeners could become program producers. "It was open to the community on an equal basis. It was quite a heterogeneous mixture of people on the air," he said. The station was open about its location, provided its telephone number to listeners and, for a studio, Reveille used the enclosed porch on the house where he lived, so that passersby could see the studio, and come in and talk, if they so wished.

The FCC took advantage of the station's openness. On May 29, FCC agents, backed by Los Angeles cops, showed up at Reveille's door, and informed him that he was breaking the law. Reveille responded that they were violating the law because Congress gave the FCC jurisdiction over interstate and foreign communications, not micro-radio, where signals barely travel two miles. The police responded to Reveille's comments by grabbing and handcuffing him. He was released when they and the FCC agents left.

Despite the FCC visit, Radio Free Venice remained on the air. "What wasn't important was the station, but to challenge the FCC," Reveille said about his decision to continue broadcasting. The FCC responded to the challenge on November 13, when two agents and four federal marshals again visited and entered Reveille's residence with guns drawn. "They ransacked the rooms of people who had nothing to do with the station," Reveille says about the raid. "They didn't take the antenna, [but] they took cash, videotapes, 160 audiotapes, files—everything they damn well pleased." Reveille never got the equipment or his personal possessions back, and the station never returned to the air (Personal communication, December 27, 1996).

As the FCC was silencing Radio Free Venice, another free station calling itself KAPW signed on in Phoenix, Arizona. The station was operated by Bill Dougan on 88.9 MHz from his home. Unlike Tom Reveille, a politically dedicated libertarian, Dougan was not involved in political activities before getting involved in radio. He had written a few letters to the editor, but not much more. This changed in 1988 when commercial station KFYI-FM dropped talk show host Tom Leykis, to whom Dougan listened almost daily. To get Leykis back on the air, Dougan initiated a boycott of KFYI advertisers; the station responded by suing Dougan for interfering with their business. Faced with the expenses of defending himself from KFYI's suit, Dougan called off the boycott (Wagner, 1994).

The experience left Dougan disenchanted with commercial radio, so he decided to start a noncommercial station, which he dubbed "Arizona's Most Controversial Station." KAPW aired a variety of materials, including tapes of "controversial" speakers such as Madalyn Murray O'Hair, Native American music, and public affairs shows—but not for long. On March 12, 1992, FCC agents showed up at Dougan's door, asking to see the transmitter. He refused to allow the agents in—or so the FCC says—but he invited in representatives of the news media, who had gathered outside his home. The FCC responded by fining Dougan $17,500 (FCC, 1996).

Dougan shut down his station, but appealed the fine in the U.S. Ninth Circuit Court of Appeals, where he argued that the FCC's restrictions on low-power broadcasting were unconstitutional. The National Lawyers Guild Committee on Democratic Communications filed a friend-of-the-court brief in that case, based largely on the research that they had done for Mbanna Kantako, but the court did not reach a decision, ruling instead that the proper jurisdiction for the case was Federal District Court (*Dougan v. FCC*, 1994).

Dougan returned to the air in 1994, after Radio Free Berkeley, defended by the Committee on Democratic Communications, beat back FCC attempts to silence that station. Dougan's new station, called KAFR or Arizona Free Radio, was created as "a refreshing change from far-right hate radio," carrying many of the same program types that appeared earlier on Free Radio Berkeley, such as a gay and lesbian show, women's programs, and punk rock music (Newberg, 1995).

Two other stations inspired by Kantako's example were Radio Free Detroit and Black Liberation Radio 2, which broadcast to Richmond, Virginia. Radio Free Detroit, although inspired by Zoom Black Magic Radio, differed from its inspiration in several ways. The station was secretive about its location and sponsorship, never recruited citizens to produce programs or otherwise participate in the station's operations, and never directly challenged the FCC, as Kantako, Williams, and Reveille had. Instead of opening the station to the public, all of the programming was produced by "the RFD collective." The station broadcast on 106.3 MHz, near the top of the FM band. The FCC apparently learned about the station from an article in *The Fifth Estate*, Detroit's alternative weekly newspaper. When the FCC showed up at the operators' door, accompanied by a few cops and a television crew trying to do a story on the station, Radio Free Detroit was silenced.

Black Liberation Radio 2 was on the air between December 29, 1994, and June 25, 1995. The station was started by Jahi Kubweza, who became "tired of being bombarded by lies." Kubeweza said, "We took it upon ourselves to show the difference between the information being made available and the information withheld" (Personal communication, January 2, 1996).

Black Liberation Radio 2 featured programs on economics, government, health, and a host of other issues, along with poetry and rap, reggae, jazz, and instrumental music. It directly challenged the FCC by operating on 91.7 MHz, 24 hours per day, 7 days per week with 30 watts of power.

FCC agents paid the station a visit on June 25 and asked to see the transmitter. "I made a mistake," Kubweza says about his decision to allow the agents in. Once in, they seized the transmitter, the antenna, and all other electronic equipment that was visible—even equipment that had nothing to do with the station. Kubweza was prosecuted and eventually convicted for operating the station (FCC, 2001).

Although the FCC believed that it could stop the growing micro-power radio revolution by issuing fines and seizing transmitters, it was wrong.

The Case of Free Radio Berkeley

Berkeley and San Francisco, birthplaces of the free speech and countercultural movements of the 1960s, became the center of the micro-radio revolution around 1993. The free-radio revolution shifted to the California Bay Area, where the National Lawyers Guild Committee on Democratic Communications was based, and where Stephen Dunifer, a former broadcast engineer for commercial radio and television stations, lived. Dunifer started Free Radio Berkeley as a direct challenge to the FCC's ban on low-power broadcasting and as a laboratory for developing and distributing a low-cost, micro-power transmitter that could be used by community groups and citizen activists.

Before putting Free Radio Berkeley on the air, Dunifer designed and tested several homemade FM transmitters in his workshop-home above an electronics repair store in West Berkeley. Dunifer's residence consisted of two bedrooms, a living room, and a workshop larger than all the other rooms combined. In the workshop, he winnowed his prototype FM transmitters down to one that was small, portable, stable, and inexpensive.

In April 1993, Dunifer began broadcasting on Sunday nights between 9 p.m. and 10 p.m. from his workshop-home, announcing, "This is Free Radio Berkeley, 88.1 on your FM dial." Shortly after Free Radio Berkeley signed on, San Francisco–based FCC agents monitored the 15-watt broadcasts, which denounced the FCC for promoting corporate interests rather than the public interest, an issue that Dunifer hammered at consistently.[1] "We are attempting to redress a greater wrong that is essentially a theft of the people's airwaves by corporate interests that have hijacked the whole thing," Dunifer said about his motivations for starting the unlicensed station (Personal communication, March 4, 1996).

Agents with the FCC's compliance bureau in San Francisco visited Berkeley on April 23, 1993, where the unlicensed station's "signals were isolated by the agent to the vicinity of 6th Street and Alliston Way" (FCC, 1995). A week later, several agents returned to Berkeley, where they parked and waited for the station to return to the air. At 9 p.m. as usual, Free Radio Berkeley signed on. When the transmissions began, the agents turned on their "close-in direction finding equipment" and locked onto the transmissions originating from Dunifer's workshop-home, which they identified as the source of the unlicensed messages.

At 9:55 p.m., one of the agents knocked on Dunifer's door and asked whether he could inspect the station's transmitter. Dunifer refused to open his door, so the agent went back to his car, where he and his cohorts waited to see what would happen next. A short time later, the agents noticed a longhaired, bearded fellow wearing wire-rimmed glasses leave the premises that they had staked out. One of the agents accosted the fellow, who refused to identify himself. The agents later identified him as Stephen Paul Dunifer, a Berkeley anarchist and radical activist.

Dunifer says that he expected the visit from the FCC. One reason for going on the air was to challenge the FCC rules prohibiting micro-power broadcasting, but before the rules could be challenged in court, he had to be cited by the FCC. "The first broadcasts were made from a fixed location to get the attention of the FCC," Dunifer says. The broadcasts were "an absolute attempt to challenge directly the FCC's regulatory structure and policies. Based on the work of the National Lawyer Guild Committee on Democratic Communications [in the Kantako case], I felt sure we had a very solid legal basis to proceed on if we could find a proper venue," he said (Personal communication, March 4, 1996).

However, once the FCC identified Dunifer's workshop-home as the source of the broadcasts, the "station went mobile," operating that way for a year and a half—until the end of 1994. "The transmitters were put into backpacks along with other portable studio equipment and were all hiked up into the hills of Berkeley," Dunifer explained. A battery was lugged along to provide electrical power for the transmitter, which went on the air Sundays from 9 p.m. to midnight, airing tapes made by community groups, local bands, and even interviews.

Because the station continued to broadcast, the FCC served a Notice of Apparent Liability for $20,000 on Dunifer on June 1, telling him that Free Radio Berkeley had been monitored broadcasting from his residence on April 25 and May 2. Louis ("Luke") Hiken, a San Francisco attorney and member of the National Lawyers Guild Committee on Democratic Communications, drafted Dunifer's response to the notice. The response noted that the FCC's fine was "grossly disproportionate to the alleged violations ... and exceeds the maximum set by statute." Moreover, the response laid out the arguments that would later be raised in U.S. District Court, where the FCC tried to get an injunction to stop Dunifer from broadcasting. It noted that FCC policies were developed "before the advent of FM broadcasting" and "failed to keep pace with ... technological advances" such as highly stable low-power FM transmitters, which provide poor people, rather than just large corporations, with access to the broadcasting spectrum (Hiken, 1993).

The FCC officials, of course, rejected all of these arguments in their brief, filed on November 8, 1993, explaining that they had the sole power to determine the public interest. In response, Hiken filed an appeal called an Application for Review in Washington, DC, on December 2, 1993.

In addition to getting the National Lawyers Guild to represent him, Dunifer did several things that the FCC did not expect. He took his case public, began showing others how they could start their own radio stations, and continued to broadcast. To publicize his case, Dunifer sent press releases to alternative, local, and national media and made himself available for interviews. The first stories about Dunifer appeared in Bay Area newspapers, such as the *San Francisco Chronicle*, which reported that Dunifer and his colleagues were "encouraging other people" to start up stations. "They offer free workshops on how to build miniature radio stations for less than $200," an article reported (Herscher, 1993). Stories about Free Radio Berkeley also appeared on CNN and in *The New York Times*, but what garnered publicity for the station was the FBI's attempt to link Bay Area radicals to the Unabomber. According to the FBI, an anonymous tipster identified Dunifer as the Unabomber, and an FBI agent decided to pay Dunifer a visit. Because of the FBI visit, Dunifer's fight with the FCC was reported in the *Washington Post*, *Los Angeles Times*, and other large daily newspapers (Noble, 1995; Achenbach, 1995; Jacobs, 1995).

Soon thereafter, another Bay Area micro-power FM station, San Francisco Liberation Radio (SFLR), appeared on 93.7 MHz. Started by activists Jo Swanson and Richard Edmondson, the station followed in the footsteps of Radio Free Berkeley, becoming mobile. During its initial months of operation, the station broadcast from different locations, hoping to avoid being tracked and silenced by the FCC. Rather than broadcasting just one night a week as Free Radio Berkeley did, SFLR was on two nights, Wednesdays and Saturdays, from 8 p.m. to 10 p.m.

After learning that Edmondson operated SFLR, the FCC issued him a Notice of Liability containing a $10,000 fine. Edmondson, like Dunifer, turned to Luke Hiken for legal assistance and then kept on broadcasting (Nessie, 1997).

The FCC's Inaction

Rather than quickly denying Dunifer's Application for Review, which would have allowed Hiken to appeal the denial in court, the FCC took a different approach. The agency let the Application for Review languish in Washington, DC, for 10 months and then filed in U.S. District Court in California for an injunction ordering Dunifer to stop broadcasting. The FCC reasoned that if it received the injunction, Dunifer could be cited for violating the court order when broadcasting, rather than for violating FCC regulations, thus avoiding a potential constitutional challenge to its rules.

However, this strategy backfired. When the FCC filed in Federal District Court for the permanent injunction, it also asked for an immediate preliminary injunction, claiming that Free Radio Berkeley's continued operation produced "immediate and irreparable harm." To this argument, Hiken responded that the station had been on for 18 months, but the FCC was only now seeking an injunction. "Why did they wait for over 18 months to bring it to this court's attention?" Hiken asked. During the 18 months, the FCC had repeatedly monitored the station, he pointed out, and had only discovered two instances where the station's signal interfered with other broadcast signals, and in one of the instances the interference was actually caused by the FCC (Hiken, 1995). Hiken also noted that other low-power stations were on the air, such as BLR in Springfield, Illinois, but that the FCC had not sought injunctions to shut them down. "If there is an emergency, why is it they haven't done anything about that [station]? There's no emergency in this case," he said (Black Hat, 1995).

Hiken also observed that the FCC in Washington had been sitting on Dunifer's appeal for a year and had not yet ruled on it. If the FCC believed that Free Radio Berkeley presented such a threat to the public interest, it should have acted on the appeal, he reasoned.

The FCC's failure to act on Dunifer's Application for Review gave him time to build more transmitters, which were eagerly grabbed by activists around the country. In San Francisco's Mission District, Radio Libre signed on during the summer of 1994 using a Dunifer-built transmitter. Started by a group of Latino street boys and white anarchists on 103.3 MHz, the station broadcast music, political commentary, and Latino community news and information (Ferris, 1995).

In Phoenix, Bill Dougan, emboldened by Dunifer's continued operation, put Arizona Free Radio back on to the air, saying, "I do want to make a federal case out of it, literally. This is a potential Supreme Court case" (Wagner, 1994). In December 1994, Black Liberation 2 took to the airwaves in Virginia. Four months later, Free Radio Santa Cruz went on the air, broadcasting from another Dunifer-built transmitter. Commenting on the sudden growth of free radio stations, Luke Hiken said, "I think this is going to get beyond the ability of the FCC to control, judging from the snowballing of people interested in setting up stations."

The FCC at a Loss

Federal District Court judge Claudia Wilken stunned the FCC on January 20, 1995, when she ruled that its request "for a temporary injunction is hereby denied." The FCC's hope that it could avoid addressing the constitutionality of its ban on low-power broadcasting was further dashed when Judge Wilken ruled that "the FCC is arguably violating its statutory mandate as well as the First Amendment by refusing" to reconsider its rules on micro-radio. On the basis of the evidence, she also concluded, "the record does not support the ... assertion" that "because Defendant's equipment is not FCC-approved, it must be considered likely to emit spurious signals without a warning" (Wilken, 1995). Wilken's ruling eventually forced the FCC to reconsider its ban on micro-radio.

The decision so stunned FCC attorney David Silberman that he insultingly informed Judge Wilken:

> Your Honor, this opens up such a can of worms. You don't realize. I mean it. Your Honor, what would happen would be that you've given carte blanche to this group of people who think they can operate a radio station without a license ... This is turning it on its head, Your Honor ... But it opens up such hazards to the public interest that I want you to realize what you're doing.

Judge Wilken replied, "I didn't find such egregious hazards on the records. I mean, if there is some further showing that you would want to make at some point, I can't prevent you from doing that" (Wilken, 1995).

The decision provided Dunifer and his associates with the opportunity to increase the station's power and hours of operation. Within weeks of the decision, the station became a full-fledged 24-hour-a-day, 7-day-a-week operation, broadcasting on 104.1 FM with 30 watts of power. "It was pretty loose at that point. People signed up on a chalk board in time slots and we started having meetings," Dunifer says about the operation (Personal communication, March 4, 1996). The station attracted an eclectic band of volunteers, including ecologists, punk rock anarchists, street activists, apolitical musicians, and Latino and African American street youths. Chris Thompson, a deejay at the station, concluded "as the months went by, two separate impulses emerged among the deejays. While Dunifer and the [activists] saw the station as a means to rally the leftist troops and politicize the listeners, the punk rock crowd and others mostly wanted to spin tunes for their friends" (Personal communication, March 4, 1996). The difference in views and lack of organization invariably led to conflicts.

Because of the conflicts, Dunifer moved the station to a north Berkeley office, where operations were overseen by a collective. The station broadcast from there between July 1996 and March 1997, after which it moved to a larger space in a low-income neighborhood, where it could be closer to its roots.

Nine months after Judge Wilken refused to issue a preliminary injunction stopping Free Radio Berkeley from broadcasting, the FCC issued its decision on Dunifer's appeal. As expected, the FCC rejected "Dunifer's argument that the Commission's rules abridge an asserted First Amendment right of free speech." The FCC added, "Mr. Dunifer's constitutional arguments directly challenge the 60-plus-year statutory approach to licensing broadcast transmissions," but failed to mention that for 60-years the FCC had defined "public interest" synonymously with commercial broadcasting (FCC, 1995).

The FCC decision contained a number of misleading assertions. For example, the FCC suggested that it might have issued Dunifer a license had he applied for one, claiming that "if Mr. Dunifer believes it would be unconstitutional for the FCC to deny him a license, he should have ... asked for a license, along with a request for a waiver of the relevant rules limiting low power FM service." However, the FCC's suggestion that it might have waived the ban on low-power station operation had the commission's procedures been followed was untrue, according to John Reed of the FCC's engineering and technology department in Washington, DC. "I've never heard of [the FCC] giving permission like that," Reed said. "There's never been a case of our approving this" (Personal communication, May 9, 1997).

To bolster its claim that it is willing to license low-power stations, the FCC wrote, "Contrary to Mr. Dunifer's argument, the Commission's rules do not prohibit all low power services. For example, the Commission's rules provide for FM translator stations and booster stations which transmit at power well below the 100 watt minimum" (FCC, 1995). In this discussion, the FCC failed to mention that translator and booster stations merely retransmit the signals of already licensed, large-power stations—and that nearly all translator and booster frequencies have been assigned to corporate broadcasters.

According to the FCC, all it needed to do to win a summary judgment was to show that the facts were undisputed (i.e., Free Radio Berkeley was on the air) and that the law was on its side (i.e., Free Radio Berkeley did not have a license to broadcast). In its request for summary judgment, the FCC argued that the Federal District Court had jurisdiction to decide the constitutionality of laws, not rules such as those developed by the FCC, and therefore must not address any of the constitutional issues raised by Dunifer.

The FCC then filed an additional brief asking the court to issue permanent injunctions against the Free Radio Berkeley collective, not just Dunifer, as well as Free Radio Santa Cruz and other stations, which the FCC asserted were operated by Dunifer. The commission requested the broad injunction so that it could avoid having to take individual free stations to court, where the constitutionality of its rules could be challenged each time.

The FCC was hoping for a speedy judgment in District Court, which it failed to get. A court decision was expected in spring 1997, but by summer the court had not acted. Because of the court's inaction, micro-power stations took to the air in almost every other major city and region of the United States. In the south, Radio Free Memphis, Free Radio The Bayou in Louisiana, and Radio Free Hiram in Georgia appeared. In the Northeast, there was Steal This Radio (New York City), Radio Mutiny (Philadelphia), and JAM-FM (Syracuse). In the Northwest, there was Seattle Liberation Radio, Radio Free Portland, and Radio Free Eugene. In the Ohio Valley region, there was Free Radio Pittsburgh, Free Radio Indianapolis, and WIBL (Hamilton, OH). In the Midwest, there was KAW-FM (Lawrence, KS), WNBK (Northbrook, IL), and KCMG-FM (Kansas City). In each instance, the stations provided services that were unavailable from commercial radio stations.

For example, Free Radio Memphis (94.7 FM) had a labor show called *Solidarity Forever*, hosted by a member of the Industrial Workers of the World. Guests on the show discussed the difficulties and needs of the labor movement. "They're not getting on there and expressing something they think someone's going to want to buy. They're getting on there and expressing things that are very important to them in an everyday sort of way," said the show's host, contrasting his guests with those appearing on commercial stations (Hanas, 1997).

Radio Free Memphis also had a feminist show, *Grrrl Power Hour*, an indie hip-hop show, and a community news program that covered stories ignored by commercial media. For example, the station aired interviews of activists attending peace demonstrations when other media ignored these activists.

Because of the defeats it suffered in Judge Wilken's courtroom, the FCC was reluctant to take direct action against free radio broadcasters, despite complaints from commercial broadcasters and lobbying by the National Association of Broadcasters (NAB). Instead the commission merely issued statements reaffirming its opposition to unlicensed radio operations (FCC Audio Services Division, 1996).

As complaints from commercial broadcasters mounted, the FCC eventually targeted for closure a few unlicensed stations in the South and Midwest—far from Judge Wilken's court. In addition to their geographic locations, the targeted unlicensed stations had several things in common: they were operated by individuals without community participation, and their programs often differed from those of most micro-radio broadcasters, which usually spoke for disenfranchised communities.

The strategy that the FCC pursued in each case was the same. FCC agents accompanied by law enforcement officials seized the stations' transmitters, rather than seeking an injunction against them, as the commission had done with Free Radio Berkeley. By seizing the transmitters, the FCC immediately put the free radio broadcasters off the air and on the defensive, requiring them to go to court to get their transmitters back, where they would be required to show that they had a legal right to operate the transmitters. Proving this in court would be impossible.

The first station the FCC targeted was Lutz Community Radio near Tampa, Florida, operated by Lonnie Kobres, a member of the "constitutionalist movement," which was incorrectly identified with the far-right militia movement. The FCC was aware for many months that Kobres's station was on the air, having first monitored its broadcasts on October 31, 1995. After the monitoring, the FCC sent Kobres letters informing him that the broadcasts were illegal.

On March 8, 1996, less than a year after the bombing of the Alfred P. Murrah federal building in Oklahoma City, which spawned a frenzy of media reports that equated "constitutionalists" such as Kobres with the Oklahoma City bombers, federal agents with search warrants raided the Lutz radio station and seized its transmitter. The widespread public antipathy to the far-right movement that resulted from the Oklahoma City bombing and the media's coverage of it made Kobres an easy target, although the FCC denied that Kobres was targeted because of his political views (Sommer, 1996).

In June 1996, the FCC raided Black Liberation 2 in Richmond, Virginia, which had been on the air for less than six months. The station was operated by Jahi Kubweza and his family, rather than a community group, and patterned after the Illinois-based free station of the same name. As with Lutz Community Radio, FCC agents visited Kubweza's home, demanded to see the transmitter, and then seized it (Kubweza, 1996).

The FCC used a similar approach to silence The Beat, a station operated by Alan Freed in Minneapolis that carried dance music. The 20-watt station, based in Freed's apartment, signed on July 21, 1996, and soon attracted an audience in Minneapolis's hip Uptown neighborhood. The station also attracted the enmity of commercial broadcasting corporations and the Minnesota Broadcasters Association, which almost immediately filed complaints with the FCC (Groebner, 1996).

In August, the FCC responded to the complaints, sending Freed a letter warning him that he could be fined and imprisoned for operating a radio station without a license. Freed responded with a letter challenging the constitutionality of the FCC's rules banning low-power radio stations. He continued broadcasting, despite the warning letter (Lambert, 1996). In October, the FCC went before a federal magistrate and asked for an arrest warrant directing the U.S. marshal to seize Freed's transmitter. The court issued the warrant and in November, the transmitter was seized.

A month later, on December 11, 1996, FCC agents from Tampa traveled to Orlando to investigate a complaint filed by local broadcasters against an unlicensed station broadcasting on 106.5 FM. Like The Beat, the Orlando station broadcast music rather than community affairs programs. As they did in Lutz, Richmond, and Minneapolis, the agents confiscated this station's transmitting equipment, thereby silencing the station (FCC Compliance and Information Bureau, 1996).

Kobres and Freed responded to the seizures by filing claims in federal court, requesting the FCC to return their equipment because the seizures were unlawful. Both challenged the constitutionality of FCC rules governing low-power broadcasting in their filings. Kobres also acquired another transmitter and put Lutz Community Radio back on the air, something neither Kubweza nor Freed attempted.

It took the U.S. District Courts in Florida and Minnesota about a year to rule on Kobres's and Freed's claims. On August 24, 1997, the court in Florida upheld the government's seizure of Kobres's transmitter. On September 5, 1997, the court in Minnesota also decided in the FCC's favor. The Minnesota court also ruled that the U.S. Court of Appeals, not District Courts, have jurisdiction over the constitutionality of FCC rules, as the FCC had argued. The Minnesota decision handed the FCC a decision that it had failed to get in Judge Wilken's court and a green light to move against free radio broadcasters in districts outside of the San Francisco Bay area.

The FCC's Offensive

It did not take long after the Florida and Minnesota decisions for the FCC to start an offensive against unlicensed broadcasters. Within weeks, the FCC was notifying unlicensed stations to close down and dispatching agents to seize the "stuff." On September 4, 1997, FCC agents and U.S. marshals raided a pirate station in Howell, New Jersey, that called itself Oldies 104.7 FM. This station differed from most micro-power stations in that it carried commercials, promoted itself on billboards, and was a member of the local chamber of commerce. The station's operator, Salvatore DeRogatis, was apparently stunned by the raid. "I thought they would never shut me down because of what had happened in California," said DeRogatis, alluding to Judge Wilken's decision, but apparently unaware that the decision applied only to that court district (*Broadcasting*, 1997; Ryan, 1997).

Two weeks later, FCC agents, backed by 12 federal marshals and 6 sheriff's deputies, seized the equipment of Community Power Radio, an unlicensed station that broadcast to African Americans in the Oak Park neighborhood of Sacramento, California (Larson, 1997).

In October 1997, the FCC also shut down several stations, including 105.5 FM in Miami, 106.5 FM in West Palm Beach, KCMG-FM in Kansas City, and Radio Free Allston, a high-profile community station in Boston (*Florida Times-Union*, 1997; Perrin, 1997). The high profile of Radio Free Alston was the result of its being operated openly with widespread public participation.

In November 1997, the FCC continued its attempts to silence unlicensed stations. FCC agents in Tampa, Florida, simultaneously raided Temple Terrace Community Radio (a.k.a. Tampa's Party Pirate), Radio Free Tampa Bay (a.k.a. 87X), and Lutz Community Radio on November 19. The raids, although consistent with what the FCC was doing in other parts of the United States, were due in part to Temple Terrace Community Radio founder Doug Brewer's increasingly brazen attitude toward the FCC. Brewer had increased the station's power to 125 watts, making it audible throughout much of Tampa, and it started carrying commercials for small businesses, including used record stores and strip joints. Brewer printed up bumper stickers promoting the station as "Tampa's Party Pirate—102.1 FM" and T-shirts reading, "License? We don't need no stinking license."

Brewer's activities were such that they were covered in a front-page story in the *Wall Street Journal*, in which Brewer challenged the FCC to take action. "It's going, it's visible, and it just plain rocks," said Brewer about the Party Pirate. Ralph Barlow, the district director of the FCC's Tampa field office, responded that Brewer's taunts were "not good" for FCC employee morale. "This guy is going off the deep end," Barlow said. "Sooner or later I'll nail him" (Orwall, 1997).

Barlow acted sooner rather than later, ostensibly on a complaint filed by commercial station WHPT-FM. At 6:30 a.m. on November 19, 1997, gun-toting police, FCC agents, and federal marshals pounded on the door of Brewer's home. Brewer awakened, thinking he had heard thunder. When he finally opened the door, Brewer was handcuffed. During the next 12 hours, FCC agents disassembled the studio of the unlicensed station, which was located in Brewer's garage, and seized everything that resembled broadcasting equipment (Cockburn, 1997; Danielson, 1997a,b).

A few miles away, FCC agents and U.S. marshals simultaneously raided the homes of Kelly Kombat and Lonnie Kobres, seizing the transmitters of 87X and Lutz Community Radio. Of the three unlicensed broadcasters arrested in Tampa that morning, only Kobres was charged with felonies for broadcasting without a license. He was charged because he continued to broadcast after the previous raid, not because of his political viewpoints, federal officials contended (Solov, 1997a). "Ninety illegal broadcasters have been shut down in the past year with no more action than sending letters or visiting them and delivering warnings," an FCC official explained about the felony charges. "Still, we do want to get across to the public that this is a serious matter, and what the consequences there are to public safety and to the broadcasters themselves" (Curtius, 1998).

The Micro-power Response

News of the FCC raids in Tampa were distributed nationwide almost immediately over the Internet to other micro-radio broadcasters, who encouraged Brewer, Kombat, and Kobres to organize a local movement protesting the FCC's actions. A national committee was established to raise money for Kobres's defense, which used the Internet to solicit funds.

In Tampa, supporters of the unlicensed stations swamped the FCC and WHPT-FM with protest calls. The calls were so frequent that the FCC and WHPT stopped answering their phones, and WHPT general manager Drew Rashbaum refused to comment about his station's complaint because of the harassment it had received from "obnoxious listeners" of the unlicensed station, as Rashbaum referred to them.

Protest demonstrations against the FCC raids were organized in Tampa. On Tuesday, November 25, more than 100 supporters of the unlicensed stations gathered in front of the FCC's Tampa office. "They're not going to get rid of us," declared Party Pirate deejay Matthew Adelman, one of the many dozens of protesters who assembled at the federal office with placards reading, "Federal Censorship Commission" and "What Good is Free Speech if You Can't Hear Us?" (Solov, 1997b).

Despite these actions, the FCC continued its assault on micro-power radio. On December 9, 1997, FCC agents visited the Old Firehouse Cafe in Anchorage, Alaska, from where Free Radio Spenard broadcast. The agents said they would return and confiscate the equipment, if the station were not silenced. "We turned it off Tuesday night after having a meeting," said a Free Radio Spenard volunteer (Dunham, 1997).

Over the Internet, the micro-power movement organized a letter writing and e-mail campaign directed at FCC Chairman William Kennard, pressuring him to change FCC policies. In addition, newspaper reports about the FCC's campaign against unlicensed broadcasters continued to be published, often carrying quotes from unlicensed broadcasters that were embarrassing to the FCC. For example, the *Florida Times-Union* of Jacksonville published a story about the FCC's crackdown on unlicensed stations that quoted Doug Brewer, who described his arrest. "It was a surprise attack. They came in with a real vengeance," he reported. "If I were a drug dealer or a murderer, that would be different story. All I had was a radio transmitter. I wasn't hurting anybody" (*Florida Times-Union*, 1997).

The pressure and continuing publicity caused the FCC in February 1998 to dust off a petition to establish a micro-radio broadcasting system that had been sitting in its files for six months. The petition that the FCC initially put on the table was as conservative as possible: It proposed that micro-broadcasters be assigned just one frequency in each broadcasting band and that, high schools and universities, not community groups, be given priority in the licensing process. The proposal also limited low-power stations to one watt. Moreover, the proposal suggested that micro-stations might also be commercial, providing access for "entrepreneurs" who are "motivated by the prospect of genuine wealth." Thus, the petition never addressed any of the inequities against which the micro-radio movement was rebelling.

Despite the conservatism of this micro-radio station proposal, the NAB, the trade, and lobby organization for commercial broadcasting industry, quickly announced its opposition to all low-power radio broadcasting. NAB President Edward Fritts said, "At a time when spectrum used for radio stations is overly congested, it would be folly to authorize hundreds of additional low-power stations that would surely cause additional interference" (McConnell, 1998). Other representatives of commercial broadcasting also spoke out against micro-radio broadcasting, confirming what had been believed by most micro-radio broadcasters all along—that commercial broadcasters were opposed to micro-radio stations not because they operated without licenses but because the stations represented competition. These stations had attracted listeners who were disenchanted with commercial radio programming. Thus, micro-radio stations, regardless of whether they were legal or illegal, threatened the very *raison d'être* of the U.S. system of corporate broadcasting.

Although commercial broadcasters opposed the licensing of low-power stations, most responses to the FCC's initial proposal favored low-power radio, and asked the FCC to expand rather than limit the service. About one year later, on January 28, 1999, the FCC issued a Notice of Proposed Rulemaking seeking comments on the creation of a low-power service for stations broadcasting with substantially greater power than it first proposed—between 10 and 1,000 watts, instead of just 1 watt. The FCC announced that it would accept comments on the rulemaking notice until August 2, and would accept reply comments until September 1 (FCC, 1999).

During the seven-month comment period, the FCC received more than 3,000 comments, far more than it received on other proposed rulemakings. The vast majority supported a low-power radio service; opposition was primarily from already-licensed broadcasters, including National Public Radio and its affiliates, and broadcast trade associations, such as the NAB. The FCC was apparently surprised by the number and diversity of comments it received, observing that comments came "from churches or other religious organizations, students, labor unions, community organizations and activists, musicians and other citizens [that] reflect a broad interest in service from highly local radio stations grounded in their communities" (FCC, 2000, 3).

Because of the widespread support for low-power radio—and the criticism that the FCC suffered in the courts and through the press—the agency announced in January 2000 that it was establishing a low-power radio service and a process to apply for low-power FM licenses. In its Report and Order, the FCC addressed technical, ownership, and operating issues (FCC, 2000). In terms of technical standards, the FCC determined that low-power stations could operate on third adjacent channels without creating "significant new interference to the service of existing FM stations," even though the NAB and other broadcasters asserted that interference would occur (FCC, 2000, 42). As for ownership, the FCC decided to grant low-power licenses to non-profit organizations, not individuals, and required the organizations to be community based (i.e., to have a local chapter or branch within 10 miles of the station they operate). Each organization could operate no more than one station in each market, a policy that the NAB asserted violated the Telecommunication Act of 1996. Lastly, the FCC decided that two classes of low-power stations would be established—10 watt and 100 watt. This policy was supported in the comments of most citizens, activists, and community organizations, which opposed establishing a new 1000-watt service that, like existing commercial stations, would not serve local communities.

Almost immediately, the NAB and other broadcast lobbyists asked Congress to overturn the FCC's Report and Order. Three members of Congress who acted at the behest of the broadcasting industry were Sen. Rod Gramms (R-MN), Rep. Michael Oxley (R-OH), and Rep. Billy Tauzin (R-LA). Gramms and Oxley sponsored nearly identical bills, which in amended form became known as the Radio Broadcasting Preservation Act of 2000, which rolled back the FCC's Report and Order. Tauzin, as Commerce Committee chair, held hearings on low-power FM that rested on two assumptions: one, the FCC had exceeded its power by creating a low-power radio service, and, two, the service would interfere with existing stations. Rep. Heather Wilson (R-NM) summarized these sentiments in a statement about the amended Radio Broadcasting Preservation Act before the House, saying, "The FCC was moving too quickly and I believe compromising the quality of the radio reception that we get in our communities" (Wilson, 2000, H2305).

The Radio Broadcasting Preservation Act of 2000 was passed by the House, and Gramm's bill (S. 3020) was inserted as a rider into the District of Columbia Appropriations Act, which was passed, and signed into law by President Clinton. This effectively derailed the FCC's policy for creating a low-power service. The bill did not eliminate low-power FM; instead, it required the FCC to "prescribe minimum distance separations to third adjacent channels," thereby barring the stations from operating on third adjacent channels, as the FCC had approved. The law essentially eliminated 100-watt stations from operating in all but the smallest markets, and restricted licensing of 10-watt stations to medium-sized and small markets with less frequency congestion and wider channel separation. The largest cities, such as San Francisco, New York, Philadelphia, Milwaukee, and Tampa, where the free radio movement found its voice, were deprived of low-power stations by the legislation.

Low-power FM stations have taken to the air in small and medium-sized markets, but the majority do not sound like, or in any way resemble, the unlicensed stations that broadcast during the late 1990s. Most of the applicants for low-power stations have been religious congregations, rather than community groups. The stations of these congregations feature biblical readings and discussions, sermons, and religious music, which were already available on FM dial.

Notes

1. FCC agent Philip Kane told the *Express* newspaper (August 13, 1993, 14) that he received complaints about Free Radio Berkeley from "several" licensed stations, which caused him to monitor and track the station. After the National Lawyers Guild newspaper, *Conspiracy*, filed a Freedom of Information Act request for copies of the complaints, Kane and the agency claimed that the "complaints or inquiries were made in person or by telephone and that no documents or other records were compiled ... and that the individuals ... had expressly requested confidentiality." See "Memorandum and Order," 10 FCC Rcd 2155 (January 13, 1995). A separate examination of a complaint about Free Radio Berkeley that the FCC claims to have received from KFOG, a commercial station in San Francisco, "appears to have been prompted by FCC prodding." The FCC received the "complaint" from the station's corporate vice president in New York, who wrote the FCC after hearing about the station at a National Association of Broadcasters (NAB) convention in Las Vegas, in which FCC officials spoke. The NAB is the trade association and lobbying group for commercial broadcasters. See Walker (1995).

References

Achenbach, J. (1995). The Hunt for Unabomb. *Washington Post*, July 20, C1.

Black Hat. (1995). Some Comments and Excerpts from *The United States vs. Stephen Dunifer. Reclaiming the Airwaves*, April/May, 3. Retrieved from http://www.totse.com/en/media/radio_free_amerika/radiofre.html, March 28, 2007.

BLR Leaflet. (n.d.). Black Liberation Radio, Decatur, 107.3 FM.

Broadcasting. (1997). FCC Officials and Federal Marshals Raided an Unlicensed Radio Station. September 8,29.

Chicago Sun Times. (1994). Police Put Down Union Protests. June 26, 27.

Cockburn, A. (1997). Free Radio, Crazy Cops and Broken Windows. *Nation*, December 15, 9.

Curtius, M. (1998). Defiant Pirates Ply the Airwaves. *Los Angeles Times*, March 5, A20.

Danielson, R. (1997a). Marshals Take Out Pirate Radio. *St. Petersburg Times*, November 20, 1A.

———. (1997b). Radio Pirates in Escalating War with Rules. *St. Petersburg Times*, November 28, 1B.

Dougan v. FCC. 75 Rad. Reg. 2nd (P & F) 214; 21 F.3d 1488 (9th Cir. 1994).

Dunham, M. (1997). "Free Radio Spenard" Pulls Plug after FCC Visit. *Anchorage Daily News*, December 11, 2D.

FCC Crosses Swords with Pirate Radio DJ. (1997), *Florida Times-Union*, December 29, A6.

Federal Communications Commission. (1995). Memorandum and Order in the Matter of Application for Review of Stephen Paul Dunifer, August 2. NAL/Acct. No. 315SF0050.

———. (1996). In the Matter of William Leigh Dougan. May 28. 11 FCC Rcd 12154.

———. (1999). Creation of a Low-Power Radio Service (Notice of Proposed Rulemaking). January 28. MM Docket 99–25.

———. (2000). Creation of a Low-Power Radio Service (Report and Order). January 20. MM Docket 99–25.

————. (2001). FM Station Operator Convicted on Criminal Charges for Operating without FCC Authorization (Press Release). September 6. Retrieved from http://www.fcc.gov/eb/News_Releases/kubweza1.html, April 2, 2007.

Federal Communications Commission, Audio Services Division. (1996). Low Power Broadcast Radio Stations. April. Retrieved (in part) from http://www.fcc.gov/mb/audio/lowpwr.html#FREE, April 2, 2007.

Federal Communications Commission, Compliance and Information Bureau. (1996). Pirate Stations Beware: FCC Shuts Down Pirate Station in Orlando, Florida. December 11. Report CI 97–7.

Ferris, S. (1995). Pirate Roils the Airwaves. *San Francisco Examiner*, January 15, B1.

Franklin, S. (1994). A City Divided—Us vs. Them. *Chicago Tribune*, June 24, 1 (business section).

Groebner, S.P. (1996). Pirate Radio Wavemaking. *Minneapolis City Pages*, September 23. Retrieved from http://citypages.com/databank/17/829/article3021.asp.

Hanas, J. (1997). Free Radio Memphis Remains on the Air. *Memphis Flyer*, November 27, 16.

Herscher, E. (1993). Do-It-Yourself Radio Broadcasts over Pirate Station in Berkeley. *San Francisco Chronicle*, June 7, A17.

Hiken, L.N. (1993). Response to the Notice of Apparent Liability, Addressed to Philip M. Kane, Acting Engineer in Charge, FCC, dated June 28.

————. (1995). Defendant's Motion in Opposition to Plaintiff's Motion for Preliminary Injunction. *United States of America v. Stephen Paul Dunifer*. United States District Court, No. C94–3542 CW. December 2.

Jacobs, P. (1995). Unabomber Probe Targets Fringe Groups, Activists. *Los Angeles Times*, July 19, A1

Lambert, B. (1996). Officials Plunder Pirate Radio Station's Equipment. *St. Paul Pioneer Press*, November 2, 1E.

Larson, M. (1997). Radio Station Shut Down by Feds Set to Start Again. *Business Journal—Sacramento*, October 10, 10.

LeBlanc, S. (1990). Revolution Radio: Dewayne Readus and WTRA Pump up the Volume Despite the FCC's Fear of a Black Radio Station. *Version*, 90, 21.

Macon County. (1997). Search Warrant in the Circuit Court for the Sixth Judicial Circuit of Illinois, Macon County, dated January 7.

McConnell, C. (1998). FCC Considers Low-Power Radio. *Broadcasting & Cable*, March 9, 19.

Nessie, N. (1997). Low Wattage, High Influence. *San Francisco Bay Guardian*, February 26, 11.

Newberg, J. (1995). Neighborhood Station Challenges Regulators, Right-Wing Programs. *Arizona Republic*, April 24, C5.

Noble, K. (1995). FBI's Search for Serial Bomber Is Unsettling for Radicals in the Bay Area. *New York Times*, August 8, 19.

Orwall, B. (1997). Mr. Brewer the Pirate Doesn't Rule the Waves, He Just Makes Them. *Wall Street Journal*, October 21, A1, A15.

Perrin, T. (1997). Radio Station Fighting for the Airwaves. *Kansas City Star*, November 13, A1.

Ryan, H. (1997). Station Silenced As Pirate. *Asbury Park Press*, September 5, A1.

Shields, S.O. & R.M. Ogles. (1995). Black Liberation Radio: A Case Study of Free Radio Micro-broadcasting. *Howard Journal of Communication*, 5, 173–183.

Solov, D. (1997a). Feds Shut Down Pirate Radio Stations. *Tampa Tribune*, November 20, 1.

————. (1997b). Pirate Radio Supporters Reclaim Spot on the Dial. *Tampa Tribune*, November 26, 10.

Sommer, D. (1996). Lutz Radio Station Equipment Seized. *Tampa Tribune*, March 9, 1.

Wagner, D. (1994). He's Back: Radio Pirate on a Mission. *Phoenix Gazette*, December 19, A1.

Walker, J. (1995). Don't Touch That Dial. *Reason*, 27 (October), 32.

Wilken, C. (1995). Memorandum and Order Denying Plaintiff's Motion for Preliminary Injunction and Staying Action. *United States v. Stephen Paul Dunifer.* No. C 94–03542 CW. January 30.

Wilson, H. (2000). Speech before the U.S. House of Representatives. *Congressional Record*, H2304–H2305.

Part 3 Archives, Curricula, and Afterthoughts

With electricity we were wired into a new world, for electricity brought the radio.

—*Theordore White*

16. Librarians of the Airwaves: Reading in the Ether

Cindy Welch

Librarians have often been among the earliest users and adaptors of technology for popular culture, and in the 1920s the new technology was radio. Children's librarians in particular were among the first wave of public broadcasters, using this new tool as a way to promote reading and library services in thousands of American homes.

> The day has long since gone when we thought a collection of books in a building was in itself an attraction and that people would automatically come to our doors. Today libraries go to the people through branches, stations, bookmobiles. We supply hospital service, books for the blind, service to shut-ins. We take books to rural schools and we keep our congressmen aware of our libraries. We circulate books in foreign languages. We cater to all classes and creeds. Our books, our magazines, our pamphlets mean nothing unless they are used. Through radio we can go to the people and give them a verbal picture of what our libraries have for them. (Nunmaker, 1948, 13–14)

Libraries and radio stations might not seem like a natural pairing, but radio as it was emerging onto the public stage on the 1920s was identified as a powerful tool with educational possibilities that complemented the life-long learning mission of the public library. "[A radio stations is] an agency for the diffusion of knowledge, the dissemination of information, and the furnishing of entertainment. It is thus comparable to the newspaper, the public forum, and the library itself" (Drury, 1931, 7).

The country was experiencing expanding economic opportunities fueled by industrialization and cheap immigrant labor, and an educated and "Americanized" populace was considered critical to both democracy and the economy. Public libraries offered free places so that adults (ages 14 and above) could further their civic education and vocational training. In fact, by 1929, New York Public Library (NYPL) had created a specialized department, the Readers' Advisor Office, that provided curricula on demand and reading lists on subjects as diverse as philosophy and plumbing (Flexner & Edge, 1934).

Children's services was another specialization that developed within the public library, in response to changing ideas about the nature and experience of childhood—and because adults used to the quiet of the library were faced with growing numbers of children seeking stories and help with school work. By the turn of the 20th century, most public libraries had a separate children's department and a dedicated staff member known as the children's librarian. These women (and a few gentlemenmen) created book collections suited to school-aged children, helped with school assignments, and offered storytelling sessions and after-school clubs. This specialization grew rapidly; the Section for Library Work with Children was created in 1901, a separate group for school librarians began in 1915, and the Young People's Reading Round Table (to serve teens) began in 1930.

On the national level, the American Library Association (ALA), established in 1876, facilitated the growth of librarianship as a profession. Members established standards and benchmarks and provided continuing education through conferences, publications, and meetings. The association acted on behalf of librarians when there were opportunities to partner with organizations (both commercial and nonprofit) whose interests—however temporarily—matched those of the library. For example, the ALA installed its first radio committee in 1926, primarily as a way to work with radio's role in adult education and literacy.

Children's Librarians on the Air

Promoting reading has always been about raising awareness. Librarians say, "Look what you can achieve/become/do/have if you learn to read." They created public relations and advertising campaigns from nearly the beginning of library service. Children's Book Week grew out of collaboration between the Boy Scouts of America, the American Booksellers Association, and the ALA and has been celebrated continuously since 1919. The 1922 John Newbery Medal, which focused attention on the increasing quality and quantity of books being written for children, and the 1938 Randolph Caldecott Medal, which celebrated outstanding illustration in children's books, are just two of the better-known examples of awareness campaigns that were designed to reach beyond libraries and librarians to involve parents, teachers, and the community.

In the 1920s, a new technology arrived that made raising awareness even easier. This technology was hailed as the first truly "mass" communication, since those who were geographically or economically separated, or separated by literacy skills, could hear the same message at the same time. The technology was radio, and it was the newest way to deliver library messages: education is a lifelong experience; reading is essential to success.

Children's librarians were on the air as early as 1922, when Pittsburgh Public Library began broadcasting storytelling for children on station KDKA. "Fairy tales and animal stories prove to be the most popular. 'The Three Bears' was repeated at the request of a little sick girl who liked that one especially" (Ahern, 1922, 502).

There may have been other libraries broadcasting at the time and certainly several who followed soon after. Reports in the *Library Journal* and *Bulletin of the American Library Association* describe programs of various types offered by public libraries in Providence, New York, Cincinnati, Grand Rapids, Chicago, St. Louis, Des Moines, and even Appleton, Wisconsin. In 1930, the ALA's Radio Broadcasting Round Table attempted to establish the scope of library broadcasting and sent out 550 surveys to libraries across the country. Of the 95 responses they received, 25 libraries were providing programs, 13 had been on the air but were no longer broadcasting—for reasons explored below—and 24 were cooperating with other organizations by providing content or ancillary materials, such as bibliographies, or publicity. Forty-five libraries were not broadcasting at all. In 1941, University of Chicago Graduate Library School faculty member Frances Henne estimated that 200 libraries across the country were involved with broadcasting, but she added that her estimate was probably on the low end.

Contributions to on-air programming took many forms, including consultations on music, performers, and stories that the station could then develop or more directly providing storytellers who did the programs themselves. Here is a sampling of programs discussed in committee reports, library literature, and related books of the 1930s and 1940s.

In 1924, the Tacoma, Washington, Public Library provided storytellers for the radio station owned by the *Tacoma Daily Ledger*. Library storytellers might be from among library friends or children's staff, but they also chose material for a "professional reader" hired by the station to do a children's series. There was a contest for Children's Book Week, in which children submitted book reviews and the winning entries were read by their young authors on the air (Use of Radio, 1924).

In 1929, Fort Wayne (Indiana) broadcast stories three nights a week:

> Three types of stories were told, a continued story for younger children (such as Winnie-the-Pooh), a continued story for older children (Robin Hood), and an evening for request stories when any story in the Public Library was told when requested. (Radio Broadcasting Round Table, 1929)

Cleveland Public Library offered a show in 1933 known as *Everyman's Treasure House* that twice a year solicited quiz questions from public school children for a kid's version of the show (Nunmaker, 1948).

Denver Public Library created *Once Upon a Time*, a Saturday morning program that started in 1935 and ran for many years. It was so successful that, after 125 kids showed up for a broadcast, the library was forced to create tickets and make them available in the children's department. This show included storytelling, fairytales, child-acted plays, and even guest speakers. Incidentally, this one had a national hookup, so scripts had to be sent to NBC for approval before broadcast (Watson, 1936).

Los Angeles created the *Radio Book Club* in 1936, in which students from a local drama school performed book dramatizations. This library followed the example set by commercial programmers; it created a membership club of its own, complete with cards. One series of broadcasts was called *Book Detective*, and clues for titles appearing on the upcoming broadcast were hidden at the library. The first three children to report the titles correctly had their names read on the air (Hyers, 1938).

In 1946, New York Public librarian Margaret Scoggins created the weekly program *Young Book Reviewers*, in which teens discussed books and interviewed authors. "We do not 'warm up' or discuss the book ... We learned in the first year that rehearsals killed the spontaneity of the broadcast and that we do better without them" (Scoggins, 1956, 2417).

Radio content could be as complex as some of the programs just mentioned or as simple as this example of a short library announcement from the St. Louis Public Library, reported by Donald Kohlstedt in a 1940 *Library Journal* article entitled "Is Library Radio Broadcasting Worth While?"

> For boys and their fathers who are interested in boat races in the park, there are books on model boat building in the children's rooms of the Public Library and its branches. Do your children have library cards? They are free to St. Louisans. (Kohlstedt, 1940, 367)

In addition to broadcast support in the form of finding stories, storytellers, and music, libraries also created bibliographies and displays to promote national and local programming. One of the biggest efforts was in 1938, in San Francisco, where a librarian created a booklist in support of Children's Book Week that was used as a source of book talks by the editor of the *San Francisco Chronicle*. The *Chronicle* then printed 60,000 copies of the list and distributed them all over the state (Lewis, 1941).

Were library broadcasts successful? Yes. The assistant librarian at the Lowell Massachusetts Public Library indicated that "the average daily circulation [in 1939] in the Children's Room used to be eighty-one and last week it jumped to 556" (Coffyn, 1939, 518). The Minneapolis Public Library "received many letters after each talk expressing appreciation" (Radio Broadcasting Round Table, 1930, 464). A survey of St. Louis listeners indicated that

[o]n November 25, 1938 ... our children's broadcast, from 4:30 to 4:45 p.m., was being received by 19 per cent of all the radio listeners of Greater Kansas City, and 25 per cent of the local group, while simultaneous broadcasts included "Let's Pretend" over KMBC, and the "Lone Ranger" over the Mutual Network. At the same time the Columbia chain station was holding only 15 per cent of the listeners in Greater Kansas City and only 10 per cent of our local group. (Kohlstedt, 1940, 367)

Kansas City radio station KCKN conducted a survey in 1940, asking 50,000 people whether they were listening to the radio and, if so, what were they listening to:

Replies were tabulated and results indicated that of all fifteen minute programs from 12:00 noon to 6:00 evening, any day of the week, the period having the greatest percentage of listeners over KCKN was from 4:30 to 4:45 on Mondays— the Public Library Storyhour. (G. Green, personal communication, July 30, 1940)

On the lighter side, Kansas City librarian Gwendolyn Green reported that "a local dentist who specialized in work with children turned on the radio in his waiting room to hear story hour then could scarcely get his patients into the chair for their appointments until the story was over" (Personal communication, July 30, 1940).

NBC president Merlin Aylesworth, as quoted in Eric Barnouw's *A Tower in Babel*, often said that "network doors were 'wide open to those who would raise the level of national culture'" (Barnouw, 1966, 262), but library broadcast programming was not without problems. As commercial radio became institutionalized, librarians found their programs shunted to undesirable time slots or even bumped completely off the air. Sometimes the local radio stations hosting programs could not compete with the national networks for airspace or time and were forced to close their doors.

Another issue was getting permissions from publishers for book dramatizations, which were very popular parts of children's radio broadcasts. At times permission was denied, or a royalty was attached that the library could not pay.

Library staff needed to learn to become scriptwriters and radio actors, and often the departure of a single staff member could shut down a library show. Sessions were given at annual conferences in an attempt to provide a mixture of demonstration and inspiration. The ALA Committee on Radio Broadcasting described its contributions to the 1938 annual conference by saying that "programs given by librarians to demonstrate actual library broadcasts drew an interested audience each afternoon" (Library Radio Broadcasting Committee, 1938, 655).

The ALA eventually started its own script exchange, so that libraries across the country could have access to scripts that had been written and audience tested, as it were. By the 1940s, a few books had been written about library involvement with radio and they often included sample scripts. Scripts could also be obtained from a Script Exchange developed by the Federal Radio Committee in the U.S. Office of Education.

There were also unanticipated challenges, for example when the audience was so excited about a book or books that had been featured on the program that they came in large numbers to the library to try to check them out. Demand outstripped supply, and there were usually not funds to purchase additional copies.

Children's Librarians on the National Stage: Collaboration and Consultation

While children's radio programming was being created at the local level, conversations about what constituted a quality program for children were taking place on a national level. The ALA was working on a national children's radio hour project, and there were many discussions about how a national program should look.

Jesse Gay Van Cleve, children's book specialist at the ALA, and the person responsible for designing the proposed national radio program for children, sent a memo to ALA executive secretary Carl Milam in which she talked about program content. She said,

> The principles upon which to build a radio program for children could well be those upon which the librarian builds the reading program ... The program should not be limited to one form but should be so designed as to admit storytelling, music, drama, science, book talks, travel and art talks, poetry—in fact, all cultural and scientific topics in which children show ready interest when an intelligent and entertaining grown-up talks to them, are material for programs. They should not feel that they are being lectured at, instructed or condescendingly talked to. (Personal communication, August, 1933)

The ALA was in contact with other organizations interested in ensuring quality programming for everyone. One of these groups was the National Advisory Council on Radio in Education (NACRE), whose director Levering Tyson met with the ALA's Section for Library Work with Children in 1931 to ask what a children's radio program should encompass, with an eye to creating such a program. Cleveland Public Library's children's librarian Effie Power thought, as did most of her peers, that the program should be "entertainment of cultural and educational value—should develop literary taste, arouse children's curiosity in right directions, stimulate and direct interest in current events, train their ears to appreciate good English and good intonation" (J.G. Van Cleve, personal communication, August, 1933).

Librarians were divided on format, with the majority coming down on the side of storytelling (45%) or music (33%) rather than comedy or drama (both 10%), and most were uniformly against slapstick. They felt the ideal program would be presented either daily or once or twice a week and should last for 30 minutes (L. Tyson, personal communication, 1931).

Staffing, stations, and funding were often scarce, and libraries collaborated with other organizations, from radio stations to networks that donated time for programs, to civic groups that donated both time and people.

In 1941, the Oklahoma City public library and the Junior League teamed up to present adaptations of children's books based on scripts originally prepared by the Pittsburgh Junior League. According to Junior Leaguer Mary Elizabeth Brittain (1941), who wrote about the program for *Library Journal*,

> Because we wanted to give the children good entertainment and at the same time encourage their interest in reading the books used on the series, we did not attempt to review the whole book on a fifteen-minute broadcast, but only to give an interesting and exciting part of the book in radio play form. At the end of each program it was suggested to the listening audience that if they had enjoyed the story the book could be borrowed at the Carnegie Library. Listening posts were established at the Carnegie and branch libraries, where the children could come and enjoy the program and, if they wished, borrow the book to read at home. Posters illustrating the book to be broadcast each week, which resulted from a participating program in the public schools, were placed in the reading rooms and served to remind the children of the broadcasts. Mrs. Hough [children's librarian] prepared a suggested reading list of books similar in interest to follow each play. (pp. 806–808)

The listening audience for this partnership program was 6,000.

The Columbia Broadcasting System's American School of the Air included a note on their 1938–1939 schedule that

> [t]his year, on the recommendation of the Board on Library Service to Children and Young People ... librarians have been appointed as consultants to work with those planning and preparing programs ... A manual will suggest ways for more effective library and radio cooperation. (Additional Columbia Programs, 1938, 520)

Another program note concerned collaboration between the National Council of Teachers of English and the ALA, for junior and senior high school students. The program, called *The Lives Between the Lines*, was created to utilize the power of literary enjoyment to deepen understanding of human beings and life in a democracy. The ALA also collaborated that same year on an elementary grades program with the National Education Association. *Songs and Stories from the Far and Near* was meant to "exchang[e] national cultures through story and song" and was designed to enrich music, literature, and social studies in elementary schools (Additional Columbia Programs, 1938, 520).

In addition to collaborations, librarians were called upon to participate at educational broadcasting conventions and to work with other groups interested in children's radio programming. Children's librarians were called upon by both commercial and nonprofit groups at the national level.

In 1933, Clare Lynch, librarian at advertising firm Young & Rubicon, wrote the ALA for a list of books they could use in creating a national program for 7- to 14-year-olds. According to Miss Lynch, "We are considering dramatizing for radio twelve to fifteen of the popular classics read by boys and girls seven to fourteen years … Shall appreciate early reply from you suggesting list of books suitable" (Personal communication, November 7, 1933).

Frances Clark Sayers, who worked for the ALA Adult Education Division, was a speaker at the first Institute of Radio Education in 1930, and Margaret Batchelder, later to become executive secretary for both the Children's and Young Adult Services Divisions at the ALA, was a panelist at the 1941 Education by Radio Conference.

Washington, DC, public librarian George Bowerman was one of several panelists at a 1934 conference organized by the National Council on Radio in Education (NCER). He spoke to the ALA's investment in children's broadcast interests, on a panel with the title "On Whom Rests the Responsibility for the Cultural Use of Radio?"

Mary Gould Davis, NYPL supervisor of storytelling, was invited to be part of the powerful Radio Council on Children's Programs, a national women's group formed in 1939 that helped write the children's section of the National Association of Broadcasters' first broadcasting code (Gordon, 1942) and also helped get five "blood and thunder" children's radio programs dropped from the airwaves (Five "Blood and Thunder," 1939).

ALA executive secretary Carl Milam commented,

> Children's librarians have become rather important informal educators. Their interest and experience are not limited to one subject or one field but are as broad as the interests of children … We believe that this experience should be used in developing a national radio program for children. On our initiative several national organizations have united in preparing a project for a series of experimental broadcasts to children which would draw upon that experience and the experience of many other groups as well. (Hyers, 1938, 82)

ALA convened more than 30 youth organizations for a town meeting in 1934 to discuss partnerships for its proposed national children's radio program. Those who attended the town meeting included representatives from the Child Study Association of America, the Boy Scouts and Camp

Fire Girls, the YWCA and YMCA, the National Education Association, the Junior League, and the Motion Picture Research Council, to name just a few.

Children's librarian-broadcasters were well respected in the educational radio field. NACRE's Levering Tyson commented in a 1931 letter to ALA children's book specialist Jesse Gay Van Cleve that he felt

> [c]hildren's librarians could be of a great deal of aid in this particular field [radio programs for children], chiefly because of their knowledge of the kind of thing that attracts children, and because of their story-telling ability or knowledge of where good story-tellers can be secured. Accordingly, it seems entirely in order to assemble information on the whole subject of children's programs on the air from a group of children's librarians. (Personal communication, June 10, 1931)

During the 1934 town meeting—which NBC and CBS also attended—Franklin G. Dunham, representing the National Broadcasting Company, solicited librarians' input for "not only advice but also for some constructive means of presenting the type of hour that children's librarians had in mind: one which would entertain a child and stimulate him to read" (Committee on Library Radio Broadcasting, 1931, 668).

Children's librarians—and librarians in general—were sometimes divided about the value of radio, but many saw such programming as an integral part of youth/library service. Faith Holmes Hyers, librarian at the Los Angeles Public Library, wrote in her 1938 book *The Library and the Radio*,

> Libraries who are utilizing the present period of insufficient and unsatisfactory programs for children to supply something wholesome and entertaining, and to build up a listening audience, are wasting neither their time nor their efforts ... While we wait for the perfect national programs for children to be evolved, many a library might be further enriching its community and interesting new borrowers in what it has for them by offering a weekly book talk or story hour. (p. 81)

Conclusion

Despite librarians' generally enthusiastic support for radio, they shared the fate of other groups who advocated for education over commercial content. Commercial programs proliferated, the industry became more sophisticated, and competitions for time and profits all but pushed libraries off the air. Although they continued to provide secondary support for broadcasts and a few were able to maintain or (more rarely) develop local programs, libraries and their association turned their attention to other aspects of broadcasting. The ALA's national children's radio hour project was abandoned in 1936 and children's librarians concentrated on evaluation of existing programs, eventually shifting their attention to sound recordings and then on to television.

What came from this interaction with radio was a new way for librarians to connect with their communities, to spread the word about the plethora of free opportunities available for literacy and learners of all ages. The profession itself was less than 50 years old, and librarians were shaping and institutionalizing their connections to society. Unlike newspapers, where economic or literacy issues separated librarians from their patrons, radio in this sense was completely egalitarian, going into homes of all cultures, economic strata, and educational experiences.

Radio's emergence also coincided with a time of great expansion in library development. Library advocates were pushing to find ways to provide service to Americans who lacked community libraries. New management configurations (regional and branch libraries), collections, and service delivery methods were being tested, and radio fit right as a way to reach beyond library walls. Radio was an informal education delivery system, and librarians saw great possibilities for using it to reach their own goals.

Librarians were active participants in shaping children's local programming. Radio was a completely new medium, and there were no models for how children's programs should be built, so children's librarians combined child psychology with knowledge of children's materials and interests and patterned their on-air programs on the successful sessions being held inside library walls.

Finally, this was an early instance of children's librarians' engagement with "technology" (in the modern sense of the word). Their work before this point had to do with books and people. Radio was a great unknown, and broadcasting's impact could be immediate and potentially overwhelming. Their work with radio equipped them to utilize and think about television and the Internet. Early conversations about both these technologies have much in common with radio broadcasting concerns—safety, psychological effects on children, and usefulness to libraries.

The experience also underlines children's librarians' sense of dedication and their willingness to use any tool that would help them accomplish their goals. In 1938, Rochester, New York, public librarian Julia Sauer, involved with the very successful School of the Air program, prodded youth librarians to embrace radio and technology, saying,

> Let us be grateful, then, for this new means of reaching children that is offered to us at a time when reading has more competitors than ever before. Let us use it sincerely, master its technique, and make it a forceful factor in our publicity programs. (p. 99)

References

Additional Columbia Programs Are Announced. (1938). *Bulletin of the American Library Association*, 32 (8), 520.

Ahern, M.E. (Ed.). (1922). A New Kind of Story Telling. *Public Libraries*, 27, 502.

Barnouw, E. (1966). *A Tower in Babel: A History of Broadcasting in the United States to 1933*. New York: Oxford University Press.

Brittain, M.E. (1941). Junior Bookshelf on the Air. *Library Journal*, 66, 806–807.

Coffyn, E.M. (1939). Lowell's Radio Series [Letter to the Editor]. *Bulletin of the American Library Association*, 33, 518.

Committee on Library Radio Broadcasting. (1931). Radio Program for Boys and Girls (Committee Report). *Bulletin of the American Library Association*, 25, 667–668.

Drury, F.W.K. (1931). *Broadcaster and the Librarian*. New York: National Advisory Council on Radio in Education.

Five "Blood and Thunder" Radio Programs for Children Dropped by Networks. (1939). *St. Louis Post-Dispatch*, December 18.

Flexner, J.M. & S.A. Edge. (1934). *A Readers' Advisory Service*. New York: American Association for Education.

Gordon, D. (1942). *All Children Listen*. New York: George W. Stewart.

Henne, Frances. (1941). Library-Radio Relationships. *Library Quarterly*, 11, 448–490.

Hyers, F.H. (1938). *Library and the Radio*. Chicago: University of Chicago Press.

Kohlstedt, D.W. (1940). Is Library Radio Broadcasting Worth While? *Library Journal*, 65, 367.

Lewis, D. (1941). *Broadcasting to the Youth of America: A Report on Present Day Activities in the Field of Children's Radio Programs*. Washington, DC: Radio Council on Children's Programming.

Library Radio Broadcasting Committee. (1938). Committee report. *Bulletin of the American Library Association*, 32, 655.

Nunmaker, F.G. (1948). *Library broadcasts*. New York: H.W. Wilson.

Radio Broadcasting Round Table. (1929). Committee report. *Bulletin of the American Library Association*, 23, 343–344.

———. (1930). Committee report. *Bulletin of the American Library Association*, 24, 464.

Sauer, J.L. (1938). Three and a Half Years on the Air. *Library Journal*, 63, 98–99.

Scoggins, M.C. (1956). Radio's Young Book Reviewers. *Library Journal*, 81, 2416–2418.

Use of Radio by Public Librarians. (1924). *Library Journal*, 49, 581–582.

Watson, K. (1936). Once-Upon-A-Time Radio Program. *Library Journal*, 61, 822–823.

17. Radio and Culture: The Modern Curriculum

BARBARA CALABRESE

In the spring of 2007, we at Columbia College, Chicago, invited the inaugural speaker of our new "Scholarship in Radio" lecture series. The person we asked happened to be Michael Keith, the editor of this volume. I had met Michael at the annual High School and College Radio Conference in Boston sponsored by the Intercollegiate Broadcasting System, where he was one of a panel of three speakers on "Culture in Radio." During the session's discussion period, I thanked the panelists for their work and announced that I hoped Michael did not mind that I was borrowing liberally (read "stealing") from his Boston College course in Radio in Culture and Society—the point being there were few such courses available at institutions around the country to draw from, which I found quite perplexing. How could this subject be so neglected, I wondered? Radio changed the world, right? That is something we have heard said about television on more than one occasion, and radio created the visual medium's programming template decades earlier. It held people in thrall and altered their behavior, lifestyle, and view of the world, as did its visually enhanced successor. Thankfully, Michael was delighted to render assistance, and he e-mailed me his syllabus to help me develop the course.

His inaugural Scholarship in Radio lecture was packed with students and faculty even though we did not require attendance. The students engaged in a lively exchange with the speaker, and following the presentation several asked me for book suggestions and reading material on various topics related to radio in society and culture. Books? Reading? Hallelujah, I could hear the heavenly choir sing. One student, in particular, gave me pause. An African American, she was writing a paper for a liberal arts class and wanted more information on black radio. I responded by recommending William Barlow's book *Voice Over: The Making of Black Radio* (1999). At that moment, I realized how much we needed a course in radio studies at Columbia.

Thus, we plan to introduce the new course in the spring of 2008. The goal of the class is to examine radio broadcasting in the context of class, gender, race, ethnicity, and sexuality and its attendant issues. Within each topic area, we will examine nonmainstream viewpoints and how radio has influenced and continues to influence multiculturalism and diversity.

Our program prides itself on its diversity. It is part of our mission and the mission of the college as a whole. A few years ago our college radio station, WCRX-FM, which is an integral part of our curriculum, earned a second-place national award from College Media Advisors for diversity on the basis of the makeup of the station's student staff and advisors, who reflected the racial, cultural, religious, lifestyle, and ethnic diversity of the community we are licensed to serve. In 2005, we were honored with an Angel Award from the Chicago Chapter of American Women in Radio and Television for having made significant increases in enrollment of women in our program. The award acknowledged our diversity and our contributions to the development of the field of radio broadcasting. However, such accolades are not sufficient for a broadcast radio curriculum to be truly relevant in today's complex media world. Courses must also reflect and celebrate student and listener diversity and multiculturalism.

This chapter considers why radio's cultural role is worthy of attention in a modern media curriculum.

The Highs and Lows of Culture

One of the members of our faculty, who worked in radio for years, notes that radio is always the "stepchild" in media. Film is often deemed high culture while radio is pop culture, or worse—given its declining interest to young people. Faculty interested in offering radio courses in programs without a radio major may have a difficult time justifying their proposals. Faculty in professional media programs cannot introduce new courses in radio in applied media programs if they are not deemed pertinent on the practical level. Likewise, we cannot get radio studies courses into theory-oriented media programs because more often than not the audio medium is viewed as unworthy of scholarly attention. Admittedly, I have never understood the high/low culture distinction. Film produces masterpieces such as *Citizen Kane*, but it also produces *Dumb and Dumber* and the cult favorite *Texas Chain Saw Massacre*. Print journalism has *The New York Times* but also produces tabloids with headlines about alien births and people who weigh more than Volkswagens. Radio (at least public stations) produces outstanding documentaries and theater, and, yes, it also produces shock jocks and banal talk radio programs. Therefore, the proverbial playing field seems about level to me.

In the first chapter of their *Radio Reader: Essays in the Cultural History of Radio*, editors Michelle Hilmes and Jason Loviglio (2002) provide a salient discussion of how and why radio, despite its estimable role in culture and society, has been neglected as an area of study (pp. 2–8). Among the reasons they cite are television's half-century of dominance in our culture and its initial and deliberate diversion of radio programs and advertising dollars to promote and develop its own programming; radio's survival strategy of turning local and spinning the hits for kids; and the entry of minority and marginalized groups into radio—which distanced the medium even further from approval by mainstream society. Radio was soon perceived by the intellectual community as little more than a frivolous device (background noise and cotton candy for the mind) or as an outdated technology unable to contribute in a meaningful way to an American collective societal vision.

A Light at the End of the Airwaves?

Hilmes and Loviglio (2002) go on to discuss the renewed interest in radio in the late 1990s as new research emerged from a variety of disciplines (pp. 8–10). Cultural research in race, feminist, and queer studies has moved into mainstream academe. Radio provides a wonderful forum to study different voices within our culture and society. Although much remains to be done, books such as the *Radio Reader* and the present volume of essays, as well as the articles in the *Journal of Radio Studies*, have convinced me that including a course on radio culture is necessary if we are to keep our curriculum current and valid. (There are many other excellent books on radio and culture; see the reference listings in other chapters in this volume.) We scramble to respond to changes in technology and content as part of our mission to prepare students for careers. However, how will they be able to make a meaningful contribution to radio if they lack the means for appreciating and understanding the cultural, political, and societal forces at work in our daily lives? Shouldn't we as educators be as insistent on giving our students the latest information from the important studies and research about their field as we are on providing them with the latest software or piece of equipment?

Furthermore, cultural studies provide not just valuable new ways to contextualize media but additional methods with which to navigate both careers and lives. Even in an applied program like ours at Columbia College, there must be courses and curricula that engage students in critical thinking, analysis, and evaluation. This is where a course in radio and culture will differ dramatically from the traditional history or survey courses in media. For example, we have an excellent Introduction to Radio course, but, by its nature, it is burdened with having to survey a whole array of information—from history to radio operations to innovations in technology and career information. There is little, if any, time to explore the vast topic of radio's influence on culture. The course stays true to its mission—an introduction.

It's Not about Political Correctness

Columbia College recently revised its liberal arts requirements to include a course in pluralism and another in global awareness. Pluralism courses are defined as including content devoted to the study of minorities and minority cultures, including race, ethnicity, and gender studies in the United States. Radio's decades-long service can provide an excellent example of both courses. When I introduced the idea of a course in Radio and Culture and Society in our department, the faculty immediately offered enthusiastic support and urged me to develop such a course as a college-wide elective to meet the pluralism requirement. Such a course offers an opportunity to discuss diversity among students who are not media majors.

Many colleges and universities now require courses in diversity. Although some critics view this movement as throwing a bone to political correctness, this is wrong-headed. Well-educated people must be citizens of the world who possess an understanding of and respect for diverse peoples and cultures. This is especially important for any program in radio or media studies. Though small, our department continues to thrive in part because of our large percentage of minority students. Radio attracts minority students—it is still the voice of the people. I am always surprised that programs trying to recruit a more diverse student population do not offer more courses and programs about radio.

Currently our enrollment of black, non-Hispanic students is 23%, which exceeds the all-college percentage of 14% as well as surpassing all the other departments in the School of Media Arts, except Journalism, which also stands at 23%. Our Hispanic population in radio is 9%, which is the same as the college percentage. We exceed all other departments in Media Arts except for Journalism (at 10%). I should note that our Journalism department houses our interdisciplinary program in Broadcast Journalism, which includes both radio and television.

The College of Radio

As we strive to support minority and local concerns, the music on our radio station is underground dance music and not the traditional rock format heard on many other college radio stations. This is based on our listening public, which largely comprises Hispanic teenagers in the immediate neighborhood. For the past three years, one of our faculty has directed a group of students in producing and broadcasting one of Richard Durham's radio plays during African American Heritage month. Every year our radio station director has all the students participate in a day-long fundraiser for the Greater Chicago Food Depository. We challenge convention by offering morning shows on the radio station hosted by two women and discourage the typical female role of giggling sidekick. We offer local programming such as *Ask the Alderman* and provide full election coverage on both local and national levels. We offer a course that requires students to develop public service campaigns for local not-for-profit organizations. This has all contributed to the success of our program, but I feel we as media faculty should do more. Developing curricula in radio cultural studies allows us to engage our students more fully in the rich history and accomplishments of minority and marginalized cultures. Moreover, it can teach them some lessons about success.

Indeed, anyone who wants to succeed in the marketplace had best not ignore minority cultures and their practices. Nowhere is this more apparent than when witnessing the phenomenal rise of Spanish-language radio. Hispanics, now the largest ethnic minority in the United States, have taught us how to succeed in radio without really trying. Spanish-language radio does what radio started out to do—serve the public's interest. For Spanish-speaking immigrants that means being able to listen to radio programs in their native language. These foreign-language stations have enjoyed great commercial success. Yet conventional commercial radio wisdom tells us we cannot have our public interest cake while eating at the table of profitability. African Americans did the same thing when they started programming black music for their listeners and invented the deejay, who talked to you, not at you—the precursor of narrowcast music formats offered by commercial radio. Yet another example is Allegheny Mountain Radio serving a geographically isolated region in Appalachia. Starting with a small community station, the company has grown from a single outlet to a network of three stations with a $300,000 budget and a listening audience of 16,000 by emphasizing programming addressing community interest and needs (Reed & Hanson, 2006, 215).

The point here is that a myriad subjects can be examined in a Radio in Culture course, and this volume—along with the growing canon of studies devoted to the medium—attests to that.

Conclusion

I return to my student who wanted to read more about the history of black radio. She was excited and inspired. A modern curriculum must do more than afford students the opportunity to play the music they want on their campus stations or teach them studio and production techniques. Students want and need information that is relevant to them and the world they live in. They want to make sense of the many competing values in our society. I want our students—in the words of Columbia's mission statement—to "author the culture of their time." I want them to get jobs, but I also want to give them the tools and the knowledge to be creative and to challenge conventional norms. I want them to take pride in radio and treat it as a meaningful profession. I want them to respect people and cultures and to live and work successfully in a global society.

Obviously, one course in Radio Culture cannot address all these desires, but it will certainly benefit and enrich students (as well as faculty) to delve into radio's profound influence on the past and present. After all, radio remains the most widely employed form of electronic media in the world even in a digital age.

References

Barlow, William. (1999). *Voice Over: The Making of Black Radio*. Philadelphia: Temple University Press.

Hilmes, Michele & Jason Loviglio. (2002). *Radio Reader: Essays in the Cultural History of Radio*. New York: Routledge.

Reed, Maryanne & Ralph E. Hanson. (2006). Back to the Future: Allegheny MountainRadio and Localism in West Virginia Community Radio. *Journal of Radio Studies*, 13 (2), 214–231.

18. Writing About Radio: A Survey of Cultural Studies in Radio

Michael C. Keith

From the inception of radio broadcasting, the medium has inspired an interesting (and recently a growing, though still limited) range of studies by both scholars and journalists. Continued attention from such government agencies as the Federal Radio Commission (FRC) and Federal Communications Commission (FCC) makes it abundantly clear that the medium has been viewed as a significant cultural part of the nation. From the earliest broadcasts, radio was expected by many to serve an egalitarian function in the world. To that end the medium was intended (by regulators if not broadcasters) to operate as a public trustee with an obligation to address the needs of its growing audience.

As might be expected, research examining radio's cultural role was scant during its formative years owing to the evolving nature of its programming as well as the lack of interest on the part of critics and academicians, who viewed radio as little more than a frivolous popular experiment. Only as President Franklin Roosevelt took to the airwaves in the early 1930s to rally the nation behind his administration's plan for economic recovery from the Depression did scholars begin to take serious notice of the medium's role as a cultural force and instrument for change.

Both domestic and foreign events in the late 1930s increased researchers' awareness of radio's effect on the lives of Americans. As the specter of world war grew in Europe, network correspondents conveyed the alarming details to listeners. Meanwhile a Halloween eve broadcast in 1938 graphically depicting an invasion of aliens from Mars caused widespread panic and clearly demonstrated the puissant hold radio had developed over the country's citizenry. Just three years after this fictional attack from outer space, the Pearl Harbor raid thrust the nation into a war in which radio would prove instrumental in galvanizing efforts to defeat the enemy.

Among the earliest works on the social and psychological relationship of listening audiences with radio broadcasting are those by Cantril (1982) and Beville (1939). Censorship and freedom of speech were on the minds of broadcasters from the medium's launch and were adequately addressed in a study by Summers (1939). In the 1940s Paul Lazarsfeld, Hadley Cantril (1982), Matthew Chappell with Claude Hooper (1944), and Frank Stanton offered benchmark studies, mostly centered on audience listening patterns and preferences. Certainly, Lazarsfeld and Kendall's 1948 book is a touchstone in terms of audience use of the medium. Meanwhile Siepmann (1950) provided valuable insight into the audio medium within a sociocultural context as the first full postwar decade got underway.

Although the years following the country's victory in World War II brought with them a great sense of promise and prosperity, they were a turning point in radio's fate. The introduction of television would mark the end of the medium's short-lived golden age and all but remove it from the radar of scholars. For the next several decades, radio would all but be a forgotten medium to communication researchers, who would turn their attention to television, disregarding radio and its new emphasis on popular music and youth.

Although not abundant, articles on radio appeared in various communication and mass media journals during this period. However, their focus was seldom on radio's cultural role; it was principally industry-centric, dealing with the business, performance, and production aspects of the medium. Barnouw's landmark three-volume broadcasting retrospective (1966, 1968, 1970), despite making no claims to be a cultural appraisal of radio, does discuss topics such as gender, race, and religion.

In the early 1990s revived interest in broader radio studies became apparent with several publications examining aspects of the medium's place in society. Vargas's (1995) book is one such example. At the forefront of this belated movement was the creation of the first academic publication devoted to the study of the medium, the *Journal of Radio Studies*. Throughout the past decade an increasing number of radio histories demonstrating an interest in radio's cultural ramifications were published—Hilmes's (1997) is a standout among them—along with several monographs (many by this chapter's author) examining specific instances of radio's role in various segments or subgroupings of the country's population.

In the new millennium radio studies has established itself as a viable field of scholarly inquiry. Coinciding with this has been the addition of radio in culture and society courses at a handful of colleges and universities, among them Boston College, Michigan State University, Brandeis University, the University of Kansas, and Brooklyn College. Douglas's (2000) estimable book, the first of the new century, offers extensive commentary on the cultural influence of radio. That same year a propitious title from UK radio scholar David Hendy (2000) assessed the cultural influence of the medium within a global context. A breakthrough collection of laudable essays pertaining to the manifold and diverse aspects of the medium's cultural history appeared in Hilmes and Loviglio's (2002) integral book and in Squier's (2003) lucent and innovative anthology, which devoted itself to an analysis of radio's consequential cultural presence. The same year, the *Radio Journal* debuted in Britain, offering further testimony to the growing global interest by scholars in the medium. And as further evidence of the mounting attraction of the field of radio studies, Bruce Lenthall (2007) published a trenchant inquiry into the cultural influence of the medium during its early years just as this book was about to go to press.

This chapter pursues the line of inquiry Michele Hilmes (2001) sets forth in her cultural history of U.S. broadcasting. Hilmes asks, "What was the context for radio's development? Out of what mixture of social, cultural, and technological force did radio emerge?" These and more questions are still in need of answers. What follows is a selective overview of publications that assume a cultural approach in their examination and assessment of the medium. It is not intended to be comprehensive or fully inclusive but does strive to traverse a good part of the terrain. Owing to space limitations, the primary emphasis here is on American studies of this topic. Rather than a chronological breakdown of the canon, topical categories are used to present cultural studies of radio, including politics, gender, race, religion, and family.

Politics

Many feel that the 1990s explosion in talk radio was responsible for changing the landscape of American politics in the early part of that decade, so it is not surprising that there is a plethora of books dealing with this subject. Among those offering worthwhile assessments of the way in which the medium and its talkmeisters influenced voters is Levin's (1987), whose telling assertions are drawn from interviews with hundreds of listeners in the Boston area. Scott (1996) also employs an extensive audience survey to determine the influence of chat hosts on public opinion. She harks back to the benign talk shows of the 1960s to underscore her claim that, three decades later, conversation radio has morphed into something that is far more scabrous and doctrinaire. Kurtz (1996) provides a candid, no-holds-barred evaluation of political talk radio's influence, as does Hutchby's (1996) monograph, while Laufer (1995) chides the format for its blatant sensationalism and political extremism.

Assessments of talk radio's cultural influence and political power are readily available in academic journals. For example, Hofstetter and Gianos (1997) examine the social hierarchy of talk radio listeners, and

Hollander (1995) analyzes national survey findings that cite talk listeners as more politically active and engaged; Armstrong and Rubin (1989) contend that talk radio promotes interpersonal communication, and Rubin and Step (2000) examine the effect of attraction, motivation, and interaction on talk radio listening. Then Hall and Cappella (2002) evaluate the influence of talk programming on the outcome of the 1996 presidential election, Page and Tannenbaum (1996) assess the nature of the public's role in this genre, and Rehm (1993) cites the value of talk radio in expanding public discourse. Finally, Chinn's (1997) book provides an incisive programming profile of a popular chat station and Barker's (2002) gives a thorough evaluation of the politics of persuasion at play on the nation's airwaves.

Several noteworthy articles focus on the influence of political talk show hosts. As might be expected given his prominence, those dealing with Rush Limbaugh far outnumber the rest. Among studies providing particular insights into and evaluations of the cultural phenomenon of this staunchly conservative talker are those by Harris et al. (1996); Kay, Ziegelmueller, and Minch (1998); Larson (1997); and Lewis (2001); Swain (1999). In their own way, each of these articles contributes further understanding as to why this particular radio talker has come to dominate the field.

Several books and articles probe the role of radio in American politics beyond the talk show venue. One of the earliest, by Frost (1937), considers whether the medium is a democratic enterprise and expresses some doubts; then Brown (1998) and Craig (2000) document the early and more recent participation of radio in political culture, as do Clark (1962), Hofstetter and Gianos (1997), Powell (1993), and Delli Carpini (1993).

Race and Ethnicity

African American presence in early radio was scant but did exist, mostly in the form of minstrelsy and ventriloquism. Several recent books examine the involvement of blacks in the medium (as well as their portrayal by it) from the 1920s through the present day. Sampson (2004) surveys the historical contribution of blacks in radio before the arrival of television, George (2003) offers a detailed account of the rise of the first black deejays, and Ely (1991) focuses on the social implications on racial attitudes engendered by *Amos 'n' Andy*. Barlow (1999) provides a solid history of black radio, emphasizing the challenges it faced in an inequitable media culture, Savage (1999) examines radio in the context of racial politics, and Williams (1998) evaluates the role of African American radio personalities in the assimilation of blacks migrating north following World War II. Cantor (1992) provides a detailed profile of the nation's first all-black station, MacDonald (1989) considers Richard Durham's *Destination Freedom* radio scripts in the context of the black protest movement,

David and Susan Siegel (2007) reveal the "untold story of how radio influenced America's image of Jews," and Hilmes and Barnouw devote portions of their substantial narratives to the implications of racial stereotyping.

Several articles and book chapters also devote themselves to the question of race in the audio medium. Carcasson and Aune (2003) evaluate the national radio broadcast of Justice Hugo Black, who employed the medium in the 1930s to respond to accusations concerning his alleged ties to the Ku Klux Klan, Newman discusses radio's overlooked "Negro market," Hattaway and Brinson report on the Alabama Negro Extension Service Broadcasts, Keith (2000) interviews several prominent figures on the question of racial bias in American radio, Meckiff and Murray (1998) consider the image of the black soldier, Shields and Ogles (1995) look at black liberation radio through the micro-station movement, and Soley and Hough (1982) investigate levels of black ownership.

Publications focusing on other ethnic minority groups are not as abundant as those devoted to African Americans. Keith (1995) offers the first detailed study of the use and application of radio by Native Americans and, in another book-length publication, Grame provides statistical data and information regarding indigenous and other ethnic broadcasting. Thus far there are fewer articles exploring Native American use of radio. Murphy reviews the nature of indigenous radio in Alaska, and Smith and Brigham (1992) discuss the evolution of Indian-language programming. Eiselein produces a Native radio listening report for CPB, Coleman examines the effects of indigenous radio in rural Alaska, and Cornette and Smith offer a study of Indian radio in the Dakotas.

In publications focusing on other ethnic radio broadcasting, Migala (1987) provides a monograph on the cultural significance of Polish American radio. Among articles on ethnic radio, Downing (1990) assesses the state of ethnic minority radio, Lum offers a retrospective of New York Chinese-language wireless radio, and Paredes discusses the surge in popularity of Spanish-language radio.

Gender and Sex

Women were for many years ghettoized by radio, writes Hilmes. The role of women was restricted in early radio, as it was in most professions in the first half of the 20th century. Radio reflected the prevailing attitude about women's subordinate place in the workforce through programs that invariably depicted women as domestic caregivers rarely to be found in careers beyond those related to home and hearth. Despite the formidable barriers against women's participation in the new medium, recent studies argue that the so-called weaker sex made important contributions to radio and in doing so helped their quest for equality. In 2001, two books provided the first thorough examinations of the experience and activities of women in radio broadcasting. Halper's (2001) pioneering monograph sheds substantial light on the contributions of women to radio within the context of cultural attitudes toward and expectations of the gender. Perhaps most important, Halper has rescued the record of some formerly forgotten pioneers. The second of these full-length studies was published in the United Kingdom and edited by Mitchell (2001). This anthology offers a range of essays on the feminist view of the medium as a tool for economic and social empowerment.

Signorielli's (1996) collection of profiles of women in mass communication provides discourse on gender discrimination and stereotyping, as do book chapters and journal articles. In two monographs (2000, 1997), Keith interviews prominent women broadcasters regarding the challenges and bias they encountered in a male-dominated profession. In the latter study (1997), Keith details the experiences of female deejays and engineers in commercial underground radio as well as their contributions to this unique and culturally sentient programming genre. Mata (1994) discusses the social influence of women in popular radio, Ruffner (1972–1973) probes women's attitudes as reflected by the medium, and Goodlad offers a thoughtful exegesis of gendering in alternative radio.

Disquisitions on gay and lesbian presence in radio are scarce. This may well be a reflection of society's long-standing reluctance to address homosexual issues. Johnson and Keith (2001) offer the first book-length study of alternative lifestyle groups determined to enhance awareness of their tenuous social footing through radio broadcasts, and Alwood focuses part of his examination of gays and lesbians on their portrayal by radio news media. A handful of journals feature articles on the subject; Tulloch and Chapman (1992) review broadcast debates about AIDS, and Barnhurst (2003) documents election-year coverage of gay and lesbian issues on public radio.

Community and Family

An area of interest to media scholars has been the effect of radio on community and family. That is to say, what part has the medium played in the evolution and configuration of these core institutions? Given radio's mandated responsibility as public trustee, it has attempted (not always willingly or successfully) to provide programming that reflects public issues, needs, and interests.

Several books concentrate on the nature of the interface between the medium and the communities to which stations are licensed. Fairchild (2001) assesses the levels of access and equity in community radio, Keith (1997) chronicles the deeds and altruistic agenda of counterculture outlets,

Milam (1998) espouses the virtues of service and activism, Lewis and Booth stress the potential of the medium for constructive public communication, Jacob J. Podber (2007) investigates the influence of radio in Appalachia, and, in a very early study, Atkinson examines network contributions to the community through educational programming.

The micro-radio movement, with its passion for neighborhood service, has inspired a handful of full-length works and book chapters. Soley (1999) discusses so-called free radio from a civil disobedience perspective, Dicks and McDowell (2000) attempt to shed light on the rise in unlicensed audio broadcasting, Ruggiero (1999) and McChesney analyze the efforts of media giants in banning low-power community-oriented stations, Bensman (2000) uses the movement as a contemporary backdrop to his history of broadcast regulation, Walker (2001) devotes chapters of his alternative retrospective of radio to the rise and agenda of low-power FM, Huntemann evaluates the politics of the micro medium, and Carpenter (2004) chronicles her experiences operating low-power illegal outlets in two California cities.

A number of journal articles have explored radio's community service and involvement. Rowland (1997) discusses the meaning of the public interest standard, Ehrlich and Contractor (1998) probe the place of shock programming in the context of "community service," Smith (1994) looks back at the FCC's first public interest campaign designed to eliminate fraudulent medical ads, and Surlin (1972) expounds on the approach to community ascertainment legislation by a minority station.

The medium's contribution to life in rural America has inspired recent journal studies. Riney-Kehrberg examines the listening habits of Kansas farm women—taking a lead from much earlier works on the subject appearing in the 1940s and 1950s. Likewise, echoing earlier studies, Craig (2001) looks at the medium's companion role to farmers, and Podber (2001) investigates early radio in rural Appalachia.

Radio's place in family life has generated a modicum of interest among scholars. Levin (1974) produced an astute monograph on applying the medium in family planning, and Gruenberg (1935), Clark (1940), Herzog (1941), and Lyness (1950) offer early studies in the relationship of children with radio, focusing on the way particular broadcasts modify the behavior and habits of young listeners. Runco and Pezdek (1984) examine the medium's influence on children's creativity and thought processes, and Dennis (1998) investigates the effects of golden age radio programs on children and comes up with some compelling conclusions. Greenfield and Beagles-Roos (1988) argue radio's greater cognitive effect on children. Roberto et al. (2002) offer insights and implications from a radio-based health communication query. Hammond, Freimuth, and Morrison (1990) also examine health messages, but as pertains to teens, and Christenson and DeBenedittis (1986) add further discourse on children's use of radio.

War

A number of strong volumes offer insight into radio's part and participation during wartime. Most focus is on World War II. Blue (2002) uses radio drama to reveal the presence of censorship during and after the global conflict, Sweeney (2001) likewise provides a study on wartime censorship, and Horten (2002) concentrates on the cultural politics of propaganda. Bergmeier and Lotz (1997) tell the story of how the Nazis used American music for propaganda purposes. Berstein and Lubertozzi (2003) focus on the war work of Edward R. Murrow and his "boys," and Morley (2001) explores the acrimonious squabble between Armed Forces Radio and the BBC. Chapters in tomes by MacDonald (1979), Hilmes (1997) and Barnouw (1968) also devote considerable print space to wartime radio. Rolo (1942) and Dryer (1942) were the first to inquire into the relationship between the medium and World War II, although both offer their own take on the subject. A number of news and war correspondents (Shirer, Severied, Cronkite) disseminated printed accounts regarding their days covering the war for the networks and these can be useful in gaining a further appreciation and awareness of the medium's valuable function during wartime.

There are fewer articles than might be expected on this broad subject in communication journals. Fay (1999) notes the decline of foreign-language broadcasting during World War II, Garay (1995) looks at government regulation during this period, and Heyer (2003), Morson (1979), and Koch (1970) analyze the war themes in Orson Welles's 1938 alien invasion broadcast. Two books provide good coverage of the U.S. external services during the cold war. Urban (1998) produces a memoir of his time as director of Radio Free Europe, and Critchlow (1995) gives a telling insider's account of cold war broadcasting at Radio Liberty. Indeed, there is a large literature on radio as propaganda instrument, much of it historical.

Religion

The topic of religion has long been of interest to radio studies scholars; many inquiries date back to the late 1940s. Religion's presence on the dial and its impact on audiences has been the subject of several recent monographs. Hangen (2002) presents a concise depiction of the development of evangelical religion coinciding with radio's own rise, Apostolidis (2000) offers a careful portrait of conservative evangelical talk radio, Lochte surveys the rise of Christian networks and their faith-oriented missions, and Warren (1996), Carpenter (1998), and Marcus (1986) provide well-informed studies of the infamous radio priest Charles Coughlin. Dorgan (1993) offers an account of grassroots radio religion in Appalachia, Erickson (1992) has assembled a directory of the programs and personalities of inspirational radio, and Rumble and Carty (1979) have collected in three volumes the transcripts of two radio priests who conducted a call-in show a half-century ago. These prove to be propitious, if not curious, records of the religious and moral concerns and fixations of the listening audience.

There have been a number of salient essays devoted to the topic. A sampling would include Johnstone's (1972) inclusive survey of the audience for religious radio, Schultze's (1988) probe into evangelical broadcasting, and Casey and Rowe's (1996) examination of the fantasy themes of Father Coughlin, and, in an earlier article, their consideration of the radio priest's rhetorical themes.

Further Topics

Other astute inquiries into radio's cultural role include Coville and Lucanio's (2002) discourse on the romance and impact of technology, Schiffer's (1992) thought-provoking and paradigmatic case study of the effect of radio's portability, and Nachman's (1998) study of golden age programs as cultural force.

Crisell (1994) appraises the medium's role in popular culture development, Fornatale and Mills (1980) critique post-television radio's reinvention, Fones-Wolf (2006) probes the use of radio by labor unions, Fowler and Crawford (2002) examine border radio, Hilliard and Keith's (2003) monograph is on obscene and indecent broadcast discourse, and Edwards and Singletary (1989) review radio music subcultures. Smethers and Jolliffee (2000) survey the live music era on rural Midwestern radio stations, Keith (2001) audits nocturnal programming, Rothenbuhler (1996) analyzes commercial radio as communication, and Smead (1959) and Benjamin (2001) study the relationship between freedom of speech rights and public interest responsibilities and obligations.

In the Air Ahead?

Despite the recent promising rise in the output of studies dealing with radio's place in American culture, it remains an underreported area in media research. The overall neglect of radio by scholars until recently has resulted in a gap in the appreciation and understanding of the significant way the medium has contributed to the lives of its listeners and the world it serves. Particularly lacking are studies that go beyond the recent crop of archetypal monographs focusing on the use of the medium by specific disenfranchised segments of society. Certainly, further research might be undertaken in counterculture, indigenous, gay and lesbian, extremist, and minority radio, as well as in a host of other elided areas. Today the likelihood that this will happen is better than it has been due to the existence of a first-rate journal and the widening awareness among communication scholars and the academic community as a whole of the significant place of radio in American culture.

Note

An earlier version of this chapter appeared in Donald Godfrey's *Methods of Historical Analysis in Electronic Media*, Lawrence Erlbaum, 2006. It is reprinted here with permission from Taylor & Francis.

References

Ackerman, William C. (1945). The Dimensions of American Broadcasting. *Public Opinion Quarterly.*

Apostolidis, Paul. (2000). *Stations of the Cross: Adorno and Christian Right Radio.* Durham, NC: Duke University Press.

Armstrong, Cameron B. & Alan M. Rubin. (1989). Talk Radio As Interpersonal Communication. *Journal of Communication*, 39 (2), 84–94.

Barfield, Ray. (1996). *Listening to Radio: 1920–1950.* Westport, CT: Praeger.

Barker, David C. (2002). *Rushed to Judgment?* New York: Columbia University Press.

Barlow, William. (1999). *Voice Over: The Making of Black Radio.* Philadelphia, PA: Temple University Press.

Barnhurst, Kevin G. (2003). Queer Political News: Election Year Coverage of the Lesbian and Gay Communities on National Public Radio, 1992–2000. *Journalism*, 4 (1), 5–28.

Barnouw, Erik. (1966). *A Tower in Babel: A History of Broadcasting in the United States to 1933.* New York: Oxford University Press.

———. (1968). *The Golden Web: A History of Broadcasting in the United States, 1933–1953.* New York: Oxford University Press.

———. (1970). *The Image Empire: A History of Broadcasting in the United States, from 1953.* New York: Oxford University Press.

Beck, Debra Baker. (1998). The "F" Word: How the Media Frame Feminism. *NWSA Journal*, 10 (1), 139–155.

Bensman, Marvin R. (2000). *The Beginning of Broadcast Regulation in the Twentieth Century.* Jefferson, NC: McFarland.

Beville, Hugh Malcolm, Jr. (1939). *Social Ramifications of the Radio Audience.* Princeton, NJ: Princeton Office of Radio Research.

Bergmeier, Horst J.P. & Rainer E. Lotz. (1997). *Hitler's Airwaves: The Inside Story of Nazi Radio Broadcasting and Propaganda Swing.* New Haven, CT: Yale University Press.

Berstein, Mark & Alex Lubertozzi. (2003). *World War II on the Air: Edward R. Murrow and the Broadcasts that Riveted a Nation.* Naperville, IL: Sourcebooks.

Blue, Howard. (2002). *Words at War: World War II Era Radio Drama and the Postwar Broadcasting Industry Blacklist.* Lanham, MD: Rowman & Littlefield.

Brown, Robert J. (1998). *Manipulating the Ether: The Power of Broadcast Radio in Thirties America.* Jefferson, NC: McFarland.

Cantor, Louis. (1992). *Wheelin' on Beale: How WDIA-Memphis Became the Nation's First All-Black Radio Station and Created the Sound That Changed America*. New York: Pharos Books.

Cantril, Hadley. (1982). *Invasion from Mars*. Princeton, NJ: Princeton University Press.

Carcasson, Martin & James Aune. (2003, May). Klansman on the Court: Justice Hugo Black's Radio Address to the Nation. *Quarterly Journal of Speech*, 89 (2), 154–170.

Carpenter, Ronald H. (1998). *Father Charles E. Coughlin: Surrogate Spokesman for the Disaffected*. Westport, CT: Praeger.

Carpenter, Sue. (2004). *40 Watts from Nowhere*. New York: Scribner.

Carroll, Raymond L., Michael I. Silbergleid, & M. Beachum. (1993). Meanings of Radio to Teenagers in a Niche-Programming Era. *Journal of Broadcasting and Electronic Media*, 37 (2), 159–76.

Casey, Michael & Aimee Rowe. (1996). Driving Out the Money Changers: Radio Priest Charles E. Coughlin's Rhetorical Vision. *Journal of Communication and Religion*, 19, (1, March), 37–47.

Chappell, Matthew N. & Claude E. Hooper. (1944). *Radio Audience Measurement*. New York: Stephen Daye.

Chinn, Sandra Hardy. (1997). *At Your Service—KMOX and Bob Hardy: Pioneers of Talk Radio*. Richmond: Virginia Publishing.

Christenson, Peter G. & Peter DeBeneditis. (1986). Eavesdropping on the FM Band: Children's Use of Radio. *Journal of Communication*, 36 (2), 27–38.

Clark, David. (1962). Radio in Presidential Elections. *Journal of Broadcasting*, 6 (3), 229–238.

Clark, W.R. (1940). Radio Listening Habits of Children. *Journal of Social Psychology*, 12.

Coville, Gary & Patrick Lucanio. (2002). *Smokin' Rockets: The Romance of Technology in American Film, Radio, and Television, 1945–1962*. Jefferson, NC: McFarland.

Craig, Douglas B. (2000). *Fireside Politics: Radio and Political Culture in the United States, 1920–1940*. Baltimore, MD: Johns Hopkins University Press.

Craig, Steve. (2001). The Farmer's Friend: Radio Comes to Rural America, 1920–1927. *Journal of Radio Studies*, 8 (2), 330–346.

Creedon, Pamela J. (Ed.). (1993). *Women in Mass Communication*, 2nd edition. Newbury Park, CA: Sage.

Crisell, Andrew. (1994). *Understanding Radio*. Studies in Culture and Communication. New York: Routledge.

Critchlow, James. (1995). *Radio Hole-in-the-Head: Radio Liberty, an Insider's Story of Cold War Broadcasting*. Lanham, MD: Rowman & Littlefield.

Davidson, Randall. (2006). *9XM Talking: WHA Radio and the Wisconsin Idea*. Madison: University of Wisconsin Press.

Delli Carpini, Michael X. (1993). Radio's Political Past. *Media Studies Journal*, 7 (3, Summer), 23–35.

Dennis, Paul M. (1998). Chills and Thrills: Does Radio Harm Our Children? *Journal of the History of the Behavioral Sciences*, 34 (1), 33–50.

Dicks, Steven J. & Walter McDowell. (2000). Pirates, Pranksters, & Prophets: Understanding America's Unlicensed "Free" Radio Movement. *Journal of Radio Studies*, 8 (2), 329–341.

Doherty, Thomas. (2003). *Cool War, Cool Medium*. New York: Columbia University Press.

Dorgan, Howard. (1993). *The Airwaves of Zion: Radio and Religion in Appalachia*. Knoxville: University of Tennessee Press.

Douglas, Susan J. (2000). *Listening In: Radio and the American Imagination*. New York: Times Books.

Downing, John D. (1990). Ethnic Minority Radio in the United States. *Howard Journal of Communication*, 2 (2, Spring), 135–148.

Dryer, Sherman Howard. (1942). *Radio in Wartime*. New York: Quadrangle.

Edwards, Emily D. & Michael W. Singletary. (1989). Life's Soundtracks: Relationships between Radio Music Subcultures and Listeners' Belief Systems. *Southern Communication Journal*, 54 (2, Winter), 144–158.

Ehrlich, Matthew C. & Noshir S. Contractor. (1998). "Shock" Meets "Community Service:" J.C. Corcoran at MOX. *Journal of Radio Studies*, 5 (1), 22–35.

Ely, Melvin Patrick. (1991). *The Adventures of Amos and Andy: A Social History of an American Phenomenon*. New York: Free Press.

Erickson, Hal. (1992). *Religious Radio and Television in the United States, 1921–1991: The Programs and Personalities*. Jefferson, NC: McFarland.

Fairchild, Charles. (2001). *Community Radio and Public Culture: Being an Examination of Media Access and Equity in the Nations of North America*. Cresskill, NJ: Hampton Press.

Fisher, Marc. (2007). *Something in the Air: Radio, Rock, and the Revolution That Shaped a Generation*. New York: Random House.

Fones-Wolf, Elizabeth. (2006). *Waves of Opposition: Labor and the Struggle for Democratic Radio*. Champaign-Urbana: University of Illinois Press.

Fornatale, Peter & Joshua E. Mills. (1980). *Radio in the Television Age*. Woodstock, NY: Overlook Press.

Fowler, Gene & Bill Crawford. (2002). *Border Radio: Quacks, Yodelers, Pitchmen, Psychics, and Other Amazing Broadcasters of the American Airwaves*. Austen: University of Texas Press.

Frost, S.E., Jr. (1937). *Is American Radio Democratic?* Chicago: University of Chicago Press.

Ganzert, Charles F. (2003). All-Women's Radio at WHER-AM in Memphis. *Journal of Radio Studies*, 10 (1), 80–92.

Garay, Ronald. (1995). Guarding the Airwaves: Government Regulation of World War II American Radio. *Journal of Radio Studies*, 3, 130–148.

Garner, Ken. (Ed.). (2003–2004). *The Radio Journal*. Glasgow, UK: Glasgow Caledonian University.

George, Martha Washington. (2003). *Black Radio ... Winner Takes All: America's 1st Black Deejays*. Philadelphia, PA: Xlibris Corporation.

Greenberg, Bradley S. & Rick Busselle. (1997). Reporting Rape: The Impact of Relationships and Names on Radio Listener Judgments. *Journal of Radio Studies*, 4, 45–59.

Greenfield, Patricia & Jessica Beagles-Roos. (1988). Radio vs. Television: Their Cognitive Impact on Children of Different Socioeconomic and Ethnic Groups. *Journal of Communications*, 38 (2, Spring), 71–92.

Gruenberg, Sidonie Matsner. (1935). Radio and the Child. *Annals of the American Academy of Political Science*, 177 (January), 123–131.

Hall, Alice & Joseph N. Cappella. (2002). The Impact of Political Talk Radio Exposure. *Journal of Communication*, 52, 332–350.

Halper Donna L. (2001). *Invisible Stars: A Social History of Women in American Broadcasting*. Armonk, NY: M.E. Sharpe.

Hammond, Sharon Lee, Vicki S. Freimuth, & William Morrison. (1990). Radio and Teens: Convincing Gatekeepers to Air Health Messages. *Health Communication*, 2 (2), 59–67.

Hangen, Tona J. (2002). *Redeeming the Dial: Radio, Religion, and Popular Culture in America*. Chapel Hill: University of North Carolina Press.

Harris, Chad, Vicki Mayer, Catherine Saulino, & Dan Schiller. (1996). The Class Politics of Rush Limbaugh. *Communication Review*, 1 (4), 545–564.

Hendy, David. (2000). *Radio in the Global Age*. London: Polity Press.

Herzog, Herta. (1941). *Children and Their Leisure Time Listening to the Radio: A Survey of the Literature in the Field*. New York: Office of Radio Research, Columbia University.

Heyer, Paul. (2003). A Reassessment of Orson Welles' 1938 *War of the Worlds* Broadcast. *Journal of Communication*, 28 (2), 149–165.

Hilliard, Robert L. & Michael C. Keith. (2003). *Dirty Discourse: Sex and Indecency in American Radio*. Armonk, NY: M.E. Sharpe.

———. (1999). *Waves of Rancor: Tuning in the Radical Right*. Armonk, NY: M.E. Sharpe.

———. (2001). Farm and Rural Radio: Some Beginnings and Models. *Journal of Radio Studies*, 8 (2), 321–330.

Hilmes, Michele. (1997). *Radio Voices: American Broadcasting, 1922–1952*. Minneapolis: University of Minnesota Press.

———. (2001). *Only Connect: A Cultural History of Broadcasting*. Thousand Oaks, CA: Wadsworth Publishing.

Hilmes, Michele & Jason Loviglio. (2002). *Radio Reader: Essays in the Cultural History of Radio*. New York: Routledge.

Hofstetter, C. Richard & Christopher Gianos. (1997). Political Talk Radio: Actions Speak Louder Than Words. *Journal of Broadcasting and Electronic Media*, 41 (4), 501–515.

Hollander, Barry A. (1995). Influence of Talk Radio on Political Efficacy and Participation. *Journal of Radio Studies*, 3, 23–31.

———. (1996). Talk Radio: Predictors of Use and Effects of Attitudes about Government. *Journalism and Mass Communication Quarterly*, 73 (1), 102–113.

———. (1999). Political Talk Radio in the 90s: A Panel Study. *Journal of Radio Studies*, 6 (2), 236–245.

Horten, Gerd. (2002). *Radio Goes to War: The Cultural Politics of Propaganda during World War II*. Berkeley: University of California Press.

Hutchby, Ian. (1996). *Confrontation Talk: Arguments, Asymmetries, and Power on Talk Radio*. Mahwah, NJ: Lawrence Erlbaum Associates.

Johnson, Frank W., Jr. (1993). The Development of Black Radio Networks in the United States: 1943–1993. *Journal of Radio Studies*, 2, 173–187.

Johnson, Phylis & Joe S. Foote. (2000). Alternative Radio: Other Voices beyond the Mainstream. *Journal of Radio Studies*, 7 (2), 282–286.

Johnson, Phylis & Michael C. Keith. (2001). *Queer Airwaves: The Story of Gay and Lesbian Broadcasting*. Armonk, NY: M.E. Sharpe.

Johnstone, Ronald L. (1972). Who Listens to Religious Radio? *Journal of Broadcasting and Electronic Media*, 16 (1), 91–102.

Kay, Jack, George Ziegelmueller, & Kevin Minch. (1998). From Coughlin to Limbaugh: Fallacies and Techniques of Propaganda in American Populist Talk Radio. *Journal of Radio Studies*, 5 (1), 9–21.

Keith, Michael C. (1995). *Signals in the Air: Native Broadcasting in America*. Westport, CT: Praeger.

Keith, Michael C. (1997). *Voices in the Purple Haze: Underground Radio and the Sixties.* Westport, CT: Praeger.

———. (2000). *Talking Radio: An Oral History of Radio in the Television Age.* Armonk, NY: M.E. Sharpe.

———. (2001). *Sounds in the Dark: All Night Radio in American Life.* Ames: Iowa State University.

Koch, Hoard. (1970). *The Panic Broadcast: Portrait of an Event.* Boston, MA: Little Brown.

Kurtz, Howard. (1996). *Hot Air: All Talk, All the Time.* New York: Crown.

Larson, Charles U. (1995–1996). Radio, Secondary Orality, and the Search for Community: A Case Study of "A Prairie Home Companion." *Journal of Radio Studies*, 3, 89–105.

Larson, Mary Strom. (1997). Rush Limbaugh: Broadcast Demagogue. *Journal of Radio Studies*, 4, 184–197.

Laufer, Peter. (1995). *Inside Talk Radio: America's Voice or Just Hot Air?* New York: Carol.

Lazarsfeld, Paul F. & Patricia L. Kendall. (1948). *Radio Listening in America: The People Look at Radio—Again.* New York: Prentice-Hall.

Lenthall, Bruce. (2007). *Radio's America: The Great Depression and the Rise of Modern Mass Culture.* Chicago: University of Chicago Press.

Levin, Harry Leon. (1974). *The Use of Radio in Family Planning.* Oklahoma City: World Neighbors.

Levin, Murray B. (1987). *Talk Radio and the American Dream.* Lanham, MD: Rowman & Littlefield.

Lewis, Justin. (2001). *Constructing Public Opinion.* New York: Columbia University Press.

Lewis, Tom. (1993). Triumph of the Idol: Rush Limbaugh and a Hot Medium. *Media Studies Journal*, 7 (3), 51–61.

Loche, Bob. (2006). *Christian Radio: The Growth of a Mainstream Broadcasting Force.* Jefferson, NC: McFarland.

Lyness, Paul I. (1950). Radio's Habits of the Young Audience. *Broadcasting*, September 25.

MacDonald, J. Fred. (1979). *Don't Touch That Dial: Radio Programming in American Life from 1920–1960.* Chicago: Nelson-Hall.

———. (1989). *Richard Durham's Destination Freedom: Scripts from Radio's Black Legacy, 1948–50.* Westport, CT: Praeger.

Marcus, Sheldon. (1986). *Father Coughlin: The Tumultuous Life of the Priest of the Little Flower.* Boston, MA: Little Brown.

Mata, Marita. (1994). Being Women in the Popular Radio. In Pilar Riano (Ed.), *Women in Grassroots Communication.* Thousand Oaks, CA: Sage.

Meckiff, Donald & Matthew Murray. (1998). Radio and the Black Soldier during World War II. *Critical Studies in Mass Communication*, 15 (4), 337–356.

Merrick, Beverly G. (1997). Mary McBride, Talk Show Host: The Perfect Proxy for Radio Listeners. *Journal of Radio Studies*, 4, 146–165.

Migala, Joseph. (1987). *Polish Radio Broadcasting in the United States.* Boulder, CO: East European Monographs.

Milam, Lorenzo Wilson. (1988). *Original Sex and Broadcasting: A Handbook for Starting a Radio Station for the Community.* San Francisco: Mho & Mho Works.

Mitchell, Caroline. (2001). *Woman and Radio: Airing Differences.* London: Routledge.

Morley, Patrick. (2001). *"This Is the American Forces Network": The Anglo-American Battle of the Air Waves in World War II.* Westport, CT: Praeger.

Morson, Gary Saul. (1979). The War of the Well(e)s. *Journal of Communication*, 29 (3), 10–20.

Nachman, Gerald. (1998). *Raised on Radio*. New York: Pantheon.

Page, Benjamin I. & Tannenbaum, Jason. (1996). Populist Deliberation in Talk Radio. *Journal of Communication*, 46 (2), 33–54.

Podber, Jacob J. (2001). Early Radio in Rural Appalachia: An Oral History. *Journal of Radio Studies*, 8 (2), 388–410.

———— (2007). The Electronic Front Porch. Macon, GA: Mercer University Press.

Powell, Adam Clayton, III. (1993). You Are What You Hear. *Media Studies Journal*, 7 (3), 71–76.

Rehm, Diane. (1993). Talking Over America's Electronic Backyard Fence. *Media Studies Journal*, 7 (3), 63–69.

Roberto, Anthony J., G. Myers, A.J. Johnson, C.K. Atkin, & P.K. Smith. (2002). Promoting Gun Trigger-Lock Use: Insights and Implications from a Radio-Based Health Communication Intervention. *Journal of Applied Communication*, 30 (3), 210–230.

Rolo, Charles. (1942). *Radio Goes to War: The "Fourth Front."* New York: Putnam.

Rothenbuhler, Eric W. (1996). Commercial Radio As Communication. *Journal of Communication*, 46 (1), 125–143.

Rowland, Willard D., Jr. (1997). The Meaning of "the Public Interest" in Communications Policy. *Communication Law and Policy*, 2 (4), 363–396.

Rubin, Alan M. & Mary M. Step. (2000). Impact of Motivation, Attraction, and Parasocial Interaction on Talk Radio Listening. *Journal of Broadcasting and Electronic Media*, 44 (4), 635–654.

Ruffner, Marguerita Anne. (1972–1973). Women's Attitudes towards Radio. *Journal of Broadcasting and Electronic Media*, 17 (1), 85–94.

Ruggiero, Greg. (1999). *Microradio & Democracy: (Low) Power to the People*. New York: Seven Stories Press.

Rumble, Fr. Leslie & Fr. Charles M. Carty. (1979). *Radio Replies: Three Volume Set*. San Francisco: Tan Books.

Runco, Mark A. & Kathy Pezdek. (1984). The Effect of Television and Radio on Children's Creativity. *Human Communication Research*, 11 (1), 109–120.

Sampson, Henry T. (2004). *Swingin on the Ether Waves*. Lanham, MD: Rowman & Littlefield.

Savage, Barbara Dianne. (1999). *Broadcasting Freedom: Radio, War, and the Politics of Race, 1938–1948*. Chapel Hill: University of North Carolina Press.

Schiffer, Michael Brian. (1992). *The Portable Radio in American Life*. Tucson: University of Arizona Press.

Schultze, Quentin J. (1988). Evangelical Radio and the Rise of the Electronic Church, 1921–1948. *Journal of Broadcasting and Electronic Media*, 32 (3), 289–306.

Scott, Gini Graham. (1996). *Can We Talk? The Power and Influence of Talk Shows*. New York: Perseus.

Shields, Steven O. & Robert Ogles. (1995). Black Liberation Radio: A Case Study of Free Radio Micro-broadcasting. *Howard Journal of Communication*, 5 (3), 173–183.

Siegel David S. & Siegel Susan. (2007). *Radio and the Jews*. Yorktown Heights, NY: Book Hunter Press.

Siepmann, Charles A. (1950). *Radio, Television, and Society*. New York: Oxford University Press.

Signorielli, Nancy. (Ed.). (1996). *Woman in Mass Communication*. Westport, CT: Greenwood Publishing.

Smead, Elmer E. (1959). *Freedom of Speech by Radio and Television*. Washington, DC: Public Affairs Press.

Smethers, J. Steven & Lee B. Jolliffee. (2000). Singing and Selling Seeds: The Live Music Era on Rural Midwestern Radio Stations. *Journalism History*, 26 (2), 61–70.

Smith, Bruce L. & Jerry C. Brigham. (1992). Native Radio Broadcasting in North America: An Overview of Systems in the United States and Canada. *Journal of Broadcasting and Electronic Media*, 36 (2), 183–194.

Smith, F. Leslie. (1994). Quelling Radio's Quacks: The FCC's First Public Interest Programming Campaign. *Journalism Quarterly*, 71 (3), 594–608.

Socolow, Michael J. (2002). Questioning Advertising's Influence over American Radio: The Blue Book Controversy of 1945–1947. *Journal of Radio Studies*, 9 (2), 282–302.

Soley, Lawrence C. (1999). *Free Radio: Electronic Civil Disobedience*. Boulder, CO: Westview.

Soley, Lawrence & George Hough III. (1982). Black Ownership of Community Radio Stations: An Economic Evaluation. *Journal of Broadcasting*, 22 (4), 455–467.

Squier, Susan Merrill. (Ed.). (2003). *Communities of the Air: Radio Century, Radio Culture*. Durham, NC: Duke University Press.

Sterling, Christopher H. (Ed.). (2004). *Encyclopedia of Radio*, volume 3. Chicago: Fitzroy Dearborn.

Summers, Harrison B. (Ed.). (1939). *Radio Censorship*. New York: H.W. Wilson.

Surlin, Stuart H. (1972). Ascertainment of Community Needs by a Black-oriented Radio Station. *Journal of Broadcasting*, 16 (4), 421–429.

Swain, William N. (1999). Propaganda and Rush Limbaugh: Is the Label the Last Word? *Journal of Radio Studies*, 6 (1), 27–40.

Sweeney, Michael S. (2001). *Secrets of Victory: The Office of Censorship and American Press and Radio in World War II*. Chapel Hill: University of North Carolina Press.

Tulloch, John & Simon Chapman. (1992). Experts in Crisis: The Framing of Radio Debate about the Risk of AIDS to Heterosexuals. *Discourse and Society*, 3 (4), 437–467.

Urban, George R. (1998). *Radio Free Europe and the Pursuit of Democracy*. New Haven: Yale University Press.

Vargas, Lucila. (1995). *Social Uses and Radio Practices: The Use of Participatory Radio by Ethnic Minorities in Mexico*. Boulder, CO: Westview.

Walker, Jesse. (2001). *Rebels of the Air: An Alternative History of Radio in America*. New York: New York University Press.

Warren, Donald. (1996). *Radio Priest: Charles Coughlin, the Father of Hate Radio*. New York: Free Press.

Williams, Gilbert A. (1998). *Legendary Pioneers of Black Radio*. Westport, CT: Praeger.

19. Slow Fade? Seeking Radio's Future

Christopher H. Sterling

During nearly nine decades on the air, American radio broadcasters have generally emphasized a "big house fits all" approach to their program service—or what is today often termed "mainstreaming." Put another way, for most of its history, broadcasting has been a classic *mass* medium, seeking to gather in the most listeners by reflecting the main cultural tenets of the country at any given time. More recently, program decisions have reflected a narrower view of that role by endlessly duplicating the three or four most popular music and talk formats. Radio time is still sold to advertisers on the basis of the medium's broad (ideally youthful) appeal and reach.

By the early 21st century, however, it seems increasingly evident that radio's one-time mass audience is splintering. This breakup is largely due to the audience morphing into a collection of smaller and more focused cultural groups, which increasingly seek what they want to hear on niche audio services, some of them self-programmed. Radio broadcasting's days of monolithic mass cultural appeal appear to be numbered. The signs are everywhere.[1] Indeed, many one-time listeners have already turned away from radio. This is but one indicator that in some of its decisions, the business has almost been asking for trouble. And while that trouble is in sight, it may not be too late to turn the medium around.

Economics: Mainstream Bean Counting

As a substantial commercial enterprise now spread across 10,000 stations (plus another 2,800 noncommercial licensees), radio broadcasting is best assessed first using the economic rubric most of its owners apply. After all, commercial broadcasting is first and foremost a business seeking a profit like any other.

Over the dozen years leading up to this book's appearance, the radio business has been characterized by continuing consolidation and the generation of short-term profits. That has led, in turn, to a declining emphasis on any local sound in favor of largely similar programming across the nation, far less news and public affairs (which is expensive to develop and maintain), and declining industry employment as a result of automated operations. To the degree the business still reflects American culture, it is generally narrowly conservative, leaving out a variety of minority groups and interests it once included.

The Telecommunications Act of 1996 is correctly accused of having greatly accelerated the ownership consolidation that underlies these trends. Provisions in that law instructed the Federal Communications Commission (FCC) to lift its existing cap on station ownership (then no more than 20 AM and 20 FM outlets in the country). While perhaps not intended, the effect of this was a rapid concentration of ownership such that Clear Channel, which became the largest radio company, controlled more than a thousand stations within five years (Sterling, 2006). Several other radio firms owned between 150 and 200 stations.[2] Virtually all were programmed in similar fashion—the top three or four music or talk formats heard almost everywhere. With ownership concentration came a growing sameness in the medium's programming.

Of more immediate importance to most listeners, however, is that radio's consolidation has also taken place locally. Individual market "clustering" of multiple stations under a single owner has had far more effect on what radio listeners hear—or do not hear. Where for decades FCC rules had limited one owner to no more than a single AM and FM station in the same market, the 1996 law allowed owners of stations in the largest cities to own and program up to eight outlets, with a declining cap for smaller communities. A half-century ago, Peter O. Steiner, later a Nobel Laureate, used his dissertation research to argue that one owner of multiple stations in a city would provide more diversified programming than multiple owners (Steiner, 1949). Current practice in the business suggests he was right—to a point. The problem is that diversity seems to mean four or five formats and rarely more. Duplication is rife.

However, such clustered operations save money, chiefly by sharply reducing the number of people required. Multiple stations can broadcast from one location, with one small engineering staff, a single sales force, (perhaps) one news staff, and a single administrative group. Indeed, by employing the technology of voice tracking, one deejay can provide the "local" voice of multiple stations in different locations. In many areas, commercial radio has become a remotely operated automatic system of generating sound.

The classic and oft-cited example is Minot, North Dakota. Back in early 2002, a train derailed, sending out dangerous clouds of noxious gas. However, when authorities contacted the several stations in town to pass a warning to listeners, they found nobody home—not one live employee at any of the stations (most then controlled by Clear Channel). The stations were operating on automatic pilot with pre-taped announcements, music, and advertising (Klinenberg, 2007; Shafer, 2007). Several of radio's changing roles are evident in this event. First among them is the fading of radio journalism.

For decades, radio was the medium to which most people first turned for breaking news—a habit learned in the 1930s and imprinted during and after World War II. Well into the 1980s, most stations offered at least occasional newscasts, often five minutes on the hour, especially in morning and evening drive time. Stations offered news as good business—advertisers and listeners alike were interested. That the FCC considered news to be a part of the public interest responsibility of broadcast licensees was a minor reason for providing it. News was an expected—and often profitable—part of radio's menu.

Over the past dozen years or more, all this has changed. Now news is more often seen as a cost center, and a cost that needs to be at least contained if not eliminated. The result is that thousands of stations now provide no news whatever. Their managers argue they do not have to, as other stations in the same market already provide news. Often that "other" station is a noncommercial operation, perhaps one affiliated with National Public Radio (NPR). And if news is disappearing from commercial stations, understand that broader public affairs programming (often of interest to few and rarely moneymaking) is becoming even more scarce.

The demise of news is part of a larger trend the industry generally ignores—the demise of localism, once a cornerstone of American radio (Hilliard & Keith, 2005). Though localism is still touted by industry spokespeople when competition looms (as with cries to "save free local radio"), American radio today consists of locally based outlets providing national content. These are not networks per se but stations across the country providing largely the same three to four music formats with minor variations. Others—chiefly AM outlets—offer talk (some of this is news, but most is talk, including a good deal of right-wing religion and politics). Huge swaths of *possible* radio content that reflect the variety of cultures in the country today find few places on the air, though many once did, as earlier chapters attest. Only the largest cities offer much variety, and even there radio's menu remains severely limited. A few legacy AM stations—Boston's WBZ is one good example—provide a broad service that still emphasizes news and the community. However, generally, the bottom line–oriented business overemphasizes a narrowly conservative view of the mainstream rather than offering a broader variety of more specialized appeals.

Religious programming is an excellent example of how radio has changed. From radio's very inception in the 1920s, stations carried church services or programs. Well into the 1960s, religion on the air meant a balanced presentation of Catholic, Protestant, and often Jewish programs, most of which had their radio costs sustained by the station, as few were sponsored. The difference today could not be starker. Radio religion now nearly always means right-wing evangelical programming and often outright station ownership. Conservative radio is profitable, too, whether from on-air fund raising or advertising. Indeed, most religious programs on radio today pay for their time on the air (Hangen, 2002; Lochte, 2006). They can readily afford it.

There is, of course, one important exception to this rather dismal picture—noncommercial radio. Noncommercial stations are divided into two large categories: the larger market public radio stations that carry NPR and other program services, and a thousand or more local community or college outlets that rely almost totally on donations from listeners. Together, these nearly 3,000 broadcasters provide a good deal of the cultural variance missing from commercial stations. NPR's *Morning Edition* is the single most listened-to radio program in the country (not, as many think, Howard Stern's sexist rants on Sirius satellite radio). To varying degrees, these noncommercial stations are radio's saving grace, with their provision of news and community affairs, funky off-beat music and even drama, and a host of other cultural formats that long ago disappeared from the majority of commercial stations.

Technology: A Two-Edged Blade

Both sides of the business—commercial and noncommercial—are facing a wave of technical change that will transform the face of radio in coming years. The changes are placing more power in the hands of listeners. As usual, younger listeners got the message first—as new options became available, they could program their own audio listening instead of listening only to what a radio station might bring them. The audio experience (what editor Michael Keith terms "soundcasting") is generally becoming both more interactive and less passive. But technology offers real options for existing broadcasters as well as radio's competitors.

It is easy to get excited about what is coming—indeed, about what is already here. Yet, time and again, we tend to overestimate short-term change wrought by technology while underestimating its longer-range impact. Examples of such missteps abound (Rohlfs, 2001). Whether this is because we are impatient for change or because short-term profit seeking is driving decisions is not clear. But the result is obvious—some technologies are given only a brief window in which to achieve success before their place is taken by something newer and possibly more capable. If we examine the ongoing digital revolution, we can see numerous examples. As this is written, much of the focus is on the burgeoning number of iPods and other MP3 players, which are turning many of their users away from regular broadcast listening. Why tune to somebody else's programming (even on a tiny portable receiver) when you can put all your favorite songs on your own device for listening at any time?

Satellite radio developed out of an assumption that the technology could provide a far broader menu of choices for listeners with different interests who were scattered across the country. Although the total audience for satellite radio is but a fraction of that tuned to legacy broadcast radio, the 130 channels programmed by both XM and Sirius offer a variety unavailable otherwise even in the largest cities.[3] Multiple channels of different kinds of jazz, classical music, even old-time radio demonstrate how both mainstream and niche interests can be served by satellite providers that can reach widely scattered audiences willing to pay for the service.

Perhaps the greatest potential threat to existing over-the-air radio comes from the Internet. Audio streaming (whether by broadcasters or Internet-only services) is one rapidly expanding way of creating a national or global market for widespread specialized interests. Anyone with Internet access can now listen to literally a world of broadcasting, and in a plethora of languages. Podcasting or minicasting, which combines Internet service and iPods into a kind of "each to his own" broadcast blog, has also proven hugely popular, though it is too early to tell whether it will survive long term. An early 2007 copyright royalty decision may clip the wings of many Internet-based music services, though appeals were underway as this was written (Copyright Royalty Board, 2007).

Turning to the other side of technology's blade, radio managers—the more enlightened ones at least—are responding to all of this. On the one hand, the primary broadcast trade association (the National Association of Broadcasters) tries to fend off, obstruct, or delay newer technologies when it can.[4] In the meantime, more AM and FM outlets are converting to the new HD radio digital technology that both improves signal quality and expands options for multiple programs on a single channel (HD Radio, n.d.). Such an ability to compete with multiple channels in what is increasingly a multichannel media world is essential to radio's long-range survival. At the same time, leaders of a number of major radio firms are calling for a reversal of some of the business's most sacrosanct patterns. To the surprise of many of their brethren, they are urging lower commercial loads (advertising minutes per hour) and thus the provision of more "real content" (what listeners really want to hear) on the air (Larson, 2004). They seek to rebuild radio as a viable choice that will attract and retain listeners as opposed to a mere commercial billboard catering to a dwindling audience.

Policy: Radio's No Longer on the Menu

With one or two exceptions, radio has not been subject to serious policy concern for at least a decade. Surely, this neglect on the part of government is yet another sign of the medium's declining public impact and importance. Of course, one could also argue that the radio industry has been so largely successful in defanging the FCC, that the agency has precious little clout to bring to bear on the medium. It wasn't always thus.

Back in 1981, one of the FCC's biggest and most controversial issues was a proceeding called "radio deregulation." This had begun in the late 1970s and by the mid-1980s had expanded to include television. It seemed a huge deal at the time—there were hundreds of comments filed. The eventual decision abandoned nonentertainment program guidelines (minimal amounts of news and public affairs), advertising guidelines (minutes per hour), specific logging requirements, and the need to ascertain listener concerns at the time of licensing and renewals of license. These were all felt to constrict broadcasters from offering programs the marketplace—listeners—wanted (FCC, 1981).

In place of these, the FCC created a new "public file" requirement (FCC, 1999). About a dozen categories of documents and information are to be retained at every station (radio and television), available for public inspection during normal business hours. Well intentioned, the public file is in reality a bust—almost no listener is aware of such a file, let alone seeks one out, and many stations toss the required material in a box and ignore it. Of course, the 1996 Telecommunications Act changed the situation with respect to station renewals—virtually guaranteeing a license will be renewed save for some awful mistake on the part of a station owner or manager (Sterling, 2006). Indeed, no license has been refused in the dozen years since the Act passed. Given essentially a permanent license, stations need not worry much about public files the public could care less about.

There is one exception to this regulatory neglect—a punitive approach to indecent programming. This has remained a fairly constant focus of the commission, with active concern rising and falling in biorhythm fashion. Perceived smut on the air is both a culturally and politically sensitive issue and is thus never far from government attention. This is not the place to debate what is presently perceived as permissible save to note that the debate suggests too many stations seem willing to drive to the lowest common denominator in search of listeners and advertiser dollars (Hilliard & Keith, 2003; Pierce, 2004). FCC decisions about indecency over the past few years have served to make radio managers scared and thus blander in their program decisions (FCC, n.d.).

Among the many things hard to find on radio these days is more than lip service concern about ethnic minority service, ownership, or even access. Once a policy focus, the silence on this front in recent years has been notable.

Other chapters in this volume outline what can be done and has been done to equip radio to play a constructive role in a variety of communities in the country. Sadly, there seems less of that kind of thing all the time. Indeed, the ownership changes already noted have served to lower the proportion of stations owned by African Americans as owners are made financial offers that are hard to dismiss.

The general wind-down of most regulatory interest in radio has resulted in an industry with little sense of (or worry about) "the public interest, convenience, or necessity," the words in the Communications Act intended to define conditions for licensing and other regulation. Radio has to a growing degree regulated itself, and the result has been more of the same rather than variety.

But Has Broadcast Radio Really Run Its Course?

Over the past decade, radio's overall listening audience has slowly but steadily declined. While the audience is still huge in aggregate terms, the decline is real and quite evident. Arbitron and other ratings data show this trend clearly (Arbitron, n.d.). Over-the-air radio—both commercial and public—is serving an aging mainstream audience still committed to broadcasting. A growing proportion of younger listeners are seeking out the niche services—narrowcasting—found elsewhere. Yet over-the-air radio can still serve specific cultural interests—witness the rise in popularity of Hispanic stations as that proportion of the population grows in number and buying power.

Summing up the numerous changes discussed here, it is easy to conclude that radio is no longer unique and is thus fading. There are a growing number of competitors who offer audio service, variations on the classic "big tent" approach of terrestrial radio in years past. Radio's "same old, same old" program sound broken up with too many ads dominates—but does it have to? As suggested above, some broadcasters are realizing that their medium is in trouble *and* faces growing competitive options. Radio's audience (really many different audiences) can no longer be taken for granted.

Yet it is by no means too late to pull broadcast radio back from the abyss and reinvigorate the service. This has happened before, most particularly in the 1950s, when the rise of television transformed radio's role. Radio stumbled for a number of years until the rise of rock music and formula radio combined to create new life for the old medium. Radio still has a lot going for it—not least that it is universally available and free. As demonstrated on earlier pages of this volume, the medium has provided good service for a variety of cultural groups and interests over the years. Some are still served today. More can be tomorrow.

Notes

1. A word of caution before going farther. I *used to* love American radio. Like many of my generation, I first tuned in just at the end of the glory years, when you could still hear drama (and eventually just daytime soap operas) and a good deal of variety on the air. I first broadcast at age 16 on a local rocker in Madison, Wisconsin, as part of a high-school business program. I was an announcer at a public radio station all through college and grad school. I studied the field and I have written and taught about the business for nearly 40 years. I knew the business pretty well. But I rarely listen to legacy radio broadcasting anymore. Instead, I tune into my CDs or satellite radio and almost never to over-the-air service. Radio's now-narrow menu of content is not aimed at me (I am too old) and the ads seem never-ending—and loud. If I want news, the Web or possibly cable news services are my usual sources. Sadly, I find most American radio to be chatty drivel, driven by the bottom line, overloaded with one-sided conservative political and religious talk, and with no interest in (let alone understanding of) what a real public service business might be.
2. Perhaps the best way to stay current on radio's changing patterns of ownership is to consult the online weekly *Who Owns What*, which compares group owners by number of stations owned, total revenues, and total audience size. Such measures provide different orderings of the top 10 and top 20 group owners.
3. And this will remain true whether or not the two companies merge, as was pending when this chapter was written.
4. For a recent selection of typical NAB filings with the FCC, see http://www.nab.org/AM/Template.cfm?Section=Legislative_and_Regulatory (accessed March 14, 2007).

References

Arbitron. (n.d.). Persons Using Radio Report. Retrieved from http://wargod.arbitron.com/scripts/ndb/ndbradio2.asp, March 14, 2007.

Copyright Royalty Board. (2007). Determination of Rates and Terms for Webcasting for the License Period 2006–2010–in [Docket No. 2005–1 CRB DTRA] Digital Performance Right in Sound Recordings and Ephemeral Recordings. Retrieved from http://www.loc.gov/crb/proceedings/2005–1/rates-terms2005–1.pdf, March 14, 2007.

Federal Communications Commission. (n.d.). Obscene, Indecent, and Profane Broadcasts: FCC Consumer Facts. Retrieved from http://www.fcc.gov/cgb/consumerfacts/obscene.html, March 14, 2007.

———. (1981). Report and Order [BC Docket 79–219], adopted January 14, 84 FCC 2d 968.

———. (1999). The Public and Broadcasting. Retrieved from http://www.fcc.gov/mb/audio/decdoc/public_and_broadcasting.html#TOC, March 14, 2007.

Hangen, Tona J. (2002). *Redeeming the Dial: Radio, Religion & Popular Culture in America*. Chapel Hill: University of North Carolina Press.

HD Radio Web site. Retrieved from http://www.hdradio.com, March 14, 2007.

Hilliard, Robert L. & Michael C. Keith. (2003). *Dirty Discourse: Sex and Indecency in American Radio*. Ames, IA: Blackwell.

———. (2005). *The Quieted Voice: The Rise and Demise of Localism in American Radio*. Carbondale: Southern Illinois University Press.

Klinenberg, Eric. (2007). *Fighting for Air: The Battle to Control America's Media.* New York: Holt.

Larson, Mark. (2004). Radio Giant Reducing Ads to Gain Listeners. *Sacramento Business Journal,* September 10. Retrieved from http://www.bizjournals.com/sacramento/stories/2004/09/13/story6.html, March 14, 2007.

Lochte, Bob. (2006). *Christian Radio: The Growth of a Mainstream Broadcasting Force.* Jefferson, NC: McFarland.

Pierce, Charles P. (2004). Hot Button Issue. *Boston Globe Magazine,* July 18.

Rohlfs, Jeffrey H. (2001). *Bandwagon Effects in High Technology Industries.* Cambridge, MA: MIT Press.

Shafer, Jack. (2007). What Really Happened in Minot, N.D.? The Whole Story about That Toxic Spill and the Clear Channel Monopoly. *Slate,* January 10. Retrieved from http://www.slate.com/id/2157395/pagenum/all/#page_start.

Steiner, Peter O. (1949). Workable Competition in the Radio Broadcasting Industry. Dissertation, Harvard University, Department of Economics, Cambridge, MA (reprinted by Arno Press Dissertations in Broadcasting, 1979).

Sterling, Christopher H. (2006). Transformation: The 1996 Act Reshapes Radio. *Federal Communications Law Journal,* 58 (June), 593–602.

Contributors

Roberto Avant-Mier is assistant professor of communication at Boston College and the author of several articles on Mexican popular culture and media. His lifelong obsession with radio is also related to professional experiences in commercial AM and FM stations and in college radio.

Louise Benjamin is associate professor of communication at the University of Georgia and the author of *Freedom of the Air and Public Interest: Establishing a First Amendment Rights on Broadcasting to 1935* as well as several journal articles. Among her other appointments, she served as interim director of the Peabody Awards.

Susan Brinson is professor of communication at Auburn University. Her research interests include the history of broadcasting, the history of broadcast regulations, and the historical contributions of women in the broadcasting industry. She recently published *Personal and Public Interests: Frieda B. Hennock and the Federal Communications Commission; The Red Scare, Politics and the Federal Communications Commission, 1941–1960;* and *Transmitting the Past: Historical and Cultural Perspectives on Broadcasting.* She is editor of the *Journal of Broadcasting and Electronic Media.*

Donald Browne is a professor of communication studies at the University of Minnesota and the author of a half-dozen books, among them *Electronic Media and Indigenous People: A Voice of Our Own?* and *Ethnic Minorities, Electronic Media, and the Public Sphere: A Comparative Study.* He is the recipient of several awards for teaching and research.

Barbara Calabrese is chair of the Radio Department at Columbia College Chicago. She has taught in higher education for 25 years and has produced programs for commercial and public radio stations. In 2005, she and her department were honored with an Angel Award from the Chicago chapter of American Women in Radio and Television.

Frank Chorba is a professor of mass media studies at Washburn University and the founding editor of the *Journal of Radio Studies.* He has chaired several academic organization groups, among them the Broadcast Education Association's radio division and American Culture/Popular Association's radio interest group.

Douglas Craig is a reader in history at the Australian National University and the author of *After Wilson: The Struggle for the Democratic Party, 1920–1934* and *Fireside Politics: Radio and Political Culture in the United States, 1920–1940*. He is currently writing a double biography of Newton D. Baker and William G. McAdoo.

Corey Flintoff is a news anchor and foreign correspondent for NPR. He has reported from more than a dozen countries, including Iraq, Saudi Arabia, Israel, Jordan, South Korea, and Haiti. He has also taught journalism in the United States and overseas, including in Kosovo and Mongolia, and is the recipient of numerous awards.

Elizabeth Fones-Wolf is a professor of history at West Virginia University. She is the author of *Selling Free Enterprise: The Business Assault on Labor and Liberalism, 1945–1960* and *Waves of Opposition: Labor and the Struggle for Democratic Radio*.

Donna Halper is a radio consultant and award-winning teacher. She has authored several books, including the first book-length study of the role of women in the development and evolution of radio, *Invisible Stars: A Social History of Women in American Broadcasting*. She is the recipient of numerous civic awards.

Tona J. Hangen teaches American studies and history at Brandeis University and is the author of *Redeeming the Dial: Radio, Religion, and Popular Culture* as well as several articles and chapters on religion, media, and culture. Currently she is working on a book about the United Nations in popular culture and American politics.

Robert L. Hilliard is a professor at Emerson College and the former head of the FCC's educational broadcasting branch. He is the author of more than two dozen books, among them *Dirty Discourse: Sex and Indecency in Broadcasting*; *The Quieted Voice: The Rise and Demise of Localism in American Radio*; and *Waves of Rancor: Tuning In the Radical Right* (all coauthored with Michael C. Keith). His textbook *Writing for Television, Radio, and New Media* has been one of the leading books on the subject for nearly half a century.

Phylis Johnson is associate professor of radio and television at Southern Illinois University and the author of several journal articles and a book (coauthored with Michael C. Keith), *Queer Airwaves: The Story of Gay and Lesbian Broadcasting*. She has also worked in various positions at radio stations.

Michael C. Keith is the editor of this book and a member of the Communication faculty at Boston College. He is the author of several books on electronic media, including *Voices in the Purple Haze: Underground Radio and the Sixties; Sounds in the Dark: All-Night Radio in American Life*; and *Talking Radio: An Oral History of American Radio in the Television Age*. His textbook, *The Radio Station*, is widely used throughout the world.

Peter Laufer is an award-winning professional journalist, producer, and radio host as well as the author of countless articles and more than a dozen books, including *Inside Talk Radio: America's Voice or Just Hot Air?; Mission Rejected; Iron Curtain Rising;* and *Shock and Awe: Responses to War.*

Larry Miller is a pioneer of commercial underground radio with a broadcast career that spans nearly 50 years. He is best known for his work in FM radio, starting in 1967 at KMPX in San Francisco and moving on to WABX in Detroit, KLOS in Los Angeles, WPLJ in New York, and WCOZ in Boston. He currently teaches at the New England Institute of Art in Boston and is heard on WMBR's *Lost and Found.*

Bruce Smith is a professor in the School of Journalism and Mass Communication at Texas State University. He has served as chair or director of several mass communication departments from Alaska to Texas and has 20 years of professional broadcast experience.

Lawrence C. Soley is the Colnik Professor of Communication at Marquette University and the author of several books, including *Clandestine Radio Broadcasting: A Study of Revolutionary and Counterrevolutionary Electronic Communication; Radio Warfare: Oss and CIA Subversive Propaganda;* and *Free Radio: Electronic Civil Disobedience.* As an alternative journalist, he won the Society of Professional Journalists' Sigma Delta Chi Award and the Project Censor Award for articles in *Mother Jones, CAQ,* and *Dollars and Sense* magazines.

Christopher H. Sterling is a professor of media and public affairs at the George Washington University. He edited the *Encyclopedia of Radio,* and he coauthored *Sounds of Change: FM Broadcasting in America* and *Stay Tuned: A Concise History of American Broadcasting.* He has more than 20 monographs and countless articles to his credit, and he founded and continues to edit *Communication Booknotes Quarterly.*

Cindy Welch is a doctoral candidate at the Graduate School of Library and Information Science at the University of Illinois, Champaign-Urbana. Her particular areas of research include the history of youth services in public libraries and public libraries' involvement with technology and culture.

Index